KU-247-465

New Concepts for Sustainable Management of River Basins

Edited by

P.H. Nienhuis, R.S.E.W. Leuven and A.M.J. Ragas

Backhuys Publishers, Leiden, 1998

UNIVERSITY OF HERTFORDSHIRE
HATFIELD CAMPUS LRC
HATFIELD AL10 9AD 302766

BIB
ISBN 9073348811

CLASS 333 73 NGO

LOCATION G WL

BARCODE 4408078754

ISBN 90-73348-81-1

© 1998 Backhuys Publishers, Leiden, The Netherlands

All rights reserved. No part of this book may be translated or reproduced in any form by print, photoprint, microfilm, or any other means without the prior written permission of the publishers, Backhuys Publishers, P.O. Box 321, 2300 AH Leiden, The Netherlands.

Printed in The Netherlands

44 0507875 4

New Concepts for Sustainable Management of River Basins

University of
Hertfordshire

Learning and Information Services
Hatfield Campus Learning Resources Centre
College Lane Hatfield Herts AL10 9AB
Renewals: Tel 01707 284673 Mon-Fri 12 noon-8pm only

This book is in heavy demand and is due back strictly by the last
date stamped below. A fine will be charged for the late return of
items.

ONE WEEK LOAN

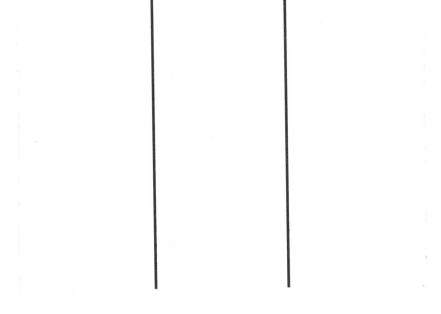

CONTENTS

PREFACE

The Department of Environmental Studies of the University of Nijmegen officially started its activities in 1991; it has three main tasks: undergraduate and graduate environmental education, scientific research and social service. The key subjects of the research programme are: (1) sustainable environmental management of lowland river basins, including estuaries, coastal lagoons and connected wetlands, and (2) setting and application of environmental quality objectives.

Our department celebrated its fifth anniversary in organizing a symposium on new concepts for sustainable management of lowland river basins on November 29, 1996. The results of the plenary lectures, poster presentations, workshop contributions and discussions are presented in this book. In order to get a well balanced picture of the Dutch knowledge regarding river basin management, a complementary number of representative authors were invited to publish their views for inclusion into our book. Following this procedure took us more time before the book could be published, but the advantage is that the manuscript now covers the knowledge of almost all the scientific players in the Dutch field of integrated river management, both from governmental and non-governmental organizations, including universities.

We would like to thank all colleagues of our department for their help with organizing the symposium. Special thanks are due to the following referees of one or more chapters in this book: B.G.W. Aarts (Department of Environmental Studies, University of Nijmegen), Dr. G.H.P. Arts (Institute for Forestry and Nature Research, Leersum), J.A. van Ast (Erasmus Centre for Environmental Studies, Erasmus University Rotterdam), B.A. Bannink (National Institute of Public Health and the Environment, Bilthoven), Dr. H. van Dijk (Health Council of the Netherlands, Rijswijk), Prof. Dr. J. Dogterom (International Centre of Water Studies, Amersfoort), Prof. Dr. C. den Hartog (Department of Ecology, University of Nijmegen), Dr. R. Heijungs (Centre of Environmental Science, Leiden University), Dr. M.A. Hemminga (Centre for Estuarine and Coastal Ecology, Netherlands Institute of Ecology, Yerseke), Dr. J.L.M. Hermens (Research Institute of Toxicology, Utrecht University), Dr. L.W.G. Higler (Institute for Forestry and Nature Research, Leersum), Dr. A.H.L. Huiskes (Centre for Estuarine and Coastal Ecology, Netherlands Institute of Ecology, Yerseke), Dr. H. Hummel (Centre for Estuarine and Coastal Ecology, Netherlands Institute of Ecology, Yerseke), D.M. de Jong (Department of Environmental Policy Sciences, University of Nijmegen), Dr. R.H.G. Jongman (Department of Physical Planning and Rural Development, Wageningen Agricultural University), J.C.M. Klaver (Department of Environmental Policy Sciences, University of Nijmegen), Dr. F. Klijn (Delft Hydraulics, Delft), L.W.J. Knippenberg (Third World Centre, University of Nijmegen), L. Lamers (Department of Ecology, University of Nijmegen), Prof. Dr. C. van Leeuwen (Research Institute for Toxicology, Utrecht University), Prof. dr. L. Lijklema (Water Quality Management and Aquatic Ecology, Wageningen Agricultural University), C.J.M. Musters (Institute of Evolutionary and Ecological Sciences, Leiden University), Dr. E. Mostert (Centre for Comparative Studies on River Basin

Management, Delft Technical University), Prof. Dr. N. de Pauw (Laboratory for Biological Research in Aquatic Pollution, University of Ghent), Dr. G.B.M. Pedroli (Integrated River Management, Delft Hydraulics), Dr. R. Reijnen (Institute for Forestry and Nature Research, Wageningen), Dr. J.A.A.R. Schuurkes (Arcadis Heidemij Advies, Arnhem), Prof. Dr. K.M. Skarzynska (Department of Soil Mechanics and Earth Sciences, University of Agriculture in Kraków), Prof. Dr. Ir. F. de Smedt (Laboratory of Hydrology, University of Brussels), Dr. J. Stapel (Centre for Estuarine and Coastal Ecology, Netherlands Institute of Ecology, Yerseke), Dr. H. Strijbosch (Department of Environmental Studies, University of Nijmegen), Prof. Dr. G. van der Velde (Department of Ecology, University of Nijmegen), Dr. J.T.A. Verhoeven (Department of Plant Eology and Evolutionary Biology, Utrecht University), Ir. J. Verloop (Technical Committee for Soil Protection, Den Haag) and Prof. J. Wessel (Centre for Comparative Studies on River Basin Management, Delft Technical University).

A sad event is the death of one of our authors, Dr. S.P. Klapwijk, before the end of the project.

The consultancy firms Royal Haskoning Group (Haskoning Ingenieurs- en Architectenbureau, Nijmegen) and Arcadis (Arcadis Heidemij Advies, Arnhem), and the Dutch Association of Water Boards (Unie van Waterschappen, Den Haag) supported the symposium and publication of our book financially. Last, but not least, we wish to thank R.M.M. Delmee for secretarial support.

Nijmegen, May 19, 1998

P.H. Nienhuis
R.S.E.W. Leuven
A.M.J. Ragas

The city of Nijmegen is situated along the river Waal (main branch of the river Rhine in the Netherlands).
(photograph P.J.M. Van den Heuvel)

Advancing industrial developments along the river Waal at Millingen. In the foreground a fragment of softwood floodplain forest.
(photograph H.M. Van de Steeg)

Extreme highwater on the river Meuse in January 1993. The centuries-old method of "sandbagging" prevents the village of being flooded.
(photograph RIZA, Arnhem)

Ecological restoration along the river Waal at the Varikse Plaat in 1996. The yellow dragline is in the early stages of nature rehabilitation far more common than the "target variable", the Black stork.
(photograph RIZA, Arnhem)

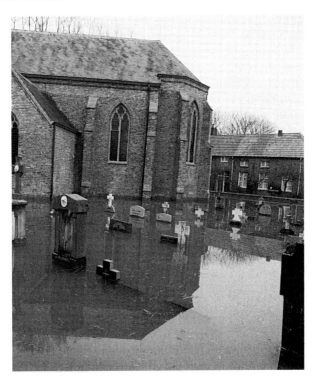

Highwater on the river Waal in the eighties. The graveyard and the church of the village of Kekerdom, situated in the floodplain of the river, have been flooded.
(photograph H.M. Van de Steeg)

Highwater on the river Waal in the eighties. The village of Kekerdom is to be seen at the horizon.
(photograph H.M. Van de Steeg)

A branch of the Lower Rhine is provided with movable barrages. This is the weir at Driel.
(photograph RIZA, Arnhem)

The river Meuse in the Netherlands has several weirs. The weir at Linne is provided with a fish-lad-
der to allow the free passage for riverine fish.
(photograph J. Koolen)

The floodplain forest at the Ooijpolder near Nijmegen during winter.
(photograph R.S.E.W. Leuven)

Remnants of a hardwood floodplain forest along the river IJssel (a branch of the river Rhine in the Netherlands).
(photograph RIZA, Arnhem)

The river Meuse near Verdun (France) bears still some characteristics of the "natural river".
(photograph RIZA, Arnhem)

The Common Meuse, a river bordering The Netherlands and Belgium, carries great potentials for ecological rehabilitation.
(photograph RIZA, Arnhem)

The river Loire (France) provides reference images for ecological rehabilitation of rivers in the Netherlands.
(photograph RIZA, Arnhem)

The river Meuse between Roermond and Belfeld (The Netherlands).
(photograph RIZA, Arnhem)

Inland pool along the river Waal in the Ooijpolder near Nijmegen (The Netherlands).
(photograph R.S.E.W. Leuven)

The river Waal (Rhine) at the Plaat van Ewijk in the Netherlands.
(photograph J. Koolen)

GENERAL INTRODUCTION

P.H. Nienhuis, R.S.E.W. Leuven & A.M.J. Ragas
*Department of Environmental Studies, Faculty of Science, University of Nijmegen,
P.O. Box 9010, 6500 GL Nijmegen, The Netherlands*

Rivers function as arteries and veins on the worlds continents, they are among the most valuable but also most abused resources on earth. In the course of human history intensive use has been made of river resources, and consequently the quality of the river ecosystems slowly degraded. River degradation in Europe became particularly manifest following the industrial revolution: the river Thames was already extremely polluted in the first half of the nineteenth century, culminating around the fifties of this century in public nuisance from hydrogen sulfide (Gameson & Wheeler 1977), the river Rhine reached its worst level in the late sixties and early seventies of this century (Tittizer & Krebs 1996), and the river Vistula in Poland may not have reached its most polluted status yet (Makinia et al. 1996). All over Europe large rehabilitation programmes have been started, and there is now a greater interest in river protection and conservation, based on ecological and socio-economic arguments, than there was ten to twenty years ago. Not all rehabilitation programmes are equaly successful, and the number of environmental problems still to be solved is substantial. The call for management strategies combining a number of human demands and functions with the ecological values of rivers is becoming more and more manifest.

"New concepts for sustainable management of river basins" is the rather pretentious title of this book. The title, however, is also a realistic one, because "sustainability" and "sustainable development" is daily talk now, and river basin management should also be checked on its "sustainability" standards. An almost classic starting point is to quote from the report by the World Commission on Environment and Development: "Sustainable development is to ensure that humanity meets the needs of the present, without compromising the ability of future generations to meet their own needs" (WCED 1987). To "sustain" is to hold, keep up, keep alive, literally "able to last". The concept of sustainable development does imply limits imposed by the present state of technology and social organisation on environmental resources, and by the ability of the biosphere to absorb the effects of human activities.

In most European countries water quality of rivers has been monitored for many years. However, as pollution has both physico-chemical and biological effects on the receiving river ecosystems, the quality of the water can be assessed in many different ways, and there are numerous methods in use throughout Europe. An arbitrary river quality classification varies between "good quality", i.e. nutrient poor, saturated with dissolved oxygen, containing a rich invertebrate fauna, and suitable spawning grounds for salmonid fish, and "bad quality", suffering from excessive

New concepts for sustainable management of river basins, pp. 1–6
edited by P.H. Nienhuis, R.S.E.W. Leuven and A.M.J. Ragas
© *1998 Backhuys Publishers, Leiden, The Netherlands*

organic pollution, prolonged periods of very low oxygen concentration or total deoxygenation, anaerobic sediments, and severe toxic input, and consequently devoid of fish. Applying this classification, about a quarter of the European river reaches are classified as having poor or bad water quality. The catchments of the large rivers Rhine, and especially Meuse and Scheldt score below average: 25 to 37 per cent of the reaches have still poor to bad water quality. The cleanest rivers in Europe are to be found in the periphery of the continent: Iceland, Scotland and Ireland (Stanners & Bourdeau 1995). On the basis of these facts the present management practice of most European rivers does not deserve the label "sustainable".

River regulation is a general term describing the physical changes that people impose on watercourses leading to the destruction of the original ecosystems, such as land drainage, flood protection, the building and maintenance of reservoirs, dams and weirs, channelisation to serve navigation and transport over water, water abstraction for industrial, agricultural and drinking water purposes, wastewater discharge, and so on. Many of the rivers in Europe have now been regulated, to the greatest extent in Western and Southern Europe, where the percentage of rivers that are still in a natural state is very low, 0 to 20 per cent. By contrast, in countries such as Poland, Estonia and Norway, many rivers still have 70 to 100 per cent of their reaches in a natural state. River regulation often causes major changes in biological river processes, primarily in the flow regime and the transport of dissolved and particulate organic matter. The effects are seen not just locally, but may be extensive, especially in the downstream reaches of the river (Stanners & Bourdeau 1995). Up to now river regulation in Europe is characterized by a dominant technological approach, and certainly not by a sustainble use of environmental resources.

In general, restoration of large rivers to pristine conditions is not feasible, but in many cases there is still considerable potential for rehabilitation, that is the partial restoration of riverine habitats and ecosystems. Renewal of physical and biological interactions between the main channel, backwaters, and floodplains, is central to the rehabilitation of large rivers. According to Nielsen (1996), during the last decade the increasing European trend to extensify agricultural production and to set-aside agricultural land in floodplains has increased awareness of the value of river and watershed restoration for integrated catchment management. Moreover, awareness is also increasing that the re-instatement of naturally functioning river floodplain systems may benefit catchment management by increasing nutrient retention, overcoming the problem of reduced summer discharge, increasing floodwater storage capacity, reducing river maintenance costs and providing better amenity and recreation facilities.

Experience with the rehabilitation of large rivers is rare relative to smaller streams, due to the large number of interwoven societal demands on the river, the connected economic costs and the complexity of the physical and biological systems involved. Proposals and concepts for large river restoration are much more abundant than are demonstrations in the field. However, it has been demonstrated that localized rehabilitation projects can be successful. The challenge for those policy makers who are in the position to value rivers, is to readdress this imbalance while protecting larger rivers from further degradation (Gore & Shields 1995).

Several large European rivers have catchment areas shared between a number of countries (e.g. Rhine, Meuse and Scheldt), and in some cases collaboration between riparian countries has been initiated to protect water resources. The Netherlands receives 85 per cent of its water from transboundary rivers. From the analysis of Dieperink (1997) it appears that the necessity of transboundary management of the river Rhine was recognized for shipping already at the end of the eighteenth century. The transboundary pollution aspect was given attention in 1932, when the Dutch government protested against emissions of residual salt into the French part of the river. After World War II, the pollution of the river increased tremendously, and in 1950 the International Rhine Commission started to study wastewater and water quality problems. The international cooperation against pollution was strengthened in the course of the years in formal international agreements. A new milestone was reached in 1986, after the Sandoz accident, when chemical spills killed a considerable part of the Rhine ecosystem. To accelerate ecological improvements in the Rhine, ministers from riparian countries decided in 1986 to establish the Rhine Action Programme, having as an aim that the ecosystem of the Rhine must become a suitable habitat again, to allow the return to this great European river of the higher animal species which were once present here, and have since disappeared (such as the salmon; Van Dijk *et al.* 1995).

The recent switch from technological river management to ecological river management is a historical change. There have always been ecologically minded visionaries in environmental management, but their voices have not been heard until recently. Ecology scores better nowadays than it did decades ago. One of the reasons for that change is the costly mistakes that have been made in the past by ignoring natural processes when designing dams, levees, channel stabilization and flood protection schemes. Another factor behind the higher valuation of ecology is the rise of the environmental impact assessment (EIA). Environmental impact legislation in the European Union and many other countries now makes it mandatory to carry out formal EIAs of any major scheme likely to alter river systems. This includes dams and channel realignments, the physical planning of floodplains and dike reinforcement projects. The outcome of this process is a generation of engineer-designers who simply have to know about ecology, hydrology, soil science, environmental economics, sociological processes, and planning and land use changes (Hey 1995).

River management, whether it is technologically or ecologically sound, is always based on policy considerations. In some cases the policy making process that shapes river management may become an aim in itself. In 1998 the pretentious "Ecological Dow Jones Index", summarizing the "health" of the river ecosystem in a few transparant indices, and introduced in 1989 (V&W 1989, Ten Brink & Woudstra 1991) finds only a regional Dutch application. The larger neighbouring countries, Germany, France and the United Kingdom all use diverging systems for integrated river management (Harper & Ferguson 1995). Besides this international confusion, the general question is whether the "data-rich but information-poor" syndrome in water quality management, formulated by Ward *et al.* (1986), has been overcome yet. The answer is no: a fact is that most river-monitoring systems are descriptive and at a maximum prescriptive but not predictive. In reality calamities are still determining the agenda of the water manager. The Rhine and Meuse floods of 1993 and 1995 provide a near-perfect laboratory experiment for crisis management. The main objective was to enhance systematic understanding of national differences and similarities in flood management (Rosenthal & Hart 1998). The most recent floods in 1997 in the Czech Republic, Poland and Germany demonstrated once again the continued vulnerability of modern societies to natural hazards.

A number of European policy documents on multifunctional water management appeared in the eighties (Higler & Van Liere 1997, Nienhuis & Leuven 1998). These documents functioned as inspiring sources for the development of concepts and instruments for integrated water management of lowland river basins. The excitement about the first spectacular results, however, is fading away. Considering the complexity of the remaining environmental problems in river catchments, it is becoming more and more difficult to gain positive and predictable results. To give an example: in the lowland section of the Rhine-Meuse catchment the emissions of harmful elements are decreasing slowly, and continuously, but the emissions of some heavy metals and nutrients on the Dutch surface waters are slightly increasing again (comparison of 1994 and 1995; Anonymous, 1998). The curve of the societal costs of integrated water management against the results gained, shows signs of diminishing returns. Several Western European riparian states have recently started to lift the strict environmental quality objectives (EQO) for surface water, that are defined in policy plans and legislation. They are being replaced by targets that merely function as guidelines, but which are not legally binding. The development of new concepts and instruments for river management demands ingenuity and optimal mobilisation of the potential of centres of knowledge. Universities should play a prominent role in this process. A recent Dutch initiative should be mentioned here: the foundation of the Dutch Centre of River Science, where governmental organisations and universities together bundle their knowledge in order to be prepared to face future challenges in river management.

The development of new concepts for river management is a continuous challenge for river scientists. Evenly important, however, is the recognition and application of recently published concepts in empirical studies. In fact a considerable number of integrated river concepts have recently been published (for a review see Townsend 1996), and the empirical large-scale testing of the models, connected to the political willingness of catchment-scale restoration are forming the real bottlenecks in the societal process.

The aim of the present book is (1) to present a comprehensive overview of research projects of the staff members of our department, (2) to publish the Dutch body of knowledge and experiences regarding integrated river basin management, and (3) to serve the public debate leading to new scientific concepts and tools for sustainable management of river basins. The manuscripts in the book are divided over three sections, (1) habitat quality, and (2) water quality, as two sides of the environmental quality of river basins, and (3) integrated river basin approaches.

(1) Habitat quality is exemplified as the environmental quality of a spatial unit, either defined at the level of the landscape, ecosystem, ecotope or habitat. Habitat quality is also expressed at the level of the occurrence or absence of populations of specific plants or animals or vegetation units. Habitat quality is rather recently recognized as an important item in river basin management; it strongly focuses on the ecological integrity of the (mostly physically disturbed) land- or water-units, based on widely accepted conservation criteria such as naturalness, representativeness, (bio)diversity and rarity (Boon 1993).

(2) Water quality covers the classical restoration issues, viz. environmental pollution and water- and sediment quality, and focuses in this book on effects of emis-

sions of chemical elements, such as heavy metals and nutrients, but also on diffuse loadings and their (cumulative) impact on the receiving water bodies and on populations of plants and animals. In the policy process of recognition, assessment and control of water quality problems, an evaluation of specific quality objectives for water systems, such as rivers, is given, together with immission assessment procedures for discharge permitting.

(3) Integrated river basin management (IRBM) is the ideal arrangement for which everybody strives, but few attain (cf. Clayton & O'Riordan, 1995). And this is also the case in our book. The presented case studies bear all a preliminary attitude. They suffer all from lack of cohesion between ecological, economic and sociological arguments, and the likely possibility that the planning procedures become a self-fulfilling prophecy for policymakers. How to attain IRBM is still a matter of much debate, especially concerning international rivers, subject to their own national management regimes. It took river scientists a long time to move from a position of "investigating and understanding the system", to one of focusing on aspects critical for "management". Consequently, according to Robinson (1994), a disproportionate amount of time and valuable resources were spent worldwide, investigating matters that could never contribute to effective management of the river system.

Notwithstanding this critical approach we are convinced that the struggle for sustainable management of entire river basins is the only way to reach full understanding of rivers as dynamic, open systems, that should be considered as ecological continua from the source to the sea. IRBM, i.e. to conserve, enhance, and, where appropriate, restore the total river environment through effective land and resource planning, across the whole catchment area (Gardiner & Cole 1992), is the means to reach sustainability.

References

Anonymous. 1998. Emissie naar water en lucht 1995. H2O n31 (2):9 (in Dutch).

Boon, P.J. 1993. Essential elements in the case for river conservation. In: P.J. Boon, P. Calow & G.E. Petts (eds) - River conservation and management. Wiley, Chichester, pp. 11-33.

Clayton, K. & O'Riordan, T. 1995. Coastal processes and management. In: T. O'Riordan (ed.) – Environmental Science for Environmental Management, pp.151-164. Longman, Singapore.

Dieperink, C. 1997. Tussen zout en zalm. Lessen uit de ontwikkeling van het regime inzake de Rijnvervuiling. Ph. D. Thesis, University of Utrecht, pp. 1-425.

Gameson, A.L.H. & Wheeler, A. 1977. Restoration and recovery of the Thames estuary. In: J. Cairns Jr., K.L. Dickson & E.E. Herricks (eds) - Recovery and restoration of damaged ecosystems, pp. 72-101. University Press Virginia, Charlottesville, VA, USA.

Gardiner, J.L. & Cole, L. 1992. Catchment planning: the way forward for river protection in the UK. In: P.J. Boon, P. Calow & G.E. Petts (eds) – River Conservation and Management. John Wiley, Chichester, pp. 397-406.

Gore, J.A. & Shields, J.F.D. 1995. Can large rivers be restored ? BioScience 45: 142-152.

Harper, D.M. & Ferguson, A.J.D. (eds). 1995. The ecological basis for river management. Wiley, Chichester. pp. 1-614.

Hey, R. 1995. River processes and management. In: T. O'Riordan (ed.) - Environmental Science for Environmental Management. Longman, Singapore. pp. 131-150.

Higler, L.W.G. & Van Liere, L. 1997. Freshwater quality in Europe: tales from the continent. In: P.J. Boon & D.L. Howell (eds) – Freshwater quality: defining the indefinable? The Stationery Office, Edinburgh, pp. 59-68.

Makinia, J., Dunnette, D. & Kowalik, P. 1996. Water pollution in Poland. Europ. Wat. Pollut. Control 6: 26-33.

Nielsen, M.B. 1996. River restoration: report of a major EU Life demonstration project. Aquat. Conserv.: Marine Freshwat. Ecosyst. 6: 187-190.

Nienhuis, P.H. & Leuven, R.S.E.W. 1998. Ecological concepts for the sustainable management of lowland river basins: a review. In: P.H. Nienhuis, R.S.E.W. Leuven & A.M.J. Ragas (eds) - New concepts for sustainable management of river basins. Backhuys Publishers, Leiden, pp. 7-33.

Robinson, S.J. 1994. Integrated approaches to the management of whole river systems. In: M.C. Uys (ed.) - Classification of rivers and environmental health indicators. Water Research Commission Report No. TT 63/94: 301-312. Cape Town, South Africa.

Rosenthal, U. & Hart, P. (eds). 1998. Flood response and crisis management in Western Europe. A comparative analysis. Springer, Berlin, 236 pp.

Stanners, D. & Bourdeau, P. (eds). 1995. Europe's Environment. The Dobris Assessment. European Environment Agency Copenhagen, Earthscan Publications, London.

Ten Brink, B.J.E. & Woudstra, J.H. 1991. Towards an effective and rational water management: the Aquatic Outlook Project - integrating water management, monitoring and research. Europ. Wat Pollut. Control 1: 20-27.

Tittizer, T. & Krebs, F. (Hrsg). 1996. Ökosystemforschung der Rhein und seine Auen - eine Bilanz. Springer Verlag, Berlin, pp.1-468.

Townsend, C.R. 1996. Concepts in river ecology: pattern and process in the catchment hierarchy. Arch. Hydrobiol. Suppl. 113, Large Rivers 10: 3-21.

Van Dijk, G.M., Marteijn, E.C.L. & Schulte-Wulwer-Leidig, A. 1995. Ecological rehabilitation of the river Rhine: plans, progress and perspectives. Regul. Rivers: Res. Manag. 11: 377-388.

V&W. 1989. Derde Nota Waterhuishouding - Water voor nu en later. Ministerie van Verkeer en Waterstaat (V&W), Rijkswaterstaat, Den Haag, The Netherlands (in Dutch).

Ward, R.C., Loftis, J.C. & McBride, G.M. 1986. The "data-rich but information-poor" syndrome in water quality monitoring. Environment. Manag. 10: 291-297.

WCED. 1987. Our Common Future, pp. 1-11. World Commission on Environment and Development, Oxford University Press, Oxford.

ECOLOGICAL CONCEPTS FOR THE SUSTAINABLE MANAGE-
MENT OF LOWLAND RIVER BASINS: A REVIEW

P.H. Nienhuis & R.S.E.W. Leuven
Department of Environmental Studies, Faculty of Science, University of Nijmegen,
P.O. Box 9010, 6500 GL Nijmegen, The Netherlands

Abstract

This paper reviews the state of the art of ecological theory in the framework of river management and restoration. The paper focuses not on the classical restoration issues (environmental pollution) but rather on physical disturbance and ecological integrity of ecosystems, thus confronting international ecological theories with Dutch river management practice. A considerable number of holistic ecological concepts for river management have been published recently. There is only restricted need for the development of new concepts, but what counts is the reconnaissance and application of ecological principles and the ambition of scientists to cooperate internationally at the catchment level. The policy and planning process of integrated river management becomes an aim in itself, which is in sharp contrast with ecological objectives of holistic streamflow management, comprising extremely high and low benchmark discharges, and restoration of lateral and longitudinal connectivity and integrity of river systems. The Dutch policy regarding ecological restoration of rivers finds itself in an advanced, but internationally isolated position. Ecologically the Dutch policy vision "Space for the river" can only be interpreted as widening the floodplains of Rhine and Meuse, and having overflows available in case of extreme river floods.

1. Introduction

Floodplain river ecosystems are among the most valuable and most abused resources on earth. In the unaltered, natural state, they are dynamic in space and time, forming an environmental mosaic inhabited by aquatic, semi-aquatic and terrestrial species. The high biodiversity and productivity of natural floodplains and river ecosystems can be attributed to complex habitat structure, high flux rates of nutrients and organic matter, more or less predictable shifts in environmental conditions and the evolution of adaptive strategies to exploit the spatio-temporal heterogeneity. Floodplains link running waters with standing waters, terrestrial systems with aquatic systems and surface waters with ground waters. The driving force that maintains ecological connectivity and integrity is disturbance induced by fluvial dynamics of flooding. Only recently have aquatic ecologists come to fully appreciate the functional dynamics of floodplain rivers. This recognition reflects the concentration of stream ecologists in parts of the world where riverine reaches have long been regulated and constrained by engineering works (Ward 1995). Large rivers, like Rhine, Meuse and Scheldt, are dynamic, four-dimensional, open systems

New concepts for sustainable management of river basins, pp. 7–33
edited by P.H. Nienhuis, R.S.E.W. Leuven and A.M.J. Ragas
© *1998 Backhuys Publishers, Leiden, The Netherlands*

that should be considered as ecological continua, from the source, via the upper and lower section, down to the receiving estuary and coastal waters.

In reality the rivers and floodplains of Europe, and particularly those of Western Europe, have been modified drastically during the past centuries. Almost eighty percent of the total water discharge of the main European rivers is more or less strongly affected by water regulation measures (Dynesius & Nilsson 1994). The main measures are visible in flow regulation, canalization, habitat fragmentation, land reclamation and consequent destruction of original habitats, and water and sediment pollution. In practice the large (European) rivers are already for more than 500 years manipulated systems, having lost their naturalness and ecological integrity. The habitat diversity of Rhine and Meuse has decreased considerably. The indigenous flora an fauna of the large rivers has partially been replaced by allochthonous species. The overall process of disturbance by human influences has led to a levelling down of the original ecosystems (Tittizer & Krebs 1996).

Since the late 1970s, however, there has been a change of attitude towards integrated river management in several European countries. There is now a greater interest in river protection and conservation, based on ecological and socio-economic arguments, for instance in the maintenance of habitats and in the supplying of good-quality drinking water. Water treatment in the framework of integrated water management programmes, drastically diminishing the pollution caused by point sources, appeared to be successful in the initial stages in several countries (e.g. Rhine Action Programme, Schulte-Wulwer-Leidig 1995, Hendriks *et al.* 1997). But in a later stage the complexity of the remaining environmental problems has been governed by the law of the diminishing returns: the curve of the public costs of integrated river management versus the results gained, shows a decreasing trend. Europe-wide unsolved problems regard (1) the effects of diffuse sources on the receiving water bodies, containing dispersed, persistent pesticides and fertilizers, (2) the heterogeneity of accumulations of toxicants in the watermass and particularly in the underwater sediments "archive", (3) the effects of combinations of pollutants on plant and animal populations and ecosystems, (4) conflicting public functions (e.g. transport over water, water sports, nature conservation), (5) flood alleviation following increased and uncontrolled river discharges, and (6) the reconstruction during the rehabilitation process of the minimum structure for the healthy functioning of degraded ecosystems. Progress in these directions will be achieved only through knowledge of the dynamics of interactive processes among rivers, the connection between rivers and estuaries, their floodplains and groundwaters and the construction of a conceptual framework for preserving near-natural systems and restoring degraded ones (De Vries *et al.* 1996).

This paper will review the state of the art of ecological theory on river management and restoration in relation to the practice of Dutch integrated river management. This contribution will not focus on the "classical" restoration issues, viz. environmental pollution and water- and sediment quality, but rather on recently recognized items such as physical disturbance i.e. the ecological integrity of habitats, species populations and ecosystems (habitat quality). The manuscript will concentrate on the situation in the Netherlands, lowland floodplain of the large European rivers Rhine and Meuse, and particularly on the Rhine and its tributaries. Dutch policy makers and river managers have recently put much energy in the development of a policy framework for integrated river management (V&W 1996). The general aim of this review is to confront and verify the Dutch policy plans in a broader international context of recent ecological theories. Three research questions will be answered: (1) What is the state of the art in Dutch integrated river management and policy plans?; (2) What is the state of the art of international ecological concepts for river management and restoration?; (3) What are the results of the confrontation and verification of international ecological theories and Dutch river management practice?

2. State of the art of Dutch integrated river management

2.1. The historical background

It is a known fact that almost all large European rivers are heavily influenced by man. The deterioration of the Rhine already started in the early Middle Ages. Already during the period 800-1200 considerable areas in the Rhine flood plains were deforested, owing to an increasing demand of wood for building and fuel purposes. Flood defence dikes were built from 1000 onwards. Canalization started already in the late fourteenth century. In the early 18th century almost all beech and oak forests were cut down, and replaced by grassland and cattle, the picture which we know so well nowadays. In the nineteenth century the Rhine changed at an accelerated speed: flood defences, flood control dams, barrages and hydroelectric power stations were built in the upper Rhine. Industrialization took place in the Middle and Lower Rhine: the construction of traffic roads, human and industrial settlements, large factories for steel and chemicals. Channelization is the most impressive human disturbance of the riverbed. Nowadays the river Rhine is a completely man-manipulated river (Tittizer & Krebs 1996). Downstream the completion of the Haringvlietdam in 1970 meant a physical barrier between the rivers Rhine and Meuse and the North Sea. The presence of this dam revealed extremely detrimental effects on the ecology of the former estuary, and in a wider context on the ecology of the entire rivers Rhine and Meuse, and the coastal strip along the Netherlands (Nienhuis 1996, Smit *et al.* 1994).

From the early human settlements until the Middle Ages the composition of the water in the river was hardly influenced by humans. The massive cutting down of trees in the Middle Ages, introduced erosion, and changed the sediment load of the river. From 1920 to 1990 the human population in the Rhine catchment increased from 5 million people to 45 million people, causing an exponentially increasing impact on water quality and habitat occupation. The maximum pollution of the river occurred in the sixties and early seventies of this century. Since 1975, however, a positive turn in water quality and in the composition of species can be observed (Tittizer & Krebs 1996).

The variety of river biota is currently increasing again, largely as a result of the return of original occupants. The variety of species is also being enlarged by immigrants. Many of these species come from a brackish environment and southern areas (Breukel & Bij de Vaate 1996). The occurrence of several brackish-water species in the freshwater stretch of the river Rhine is a result of the increasing salinity of the river, and concomitant rise in temperature of the riverwater (approximately 2-3 °C).

At present the Rhine contains 10 to 15 times its natural salt content. In 1874 the yearly mean-salinity at the German-Dutch border was 13 mg Cl⁻ per liter; in 1988 it was 150 mg per liter with maximum levels up to 234 mg Cl⁻ per liter (Den Hartog *et al.* 1989). In addition, the continuously increasing integration of river systems which used to be separated, plays a part in the distribution of flora and fauna, e.g. the channelization between the river Danube and the river Rhine connects the Black Sea with the North Sea.

Notwithstanding existing international Rhine treaties (V&W 1989) only recently there is a growing concern for the restoration and maintenance of river ecosystems, a policy which is strongly incident-driven. A striking example is the Sandoz fire in 1986 in Schweizerhalle, near Basel on the river Rhine. The fire evoked substantial chemical pollution and consequent massive mortality of fish and invertebrates in extensive streches of the Rhine. This accident appeared to be the turning point in river management (Rhine Action Programme): from that time onwards it was not only water quality that counted, but the integrity of Rhine ecosystems was at stake. Already in December 1986 the ministers of the Rhine states, joined in the International Commission for the Protection of the Rhine, decided that the ecosystem Rhine should be restored in the year 2000 to such a level that extinct species (e.g. the salmon) should have returned, that the quality of the water as drinking water should be guaranteed, and that the discharge of pollutants should have been drastically reduced (Schulte-Wulwer-Leidig 1995). Further recovery of the river biota depends on continued repression of pollution, but also on the development of more natural habitats and an increase in morphological dynamics of the river catchment (Breukel & Bij de Vaate 1996).

2.2. The Dutch policy plans for integrated river management

The historical overview presented in section 2.1. is necessary to understand the position of the Dutch river managers. It points to the dominant feature of river management: to avoid flooding and to guarantee safety for the human population. In dealing with the most recent trends in Dutch policy plans for river management, it should be realized that the deteriorated large rivers as we know them nowadays leave only little space for restoration measures without violating the basic rule of safety.

In preparation for the Fourth Dutch Water Management Policy Plan, which should appear in 1998, the Ministry of Transport, Public Works and Water Management, performed so-called "Aquatic Outlook" policy reports (Luiten 1995, Duel *et al.* 1996, Postma *et al.* 1996, Rademakers *et al.* 1996). The reports provide insight into the physical, chemical and ecological conditions of Dutch surface waters, the rivers included. The ecological condition of the Dutch rivers is described and presented, using the so-called AMOEBA-methodology. AMOEBA stands for A general Method Of Ecological and Biological Assessment (Ten Brink & Hosper 1989). The method can be used to describe three situations of a specific river branch, (1) the current situation, (2) the historic reference situation, and (3) the target situation, presuming improvement by active management. The target variables in the AMOEBA-approach are mainly conspicuous and characteristic plant and animal species, historically occurring in the river water or floodplain, and now rare or suppressed owing to dominant human impact. AMOEBA is a policy instrument: the choice of the target variables is partly made on the basis of the "cuddliness" of the species. Whether a conspicuous, cq. characteristic species is to be regarded as a keystone species in the foodweb of the ecosystem, or as an essential species to keep the foodweb running, is an ecological question beyond the policy choice. The strength of AMOEBA is the graphical presentation, giving in one short view the ecological status ("health") of a river segment (Fig. 1). The weakness is the insufficient ecological underpinning, and the ignorance of (autonomous) ecological developments (e.g. the increasing dominance of exotic species, such as *Corophium curvispinum*). The AMOEBA is a static policy instrument, not counting the dynamic caprices of the climate (sequences of severe winters or hot summers) and the stochastic occurrence of extremely high river discharges, altering the geomorphological and hence the vegetational pattern of the flood plains.

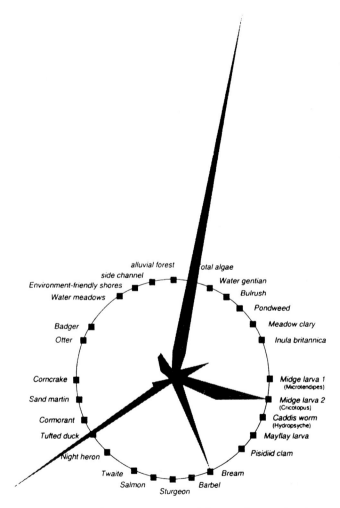

Fig. 1. AMOEBA of the lower Rhine ecosystem, containing a reference situation around 1930 (circle) with target variables (black squares) and the current status of the target variables (indicators) in 1988 (radial graph) (Van Dijk *et al.* 1995)

The historic reference situation necessary as a blueprint for ecological restoration, is a matter of much debate. Recent geological research in natural river levees of fluvial areas along the Dutch river Rhine revealed pollen diagrams from cores dated around 2700 cal year BP. The profiles showed an almost closed hardwood floodplain forest with small open spots in the vegetation, either caused by minor human activities or by natural grazing (De Klerk *et al.* 1997). These data will be used as palaeo-reference ecosystems for nature development projects currently in progress on embanked floodplains in the Netherlands, where agricultural lands will be transformed into new nature areas (De Bruin *et al.* 1987, Helmer *et al.* 1992, Lenders *et al.* 1997). To re-establish these "near-natural wilderness areas" means allowing the natural process of vegetation succession in river floodplains for almost 200 years without human intervention. This is virtually impossible because it is in contrast with the natural evolution of the river catchment (cf. section 3.4.; Ripl *et al.* 1994) and conflicts with several other functions of the rivers, viz. safety reasons (flood protection) and shipping. Going back to the Middle Ages when the rivers freely meandered and were lined with extensive hardwood floodplain forests, without any human impact is an illusion. In practice the future target situation is enclosed by some boundary conditions, of which the most rigid one is safety for the population and their goods. Nowadays Dutch river stretches are harnassed by high dikes, avoiding flooding of the hinterland in case of extremely discharges of river water. One of the policy-driven boundary conditions of the target image is that ecological rehabilitation may not lead to higher Standard Highwater Levels in the river. This means that river lowland forests, following their natural succession, would dominate after roughly 30 years, are only allowed to develop over very limited areas, bound by safety precautions. Nature development means in this context a contradictio in terminus: the spontaneous developments of nature leading to softwood and hardwood forests in the flood plains should continuously be managed and removed by grazing and cutting.

The current policy of the Dutch government is that the total area of "natural" landscape in the floodplains of the Rhine branches and along the Meuse will increase to approximately 18,000 hectares in 2015 (RIVM 1997) owing to active management in which agricultural land (mainly cultivated meadows) will be transformed into natural grassland, wetlands, dynamic braided or secondary river branches, and restricted areas of softwood and hardwood floodplain forests. This is theoretically a major step into the direction of the nature target model. The optimum nature target model is bound by societal choices, which can be either a continuation of the present-day policy of economic priorities or a future scenario aiming at sustainable ecological development (RIVM 1997).

2.3. The River Ecotope System

The River Ecotope System (RES; Rademakers & Wolfert 1994) classifies 18 riverecotopes and 65 sub-ecotopes that occur in the river beds and floodplains of the rivers Rhine and Meuse in the Netherlands and adjacent parts of Belgium and Germany. The spatial relations between ecotopes and their surrounding express themselves in the transport of elements and organisms, creating a functional system of higher order, the landscape. Ecotopes are defined as spatial ecological units (scale 1:25,000 to 1:100,000) of which the composition and development are determined by their abiotic, biotic and anthropogeneous factors. In contrast with ecosystems (see section 3.2.) ecotopes are concrete, easily to be mapped and monitored units that cover the entire landscape. As such the RES offers a base for future policy-oriented research and design projects within the project "Ecological Rehabilitation of the Rivers Rhine and Meuse". The RES is to be used on national and regional levels by policy makers, landscape architects and those involved in nature and river management (cf. Reijnen *et al.* 1995). Ecotope designation should have relevance for the operative nature policy. Ecotopes without policy relevance, because they are too small and insignificant, should be grouped together with more significant ecotopes.

In the Aquatic Outlook the RES makes sense by its ecological relevance in terms of ecosystem structure and biodiversity. However, these ecotopes are clustered in 8 groups, in order to improve the intercomparison between the different river branches. This reduction is in ecological terms a simplification of the natural diversity on community-ecosystem level, but can be legitimized by policy considerations. In the latter case the 8 clusters could as well be simply designated as basic landscape types, without applying the long-winded procedure of distinguishing ecotopes.

The combination of (1) the AMOEBA-approach in which a summation of target species demonstrates the species oriented target image and (2) a graphic presentation of the surface area of ecotopes designating the present situation, the historic reference situation and the future, policy directed target situation, is used to describe the ecological status of a river branch. Following a theoretical and static approach, habitat suitability indices have been calculated, in which for every target species is indicated which ecotopes can be considered as habitat, and to what extent -measured in surface area- ecotopes are suitable as habitat (Postma *et al.* 1996). These calculated indices have their practical value (Lenders et al. 1998), but projected on tangible, physical landscapes their use is limited. The high floods of 1993 and 1995 demonstrated the dynamic nature of Dutch rivers: an enormous amount of sand was displaced by the river, sand dunes were formed on the river levees, layers of silt were deposited and diaspores distributed widely, literally overruling the published mapping of ecotopes.

2.4. "Space For The River" policy

The governmental policy to allow the rivers to take more physical space, in order to avoid emergency scenarios during extremely high discharges of the river, and consequent high water levels in the river ("Space for the river"; VROM & V&W 1996) has farreaching consequences for the present river management. Generally each raising of the water level caused by actions of man (building of houses; reclamation of wetlands; forest growth; etc.) must be compensated for in a sustainable manner. The use of the winterbed of the river is severely restricted: existing man-made constructions, such as farmhouses and stone-factories may be maintained, but no expansion of building sites is allowed; ecological restoration comprising the natural development of floodplain forests, creating resistance and roughness of the winterbed may not interfere with the unimpeded discharge of riverwater, causing higher water levels than the calculated Standard Highwater Levels, connected to specific risk assessment levels. Compensating measures might be:(1) heightening of the existing winter dikes; (2) lateral compensation by landinwards rebuilding of the winterdike; (3) creating inland inundation fields, to be used in case of extremely high river discharges; (4) lowering (excavating) the river floodplains over very large distances. The second and third option are largely ignored in policy documents, owing to the fact that already centuries ago the now landinwards area, the former floodplain, has been reclaimed, completely cultivated and densely populated and economically and legally fully occupied.

The first option is under serious policy consideration now. To heighten and strengthen the main dike is "business as usual"; until the year 2000 roughly 450 km of river dikes have still to be reinforced and heightened at the safety level of 1/1250 per year. The recent high water levels occurring in the rivers (1993 and 1995) have biased the existing models: the "design discharge" (a theoretical calculated discharge of the river, acting as a standard for the height of the main dikes along the river, guaranteeing the accepted degree of protection against flooding: 1/1250 yr) calculated for the year 2001 within the framework of the Flood Protection Act (1996), has to be raised again from 15,000 m^3s^{-1} to 16,000 m^3s^{-1} (Silva & Kok, 1996). But this process of heightening and strengthening of the dikes cannot be continued forever. The public acceptance of high and unsurmountable river-walls separating the low-lying, ever compacting inhabited polders from the higher situated silted up river bed and flood plain is supposed to decrease.

The fourth option is new: to excavate the existing flood plains over very large distances, in order to create physical space for the river, especially during periods of extremely high discharges. The feasibility of this option will be discussed on the basis of ecological arguments in section 4.2.2., because it means a confrontation of future river management and ecological theory.

3. State of the art of ecological concepts for river management and restoration

3.1. The river as a temporal and spatial continuum

Townsend & Hildrew (1994) and Townsend (1996) reviewed and evaluated the diversity of ecological concepts that have been proposed so far. River ecology has moved from a static view, describing spatial patterns of organisms, populations and communities in a zone or section of a river, through a still descriptive fase in which the occurring biota were correlated with physical and chemical environmental factors, to a stage where structural linkages at various spatial and temporal scales and biological processes became the focus and explanations for patterns depended on carefully conceived causal pathways.

This historical sequence from simple descriptions of biota via correlations to causal explanatons of the relations between biotic communities and environment on an ever growing spatial and temporal scale reflects not only the history of river ecology in many countries, but also follows an inevitable technological and economic sequence inherent to the evolution of science. Modern river science on the level of an entire river catchment needs multidisciplinary approaches, sophisticated instrumentation in the field, outstanding chemical and physical laboratory equipment, computer facilities and satellite images. This explains why the knowledge of many river systems is still in its infant stage (cf. Harper & Ferguson 1995).

Ward & Stanford (1993) formulated research needs in regulated river ecology and plead for holistic, catchment based actions to mitigate the impacts on ecology and consequences of river regulation. They urged to maintain a clear commitment to scientific methods and not allow single-minded or species specific-approaches or models to dominate mitigation processes.

According to Petts (1996) most of the general scientific principles underpinning the determination of ecological needs for river management are connected to the flow regime of the river, (1) the longitudinal connectivity, (2) the floodplain flows, (3) the channel maintenance flows, comprising the minimum and the optimum flows. Wet years and concomitant high river discharges are particularly important for sustaining the gross morphology of the channel and floodplain systems. Channel form, erosion and deposition of sediment and floodplain communities structure are affected by the full range of flows, which on many rivers occurs once per twenty years. The natural frequency and duration of benchmark flows should be considered, and whenever possible preserved in determining the ecologically acceptable flow regimes (see section 3.4.: Ecologically Acceptable Flow Regime). Although extensive flooding and highly unstable channels may be incompatible with other human uses of river corridors, floodplain inundation and channel mobility within some sectors, or within the reach of a specific corridor, can have significant ecosystem benefits (Petts 1996).

3.2. Ecotope, ecosystem and habitat templet

Although the concept "ecotope" is not commonly coined in classical ecology textbooks (cf. Begon *et al.* 1986), Dutch river managers use the notion frequently. The concept ecotope is one of the oldest in landscape ecology; it signifies a spatial unit, as defined by Tansley (1935) and independently also by Troll (1963), who was the first to operationalize the concept as the smallest unit that can still be considered as a landscape. The concept has been used and reworked into an ecotope classification, elaborated for rivers and their floodplains by Rademakers & Wolfert (1994) and Wolfert (1996), but there is only restricted application for aquatic environments and brackish habitats in general, presumably because of their dynamic and changeable nature.

In the Dutch discussion Stevers *et al.* (1987) widened the definition: an ecotope is a spatial unit which is homogeneous as to vegetation structure, succession stage and main abiotic factors. Vroon *et al.* (1997) maltreated the definition further: an ecotope is a spatially bordered ecological unit of which the composition and development are determined by abiotic, biotic and anthropogenic conditions. In practice the ecotope is often reduced to an isolated basic mapping unit of less than one to several hectares.

The concept "ecosystem" was first used in print by Tansley (1935) in his paper on vegetational concepts and terms. In the course of the short history of ecology the concept of the ecosystem, although powerful and robust, became an scale-less abstraction of little use to practical nature managers. According to Odum (1971) the ecosystem is the basic functional unit in ecology. The ecosystem concept is dimensionally undefined: it may be a pond, a catchment basin, the earths' biosphere, or (quoting Odum) a window flower box. For practical environmental managers and engineers a dimensionless unit remains an abstractum, not applicable in every days practice of sustainable nature restoration (Nienhuis & Leuven 1997). The definition of an ecosystem therefore should be refined, taking into account the scale of the system. Willis (1997), in an historical analysis of the ecosystem concept, suggested the following definition: an ecosystem is a unit comprising a community (or communities) of organisms and their physical and chemical environment at any scale, desirably specified, in which there are continuous fluxes of matter and energy in an interactive open system. In this definition "ecosystem" and "ecotope", as being a specified area of land or water, are coming quite close together, in favour of the practical applicability in nature management.

Klijn (1997) held a plea for the ecosystem as the central unit in environmental management: the ecosystem concept should be operationalized in such a way that it becomes a practical tool for analyses of environmental managers. The concept ecotope is in his typology reduced to a basic mapping unit of 0.25 to 1.50 hectares, in contrast to the aggregated ecotopes of the "Aquatic Outlook". The concept ecotope is used in confusing ways by Dutch river scientists and managers (cf. Stevers et al. 1987, Rademakers & Wolfert 1994, Vroon et al. 1997, Klijn 1997; see also Zonneveld 1995): it bears unclear and contrasting definitions, and is sometimes applied for purposes not originally intended.

The habitat-approach offers a good alternative for the ecotope-approach. Southwood (1977) coined the concept "habitat" as the physical spot where an organism lives. The habitat provides the templet on which evolution forges characteristic life history strategies. Thus, through the effects of habitat conditions on the fitness of individual organisms in geological time, certain combinations of adaptations for survival and reproduction are assumed to be selected. The nature of each real community will be most accurately reflected in a framework, a habitat templet with two environmental axes, representing spatial and temporal variation (heterogeneity). In the identification of the ecological basis for river management the "habitat as a templet for organisms" has the following advantages: (1) it follows sound ecological theory (cf. Begon et al. 1990); (2) it is internationally applicable and accepted in circles of ecologists and watermanagers (see Harper & Ferguson 1995; Boon et al. 1997: SERCON (System for Evaluating Rivers for Conservation; see paragraph 3.4); Raven et al. 1997: RHS (River Habitat Survey). Table 1 gives a comparison between some river management tools in the Netherlands and in the United Kingdom, and illustrates the low degree of similarity between the two approaches. A more thorough analysis of the use of "ecotope" versus "habitat" in river management is to be recommended.

3.3. Various ecological concepts

Because biological communities integrate the effect of ecological conditions over different temporal and spatial scales, they are considered to be sensitive indicators of river health. Fish- and invertebrate-based indices have most often been used for this purpose, although attention has also been given to riparian vegetation and aquatic plants (Naiman et al. 1992, Uys 1994). The Index of Biotic Integrity (IBI)

Table 1. Comparison between river management tools in the Netherlands and in the United Kingdom (for explanation see text).

The Netherlands	United Kingdom

• Methodology
    AMOEBA
    General Method for
    Ecological Description
	• Methodology
	    SERCON
	    System for Evaluating
	    Rivers for Conservation

• Unit of space
    ecotope
	• Unit of space
	    habitat

• Spatial classification
    RES = River Ecotope System
	• Spatial classification
	    RHS = River Habitat System

is receiving much attention. This can be a fish-community based system which incorporates both structural and functional components of stream fish communities to assess the environmental quality of streams (Karr & Dudley 1981). Although the IBI has been developed in the mid-western United States, it has been successfully applied to other areas in the world (Naiman *et al.* 1992). Difficulties associated with the use of the IBI are related to the determination of natural baseline conditions (Plafkin *et al.* 1989), i.e. the reference image of Dutch watermanagers.

Ramm *et al.* (1994) developed an index for ecosystem integrity (health) (IEH) in which not only physico-chemical (i.e. water quality) and biological (i.e. species richness) variables are used, but also "aesthetic health", centring on what an individual perceives the ideal state of a river-estuary to be. The perception of the appearance of an area will vary from one person to another and from one socio-economic group to another, and thus the measurement of aesthetic health is potentially very subjective. To eliminate this problem, the ideal state of the estuarine area was taken to be the pristine state that existed before any human intervention. The parameters which accomodate most of the aesthetic impact of an estuary, where considered to be floodplain use, the appearance of the floodplain surroundings, and the degree to which the channel margins were natural. This IEH might be applied for rivers and estuaries in South Africa, relatively undisturbed by man. It certainly does not work for large European rivers, impacted by man from ancient times onwards. Good descriptions of pristine European rivers do not exist; when scientists started to make inventories of biota and landscape units, the deterioration had already considerably progressed.

According to Townsend (1996) most ecological concepts are viable and can be meshed together into the broad spatio-temporal context of the catchment hierarchy of an entire river, the unit of study for the river ecologist. Longitudinal linkages, made prominent in the river continuum (Vannote *et al.* 1980) and nutrient spiralling concepts (Webster & Patten 1979), are ubiquitous features of all rivers. The open nature of river ecosystems, characterized by disturbance and temporal variation, and with their various parts linked together by movements of water, other inorganic chemicals, organic matter and organisms, fits neatly into the patch-dynamics framework. In the patch-dynamics concept of river ecosystems different patches (functional units) in the ecosystems are dynamically linked in terms of inputs and outputs of inorganic and organic materials and organisms. The patches may occur at any scale from small (e.g. pools, runs and riffles) to large (subcatchments). Essential is the notion of a hierarchical classification of patches whose nutrient, energy and community dynamics are interlinked within the catchment hierarchy. At present we have much theory but too few rigorous tests at the catchment level to falsify Townsend's (1996) ideas.

3.4. Holistic approaches to river ecology

Present-day water resources management of large European rivers conflicts dramatically with ecologically acceptable flow regimes. Dams, reservoirs and interbasin transfers have been constructed to achieve a policy of regulated equilibrium in water supply, especially in avoiding extremely low and extremely high water flows. This policy is in flagrant contrast with the ecological objectives of holistic river management. Holistic streamflow management requires the derivation of an ecologically acceptable flow regime (EAFR) based upon sound scientific principles. The conservation or restoration of river ecosystems requires considerations of the full range of flows expierenced by the river (Petts 1996). The derivation of the EAFR involves two major steps:

1. To define a hierarchical set of ecological objectives and associated targets, based on a full review of the available hydrological, geomorphological, ecological and management information, including historical records. Dutch progress regarding this item is ongoing ("Salmon back in the Rhine"; AMOEBA; ecotope classification; reference and target images), but the cross references with foreign practice are minimal. The specification of ecological targets incorporates the concept of "acceptable" loss of habitat, species number etc. "Acceptable" loss needs a subjective decision, based on social, cultural and economic factors as well as on scientific ones. In Dutch nature policy a maximal "acceptable" loss of 5% of the species in an ecosystem is incorporated, but there is much debate about this subjective choice (cf. Bink *et al.* 1994).

2. To define the flows of river water required to meet the ecological targets, not only the current, accepted average flows, but also the "benchmark flows" reference discharges, either extremely low or high, including their frequencies and durations should be considered. As an operational minimum each river must be subdivided into four sectors and ecological targets specified for each: headwater stream, middle river, lowland river and estuary. Rivers should be viewed as longitudinal continua dominated by downstream transfers of energy and matter (Vannote *et al.* 1980). The need to sustain longitudinal connectivity is an important principle for river management.

Other scientists have also recognized the importance of a natural flow regime. Ward & Stanford (1995) stress the fact that ecological integrity in floodplain rivers is based on a diversity of water bodies with differing degrees of connectivity with the main river channel (braided rivers, active meandering rivers, oxbow lakes, etc.). To counter the influence of river regulation, restoration efforts should focus on re-establishing dynamic connectivity between the channel and floodplain water bodies.

Boon *et al.* (1997) recently developed a holistic approach in SERCON, a System for Evaluating Rivers for Conservation, a broad-based technique for river evaluation, designed to be applied with greater consistency than present methods, and to provide a simple way of communicating technical information to decision makers, especially in the United Kingdom. Its applications include the identification of important rivers for conservation and potentially the monitoring of rehabilitation schemes. SERCON evaluates data on 35 ecological and non-ecological attributes, grouped within six conservation criteria: physical diversity, naturalness, representativeness, rarity, species richness and special features. For general use a PC version and printed manual of SERCON are available.

The most far-reaching holistic theory is published by Ripl *et al.* (1994). According to them the evolution of the large European rivers after the last glaciation period is an irreversible process, starting with the post-glacial pioneer phase, followed by the climax phase, characterised by a closed cycle of primary production and decomposition, a well developed vegetation cover and consequent optimum water retention capacity (the "sponge"). The closed water cycle connected to this climax phase gave rise to a minimum loss of minerals and plant nutrients. The climax phase lasted in Northern Europe until about 1500 BC, when man began to cultivate the large river systems, exploiting the forests and developing agricultural and (later) urban-industrial practices with ever increasing intensity. This cultural phase, in which most Western and Central European rivers are in now, is characterized by an open water cycle with consequent increasing loss of water to the sea and connected high losses of sediment, and water soluble material such as nutrients. The present day intensive agricultural fertilization cannot compensate the total loss of matter.

In the view of Ripl *et al.* (1994) the cultural phase of the river catchment will necessarily be followed by the breakdown phase, characterized by a total disruption of the water cycle and a maximum loss of minerals and nutrients. Insufficiently buffered residues from past industrial and agricultural practices (heavy metals; toxic organic residues) give rise to dissolution of toxic substances, which cause the die-off of vegetation. Although the process of irreversible loss of elements, transported via the rivers to the sea, occurs naturally, this process is greatly enhanced by man and his non-sustainable management of water resources. The greater the intervention in the water balance, the faster the degradation of the catchment proceeds. In southern countries these degradation processes can escalate even more rapidly because of the higher energy input from the sun. Finally the water cycle will collapse and the process of desertification will expand. According to Ripl *et al.* (1994) the level of reality of his model is demonstrated in the ancient cultures of Mesopotamia (Iracq) and North Africa, where once florishing rivers have dried up and desertificated.

Ripl *et al.* (1994) are pessimistic about the chance on success of river restoration projects. Restructuring the catchment by ecological restoration measures such as artificial water retention and the replanting of forests will slow down the process of river breakdown, but the final phase is irreversible. We did not find advocates nor opponents of Ripl's holistic theory in the recent literature.

4. Confrontation of Dutch river management and ecological theory

4.1. Protocol for ecological restoration

Loss of bioproduction and biodiversity, especially riverine and anadromous fisheries, underscores the need for restoration of regulated rivers and enormously expensive reconstructions are underway or are being planned (Gore & Shields 1995). Even removal of large dams on large rivers is included in some restoration plans because the costs of damage to fisheries and other attributes of riverine integrity in some instances far exceed the commercial value of the dams.

In formulating a protocol for ecological restoration of large rivers a number of physical and biological facts is to be recognized, viz. the reduction and disturbance of original river habitats, and the proliferation of non-native riparian species being good competitors in the homogeneous habitats of regulated rivers (Stanford *et al.* 1996). The most significant change in the river catchment is the substantial reduction of habitat diversity. Large storage dams world-wide inundate piedmont or mountain valley floodplains, thereby severing the river continuum. Mass transport dynamics that create instream and floodplain habitats for riverine biota are drastically altered. Flood peaks are eliminated, daily discharges are more equable and temperature seasonality may be reduced or lost. The loss of upstream sediment supply and the loss of scouring flood flows, leads to storage of bedload in the reservoir and constant clear water flushing downstream artificially depletes gravel and finer sediments in the tailwaters.

A good illustration of this phenomenon is presented by the river Rhine. The natural influx of water and sediment has ceased completely owing to barrages and reservoirs up to Iffezheim, more than 300 km from the source of the Rhine. The continuous erosion of the river bed, originally compensated by sediment deposition from upstream, increased. The scouring watermass, accelerating its speed owing to channelization of the river, caused large scale erosion of the river bed. In order to compensate for this loss of sediment, since 1978 annually 180 000 m^3 of sediment is artificially dumped at the seaward side of the barrage at Iffezheim (Kuhl 1993). At many more downstream localities continuous dredging of sills and dumping at scouring sites is necessary, in order to facilitate navigation and prevent unsafe situations.

Stanford *et al.* (1996) designed a conceptual restoration protocol for large rivers, comprising several steps.

1. Describe and formalize the problem of ecological restoration at catchment scale: the entire catchment, from headwaters to the ocean, is relevant. Restoration of large, regulated rivers begins with recognition of the river continuum and evaluation of the loss of ecosystem capacity to sustain biodiversity and bioproduction. By ignoring this evidene conventional flood protection will partially remain a speculative process (Zawada 1997).
2. Restore environmental (habitat) heterogeneity but let the river do the work. Renewal of physical and biological interactions between the longitudinal sections of the river from headwater streams to the sea, and lateral parts from the main channel to backwaters, and floodplains is central to rehabilitation. Peak flows are needed to scour and rearrange substratum and reconnect floodplain habitats with the channel, i.e. to restore natural habitat heterogeneity.

Of course, restoration of overbank flows is problematic in many rivers where humans have colonized the floodplain. In these cases revetments (dikes) have often been extensively built to restrain flood flows. River-dikes tend to act as dams during very large floods on aggraded rivers and extensive scouring of floodplains occurs if revetments are breached. Recent floods of such magnitude in large rivers not only in Western Europe (e.g. Rhine end Meuse in 1993 and 1995), but also in Central Europe (Odra and Danube in 1997) provided evidence of the value of vacating floodplains to reduce the human costs and exploit natural flood pulsing (see Sparks 1995).

3. Maximize passage efficiency for biota to allow recovery of metapopulations. In many large, regulated rivers, viable populations of native species remain in segments isolated by dams. Restoration of flow and temperature seasonality and reconnection of these refugia may restore critically important core areas, revitalize metapopulation structure and rapidly lead to recovery of genetically and numerically depressed populations (Sedell *et al.* 1990).

4. Minimize the planting of cultured stocks. There is a general belief that habitat loss caused by stream regulation can be replaced (mitigated), if not enhanced by artificial propagation. While, economically important, non-native salmonid and other fisheries have been established from culture stocks in river-segments world-wide, in almost every case this practice has failed to meet its objective replacing lost fisheries (Stanford *et al.* 1996). Stocking of native and non-native fish has irresponsibly compromised native food-webs around the world (the Frankenstein Effect; Moyle *et al.* 1986). Culture operations should be avoided unless native biota are becoming extinct as a consequence of habitat loss. Even then, cultured stocks cannot be expected to re-establish if they are simply released back into the same degraded habitat in a non-continuum context (cf. "the salmon back in the Rhine").

5. Adaptive ecosystem management (Lee & Lawrence 1986) is a useful process for solving the catchment-scale problems discussed before. The authors advocate an iterative, stepwise approach that involves synthesis of available information in an ecosystem context to define the problem, public participation in goal setting (e.g. protection and restoration of native biodiversity and habitat integrity), and effective monitoring, and evaluation of management actions (cf. constructive socio-ecological management; De Vries *et al.* 1996).

The step from adaptive ecosystem management to Integrated River Catchment Management (IRCM; Robinson 1994) is small, but how to approach IRCM is still a matter of much debate, especially concerning international rivers, having their own national management regimes. It took river scientists a long time to move from a position of "investigating and understanding the science of the system", to one of focussing on aspects critical for "management". Consequently a disproportionate amount of time and valuable resources were spent worldwide investigating matters that could never contribute to effective management of the river system, in case there is an environmental problem to be solved, and limited resources are available for research (Robinson 1994).

IRCM may comprise a Decision Support System (DSS). A DSS is a conceptual model or framework designed to organize information in such a way as to assist in decision-making, preferentially having some predictive power. The development of

DSS for entire river basins is still in an initial stage worldwide (Sweerts & Glas 1995, Fedra & Jamieson 1996, Allan & Johnson 1997). DSS combines a high level of policy integration with a low level of maintaining ecological integrity of the river catchment. The same accounts for the new Dutch so called "comprehensive approaches to water management" (Van Rooy *et al.* 1996, 1997) a policy planning-cycle to reach "good and sound" goals for integrated water management. From an ecological point of view the drawbacks of these "comprehensive approaches to water management" are the too narrow national (Dutch) focus (compare the wide scope of SERCON; Boon *et al.* 1997), and the likely possibility that this planning process becomes an aim in itself for policymakers. Thus envisaged comprehensive approaches are diametrically opposed to ecological principles of river ecosystem integrity and connectivity. Ecological restoration of river systems needs rigorous application of ecological principles, not more and complicated policy planning: let the rivers do the work (cf. Stanford *et al.* 1996).

4.2. Dutch river management and ecological theory

4.2.1. Ecological restoration
Van Dijk *et al.* (1995), Schulte-Wulwer-Leidig (1995) and Hendriks *et al.* (1997) gave an overview of the progress of the ecological rehabilitation of the river Rhine. During the past twenty years water quality improved greatly owing to substantial international commitment. A number of habitat restoration projects are carried out, as well in Switzerland, France, Germany as in the Netherlands. The river habitat improvements rely heavily on local and regional planning policies, and lack a catchment-oriented holistic approach. Fig. 2 gives the tentative position of the river Rhine with regard to water quality (improving) and habitat quality (low), compared to the river Odra, which in contrast has a negative water quality, but still a high level of ecological habitat integrity (Chojnacki & Kowalski 1997). Both rivers are far from their target image, the ecologically rehabilitated and restored riverbed and floodplains.

In the Netherlands habitat restoration starts from the "stepping stone" concept (Van Dijk *et al.*, 1995), based on the assumption that local management projects should be set up along the longitudinal axis of the river Rhine at regular distances, in such a way that a connected chain of nature reserves comprising favourable conditions for the (potential) plant and animal species will be developed. This stepping stone concept demands models and concepts for the ecological target images of the entire river. According to Van Dijk *et al.* (1995) the development of such concepts is considered a major challenge for river ecologists. To our opinion it is not so much the development of new concepts as well as the reconnaissance and application of recently published concepts that counts. In fact a considerable number of integrated river-concepts have recently been published (for a review see Townsend 1996). The empirical large-scale testing of the models, connected to the political willingness of catchment-scale restoration are forming the real bottlenecks.

The drawback of the stepping stone concept can be that a standard recipee for nature development will be applied to many places, without counting the original spatio-temporal heterogeneity and ecological connectivity between the river course and the floodplains and integrity of the river and its floodplain. Basic insight is

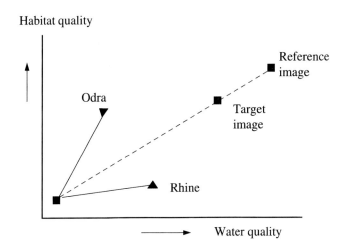

Fig. 2. The tentative position of the rivers Rhine and Odra in terms of water quality and habitat quality. Target image and reference image are fully hypothetical entities in this picture (for explanation see the AMOEBA terminology in section 2.2.).

needed into the fluvial dynamics of the entire river, the original hydrodynamics and geomorphology, i.e. the flow regime (EAFR) as the templet for habitat restoration. Once the templet has been defined, a better understanding is needed of the reference ecosystems of the entire catchment (palaeo-references). The political reality is that the societal boundary conditions (cultural and historical rights; safety risk control; shipping facilities; agricultural practices; etc.) offer too small "playing ground" to apply the holistic concept. The international approach fails because national and regional interests prevail, degrading ecological rehabilitation to a policy of tinkering.

In the framework of ecological rehabilitation a (e.g.) moorland, a raised bog or a lake can be isolated from its surrounding landscape. A large river, however, cannot be isolated in order to carry out ecological restoration measures. This means that integrated river management is only effective when measures are taken at the catchment level. Dutch river policy is far from the recognition of catchmemt scale management, although some non-conformative visions of Dutch non-governmental organizations (NGO's) for full ecological restoration of the Rhine and Meuse (Helmer *et al.* 1992) have been scrutinized by the Dutch Ministry of Transport and Public Works (Silva & Kok 1994, V&W & LNV 1994). The Netherlands are mainly formed by the coastal floodplain and estuaries of the large rivers Rhine and Meuse. The piedmont, montane and headwater sections of these rivers flow through several other autonomous countries, using different catchment management strategies. Notwithstanding the good will of the International Commission for the Protection of the Rhine, the national governments are fully responsible for the flow regime to be maintained or to be restored in their own country. Even within the Dutch section of the coastal floodplain and connected estuaries the competences among the Dutch water management authorities are not consistent: although an integrated "Managementplan for Dutch State Waters" (V&W 1993) exists, separate regional authorities are responsible, either for the management of the estuarine part of the watershed or for the lowland river section. The consequences of estuarine manipulation for the biodiversity and bioproductivity of upstream stretches, such as the effects of the presence of seawalls and barrages, is theoretically recognized (V&W 1989) but not implemented in practical management.

Several policy scenarios for the lower reaches of the rivers Rhine and Meuse have been developed and it is obvious that in theory ecologically full restoration of the estuarine conditions scores best (Smit *et al.* 1994). A programme for the removal of the polluted sediments (Dutch class 4: heavily polluted) should be followed by a gradual opening of the sluices in the Haringvlietdam, ultimately ending in a complete opening of the gates (the policy of the Rhine Action Programme:"the salmon back in the Rhine"; Schulte-Wulwer-Leidig 1995). The reality is that in 1997 an experiment for partial re-opening of the sluices has been stopped premature, because recently built inlets for drinking water appeared to be threatened by the intrusion of salt water from the North Sea. In political terms ecology is treated as an item of subordinate priority after safety for the population and the provision of safe drinking water.

According to Bradshaw (1984) restoration is the "acid test" for the science of ecology; we cannot hope to know how to put the pieces together again, unless we know how the system works. There is growing evidence that river restoration can only be successful when the ecosystem is conceptualized as a longitudinal continuum from its source down to the sea, and as a transversal gradient from the main river channel, the braided channels and wetlands up to the higher floodplains. There are many gaps in our understanding of the working of the catchment hierarchy. Approaches and technologies should be devised to uncover new patterns and processes that are relevant at the larger scale (Townsend 1996). The "acid test" in ecological restoration is no longer the lack of ecological knowledge after hundreds of case studies at the regional scale adding to conventional wisdom, but the ambition of scientists to work (internationally) at the catchment scale, together with the political willingness to give priority to EAFR and consequent ecological restoration at the catchment level.

Décamps (1996) summarizing the results of a recent symposium on the ecology of large rivers stressed the fact that lack of communication is largely recognized as an important obstacle between the scientist and the manager. Communication between natural and social scientists and between decision-makers and the public is necessary to assign realistic objectives to systems that are to be restored or rehabilitated.

De Waal *et al.* (1995) gave a review of 66 river rehabilitation projects recently conducted in Europe, among which three in the Netherlands. The most dramatic aspect of man's impact on fluvial systems is channelization, which involves the direct modification of the river channel in the past; this could explain the high percentage (75%) of rehabilitation projects dedicated to channel morphology. Roughly 40% of the restoration projects were undertaken to restore the lost riparian vegetation and wetland communities. Nature conservation and restoration was far out the most common objective of the rehabilitation schemes (85% of the projects). Most of the reviewed rehabilitation projects are executed in streams and small rivers, and are of a small scale, up to 5 km in length, and therefore only including a very small part of the catchment. This is confirmed by Muhar *et al.* (1995) who gave an overview of river restoration projects in Austria and stated that most projects are small-scale "restructuring" projects, not based on the specific characteristics of the entire river (protective bio-ecological management sensu De Vries *et al.* 1996). Consequently, uniform restoration stretches are developed, independent of the specific landscape area, river morphology, discharge regime and site specific biological communities. Although these measures improve habitat quality locally, comprehensive concepts encompassing the entire river system are lacking. Rehabilitation of large stretches of large rivers will conflict severely with non-ecology functions of the river, such as flood control, sediment transport, and urban and agricultural use and land ownership of the floodplains.

International cooperation is a prerequisite for any further progress in water management of transboundary rivers. The present day practice is that in most cases river management stops at the borders of the country through which the river flows. Only a minor percentage of the results of projects for environmental management and river rehabilitation is accessible in international journals. The great majority of research data is hidden in "grey" reports in the national language (De Waal *et al.* 1995).

4.2.2. Lowering of existing floodplains

An increase in the frequency of flooding is among the most feared, though difficult to assess impacts of climate change, and a relatively small change in hydrological characteristics can produce large changes in flood risk (Arnell 1996). Kwadijk & Middelkoop (1994) investigated changes in flood risk along the river Rhine, using a monthly simulation model and empirical relationships between monthly and peak discharge values. They found that an increase in precipitation and an increase in temperature, two consequences usually connected to global warming, could lead to major increases in both flood frequencies and the risk of inundation. Kwadijk & Middelkoop (1994) showed that the frequency of flows above 5500 m^3s^{-1}, sufficient to inundate most floodplains along the Rhine in the Netherlands, would alter dramatically if annual amounts of precipitation were to change by only ten to twenty percent.

To fight the increasing frequency of high river floods Dutch river managers are presently considering two options: either the existing dikes should be heightened again in the early decades of next century, or the level of the floodplains should be lowered over large stretches (cf. Silva & Kok 1996). In theoretical computer models the mega-hydrological consequences of floodplain excavation can be calculated, connected to safety risks. This has been done in the so called LPR-project (Landscape Planning of the river Rhine in the Netherlands; Silva & Kok 1996). In a one-dimensional simulation model water movements and morphology of the Rhine branches in the Netherlands have been studied for several scenarios. But the river is more than a drain filled with flowing water only. Geomorphologically, the behaviour of sediment, the distribution of sand and silt is very complicated to be modelled, and integrated models especially during peak-discharges do not exist.

Deposition rates during overbank sedimentation along the Dutch lowland section of the river Rhine averaged over a time interval of more than a century have been in the order of 5 to 16 mm yr^{-1}. Recent annual sedimentation rates along the main branch of the river Rhine (Waal) vary between 0.5 and 3.5 mm yr^{-1}, and in depressions up to 6 mm yr^{-1}. Lowly situated floodplains without a summer dike gain the highest sedimentation load, more than 15 mm yr^{-1}. Patterns of sediment deposition may change with varying flood magnitude. During minor floods, large accumulations of fine sediments occur in low-lying areas and depressions. High magnitude floods result in a pattern dominated by sand deposition along the main channel. In floodplains that are not bordered by a minor dike, sand deposition dominates the pattern of total sediment deposition. The amount of (fine) sand decreases exponentially with distance from the levee. At distances of over 50 to 100 m from the river main channel the deposits consist of silty clay. In these areas deposition of silt and clay in depressions can be twofold greater than on higher parts of the floodplain (Middelkoop 1997).

The most complicated and unpredictable aspect of floodplain excavation is the ecology of the riverbed. Excavation of the floodplains means an increase of flooding frequency and flooding duration and a change of the groundwater table and the sediment composition. A slight heightening of the groundwater table, connected to a slight change in flooding characteristics already leads to completely different vegetation units, and hence to different connected fauna elements (Gregory 1992, Wade 1995). Our knowledge to describe the ecological processes regarding biodiversity and bioproductivity, connected to large-scale floodplain excavation is highly insufficient. The next step, viz. quantitative ecological modelling in order to prescribe a therapy for ecological restoration or to predict and hence prevent or stimulate specific developments at the catchment level (constructive geo-ecological management; De Vries *et al.* 1996) is virtually impossible, considering the present state of ecological knowledge.

The choice whether the dikes should be heightened again or the level of the floodplain should be lowered, is a non-feasible contradiction, and there is no scientific evidence that this enterprise will succeed. Excavation of the floodplains and removal of summer dikes, as envisaged by Silva & Kok (1996) in order to create space for the river Rhine during periods of extremely high discharges, will ultimately lead to enhanced siltation and sedimentation of the floodplains. When the floodplain surface is lowered to enlarge the discharge capacity of the winter bed, increased sedimentation will lead to a rise of the floodplain surface of several dm over a period of 50 years (Middelkoop 1997) which makes the measures ineffective. Moreover, the combination of climate change and land use changes in the upper Rhine basin will lead to a twofold increase of sedimentation rates on the embanked floodplains over the forthcoming 50 to 100 years. As a result of these anthropologically induced changes, and leaving floodplain excavation out of consideration, the Lower Rhine floodplains will have been elevated by about 3 to 25 cm by the year 2050, depending on floodplain topography and local deposition of sand and silt. This will seriously reduce the discharge capacity of the winter bed.

"Space for the river" (cf. VROM & V&W 1996) can only be interpreted as widening the floodplain, having spillways and overflows, abandoned land available in case of extreme river floods. The lowland river is pressed in a too narrow straight jacket, the dikes. Deepening the winterbed does not solve the problem, unless it occurs over the entire length of the river section in a relatively short time span, which is not feasible. It is unknown what the effects are of large-scale excavating of the winterbed of the large rivers. After the removal of the vegetation layer (the first excavating action) the unchained transport of sediment at extreme river discharges may completely re-arrange the existing hydromorphological structure of the river bed, and connected ecosystems. The first step of the process, synthesis of available information in an ecosystem context, has started in 1998, by the Dutch government.

Large-scale floodplain excavation generates some dilemmas:

(1) These excavations will turn the river landscape for 20 to 30 years into a tumultuous and noisy building pit, mobilizing many caterpillar machines an excavators (already in 1994 there were nearly 200 project initiatives; Silva & Kok 1996), whereas ecological rehabilitation, as envisaged in the nature development schemes, asks for the biological rhythm of tranquility and ample time to grow to the climax stage.

(2) Large-scale excavations in the winterbed of the river increase the dynamical nature of geomorphological and ecological processes, whereas in the framework of the "highwater problem" an increase in controllability and predictability is needed; besides this argument navigation with large freight ships asks for deep, stable and controllable shipping canals, which is also counteracted by floodplain excavation.

(3) Safety for the human population versus nature development. At progressing vegetation succession the number and size of soft- and hardwood floodplain trees will increase, increasing the rugosity and resistance for water discharge of the flood plain. It is unknown, as is suggested in the "compensation principle", whether there is a negative linear relation between the volume of forests in the floodplains and the discharge capacity of the river.

(4) Excavating the flood plains enhances unwanted exposure of heavily contaminated river sludge ("class 4"), deposited by the river in former decades when water- and sediment pollution was still severe.

One of the major reasons for the continued widespread degradation of environmental conditions in streams and rivers throughout the developed world is the inadequate input, transfer and application of ecological knowledge to decisions concerning the management of rivers and their biota (De Waal *et al.* 1996, Maitland & Morgan 1997). But there is also a deficit in whole-river ecological knowledge. Notwithstanding the fact that we possess many ecological concepts now for river management (cf. Townsend, 1996), the large-scale empirical underpinning of nature development along rivers is considerably lacking, and consequently the knowledge about the ecological functioning of entire river ecosystems is restricted. The unpredictability in biological changes (invasions) connected to the almost unchangeable boundary conditions of river systems, such as increased water temperature and salinity, disrupted and fragmented habitats, and the geologically uni-directional development of the "old" river (cf. Ripl *et al.* 1994), and moreover various societal demands, leave little space for rejuvenation and "nature development". The goals for ecological restoration that could be anticipated considering the reference images, are strongly jeopardized by the multi-functional characteristics of large rivers.

Nowhere in the ecological literature we have found a plea for lowering of existing floodplains. Pleas for widening of the riverbed, and consequent vacation of the floodplains, are frequently advocated. The challenge for river managers is to protect uncolonized floodplains by re-establishing periodic overbank flooding, allowing the river to rebuild the original habitats. The role of a high flood can be defined in terms of the "work" done by the river in moving masses of sediment, and "effectiveness", i.e. the amount of channel change caused by that flood (Brookes 1995). Elsewhere, incentives will be needed to get people to vacate floodplains so that the revetments can be removed allowing reconnection of channels and floodplains. If that is not practical or desired by stakeholders, development of strategies for reconnection of several lowland floodplain wetlands and backwaters by using lateral flow control structures (sluices; culverts) may be useful (Gore & Shields 1995).

An analysis of Dutch river management shows exactly the opposite strategy: the rivers Rhine and Meuse are irreversibly canalized, and the formerly uncolonized floodplains are in recent times intensively used for the building of houses and other urban infrastructure (Hensens *et al.* 1997). The process of public participation and goal setting about large-scale excavations has not yet started in the Netherlands. The public discussion about "depoldering" (Dutch: ontpolderen), that is allowing the tidal movements to enter small areas of agricultural land along the seawall in the Dutch Delta area of the large rivers in 1996 showed that there was no public support for these proposals ("a farmer does not give back to the sea what his forefathers have gained from the sea in a toilsome way"; Kater & Van Nieuwpoort 1997). The public debate about floodplain lowering has not yet started, but massive counter actions from society are anticipated, because it is mainly agricultural land that should be "sacrificed" to the river.

4.3. Conclusions

1. Floodplain river ecosystems are among the most abused resources on earth.
2. River ecology moved from a static view to a dynamic view in which rivers are considered as spatial and temporal ecological continua.
3. Ecological knowledge at the level of plant- and animal- individuals and populations living in and around rivers is quite extensive; ecological knowledge of the structure and functioning of entire river ecosystems is restricted, and the empirical underpinning of large-scale nature development at landscape level is lacking.
4. A considerable number of (holistic) ecological concepts for river management have been published recently. There is only restricted need for the development of new concepts, but what counts is the reconnaissance and application of ecological principles and the ambition of scientists to cooperate internationally at the catchment level.
5. River management changed from sectorial, one issue-oriented to integrated, catchment oriented management, using various labels: adaptive ecosystem management; constructive socio-ecological management; comprehensive water management.
6. The policy and planning process of integrated river management may become an aim in itself; integrated management of several large European rivers is in sharp contrast with ecological objectives of holistic streamflow management.
7. Ecological restoration of river systems needs rigorous application of ecological principles, not more and complicated policy planning. Let the rivers do the work: restoration of lateral and longitudinal connectivity and integrity of ecosystems.
8. International cooperation is a prerequisite for any further progress in water management of transboundary rivers.
9. The Dutch policy regarding ecological restoration of rivers finds itself in a rather advanced, but internationally isolated position.

10. In the future the maximum discharge of the rivers Rhine and Meuse will increase; the Dutch policy choice whether the dikes should be heightened or the level of the floodplain should be lowered is an ecological dilemma. Large scale floodplain excavation will lead to a sediment balance beyond control of the river managers.
11. Ecologically "Space for the river" can only be interpreted as widening and vacating floodplains, and having spillways and overflows available in case of extreme river floods.

Acknowledgements

This manuscript benefitted from discussions with several colleagues and students from the departments of Environmental Studies and Ecology, University of Nijmegen.

References

Allan, J.D. & Johnson, L.B. 1997. Catchment scale analysis of aquatic ecosystems. Freshwater Biol. 37: 107-112.

Arnell, N. 1996. Global warming, river flows and water resources. John Wiley & Sons, Chichester, pp. 1-224.

Begon, M., Harper J.L. & Townsend C.R. 1990. Ecology: individuals, populations and communities. Blackwell, Oxford.

Bink, R.J., Bal, D., Van den Berk, V.M. & Draaijer, L.J. 1994. Toestand van de natuur 2. IKC-NBLF, Wageningen, pp.1-246 (in Dutch).

Boon, P.J., Holmes, N.T.H., Maitland, P.S., Powell, T.A. & Davies, J. 1997. A system for evaluating rivers for conservation (SERCON): development, structure and function. In: P.J. Boon & D.L. Howell (eds.) - Freshwater Quality: Defining the Indefinable ? Her Majestys Stationary Office, p. 299-326.

Bradshaw, A.D. 1984. Ecological principles and land reclamation practice. Landcape Planning 11: 35-48.

Breukel, R.M.A. & Bij de Vaate, A. 1996. Ecological effects of changes in the water quality of the Rhine. In: Monitoring Tailor-made II. An international workshop on information strategies in water management, Nunspeet, The Netherlands. WRK/LUA/RIZA, Lelystad.

Brookes, A. 1995. The importance of high flows for riverine environments. In: D.M. Harper & A.J.D. Ferguson (eds.) - The ecological basis for river management. John Wiley & Sons, Chichester, pp. 33-49.

De Bruin, D., Hamhuis, D., Van Nieuwenhuize, L., Overmars, W., Sijmons, D. & Vera, F. 1987. Ooievaar. De toekomst van het rivierengebied. Stichting Gelderse Milieufederatie, Arnhem (in Dutch).

Chojnacki, J.C. & Kowalski, W. 1997. The present status of the Lower Odra ecosystem and the Odra estuary. 3rd Annual Meeting Scientific Council ICE-PAS, Szczecin 8-9 December, 1997.

Décamps, H. 1996. The ecology of large rivers: a symposium in perspective (Krems, Austria, 1995). Arch. Hydrobiol Suppl. 113 -Large Rivers 10: 593-598.

De Klerk, P., Janssen, C.R., Joosten, J.H.J. & Tornqvist, T.E. 1997. Species composition of an alluvial hardwood forest in the Dutch fluvial area under natural conditions (2700 cal year BP). Acta Bot. Neerl. 46: 131-146.

Den Hartog, C., Van den Brink, F.W.B. & Van der Velde, G. 1989. Brackish-water invaders in the river Rhine. Naturwissenchaften 76: 80-81.

De Vries, I., Smaal, A.C., Nienhuis, P.H. & Joordens, J.C.A. 1996. Estuarine management strategies and the predictability of ecosystem changes. J. Coast. Conservation 2: 139-148.

De Waal. L.C., Large, A.R.G, Gippel, C.J. & Wade, P.M. 1995. River and floodplain rehabilitation in Western Europe: opportunities and constraints. Arch. Hydrobiol. Suppl. 101 - Large Rivers 9: 679-693.

Duel, H., Pedroli, G.B.M. & Arts, G. 1996. Een stroom natuur. Natuurstreefbeelden voor Rijn en Maas. Watersysteemverkenningen 1996. Achtergronddocument B:1-192. RIZA Werkdocument 95.173X (in Dutch).

Dynesius, M. & Nilsson, C. 1994. Fragmentation and flow regulation of river systems in the Northern third of the world. Science 266:753-762.

De Waal, L.C., Large, A.R.G., Gippel, C.J. & Wade, P.M 1995. River and floodplain rehabilitation in Wester Europe: oppotuniuties and constraqwints. Arch. Hydrobiol. Suppl. 101 - Large Rivers 9 (3/4): 679-693.

Fedra, K. & Jamieson, D.G. 1996. The "waterware" decision-support system for river-basin planning. 2. Planning capability. Hydrol. 177:177-198.

Gregory, K.J. 1992. Vegetation and river channel process interactions. In: P.J. Boon, P. Calow & G.E. Petts (eds.) - River conservation and management. John Wiley & Sons, Chichester, pp. 255-269.

Gore, J.A. & Shields J.F.D. 1995. Can large rivers be restored ? BioScience 45:142-152.

Harper, D.M. & Ferguson, A.J.D. (eds.) 1995. The ecological basis for river management. Wiley, Chichester. pp. 1-614.

Helmer, W., Litjens, G., Overmars, W., Barneveld, H., Klink, A., Sterrenburg, H. & Janssen, B. 1992. Levende Rivieren. Wereld natuur Fonds , Zeist (in Dutch).

Hendriks, A.J., Cals, M.J.R., Cazemier, W.G., Van Dijk, G.M., Higler, L.W.G., Marteijn, E.C.L., Pieters, H., Postma, R. & Wolfert, H.P. 1997. Ecological rehabilitation of the rivers Rhine and Meuse: Summary Report 1994-1995. Ecological Rehabilitation of the Rivers Rhine and Meuse, no 67-1997: 1-34. DLO / RIVM / RIZA, Lelystad.

Hensens. G., Nienhuis, P.H. & Thörig, M.H.W. 1997. Ruimte voor de Maas: veranderingen in de afvoerfunctie in relatie tot de hoogwaterproblematiek. H2O 30: 496-499+515 (in Dutch).

Karr, J.R. & Dudley, D.R. 1981. Ecological perspective on water quality goals. Environment. Management 5: 55-68.

Kater, E. & Van Nieuwpoort, J.M. 1997. Toekomstvisies op natuur in de Deltawateren. Verslagen Milieukunde nr. 138: 1-140. Vakgroep Milieukunde, Katholieke Universiteit Nijmegen (in Dutch).

Klijn, F. 1997. A hierarchical approach to ecosystems and its implications for ecological land classification. Ph.D. Thesis University of Leiden, pp.1-186.

Kuhl, D. 1993. Artificial bedload supply in river "Rhein" downstream Iffezheim. Der Bauingieur in der Wasser- und Schiffahrtsverwaltung 1993.

Kwadijk, J. & Middelkoop, H. 1994. Estimation of impact of climate change on the peak discharge probability of the river Rhine. Climatic Change 27:199-224.

Lee, K.N. & Lawrence, J. 1986. Adaptive management: learning from the Columbia River basin fish and wildlife program. Environm. Law 16: 431-460.

Lenders, H.J.R., Leuven, R.S.E.W., Nienhuis, P.H. & Schoof, D.J.W. 1997. Natuurbeheer en -ontwikkeling. Handboeken Milieukunde 2. Boom, Amsterdam, pp. 1-350 (in Dutch).

Lenders, H.J.R., Leuven, R.S.E.W., Oostinga, K.D., Nienhuis, P.H. & Van den Heuvel, P.J.M. 1998. Ecological rehabilitation of floodplains along the middle reach of the river Waal: corridors or unbridgeable barriers for target species? In: P.H. Nienhuis, R.S.E.W. Leuven & A.M.J. Ragas (eds.) - New concepts for sustainable management of river basins. Backhuys Publishers, Leiden, pp. 115-130.

Luiten, J.P.A. 1995. The ecological basis for catchment management. A new Dutch project: the Water System Explorations. In: D.M. Harper & A.J.D. Ferguson (eds.) - The ecological basis for river management. John Wiley & Sons, Chichester, pp. 453-473.

Maitland, P.S. & Morgan, N.C. 1997. Conservation Management of Freshwater Habitats. Conservation Biology Series 9: 1-233. Chapman & Hall, London.

Middelkoop, H. 1997. Embanked floodplains in The Netherlands. Geomorphological evalution over various timescales. Ph. D. Thesis University Utrecht, Netherlands Geographical Studies no. 224: 1-341. University Utrecht.

Moyle, P.B., Li, H.W. & Barton, B.A. 1986. The Frankenstein effect: impact of introduced fishes on native fishes in North America. In: R.H. Stroud (ed.) - Fish Culture in Fisheries Management. Amer. Fish Soc. Maryland, pp. 415-426.

Muhar, S., Schmutz, S. & Jungwirth, M. 1995. River restoration concepts - goals and perspectives. Hydrobiologia 303: 183-194.

Naiman, R.J., Lonzarich, D.G., Beechie, T.J. & Ralph, S.C. 1992. General principles of classification and the assessment of conservation potential in rivers. In: P.Boon, P. Calow & G. Petts (eds.): River conservationnand management. John Wiley , Chichester etc., pp.94-123.

Nienhuis, P.H. 1996. The North Sea Coasts of Denmark, Germany and The Netherlands. In: W. Schramm & P.H. Nienhuis (eds.) - Marine benthic vegetation. Ecological Studies 123: 1-470. Springer, Berlin.

Nienhuis, P.H. & Leuven, R.S.E.W 1997. The role of the science of ecology in the sustainable development debate in Europe. Verhandllungen der Gesellschaft f. Okologie 27:1-10, Springer, Heidelberg.

Odum, E.P. 1971. Fundamentals of ecology (Third edition), Saunders, Philadelphia, pp. 1-574.

Petts, G.E. 1996. Water allocation to protect river ecosystems. Regulated Rivers: Res. Managem. 12: 353-365.

Plafkin, L.P., Barbour, M.T., Porter, K.D., Gross, S.K. & Hughes, R.M. 1989. Rapid bioassessment protocols for use in streams and rivers: benthic macroinvertebrates and fish. U.S. Environmental Protection Agency, Washington D.C.

Postma, R., Kerkhofs, M.J.J., Pedroli, G.B.M. & Rademakers, J.G.M. 1996. Een stroom natuur. Natuurstreefbeelden voor Rijn en Maas. Watersysteemverkenningen 1996:1-102. RIZA-nota 95.060 (in Dutch).

Rademakers, J.G.M., Pedroli, G.B.M. & Van Herk, L.H.M. 1996. Een stroom natuur. Natuurstreefbeelden voor Rijn en Maas. Watersysteemverkenningen. Achtergronddocument A:1-173. RIZA werkdocument 95.172X (in Dutch).

Rademakers, J.G.M. & Wolfert, H.P. 1994. Het Rivier-Ecotopen-Stelsel. Ecological rehabilitation of the Rivers Rhine and Meuse, no. 61-1994: 1-77. DLO /RIVM / RIZA, Lelystad.

Ramm, A.E.L. 1988. The Community Degradation Index: A new method for assessing the deterioration of aquatic habitats. Water Research 24: 383-389.

Ramm, A.E.L., Cooper, J.A.G., Harrison, T.D. & Singh, R.A. 1994. The estuarine health index: a new approach to scientific information transfer. In: M.C. Uys (ed.) -Classification of rivers and environmental health indicators. Water Research Commission Report No.TT 63/94: 271-280. Cape Town, South Africa.

Raven, P.J., Fox, P., Everard, M., Holmes, N.T.H. & Dawson, F.H. 1997. River habitat survey: a new system classifying rivers according to their habitat quality. In: P.J. Boon & D.L. Howell (eds.) - Freshwater Quality: Defining the Indefinable ? Her Majestys Stationary Office, p. 215-234.

Reijnen, R., Harms, W.B., Foppen, R.P.B., De Visser, R. & Wolfert, H.P. 1995. Rhine-Econet. Ecological Networks in River Rehabilitation Scenarios: a case study for the Lower Rhine. Ecological Rehabilitation of the Rivers Rhine and Meuse, no. 58-1995: 1-172. DLO / RIVM / RIZA, Lelystad.

Ripl, W., Pokorny, J., Eiseltova, M. & Ridgill, S. 1994. A holistic approach to the structure and function of wetlands, and their degradation. IWRB Public. 32: 16-35.

RIVM. 1997. Nationale Milieuverkenning 4, 1997-2020. RIVM - Rijksinstituut voor Volksgezondheid en Milieu (RIVM). Samson, Tjeenk Willink, Alphen aan de Rijn, pp. 1-162 (in Dutch).

Robinson, S.J. 1994. Integrated approaches to the management of whole river systems. In: M.C. Uys (ed.) - Classification of rivers and environmental health indicators. Water rersearch Commission Report No. TT 63/94: 301-312. Cape Town, South Africa.

Schulte-Wulwer-Leidig, A. 1995. Ecological master plan for the Rhine catchment. In: D.M. Harper & A.J.D. Ferguson (eds.) - The ecological basis for river management. John Wiley & Sons, Chichester, pp. 505-514.

Sedell, J.R., Reeves, G.H., Hauer, F.R., Stanford, J.A. & Hawkins, C.P. 1990. Role of refugia in recovery from disturbances: modern fragmented and disconnected river systems. Environm. Manag. 14: 711-724.

Silva, W. & Kok, M. 1994. Natuur van de rivier. Toetsing WNF-plan Levende Rivieren. Eindrapport Minist. Verkeer en Waterstaat, Den Haag (in Dutch).

Silva, W. & Kok, M. 1996. Integrale Verkenning inrichting Rijntakken. Hoofdrapport; IVR-rapport nr.1. Ministerie van Verkeer en Waterstaat - RIZA, Arnhem en Waterloopkundig Laboratorium, Marknesse (in Dutch).

Smit. H., Smits, R. & Coops, H. 1994. The Rhine-Meuse Delta: ecological impacts of enclosure and prospects for estuary restoration. In: R.A. Falconer & P. Goodwin - Wetland Management. Inst. Civil Engineers, London.

Southwood, T.R.E. 1977. Habitat, the templet for ecological strategies. J. Anim. Ecol.46: 337-365.

Sparks, R.E. 1995. Need for ecosystem management of large rivers and their floodplains. BioScience 45:168-182.

Stanford, J.A., Ward J.V., Liss, W.J., Frissell, C.A., Williams, R.N., Lichatowich, J.A. & Coutant, C.C. 1996. A general protocol for restoration of regulated rivers. Regul Rivers: Res. Manag. 12: 391-413.

Stevers, R.A.M., Runhaar, J., Udo de Haes, H.A. & Groen, C.L.G. 1987. Het CML-ecotopensysteem, een landelijke ecosysteemtypologie toegespitst op de vegetatie. Landschap 4/2: 135-150 (in Dutch).

Sweerts, J-P.R.A. & Glas, P.C.G. 1995. The use of Decision Support Systems in Water Managenment, Delft Hydraulics, T1309. Delft.

Tansley, A.G. 1935. The use and abuse of vegetational concepts and terms. Ecology 16: 284-307.

Ten Brink, B.J.E. & Hosper, S.H. 1989. Naar toetsbare ecologische doelstellingen voor het waterbeheer: de AMOEBE-benadering. H2O 22: 612-617 (in Dutch).

Tittizer, T. & Krebs, F. (Hrsg.) 1996. Ökosystemforschung der Rhein und seine Auen - eine Bilanz. Springer Verlag, Berlin (in German).

Townsend, C.R. & Hildrew, A.G. 1994. Species traits in relation to a habitat templet for river systems. Freshwat. Biol. 31; 265-275.

Townsend, C.R. 1996. Concepts in river ecology: pattern and process in the catchment hierarchy. Arch. Hydrobiol. Suppl. 113, Large Rivers 10: 3-21.

Troll, C. 1963. Ueber Landschaft-Sukzession, Vorwort des Herausgebers. In: Bauer, H.J.-Landschaftsokologische Untersuchungen im ausgekohten Rheinischen Braunkohlenrevier auf der Ville. Arbeiten zur Rheinischen Landeskunde 19 (in German).

Uys, M.C. (ed.) 1994. Classification of rivers and environmental health indicators. Proceedings of a joint South African / Australian Workshop, February 7-14 1994, Cape Town, South Africa. Water Research Commission Report No. TT 63/94.

Van Dijk, G.M., Marteijn, E.C.L. & Schulte-Wulwer-Leidig, A. 1995. Ecological rehabilitation of the river Rhine: plans, progress and perspectives. Regul. Rivers: Res. Manag. 11: 377-388.

Vannote, R.L., Minshall, G.W., Cummins, K.W., Sedell, J.R. & Cushing, C.E. 1980. The river continuum concept. Can. J. Fish. Aquat. Sci. 37: 130-137.

Van Rooy, P.T.J.C., Van Sluis, J.W., Tolkamp, H.H. & De Jong, J. 1996. Towards comprehensive water management in The Netherlands: (4) INVERNO. Europ. Water Poll. Control 6: 22-33.

Van Rooy, P.T.J.C., De Jong, J., Jagtman, E., Hosper, S.H. & Boers, P.C.M. 1997. Comprehensive approaches to water management. In: R. Roijackers, R.H. Aalderink & G. Blom (eds.) - Eutrophication Research, 28-29 August 1997, Wageningen, The Netherlands. pp. 307-322. Agricultural University, Wageningen.

VROM & V&W. 1996. Beleidslijn Ruimte voor de Rivier, Ministerie van Volkshuisvesting, Ruimtelijke Ordening en Milieubeheer en Ministerie van Verkeer en Waterstaat, Den Haag (in Dutch).

Vroon, J., Storm, C. & Coosen, J. 1997. Westerschelde, stram of struis. Rapport RIKZ-97.023, DG Rijkswaterstaat, RIKZ, Middelburg (in Dutch).

V&W. 1989. Derde Nota waterhuishouding - Water voor nu en later. Ministerie van Verkeer en Waterstaat (V&W), SDU Uitgeverij, Den Haag, The Netherlands (in Dutch).

V&W. 1993. Beheersplan voor de Rijkswateren. Programma voor het beheer in de periode 1992-1996. Ministerie van Verkeer en Waterstaat (V&W), Rijkswaterstaat, Den Haag, pp.1-263 (in Dutch).

V&W. 1996. Achtergrondnota Toekomst voor Water. Project Watersysteemverkenningen. RIZA Nota 96.058. Rapport RIKZ 96.030, pp. 1-415. Rijkswaterstaat, Den Haag (in Dutch).

V&W & LNV. 1994. Natuur aan het werk. Achtergronddocument - Ministerie van Verkeer en Waterstaat (V&W) en Ministerie van Landbouw, Natuurbeheer en Visserij (LNV), Den Haag (in Dutch).

Wade, M. 1995. The management of riverine vegetation. In: D.M. Harper & A.J.D. Ferguson (eds.) - The ecological basis for river management. John Wiley & Sons, Chichester, pp. 307-313.

Ward, J.V. 1995. Preface: International conference: Sustaining the ecological integrity of large floodplain rivers. Regul. Rivers: Res. Manag. 11: 1-2.

Ward, J.V. & Stanford, J.A. 1995. Ecological connectivity in alluvial river ecosystems and its disruption by flow regulation. Regul. Rivers: Res. Manag. 11: 105-119.

Ward, J.V. & Stanford, J.A. 1993. Research needs in regulated river ecology. Regul Rivers: Res. Manag. 8: 205-209

Webster, J.R. & Patten, B.C. 1979. Effects of watershed perturbation on stream potassium and calcium dynamics. Ecol. Monogr. 19: 51-72.

Willis, A.J. 1997. The ecosystem: an evolving concept viewed historically. Functional Ecology 11: 268-271.

Wolfert, H.P. 1996. Rijkswateren-Ecotopen-Stelsels: uitgangspunten en plan van aanpak. RIZA Nota nr. 96.050 (in Dutch).

Zawada, P.K. 1997. Palaeoflood hydrology: method and application of flood-prone Southern Africa. S. Afr. J. Sci. 93: 111-132.

Zonneveld, I.S. 1995. Land Ecology. An Introduction to Landscape Ecology as a base for Land Evaluation, Land Management and Conservation. pp. 1-199. SPB Academic Publishing, Amsterdam.

THE ROLE OF REFERENCE AND TARGET IMAGES IN ECOLOGICAL RECOVERY OF RIVER SYSTEMS: LINES OF THOUGHT IN THE NETHERLANDS

H.J. R. Lenders[1], B.G.W. Aarts[1], H. Strijbosch[1] & G. Van der Velde[2]

[1] Department of Environmental Studies, Faculty of Science, University of Nijmegen, P.O. Box 9010, 6500 GL Nijmegen, The Netherlands; [2] Department of Ecology, Laboratory of Aquatic Ecology, Faculty of Science, University of Nijmegen, P.O. Box 9010, 6500 GL Nijmegen, The Netherlands

Abstract

In this paper the concept of ecological recovery is subjected to closer examination, with special attention to river systems. The question is raised whether ecological recovery should be regarded as *restoration* or as *rehabilitation* and some philosophical and ecological considerations are presented with respect to the type of nature that can be aimed at. Subsequently, the role of reference and target images as conceptual tools for ecological recovery and their mutual relations are explained. After an analysis of a number of projects/plans involving ecological recovery of (parts of) rivers in the Netherlands, the paper concludes with a proposal for a coherent conceptual model for ecological recovery (of river systems) which includes the above considerations.

1. Introduction

In many European countries, including the Netherlands, ecological recovery is one of the major objectives of present day policies regarding rivers. In modern river management, this objective is considered to be almost as important as the discharge of water, ice and sediment, navigation and protection against flooding. Although ecological recovery is already being put into practice by improving water quality and redesigning floodplains, a clear and unambiguous concept is lacking. The "Ecological Master Plan for the River Rhine" formulates the following conceptual focal points with respect to ecological recovery: "restoration of the main stream, as the backbone of the complex Rhine ecosystem, with its main tributaries as habitats for migratory fish" and "protection, preservation and improvement of ecologically important reaches of the Rhine and the Rhine valley with a view to increasing the diversity of indigenous animals and plants" (Van Dijk & Marteijn 1993). When we take a closer look at these politically determined focal points, some aspects turn out to be quite restricted ("habitats for *migratory fish*"), others rather ambitious ("protection, preservation *and* improvement" and "*increasing* the diversity") or even unclear ("*indigenous* animals and plants" and "restoration"). In order to set unambiguous and realistic goals for river management, the concept of ecological recovery must be made more concrete, taking into consideration that certain features of

New concepts for sustainable management of river basins, pp. 35–52
edited by P.H. Nienhuis, R.S.E.W. Leuven and A.M.J. Ragas
© *1998 Backhuys Publishers, Leiden, The Netherlands*

the original river ecosystem have been irreversibly affected. Furthermore, managers of ecological recovery projects have to accept that most rivers also have to fulfil economic and social functions. Reference and target images may prove to be helpful tools in elaborating the concept of ecological recovery and making it operational. This article takes a closer look at the concept of ecological recovery and focuses on the role of reference and target images in the elaboration of this concept. Finally, we will construct a coherent conceptual model for ecological recovery.

2. Ecological recovery: restoration or rehabilitation?

The first step in making ecological recovery more concrete is to determine whether this concept concerns ecological *restoration* or ecological *rehabilitation*. As will become clear from the following, answering this question is more than just a matter of semantics. Cairns (1982, 1991 in Tapsell, 1995) defines ecological *restoration* as "the complete structural and functional return to a pre-disturbance state". In many approaches, however, ecological restoration does not exclusively refer to a "pre-disturbance state", but implies – by analogy to restoration in architecture – bringing back an ecosystem to a "former state". This means that the *pattern* – at least in the first instance – is more important than its *functioning*. The use of these approaches requires an answer to the question which "former state" we would like to restore: are we aiming for a system that existed, for example, in prehistoric times, during which the river system was not subjected to human influence at all, or are we satisfied with a situation that existed in the Middle Ages or in the nineteenth century? There appears to be no scientific answer to this question. However, no matter what definition is used, ecological restoration does not seem to take into account that certain features of river systems are affected or altered irreversibly in comparison with the former situation (e.g. disturbed geological structures and changed climatological conditions). Furthermore, in modern society, rivers have to fulfil other functions than merely ecological ones (Petts *et al.* 1989). Therefore, ecological recovery has to be achieved within the framework of several other present and future functions which the system did not have to fulfil in (pre)historic times. For these reasons, aiming at restoration does not seem to be a viable option (cf. Tapsell 1995) and we will have to find new ways to achieve ecological recovery.

The second option, ecological *rehabilitation*, is defined by Tapsell (1995) as "the partial structural and functional return to a pre-disturbance state". The adjective "partial" in this definition refers to desired features only, thus implying that ecological rehabilitation does take into account man-related functions besides the ecological state of the system. However, by using the term "pre-disturbance state" this definition evokes the same questions as that of ecological restoration. In our opinion, a more important distinguishing characteristic of ecological rehabilitation in comparison with ecological restoration is that rehabilitation merely implies returning structural and/or functional space to nature, thereby taking into account the boundaries set by social demands (e.g. safety and navigation) and desires (e.g. recreation), rather than returning the system to a former state. This interpretation of ecological recovery will be used throughout the remainder of this article. In fact, Tapsell (1995) distinguishes a third option: *enhancement*, defined as "any improvement of a structural or functional attribute", thereby not referring to a pre-disturbance situation. However, we regard *ecological rehabilitation* and *enhancement* as defined by Tapsell as two variants of the same concept.

In the current scientific literature concerning environmental philosophy, there is an ongoing debate about whether ecological restoration (sic!) is possible at all, and to what extent man is able and allowed to play a role in recovering ecosystems (Katz 1992, 1996; Scherer 1995). Even if we decide that restoration is not an option for ecological recovery (as we have concluded above), but rehabilitation is, we still have to deal with dilemmas concerning the role that man is allowed to play and the type of nature we should be aiming at. In fact, it should first be clear whether man is or is not an intrinsic part of nature, and whether *patterns* or *processes* should be the principal goals of ecological recovery. The first question addresses a philosophical issue, the second an ecological one.

If man is considered to be an intrinsic part of nature (referred to as *man-inclusive* nature), he should be allotted an inherent role in the functioning of ecosystems and, consequently, in ecological recovery as well. If not (*man-exclusive* nature), then the role man plays within the ecosystem should be eliminated and his influence on the system should be restricted to, at most, external management only. As regards the type of nature that is to be aimed at, one can distinguish *nature-in-balance*, in which patterns (and especially their maintenance) are the main issue, and *nature-in-flux*, in which natural processes as driving forces of nature are considered to be of primary importance. By confronting these philosophical and ecological approaches, four (extreme) types of nature as goals for ecological recovery can theoretically be distinguished (Figure 1).

In most policy and management documents dealing with the ecological recovery of river systems in the Netherlands, the choice between *man-exclusive* and *man-inclusive* nature is not discussed explicitly. However, the underlying view usually seems to be: "the less human interference river systems are subjected to, the more natural they are", thus implicitly referring to man-exclusive nature. Furthermore, most plans for ecological recovery of rivers in the Netherlands see river processes like erosion and sedimentation and the process of extensive grazing by large, (semi-) wild herbivores as the main driving forces for ecological rehabilitation. This can be regarded as an implicit choice for a nature-in-flux approach. Aiming at man-exclusive nature-in-flux is especially popular among a specific group of Dutch scientists who have had great influence on the development of the concept of ecological recovery of river systems in the Netherlands (see e.g. De Bruin *et al.* 1987 and WWF 1992). Regarding in particular the choice for man-exclusive nature, however, one should keep in mind that this approach is not necessarily a widely accepted idea in society. Several studies in the Netherlands have shown that preference is often given to man-inclusive nature (mostly of the in-balance type; e.g. Natuurbeschermingsraad 1993 and Van den Berg *et al.* 1996).

Man has seriously affected the ecological functioning of river systems, especially by means of civil engineering, land transformation and pollution. In some cases, ecological functioning was eliminated deliberately; in other cases it was the outcome of ill-considered actions whose consequences could not be foreseen due to the unpredictable and unknown nature of the system at that time (chaotic behaviour, intrinsic dynamics). However, ecological recovery, regardless of whether it aims at

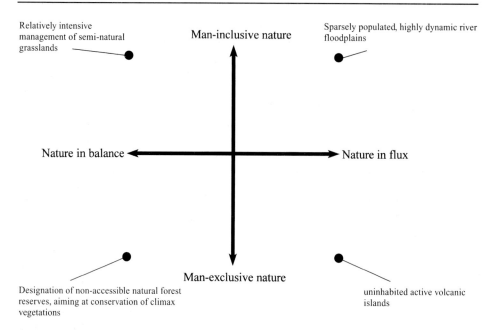

Relatively intensive
management of semi-natural
grasslands

Man-inclusive nature

Sparsely populated, highly dynamic river
floodplains

Nature in balance

Nature in flux

Man-exclusive nature

Designation of non-accessible natural forest
reserves, aiming at conservation of climax
vegetations

uninhabited active volcanic
islands

Fig. 1. Relation between philosophical and ecological conceptions of nature, with an indication of
four (extreme) types of nature and the human interference they are subjected to.

man-inclusive or man-exclusive nature and nature-in-balance or nature-in-flux, also
demands more or less constant engineering intervention in order to maintain desired
patterns or processes and, at the same time, safeguard other functions such as navigation and the discharge of water, ice and sediment. In fact ecological recovery is
in all cases characterised by a strong belief in techno-ecological techniques. This
relatively new form of engineering may or may not be well-considered from an ecological point of view, but the question still remains whether, and if so to what extent,
we can foresee its consequences. Furthermore, in accordance with philosophical
custom, techno-ecological engineering should be seen in the light of questions such
as: does man have the ethical right to intervene in the river system again?; does such
an attitude not suggest the pliability of nature and are we not legitimising further
civil engineering that affects ecosystems, stimulated by the idea that "we can always
recover nature anyway"? However, in the everyday practice of policy making and
river management, the dilemma of aiming at man-exclusive nature versus required
human interventions does not seem to be an issue. Ecological recovery is only
believed to be feasible if it is initiated and managed by man. Therefore, some constant level of human interference seems to be beyond discussion.

The above considerations on principles of ecological recovery can help us to
point out the dilemmas of ecological recovery more clearly and assess its consequences. If we aim at *nature-in-flux*, whether it concerns the man-inclusive or the
man-exclusive variant, these consequences will be unpredictable for (man and)
nature. It is clear that (extreme) variants of nature-in-flux approaches may offer the
best opportunities for ecological recovery in terms of natural processes, but by

allowing such processes, other man-related functions of the river system (such as navigation) will be seriously endangered. Furthermore, the question should be raised whether deploying natural processes as driving forces for ecological recovery will actually offer the best opportunities to maintain or even increase the diversity of indigenous animals and plants (one of the principal goals of ecological recovery, see section 1), since the outcome in terms of biological diversity targets will also be relatively unpredictable (Bal *et al.* 1995). Apart from the question how biological diversity goals can be expressed and valued (see Box 1), other strategies may turn out to contribute equally or even more to this goal. Aiming for *nature-in-balance* may offer good opportunities to safeguard or even increase (a relatively predictable) biological diversity as well and, at the same time, take other river system functions into account. This does mean, however, that a more or less self-regulating river ecosystem (another important goal in the ecological recovery of river systems in the Netherlands) will not turn out to be feasible.

Nature-in-flux or nature-in-balance and man-exclusive or man-inclusive nature are extremes in two wide ranges of possibilities. In practice, river management authorities in the Netherlands have chosen a middle course that can be paraphrased as *process management*. Natural processes are accepted up to a certain degree and even intentionally deployed in order to mould the river system according to our wishes regarding the catchment area level (thus striving for a nature-in-balance kind of river system and safeguarding other functions) and to initiate a more or less unrestricted development of nature on lower levels, e.g. parts of floodplains, utilising its own driving forces (nature-in-flux). Remarkably, at the beginning of nearly every new project of ecological recovery of (parts of) river systems in the Netherlands, an image of an ecosystem resembling man-exclusive nature-in-flux seems to be the starting point (see also section 4). In the process of elaborating these initially rather abstract plans into concrete designs, this image often shifts towards either man-exclusive or man-inclusive nature-in-balance. In other words, the goals set for ecological recovery seem to evolve during the planning process from a more or less self-regulating ecosystem towards an ecosystem (at least partly) regulated and/or managed by man.

3. Reference and target images: a delineation and their mutual relations

Reference and *target images* are considered to be useful tools for making ecological recovery practicable (Pedroli *et al.* 1996). In the current Dutch literature on this subject, widely divergent meanings are assigned to the concepts of *reference* and *target images* (see e.g. During & Joosten 1992 and Buys 1995). Most authors, however, interpret *reference images* (also referred to as *Leitbild concept*, Kern 1992; Tapsell 1995) as *ideal* solutions, ignoring current conditions (Tapsell 1995). However, since other demands on the system also have to be met, reference images can only function as sources of inspiration, on which the development towards the target image is based (e.g. Bal *et al.* 1995 and Pedroli *et al.* 1996). Reference images can be constructed on the basis of historical data (*palaeoreferences*), data derived from actual situations elsewhere (*actuoreferences*), knowledge about system functioning in general (*system theoretical references*) or a combination of these three sources (Petts & Amoros 1996).

The *target image* can be regarded as the embodiment of what we consider feasible policy and management goals along temporal and spatial scales. These goals, which are the result of scientific, political and social discussions on the subject, provide the direction for measurements to be taken. At the same time, however, these goals necessitate a reconsideration of the reference image used, since the reference image has to function as a *realistic* source of inspiration. Hence, in practice we are dealing with an iterative process: a priori chosen reference images determine the options for the goals to be set, expressed as target images, and the chosen target image in its turn compels one to reconsider of the reference image. Therefore, both reference and target images ultimately result not only from scientific considerations, but also from political and societal choices. To a large degree, these choices are determined by what we call *society images* (i.e. conceptions of how one thinks society is or should be structured) and by *views on functions* (i.e. conceptions of the potential contribution of a particular function to a desired structure of society). From the perspective of ecological recovery of river systems, the views on the function of "nature and its management" are of particular interest. It is obvious that the elaboration of views on "nature and its management" is closely related to the philosophical and ecological conceptions of nature described in the foregoing section. Van Amstel *et al.* (1988) distinguish five principal variants of this type of views in the Netherlands: 1) the classical nature management view, 2) the nature development view, 3) the functional nature view, 4) the sustainable technology view and 5) the ecosophical view. Some characteristics of these views are listed in Table 1. In the Netherlands, views 1, 2 and 3 appear to exert a particularly great influence on the choice and construction of reference and target images for ecological recovery.

The debates on the elaboration of target images are often heated. The reason for these fierce discussions is that the necessary space for a particular function (whether it concerns recreation, navigation or nature) has to be reclaimed from and defended against other functions (e.g. agriculture, forestry or industry). These discussions are not only going on *between* functions, but also *within* functions. For instance, depending on one's view of "nature and its management", several types of nature target images can be dealt with regarding one specific location.

In the course of time, the number of functions and their demand for space in river systems have grown (Smit *et al.* 1997). Since every view on every function has its own demands and wishes regarding the ideally required area, so called *function-related target images* (derived from *function-related reference images*) are often used initially (e.g. nature target images and recreation target images). These function-related target images can be regarded as the *maximum achievable* (not *ideal!*) solutions under prevailing conditions (cf. Tapsell 1995). After a process of claiming space and adjusting demands and wishes, these function-related target images ultimately have to be brought together into a coherent *integral target image*, upon which all, or at least most, parties involved can agree. This integral target image is considered to be the most *feasible* solution. Within such an integral target image, the available space has to be divided among the individual functions with due regard for mutual demands and wishes, desired surface areas and the spatial configuration of each function.

These theoretical considerations on the relations between reference images, function-related target images and integral target images and the way they are influ-

Table 1. Characteristics of the five main views on nature and nature management (after Van Amstel *et al.* 1988; Lenders *et al.* 1997).

Criterion	View on nature and nature management				
	Classical	Nature development	Functional	Sustainable technology	Ecosophical
Primarily directed at nature or at society	nature	nature	intermediate	society	society
Main reference	historical (ca. 1870)/ actuo	historical (prehistoric)/ actuo	system theoretical	system theoretical	system theoretical
High and low dynamic functions	separated	separated	interwoven	separated	interwoven
Man-inclusive or man-exclusive nature	inclusive	exclusive	inclusive	indifferent	inclusive
Nature-in-balance or nature-in-flux	balance	flux	balance	indifferent	balance
Ecosystem scale	intermediate	large	intermediate	large	small
Human contribution to nature management	relatively large	relatively small	very large	indifferent	relatively large
Ideas concerning techno-ecological engineering	preferably not used	accepted for external use	fully accepted	main tool	not accepted
Other human influences on nature accepted	no	no	yes	no	yes
Ideas concerning biological diversity	main goal	will develop spontaneously from natural processes	dependent on function and use of the system	will increase spontaneously or as a result of nature management	safeguarded as a result of a small scale society

enced by social factors, are summarised in Figure 2. For the sake of convenience, not all possible function-related reference and target images other than "nature" have been presented; they are represented by only one function. Furthermore, the impact of the society image used and relevant views on this particular function have been omitted.

The target image concept can be characterised by various qualities, depending on the intended application. The first quality refers to the *intended purpose* of the target image. Three main types of purpose can be distinguished: 1) the target image as a quantitative standard which has to be achieved; 2) the target image as a depiction of goals at which developments have to aim and 3) the target image as a framework within which consensus between all parties concerned can be reached. The second quality concerns the *level of abstraction*. Two main levels can be distinguished: 1) universally applicable target images and 2) area-specific target images. Finally, the target images can be characterised with regard to the *subject matter*: 1) monofunctional (which with respect to ecological recovery would be a nature target image) or 2) integral, including all functions involved.

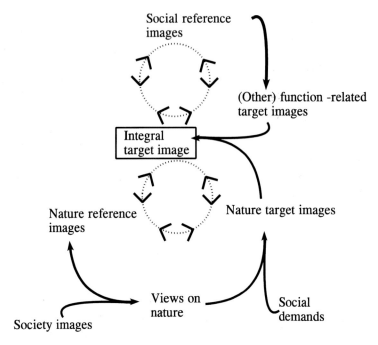

Fig. 2. Relations between function-related reference and target images and an integral target image. The circular two-sided arrows represent the iterative process of mutual influence; the other arrows point out the main relational links.

4. An analysis of river management policy in the Netherlands

In order to gain insight into the state of affairs with respect to the use and character of reference and target images in everyday practice of river management in the Netherlands, twelve projects or plans for ecological recovery of (parts of) rivers and their catchment areas in the Netherlands have been subjected to an analysis. The analysis was carried out by examining relevant documents and interviewing persons involved in the planning process. Seven of these projects/plans concern private initiatives or public policies regarding the entire Dutch part of one or more rivers or their catchment areas (for example "Living Rivers", WWF 1992 and the "Specific Elaboration for the River District", Stuurgroep NURG 1991). These projects/plans will be referred to as "catchment area" projects. The remaining five projects concern plans for the ecological recovery of specific regions (for example the "Gelderse Poort" and "Fort St. Andries" along the river Waal) and will be referred to as "region-specific" projects. It is especially with regard to these last types of project that supplementary information was gathered by interviewing persons involved. The twelve projects/plans that have been analysed are listed in Table 2.

The projects/plans were analysed using 19 criteria (see Table 3). As regards the reference images, the extent to which a reference image had been elaborated (1.a.) and the types of data used to construct the reference image (1.b.I. to 1.b.III.) were determined. The target images were also analysed with regard to the extent to which they had been elaborated (2.a.). Furthermore, the intended purpose (2.b.I. to 2.b.III.), the level of abstraction (2.c.I. and 2.c.II) and the subject of the target image (2.d.I. and 2.d.II.) were determined. Criteria 3.a. to 3.e. were used to determine which of the five views on "nature and its management" had been used when constructing the reference image and defining the target image. Finally, the projects were analysed on whether they comprised biological diversity goals in terms of (sub)species and/or in terms of ecosystems (4.a. and 4.b.). The projects were evaluated by assigning 0, 1 or 2 points to each of these 19 criteria. If a criterion was not met, 0 was assigned; if it was met to a certain degree, but not fully, 1 point was allocated and if it was fully met, 2 points were given. For three categories ("Catchment area" projects, "Region-specific" projects and "Total"), an index per criterion, ranging from 0 to 10, was calculated according to the following formula:

$$\text{Index } (x) = \frac{10 \times \sum_{i=1}^{i=n} \text{score(act)}_i}{\sum_{i=1}^{i=n} \text{score(act)}_i} \tag{1}$$

with x = analysed criterion, n = number of relevant projects, score(act) = the actual score obtained for that particular criterion in the analysed project and score(max) = the maximum possible score for that particular criterion. The indices (see Table 3) can be regarded as an expression of the extent to which the criteria are met.

As the analysis is based on the examination of a limited number of documents and interviews, it should be regarded as tentative. Therefore, conclusions from the results can only be drawn very cautiously. Nevertheless, the following tendencies might be derived from the analysis.

In general, the reference image and target image concepts seem to have been elaborated quite well in ecological recovery projects. In some cases, however, the definition and/or substantiation of the reference image concept lack clarity. The difference in the use of the reference image concepts in "catchment area" projects and in "region-specific" projects is striking. Apparently, reference images are rarely mentioned or made concrete in "region-specific" projects. Actuoreferences are seldom used in all types of projects, while palaeoreferences are mainly used in "catchment area" projects. Swart & Van der Windt (1996) state that, while aiming for nature-in-flux, there is little sense in using palaeoreferences or even any reference at all, because of the unpredictable behaviour of the system under such circumstances. Our analysis, however, did show that projects in which nature target images strongly resemble nature-in-flux make extensive use of reference images; projects in which more nature-in-balance type target images are aimed at often appear to be lacking reference images entirely.

Target images, especially those of "catchment area" projects, rarely seem to function as quantitative standards. In nearly all cases, they mainly function as a depiction of goals at which developments have to be directed. In "region-specific" projects, the target image also often seems to function as a framework within which consensus has to be reached, which can probably be regarded as the result of discussions on the claims for space and the demands and wishes of the functions in

Table 2. The twelve analysed projects/plans that involve ecological recovery of (parts of) rivers and their catchment areas in the Netherlands with some characteristics.

Project/plan	Main initiator or coordinator	Status	Reach
"Plan Ooievaar"	De Bruin *et al.* (1987)	private initiative	catchment area
Living Rivers	World Wildlife Fund	private initiative	catchment area
National policy on water management	Ministry of Transport, Public Works and Water Management	public policy	catchment area
The Rhine and its tributaries	Institute for Inland Water Management and Waste Water Treatment (RIZA)	public policy	catchment area
"Oeverture"	Ministry of Transport, Public Works and Water Management - Gelderland	public policy	catchment area
"Een stroom natuur"	Institute for Inland Water Management and Waste Water Treatment (RIZA)	public policy	catchment area
Specific Elaboration for the River District	Ministry of Housing, Physical Planning and Environment	public policy	catchment area
"Duursche Waarden"	Ministry of Agriculture, Nature Management and Fisheries - Gelderland	public policy	region-specific
"Noordoever Nederrijn"	Province of Utrecht	public policy	region-specific
"Gelderse Poort"	Province of Gelderland	public policy	region-specific
"Fort St. Andries"	Province of Gelderland	public policy	region-specific
"Grensmaas"	Province of Limburg	public policy	region-specific

Table 3. Analysis of ecological recovery projects in the Netherlands using 19 criteria. C = "Catchment area" projects (n=7); R = "Region-specific" projects (n=5); T = Total (n=12). The assessment is expressed as an index on a scale of 0 to 10, calculated according to formula 1.

Criterion			C	R	T
1. Reference image	a. elaboration		7.9	2.5	5.9
	b. type of reference	I. palaeoreferences	8.6	4.0	6.7
		II. actuoreferences	1.4	2.0	1.7
		III. system theoretical ref.	4.3	6.0	5.0
2. Target image	a. elaboration		7.9	7.0	7.5
	b. intended purpose	I. quantitative standard	1.4	4.0	2.5
		II. direction of development	9.3	9.0	9.2
		III. consensus framework	0.7	6.0	2.9
	c. level of abstraction	I. universally applicable	8.6	0.0	5.0
		II. area-specific	6.4	10.0	7.9
	d. subject matter	I. nature	9.3	9.0	9.2
		II. integral	2.9	7.0	4.6
3. View on nature	a. classical		2.1	7.0	4.2
	b. nature development		9.3	10.0	9.6
	c. functional		5.0	7.0	5.8
	d. sustainable technology		2.1	1.0	1.7
	e. ecosophical		0.0	0.0	0.0
4. Biological diversity	a. (sub)species		4.3	7.0	5.4
	b. ecosystems		6.4	10.0	7.9

question. Divergent demands and wishes are probably also the main reason why integral target images seem to be lacking in "catchment area" projects. In the drawing up of these types of project plan, area-specific demands and wishes of different functions are not yet being taken into consideration or discussions on the actual claim for specific functions have not been settled yet. Nature target images on the other hand, have been formulated in nearly all projects.

With the launching of the "Plan Ooievaar" (English: "Stork Plan", a private initiative involving a complete redesign of the Rhine basin and its tributaries in the Netherlands; De Bruin *et al.* 1987), the nature development view, which aims at realising self-regulating processes, received an important boost. Hence, it is not surprising that this view plays a major role in most ecological recovery projects drawn up after "Plan Ooievaar" was published. The functional nature view also profited from "Plan Ooievaar" by combining nature with other functions (especially recreation and excavation of sand and clay). At the same time, the influence of the classical nature management view, which was the main view on flood plain management before the publication of "Plan Ooievaar", declined. In the "region-specific" projects, however, this last view appears to have regained some influence. In the wake of this "revival", the functional nature view gained further influence by trying to find new ways of combining nature and agriculture. The sustainable technology view and the ecosophical nature view seem to have little significance.

Biological diversity goals are often a part of target images for ecological recovery, especially in the "region-specific" projects. Remarkably, the goals have in most cases been set at the ecosystem level. Furthermore, it is striking that biological diversity goals often concern the terrestrial sections of the river system and water bodies in the floodplains (e.g. former meanders, oxbow lakes, break-through lakes and clay, sand and gravel pits), but rarely the river itself (see also Van den Brink *et al.* 1996).

5. Elaborating a coherent conceptual model for ecological recovery

As mentioned above, the opportunities for ecological recovery of rivers are limited by two main factors: features of the system that have been irreversibly affected, and the limiting boundaries and wishes set by society. From the point of view of ecological recovery, these factors can be referred to as (basically) non-manipulatable and manipulatable system features, respectively. On the face of it, the difference between limiting *boundaries* and limiting *wishes* set by society is of no importance in exploring the opportunities for ecological recovery. After all, it is theoretically possible that we give up safety and economic interests in the river basin and move inhabitants to higher altitudes. In practice, however, we will encounter great difficulties in trying to do so. Therefore, the difference between limiting boundaries and wishes set by society appears to be of major significance in the choice of realistic nature target images and hence also for (reconsidering) the choice of the reference image. In this final section we will propose a coherent conceptual model for ecological recovery, taking into account the opportunities and restrictions set by social wishes and demands, irreversibly affected and changed system features and targets for ecological recovery in terms of a nature quality index.

Recently, a national debate on development of "new" nature (read: ecological recovery) in the Netherlands was rounded off (Anonymous 1996). This so-called Rathenau debate showed that lack of public support is one of the greatest problems facing ecological recovery projects. The local public often feels that their ideas concerning nature and their interests (whether they conflict with the nature development plan in question or not) are insufficiently taken into account. Furthermore, developers are confronted with a large, new group of users of the countryside who do not live in the area itself: day trippers and tourists. This group is already exerting a great influence on the countryside and will probably do so increasingly during the coming decades. Making people enthusiastic for the beauty and value of nature can be a prerequisite for the creation and maintenance of public support for ecological recovery projects. However, as mentioned above, naturalists, responsible authorities, the local population, day trippers and tourists may all impose different demands on the countryside, based on their own reference images of nature. Due to these conflicting demands, it may be difficult to arrive at a collective target image for a particular area. As a consequence, recent ecological recovery projects often show a mixture of nature target images (see e.g. the extent to which different views on "nature and nature management" can be observed in "region-specific" projects; Table 3). In order to increase social involvement, it is advisable to allow citizens to participate in the whole process of choosing reference and target images (see also Tapsell 1995). Therefore, the options and social consequences for a variety of possible target images must be made clear in advance. It is known that people are not likely to choose a target image they are unfamiliar with. Instead, most people are inclined to try and conserve the landscape that surrounds them and to which they are accustomed to. At most, they may be willing to return to the romantic landscape which existed at the end of the nineteenth century. If one wants to break away from this traditional and (literally) conservative attitude in order to favour more feasible strategies for ecological recovery, it may be convenient to start model projects, which show people the possible outcome of a *range of different* strategies and thus enable them to make an *informed* choice.

The process of making collective choices can be greatly enhanced by a conceptual model that shows the relation between the manipulatable and non-manipulatable system features and the degree of ecological recovery (expressed by means of a "nature quality index", e.g. a biological diversity index; see Box 1) and that also gives insight into the social consequences of certain choices. Figure 3 presents such a conceptual model by means of a reference/target image diagram; in Box 2 this diagram is illustrated by means of a metaphor. In the reference/target image diagram, point 1 represents a palaeoreference. It may be noted that the model can be applied to actuoreferences and system theoretical references as well. However, in order to facilitate the explanation of the model, we have chosen a palaeoreference. The reference image should be selected by making clear choices regarding man-inclusive or man-exclusive nature and nature-in-balance or nature-in-flux or intermediate situations in both choices. The outcome of such a selection could, for instance, be a previously existing, dynamic river system in which there was no human influence at all. The quality of nature (plotted on the y-axis) in former days is a result of a particular constellation of manipulatable (z-axis) and non-manipulatable (x-axis) system features at that time. At point 2 in time (the present situation) the quality of nature is relatively low, as a result of reversible and irriversible changes. It should be noted that, if this is not the case, there would be no need for ecological recovery of the system. Doubtlessly, the system's features will be subjected to manipulatable and non-manipulatable changes in the future as well. Once non-manipulatable events take place (for instance, climatological changes), man cannot reverse them (cf. Tapsell 1995). At most, he can influence the rate at which these changes occur. In formulating a target image, we will have to try to estimate these changes with respect to the probability they will occur and the extent to which they will influence the system.

Box 1. Some considerations on determining practicable and relevant measures for biological diversity goals in ecological recovery projects.

In most plans concerning ecological recovery of river systems the diversity of animal and plant species plays an important role in setting goals. According to the Convention on Biological Diversity, which resulted from the 1992 Rio "Earth Summit", *conservation* should be the principal target as regards biological diversity. However, in the "Ecological Master Plan for the River Rhine" and, for that matter, in many other plans concerning ecological recovery of river systems, targets have been set more ambitiously. These plans often aim at *increasing* the diversity of animals and plants. Making biological diversity operational for ecological recovery requires clear and workable definitions and methods to express and value this concept.

Defining and handling biological diversity
As is the case with other goals of river management, the concept of biological diversity needs to be specified at an appropriate level in order to make it practicable. In the Convention on Biological Diversity, it is specified as "the variability among living organisms (...) including (...) ecosystems and the ecological complexes of which they are part; this includes diversity within species, between species and of ecosystems". This broad definition implies that the Convention aims at preserving biological diversity at a genetic level as well as at the levels of species and ecosystems. However, this does not facilitate making biological diversity targets operational. Therefore, we will have to take a closer look at the different levels of biological diversity and attempt to determine which level or levels seem to be the most appropriate ones in ecological recovery.

Making biological diversity targets operational at a genetic level appears difficult, if not impossible, since every plant or animal population, or even individual for that matter, can be considered genetically unique and therefore, according to the Convention, worthy of conservation. Clearly, it is not the intention to preserve every plant or animal population or individual, since this would make the use of plants and animals as resources for human ends impossible. With respect to "diversity within species", the Convention probably refers to the genetic or ecological type of a particular species and/or subspecies. However, determining whether a population or (a group of) individuals represents a particular genetic type is equally difficult or impossible. Using ecotypes and/or subspecies as criteria for "biological diversity within species" on the other hand appears to be a more realistic option, since there seems to be sufficient scientific consensus in marking out these terms. Putting biological diversity targets into practice in terms of ecosystems results in other difficulties. There is no standard practice in defining ecosystems; an ecosystem can vary from a drop of water to the entire world (Gaia). Some scientists even deny the existence of ecosystems at all (e.g. Hengeveld 1990). In this respect, it is revealing that the expression of nature management targets in terms of ecosystem characteristics invariably leads to heated debate. For that matter, it is totally unclear whether an ecosystem can be "sustainable" or even "stable" (Pimm 1991). Nevertheless, nature management and river management authorities in the Netherlands have developed ecosystem based classifications for management purposes,

Box 1. Continued.

called *nature target types* and *river ecotopes*, respectively (Bal *et al.* 1995; Rademakers & Wolfert 1994). According to Duel *et al.* (1996), the advantages of these approaches in comparison with species or subspecies are that nature target types and river ecotopes can be quantified and monitored more easily. However, it should be noted that in determining whether the management goals are achieved by means of nature target types or river ecotopes, the presence and/or abundance of selected species or subspecies (referred to as *target species*) are the main standards. Hence, it seems that subspecies and species are the best operational units to quantify and measure biological diversity (see also Hoogeveen 1994).

Expressing and valueing biological diversity
It is not only the broad definition that complicates the handling of the concept of biological diversity. In order to determine whether biological diversity is "increasing" or not, it is insufficient to simply count species and the numbers in which they are present, since the presence of, for example, rare or legally protected species is generally valued more than the presence of large numbers of common species. Furthermore, programs for measurement and monitoring of biological diversity require a selection of relevant species, since including all species in such programs would be highly impractical (e.g. Ten Brink 1997). Subsequently, questions arise with respect to the criteria that should be used for such a selection. For this purpose, a variety of criteria can be used: economic potential, effort required for inventory and monitoring (Pearson 1994), ecological significance (Ten Brink & Hosper 1991; Van den Brink *et al.* 1996), rarity and/or the extent of decline (Bal *et al.* 1995), the legal protection status of species (e.g. Lenders in prep.), and so on. In conclusion, it should be noted that different management strategies can lead to different species spectra in the same area. This evokes questions on how these spectra can be valued and which of these spectra best suits the safeguarding of biological diversity (see for example Van der Velde *et al.* 1994). These questions demand the development of a tool, for instance an index, by means of which the value of species spectra can be expressed and compared.

In order to actively initiate ecological recovery, we will have to look for possibilities on the z-axis of the diagram. It is not very likely that we will choose a situation that matches z4, because under these circumstances (which resemble z1 and therefore represent a situation without, for example, winter and summer dikes) the situation does not correspond to our current social wishes and possibilities. However, we can opt for situation z3, which, with regard to the manipulatable system features, lies between the present and the former situation (for example a situation in which we maintain the winter dikes but eliminate the summer dikes). However, in doing so, it should not be expected that the quality of nature that may be achieved will equal the quality of the reference period. After the choices concerning the manipulatable system features have been made, we can reconsider the reference image and choose another one that matches the expectations in terms of the feasibility of the manipulatable features. This new reference image can then be used as the basis of our target image.

It should be noted that the quality of nature in situations 3 and 4 has been assessed in relation to the reference image. In conclusion, a few remarks concerning this assessment should be made. Firstly, the kind of nature that may be achieved will be different to that during the reference period, due to irreversible changes in the system's features. This is one of the main reasons why the nature quality standard on the y-axis does not exist as an absolute figure, but must be seen as a (relative) index. The impossibility of ecological restoration, as argued in the opening

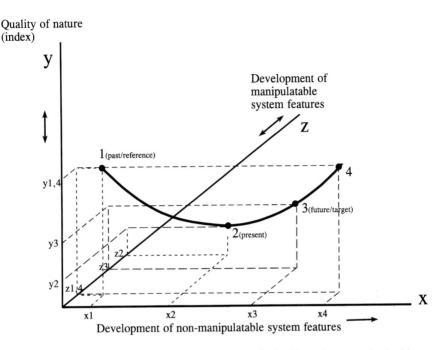

Fig. 3. A conceptual model for the relations between manipulatable and non-manipulatable system features and the quality of nature. For explanation see text and Box 2.

paragraphs of this article, can also be seen in this light. Ecological restoration aims at "identical" nature, ecological rehabilitation for "equivalent" nature. Secondly, the developments after situation 2 are estimates, which are based on the scientific state of knowledge of ecological relations; reality can be more recalcitrant, but also more supporting. Therefore, the quality of nature (y3 or y4) may be lower or higher than suggested in this diagram. It may even be higher than the quality of the reference period ("*increased* biological diversity"). In our opinion, it is impossible to make an accurate forecast of the system's features (at least in the long term) because of insufficient knowledge about the ecological relations within the system, concerning the nature, extent and rate of irreversible system changes in the future, and about possible chaotic behaviour of the system. In plans involving ecological recovery of river systems, this unpredictability should be explicitly taken into account in order to avoid expectations which can not be fulfilled.

Box 2. An illustration of the conceptual model for ecological recovery: the Maria Callas metaphor.

The conceptual model for ecological recovery in Figure 3 can be exemplified by means of a metaphor, based on the life of Maria Callas. Maria Callas was one of the most famous soprano singers, and her voice has charmed millions of opera devotees. Maria had an eventful life which, without doubt, exerted great influence on her development as an opera singer. She was born in New York in 1923 from Greek parents. They would rather have had a

Box 2. Continued.

boy child to compensate the loss of their three-year-old son, who died as a result of a typhus infection. At the age of five, Maria was involved in a car crash, as the result of which she was in a coma for 22 days. Her parents divorced, and as a consequence, Maria moved to Greece with her mother at the age of 14, although she was much more attached to her father. In Athens she attended a school of music and made her debut as a professional opera singer in 1942. Maria returned to the United States and had some bad experiences with several impresarios. In 1947 she moved to Italy where she met the rich businessman Meneghini. He became her personal Maecenas and lover and they were married in 1949. Progressively, she attained fame as an opera singer. In 1958 she met the Greek shipowner Onassis, fell in love with him and left her husband. In the mid-sixties – Maria was then living in Paris – her voice started to deteriorate and her popularity rapidly declined. When Onassis next married Jackie Kennedy, John F. Kennedy's widow, she suffered a mental breakdown. In the early seventies, she obtained an official divorce from Meneghini. Maria died in 1977, alone in her apartment in Paris, according to the official reading, as a result of a heart attack. She was cremated and her ashes were scattered in the Aegean Sea during a storm.

Why this portrayal of Maria's life? Well, suppose we would like to enjoy the glorious voice of Maria Callas again. Would this be possible? Maria Callas has died and even if we had advanced cloning techniques or other methods of genetic engineering, Maria died childless and has been cremated and, let us assume, none of her closest relatives are alive any more. Therefore, it is by no means possible to have the unique genetic material that yielded the phenomenon of Maria Callas. Furthermore, the factor time plays an important role. The events in her life, the coma, her marriage, her encounter with Onassis, etcetera, are unique events in time and cannot be reproduced exactly. In other words, a great number of variables which have contributed to the development of her voice, have changed irreversibly and non-manipulatably. These variables are situated on the x-axis of our reference/target image diagram. Eventually, it will be impossible to reproduce the reference image exactly: we are unable to "restore" Maria Callas. However, we can – at least in theory – select a married couple from Greek origin with musical talents that live in New York. Using existing biomedical techniques, we could allow this couple to build up a corresponding family, including a "Maria Callas equivalent". We could even – still in theory – allow a three-year-old boy from this family to die from typhus. The divorce of her parents, the move to Greece, her attending a school of music, even the encounters with men in her life, could all be arranged. In other words, some variables could be repeated or at least be simulated. These variables are situated on the z-axis of our diagram and can be brought back, or just about brought back, to their original state. However, in practice we will not do so, for example because of ethical consideration: we will not inject a three-year-old boy with *Rickettsia prowazekii*, the bacteria that causes typhus, just because we would like to reconstruct the circumstances which made Maria Callas a famous opera singer. Moreover, such drastic interventions in someone's life are not necessary in order to approximate the voice of Maria Callas. We could also select gifted young girls (if necessary from American-Greek origin, in order to come close to Maria's accent) and let them be taught soprano singing by expert teachers. In other words, we choose a set of variables on the z-axis that is different from the original one. At best, we may be able to train a soprano singer who is capable of imitating Maria Callas in such a way that only opera experts can distinguish her voice from the original one. Although it is most unlikely that even this can be achieved, the voice of this "new" Maria Callas may be equally or even more esteemed than the original. However, there is little sense in assigning absolute values to the y-axis; relative values, for example by means of an index, suffice to express – in the case of our metaphor – the public's appreciation for soprano singing. Thus, we can "rehabilitate" Maria Callas and honour her in a way she deserves.

Acknowledgements

The authors would like to thank Mrs Kiki Dethmers (Department of Environmental Studies, Faculty of Science, University of Nijmegen) for her contribution to an earlier version of this article, Wouter Helmer (the "Ark" foundation/"Stroming" consultancy, Laag Keppel) for his role as an opponent during the workshop "Reference and target images for ecological recovery", Mr Barry Kelleher (Department of Ecology, Faculty of Science, University of Nijmegen) and Mr Jan Klerkx for their critical remarks and two anonymous referees, to whom we are greatly indebted for their suggestions for improvements to this article.

References

Anonymous 1996. Natuurontwikkeling: waarom en hoe? Het Rathenau debat. Natuurontwikkelingen, 5: 24-28 [in Dutch].
Bal, D., Beije, H.M., Hoogeveen, Y.R., Jansen, S.R.J. & Van der Reest, P.J. 1995. Handboek natuurdoeltypen in Nederland. Rapport IKC-Natuurbeheer nr. 11, Wageningen [in Dutch].
Buys, J. 1995. Algemene natuur. Een realistische referentie. Landschap, 12: 51-54 [in Dutch].
De Bruin, D., Hamhuis, D., Van Nieuwenhuize, L., Overmars, W., Sijmons, D & Vera, F. 1987. Ooievaar. De toekomst van het rivierengebied. Gelderse Milieufederatie, Arnhem [in Dutch].
Duel, H., Pedroli, G.B.M. & Arts, G. 1996. Een stroom natuur. Natuurstreefbeelden voor Rijn en Maas. Achtergronddocument B: Ontwikkelingsmogelijkheden voor doelsoorten. RIZA/ Grontmij/Waterloopkundig Laboratorium, Lelystad [in Dutch].
During, R. & Joosten, J.H.J. 1992. Referentiebeelden en duurzaamheid. Tijd voor beleid. Landschap, 9: 285-295 [in Dutch].
Hengeveld, R. 1990. Natuurontwikkeling. Theoretische uitgangspunten in de ecologie. Landschap, 7: 47-53 [in Dutch].
Hoogeveen, Y.R. 1994. De soortsinvalshoek in het natuurbeleid. Een beleidsaanbeveling. Werkdocument IKC-Natuurbeheer nr. 59, Wageningen [in Dutch].
Katz, E. 1992. The big lie: human restoration of nature. Research in Philosophy and Technology, 12: 231-241.
Katz, E. 1996. The problem of ecological restoration. Environmental Ethics, 18: 222-224.
Kern, K. 1992. Rehabilitation of streams in South-west Germany. In: Boon, P.J., Calow, P. & Petts, G.E. (eds.). River conservation and management. pp. 321-335. John Wiley and sons, Chichester.
Lenders, H.J.R., Leuven, R.S.E.W., Nienhuis, P.H. & Schoof, D.J.W. 1997. Handboeken Milieukunde 2: Natuurbeheer en -ontwikkeling. Boom, Amsterdam [in Dutch].
Lenders, H.J.R. (in prep.). A biological diversity indicator for river dependent ecosystems.
Natuurbeschermingsraad 1993. Natuur tussen de oren. Natuur- en landschapsbeelden en hun rol bij de ontwikkeling en vormgeving van beleid. Natuurbeschermingsraad, Utrecht [in Dutch].
Pearson, D.L. 1994. Selecting indicator taxa for the quantitative assessment of biodiversity. Philosophical transactions of the Royal Society of London. Series B, Biological sciences, 345: 75-80
Pedroli, G.B.M., Postma, R., Rademakers, J.G.M. & Kerkhofs, M.J.J. 1996. Welke natuur behoort er bij de rivier? Naar een natuurstreefbeeld afgeleid van karakteristieke fenomenen van het rivierlandschap. Landschap, 13: 97-113 [in Dutch].
Petts, G.E. & Amoros, C. 1996. Fluvial hydrosystems. Chapman & Hall, London.
Petts, G.E., Moller, H. & Roux, A.L. (Eds.) 1989. Historical change of large alluvial rivers: Western Europe. John Wiley and sons, Chichester.
Pimm, S.L. 1991. The balance of nature. University of Chicago Press, Chicago.
Rademakers, J.G.M. & Wolfert, H.P. 1994. Het Rivier-Ecotopen-Stelsel; een indeling van ecologisch relevante ruimtelijke eenheden ten behoeve van ontwerp- en beleidsstudies in het buitendijkse rivierengebied. Publicaties en rapporten van het project "Ecologisch herstel Rijn en Maas", nr. 61, RIZA, Lelystad [in Dutch].

Scherer, D. 1995. Evolution, human living and the practice of ecological restoration. Environmental Ethics, 17: 359-379.

Smit, H., Van der Velde, G., Smits, R. & Coops, H. 1997. Ecosystem responses in the Rhine-Meuse Delta during two decades after enclosure and steps toward estuary restoration. Estuaries, 20 (3), 504-520.

Stuurgroep NURG 1991. Nadere uitwerking rivierengebied. Stuurgroep NURG, Arnhem [in Dutch].

Swart, J.A.A. & Van der Windt, H.J. 1996. Verkade, Veronica of Neeltje Jans? De esthetische wending in het natuurdebat. De Levende Natuur, 97: 232-235 [in Dutch].

Tapsell, S.M. 1995. River restoration: what are we restoring to? A case study of the Ravensbourne River, London. Landscape Research, 20: 98-111.

Ten Brink, B. 1997. Biodiversiteit 7. 'Hekkensluiter loopt mondiaal voorop'. Bionieuws 7/5: 2-3 [in Dutch].

Ten Brink, B.J.E. & Hosper, S.H. 1991. Naar toetsbare ecologische doelstellingen voor het waterbeheer: de AMOEBE-benadering, H2O, 22/20: 612-617 [in Dutch].

Van Amstel, A.R., Herngreen, G.F.W., Meyer, C.S., Schoorl-Groen, E.F. & Van de Veen, H.E. 1988. Vijf visies op natuurbehoud en natuurontwikkeling. RMNO, Rijswijk [in Dutch].

Van den Berg, A.E., Coeterier, J.F & Vlek, C.A.J. 1996. Hoe mooi is ruige natuur? Verschillen tussen gebruikers in de waardering van landschapskenmerken bij natuurontwikkeling. Landschap, 13: 285-297 [in Dutch].

Van den Brink, F.W.B., Van der Velde, G., Buijse, A.D. & Klink, A.G. 1996. Biodiversity in the Lower Rhine and Meuse river-floodplains: its significance for ecological river management. Netherlands Journal of Aquatic Ecology, 30: 129-149.

Van Dijk, G.M. & Marteijn, E.C.L. (Eds.) 1993. Ecological rehabilitation of the River Rhine, the Netherlands research summary report (1988-1992). Report of the project "Ecological Rehabilitation of the rivers Rhine and Meuse", report no. 50. RIZA/RIVM/IBN-DLO/RIVO-DLO/SC-DLO, Lelystad.

Van der Velde, G., Leuven, R.S.E.W. & Lenders, H.J.R. 1994. Grenzeloze soortbescherming? De Levende Natuur, 95: 192-199 [in Dutch].

World Wildlife Fund 1992. Living rivers. WWF, Zeist.

RIVERS: KEY ELEMENTS IN EUROPEAN ECOLOGICAL NETWORKS

R.H.G. Jongman
Wageningen Agricultural University, Department of Environmental Sciences, Land Use Planning Group, gen Foulkesweg 13, 6703 BJ Wageningen, The Netherlands

Abstract

Ecological networks are products of a recent development in nature conservation and spatial planning. The principles on which they are based stem from the theory of Island biogeography and the metapopulation concept and in its planning a key role is played by the ecological corridor. They can be manifold depending on both the ecological and the societal function for which they have been developed. The planning concept of ecological networks makes use of ecological principles for land use purposes.
Rivers often play an important role in the plans that are developed for ecological networks. In several national and regional plans for ecological networks in Europe streams and rivers are the backbone of the system. In most cases the role of rivers is not stated explicitly but most plans contain river catchments implicitly. The Habitat Directive as an important instrument for nature conservation in the European Union does not show coherence yet. Development of corridors is subject of subsidiarity and depending on national and regional initiatives. The Pan-European Biological and Landscape Diversity recognises the importance of rivers as part of ecological networks and has devoted an action theme to river systems in explicit relation with the development of the European ecological network.

1. Introduction

Nature conservation policies in Europe have developed from a national to an international field of policy through various initiatives. Already in the beginning of this century international exchange and co-operation took place. Especially non-governmental organisations initiated co-operation. However, the two world wars and the political situation in, between and after those episodes hampered national development within countries and international co-operation between countries and it made national policies diversify. After the second world war the founding of International Union for Nature (IUCN) and World Wide Fund for Nature (WWF) were major incentives for co-operation. National governments started to realise that nature conservation should be a national policy item and in all Europe nature conservation became an issue. The Council of Europe was a major initiator.

In 1972 the Wetlands convention gave a first incentive to coherent international nature conservation policy. In the same decade other conventions such as the Bern and the Bonn convention were initiated. The European community embraced these initiatives and developed Community legislation through the Birds Directive (79/407/EC) and the Species and Habitats Directive (92/43/EC).

New concepts for sustainable management of river basins, pp. 53–66
edited by P.H. Nienhuis, R.S.E.W. Leuven and A.M.J. Ragas
© *1998 Backhuys Publishers, Leiden, The Netherlands*

In 1992 the Convention of Rio has been adopted and it stimulated countries to develop both national strategies and international co-operation in the field of in situ conservation. The Pan-European Biological and Landscape Diversity Strategy is the expression of a European wide wish to co-operate on the field of nature conservation.

In both the Species and Habitats Directive and the Pan-European Strategy the principle of ecological networks plays a central role. Based on the concept of island biogeography (McArthur & Wilson 1967) and the metapopulation model (Levins 1970) new insight has been gained that conservation of single isolated sites might be ineffective if these sites are too small and isolated. Corridors are needed to enhance exchanges between them for foraging, exchange of genetic material, occupation of empty habitats and recolonisation after extinction. Ecological networks are the planning and policy consequence of these scientific principles.

Rivers are both socio-economically and ecologically important as transport routes. The Rhine is the important transport route between Rotterdam harbour and Germany. The Elbe, the Danube and Volga are also of utmost importance regarding their transport function. Rivers also transport sediment from the mountains to the sea and in this way built for instance great parts of the Netherlands and Romania. They also transport species from the mountains to the sea and plant species colonise the lowland plains. Migrating fish use the rivers upstream and downstream to find good spawning grounds in the mountains. In all aspects rivers are a natural and human transport mean. Being such important corridors they also must play an important role in ecological networks.

In this contribution, I will explain the principles of ecological networks and the way in which rivers can and do play a role in them. After an introduction into the relationship of landscape ecology and nature conservation, the principles of ecological networks are treated and the potential role of river systems in it. The importance of ecological concepts for land use planning and the design of future land use will be indicated.

2. Landscape ecology and nature conservation

Landscape ecology and, embedded in it, population dynamics gave a scientific basis to nature conservation strategies. These scientific fields provided the insight that nature is a relatively dynamic system reacting on a complex of environmental and land use conditions. Land use is considered to influence the functioning of ecosystems as a whole, its self-purification capacity and the carrying capacity of the landscape (Mander *et al.* 1988, Kavaliauskas 1995). It also affects habitat quality for wild species and the potential for dispersal and migration that are vital for survival of populations especially in fragmented landscapes.

Areas with good living conditions inhabited by a sustainable population of a species (at least 100 individuals) can be defined as core areas for that species. In years with high reproductivity the species will move from these areas into other, even marginal sites (Verboom *et al.* 1991). The size needed for core areas is different for each individual species. In general, larger species need larger areas and predators need larger areas than herbivores. Area reduction will cause a reduction of the populations that can survive in a site and in this way cause an increased risk of extinction. In case of isolation, also dispersal between habitats decreases.

Nowadays, isolation is an important feature in the agricultural landscapes of north-western Europe. Even in production forests, management can cause isolation of the remnants of natural old growth forests within it (Harris 1984). Most natural and semi-natural habitat sites are remnants of a former natural area. In the time that Europe was merely covered by natural and semi-natural vegetation, species within these forests and scrubs – in general the less dynamic habitats – had no problems of dispersal or migration. Their biotopes were large and well accessible. Dynamic ecosystems were present as well, but relatively small and the species were easy colonisers and adapted to fast dispersal.

Present landscapes are characterised by the opposite situation: they are dominated by man-made dynamic habitats and the less dynamic habitats are small and isolated as are the populations in it. Natural relations have declined by the disappearance of forested corridors and river corridors on one hand and the development of human infrastructure on the other. Dispersal is important for the survival of populations. However, dispersal can only function if there are sites and means for dispersal. Restriction of species dispersal increases the chance of species extinction (Den Boer 1990).

The main landscape elements of importance for dispersal are the distance between sites, the presence of corridors and the barrier effect of landscape and land use between (Opdam 1991). Routes for species migration consist of zones that are accessible for the species to move from one site to another and back. Migration routes can be manifold, from single wooded banks to small scale landscapes and from river shores to whole rivers and coastlines. Migration is a prerequisite for many species from northern Europe to survive the winter period, for migrating fish and amphibians it is essential to reach their spawning grounds and reproduction ponds.

Modelling, field research as well as nature conservation practice show, that without species exchange apparently vital populations can get extinct on the long run. This is not the case for all species, but it is so for many species. Ecological corridors and stepping stones can be essential for long term persistence of species. They function for the persistence of multiple ecological relations through air, in the water and on the ground. Their spatial scale can differ from local to continental and global depending on species behaviour, size and season. Differences exist between species (migrating and non-migrating species) and within species (migration period and breeding period). For all categories ecological linkages are different. As the distance between suitable biotope sites increases, the possibility of species to bridge it decreases. The physical appearance of an ecological link in an agricultural land or cultural landscape is called an ecological corridor. Ecological corridors can be of all kind and that makes it difficult to define them and to realise them in practice. An ecological corridor, defined as species related structure, is monofunctional. In planning it is needed to combine corridors for different species to a multifunctional ecological corridor or corridor system.

Fig.1. Flooded land in the Pantanal, a yearly returning phenomenon in all natural floodplain areas.

European amphibians migrate some hundreds of metres or at a maximum some kilometres. Mammals are able to disperse over distances to hundreds of kilometres. For small mammals ecological corridors can be hedgerows, brooks and all kind of other natural features that offer shelter. Migration is important for grazing animals like red deer (*Cervus elapus*) and roe deer (*Capreolus capreolus*). Birds, such as swallows and storks use the European continent as part of their migration route to Africa. Salmons and sturgeons used to move up and down the European rivers.

Also flora elements can move from one site to another with help of wind, water or animals. Although plant strategies for dispersal are the least known, in many cases their distribution is clearly linked with river systems. Although little research is done on river transport and most data are anecdotal, it seems likely that rivers play an important role in plant dispersal. All river lowlands are regularly flooded. In the last century this was the case in the Netherlands for nearly the whole country (Van der Woud 1987). Until the late 1950s brook systems flooded regularly large areas in the eastern part of the country. connecting in this way all lower parts. This still is the case in natural floodplain areas such as the Pantanal in Brazil (Fig. 1). Here most of the land is annually flooded during a period of four months and all parts are connected and propagules, as far as they can float, can be transported to many places. The River Paraguay, of which the Pantanal area is a part, carries in this season large islands of plants downstream (Fig. 2).

Fig. 2. Islands of plants are carried down the Rio Paraguay, transport of biomass and diaspores in a natural river system.

3. Ecological networks

An ecological network is composed of core areas, (usually protected by) buffer zones and (connected through) ecological corridors (Bischoff & Jongman 1993). Ecological corridors and buffer zones are becoming key elements of the 'ecological network' strategy. Ecological networks are more widespread in Europe than often supposed (Jongman 1995). Reviewing recent developments concerning ecological networks, Arts *et al.* (1995) concluded that "during the last decade, the nature conservation policies in many European countries have been based on landscape-ecological research, especially concerning the role of land use and landscape structure in the survival of species and in the protection of nature reserves. Plan proposals were made to establish ecological networks on local, regional and national scales."

For the design of ecological networks, it is important to know which elements and processes are essential for the functioning of habitat sites and on which scale they function. The functioning of habitats and occurrence of wildlife species within a certain habitat is, amongst others, determined by three habitat conditions: (1) water supply and retention, (2) buffering of nutrients, energy, human disturbance and (3) dispersal and migration of organisms (Fig. 3). Water supply and retention are catchment characteristics that integrate the ecosystem in the wider landscape at the level of abiotic fluxes. They determine the type of vegetation and fauna species as well as the ecosystem dynamics. Buffering functions are local – often designed or designated – adaptations around a system. Dispersal and migration are functions that integrate an ecosystem in the wider landscape at the species level.

Within a habitat-network the optimal habitat-condition is related to persistence of landscape fluxes, such as air movements, water flows, species migration and human transport. An ecological network is successful if it sustains biological transition and landscape connectivity at all levels where fragmentation, isolation and barriers to movements and fluxes occur. Rivers and waterflows in general can play an important role in this because of their function in supplying water and transporting sediments, nutrients and organisms.

Within an ecological network ecological corridors are various landscape structures, other than patches, in size and shape varying from wide to narrow and from meandering to straight, which represent links that permeate the landscape, maintaining or re-establishing natural connectivity (Jongman & Troumbis 1995). Within an ecological network they are mostly multifunctional landscape structures. Nowadays, many ecological corridors are primarily the result of human intervention in nature: hedgerows, stonewalls, landscapes with small forests, canals and regulated rivers. Their density and spatial arrangement change according to the type of land use. Their connectivity varies from high to low depending on their spatial arrangement, internal structure and their management. Nature needs different types of ecological corridors that have a complementary role to play in an interconnected habitat island system and as it is the case for all types of land use, ecological corridors require a planning approach.

Scale in network control strategies

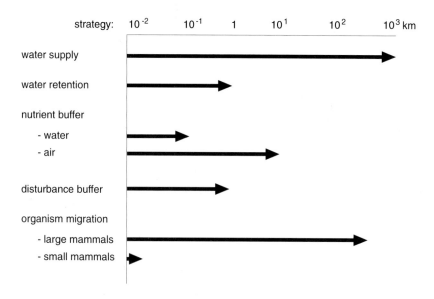

Fig. 3. External conditions for habitat functioning consisting of three groups, availability of water, buffering impacts and supporting dispersal (from J.M.J.Farjon, in Jongman & Troumbis 1995).

The nature of ecological corridors and their efficiency in interconnecting remnants and in permeating the landscape depend on the habitat site they originate from and the land use mosaic within which they are embedded and of which they consist: remnants (hedgerows), spot disturbance (railroad and power line strips), environmental resource (streams), planted (shelter beds), and regenerated (regrowth of a disturbed strip) (Forman 1983).

Four spatial types of corridors as landscape structures can be defined (Forman & Godron 1986):

1 line corridors, which are narrow strips of edge habitat, such as paths, hedgerows and roadsides;
2 strip corridors, with a width sufficient for the ready movement of species characteristic of path interiors (for example, a wide powerline corridor permitting movement of open country species through a forest);
3 stream corridors, which may function as one of the previous two, but which additionally control stream bank erosion, siltation and stream nutrient levels;
4 networks, which are formed by the intersection of corridors, this usually resulting in the presence of loops, as well as subdividing the matrix into many patches.

Box 1. EU- Habitats directive and ecological network.

The European Union adopted in 1992 the Habitats and Species Directive (EC 92/34), meant for the conservation of natural habitats and species. Core of the Habitats Directive is the development of "Natura 2000", a network of special areas for conservation (SAC's). In article 10 it is stated that national or regional governments can develop a policy to support "favourable conservation status" in the core areas. Core areas and the species in them can be supported by measures in the wider landscape. The Habitats Directive indicates that Special Areas for Conservation are sites of Community importance designated by the member states through a statutory, administrative and/or contractual act where the necessary conservation measures are applied for the maintenance or restoration, at a favourable conservation status of the natural habitats and/or the populations of the species for which the site is designated.

The conservation status of a natural habitat is favourable when:
 – its natural range and the area it covers within that range are stable or increasing;
 – the specific structure and functions which are necessary for its long term maintenance exist and are likely to continue to exist for the foreseeable future;
 – the conservation status of its typical species is favourable.

The conservation status of a species is favourable when:
 – population dynamics data on the species concerned indicate that it is maintaining itself on a long-term basis as a viable component of its natural habitats,;
 – the natural range of the species is neither being reduced nor likely to be reduced in the foreseeable future;
 – there is, and will probably continue to be, a sufficiently large habitat to maintain its populations on a long term basis.

Spatial transition from one biological community to another has attracted the interest of ecologists, geographers and wildlife and land managers for several decades. 'Ecotones', 'buffer zones' and 'natural corridors' (and related or synonymous concepts) are concepts relying on the idea of transitional zones between ecological units. These concepts for nature

Box 1. Continued.

conservation have recently been enriched by recognising their value regarding biodiversity maintenance and control of flows across the landscape. A landscape is a network of patches or habitats connected by fluxes of air, water, energy, nutrients and organisms. Interactions between habitats are thus defined by these landscape fluxes and the function of the latter for certain habitat-conditions.

If an area is a Special Area for Conservation for Natura 2000 (SAC), being a representative sample of Europe's biodiversity, however, does not mean that it stands alone. It should function as an optimal habitat for the species concerned and function without disturbances from the outside. They should even function for the wider environment as a source and refuge area for species. That means that linkage with the wider landscape is essential. This also means a link with policies for the wider countryside; policy and planning for the supporting areas mean also linkage between nature conservation, agriculture and the realisation of road and railway networks. Here, integration between national and European policies is vital.

Buffer zones and ecological corridors are management objects which may be necessary to ensure the conservation status of species and habitats within the Natura 2000 sites. There is a need to consider features required across areas, and set out the overall character of an area which is necessary to achieve a favourable conservation status. This will include consideration of the full range of ecological needs of the species involved, including movement, dispersal, migration and genetic exchange.

The Habitats Directive refers to corridors and stepping stones. We need to be neutral as to shape and extent of corridors: one important contribution they can make is to ensure a sufficient habitat to maintain populations across their total natural range. This will require decisions on location, management and pattern. This is clearly flagged in the Birds Directive (article 3(2)(b), (c) and (d)) and is part of the Habitats Directive. Article 10 states that the responsible authorities can take measures in the wider landscape to enforce the favourable conservation status and the functioning of SAC's by protecting or managing linear features such as rivers, streams, and hedgerows. It has been identified as a national or regional responsibility to decide on that.

All kind of linear elements on different scales, such as single hedgerows small streams at the lowest level and hedgerow landscapes, patchy forest landscapes and rivers on an intermediate to continental level can fulfil this function. Hedgerows, first order and second order streams are key elements on the local scale. They provide food, guidance and shelter for small mammals, birds and amphibians; they also are the wintering sites, nesting sites, spawning grounds for fish species and the transport route for river transported plant species. Larger rivers and related wetlands can provide foraging grounds for large mammal species, migrating birds and river fish on a larger, even continental scale.

The more complex a corridor is, the better it can function for different species groups and the more it is multifunctional. A high immigration rate can help to maintain species number, increase metapopulation size, prevent inbreeding, and encourage the retention of genetic variation which can be judged as the main advantage of corridors (Simberloff & Cox 1987). They increase the foraging area for wide-ranging species and provide possibilities to escape predators and disturbances. However, they also can have negative influences like the breaking of isolation that is needed for some species and exposing populations to more competitive species, the possibility of spreading of diseases, exotic species, and weeds, and disrupting local adaptations, facilitating spread of fire and abiotic disturbances.

Ecological corridors are mostly not monofunctional in an ecological nor in societal sense. They are no core areas but function in the wider landscape. In the USA and Australia, corridors are in general named 'Greenways'. In their classification they can be as wide as a watershed or as narrow as a trail (Florida Greenways Commission 1994). They can encompass natural landscape features as well as a variety of human landscape features and are from more natural to more cultural classified as:

- landscape linkages, large linear protected areas between large ecosystems including undisturbed rivers;
- conservation corridors, less protected and in many cases with recreational functions, often along rivers;
- greenbelts, protected natural lands surrounding cities to balance urban and suburban growth;
- recreational corridors, linear open spaces with intensive recreational use;
- scenic corridors, primarily protected for its scenic quality;
- utilitarian corridors, canals, powerlines that have an utilitarian function but serve natural and recreational functions as well;
- trails, designated routes for hikers, outdoor recreation that can have a function as natural corridor as well.

Rivers and small streams play an important role in this classification especially in the first two nature conservation oriented greenways.

4. Ecological networks and river systems in Europe

Rivers are both socio-economically and ecologically important as transport routes. The Rhine is the most important transport route between Rotterdam harbour and Germany. The Elbe, the Danube and Volga are also of utmost importance for their transport function. Rivers also transport sediment from the mountains to the sea and in this way they have built for instance great parts of the Netherlands and Romania. They transport species from the mountains to the sea and fish use the rivers to find good spawning grounds in the mountains. This means that in al aspects rivers are natural and human transport systems. This results in a high biological diversity not only in the rivers themselves, but also in the areas they connect.

Nowhere in Europe major river systems are protected as core areas for nature conservation. Core areas for nature conservation are usually found in those areas where man cannot have a great economic influence such as in mountains, bogs and coastal wetlands. The linkage between them is mostly the river. It is the ecological bridge and it transports sediment and species and provides water for all functions.

Rivers are always under ecological stress. The alluvial land in the delta and along the river is fertile and intensively used for agriculture. The system itself is dynamic and human use provides an extra pressure on it, partly by introducing human dynamics such as shipping, extraction and pollution and partly by preventing natural dynamics by regulation and canalisation. Due to (1) the character of rivers, a cheap transport route, (2) the administrative situation: crossing several countries, (3) the flat landscape along rivers, on which it is easy to build and (4) the availability of building material, floodplains and river deltas are intensively used. Modern river reconstruction takes place from the beginning of the 19th century on and many European river lowlands and delta's have a dense population. Less and less ecological considerations have been taken into account and the biological and landscape diversity declined strongly.

UNIVERSITY OF HERTFORDSHIRE LRC

It is difficult to protect river systems as nature conservation areas, because of their economic importance and their multifunctional character. The strategy for river protection should be to find a balance between economic use and conservation. That means that in planning land use along the river and in river management the concept of an ecological network must be included. Core areas, stepping stones along rivers and ecological corridor function of rivers must be identified (Foppen & Reijnen 1998).

Implicitly rivers do play already an important role in designs for ecological networks in Europe. In the national ecological network of the Netherlands the main rivers Rhine and Meuse are part of the core of the network together with many of their tributaries such as the Dommel, the Mark and the Vecht (Ministry of Agriculture, Nature Management and Fisheries 1990). A great part of the implementation activities takes place there and many corridors are situated along them. Also the Danish Naturverbindsele (nature corridors) as they have been designed in the regional plans of the counties are in most cases situated along the streams (Brandt 1995). In the Polish National Ecological Network the plan is the result of many different ecological datasets. However, the result appears to be based on the national river system (Fig. 4). The Lithuanian ecological network is even totally based on a catchment planning, considering rivers as the core of the regional planning units (Kavaliauskas 1995).

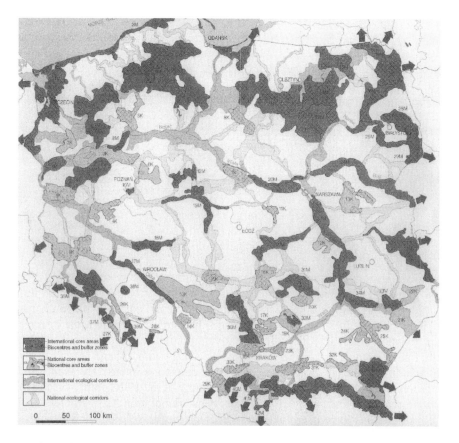

Fig. 4. The National Ecological Network of Poland (from Liro 1995).

At the European level, two developments are of importance. Within the EU the Species and Habitats Directive (92/43 EC) has been agreed on in 1991. This is the core of the EU-nature conservation policy and its main aim is to develop a network of conservation sites named Natura 2000 (Box 1). This system is, as far as it is not subject to subsidiarity, only a system of core areas. It consists of Special Areas for Conservation. Subsidiarity means that countries or regional authorities can take their responsibility and include corridors in the wider landscape, among others rivers and streams.

Box 2. Ecological networks in the Pan European Biological and Landscape Diversity Strategy.

At the conference of the European Ministers of the Environment in Sofia on October, 25 1995 a declaration was adopted in which the Ministers stated among others, that "Recognising the uniqueness of landscapes, ecosystems and species, which include, inter alia, economic, cultural and inherent values, we call for a Pan-European approach to the conservation and sustainable use of shared natural resources. We endorse the Pan-European Biological and Landscape Diversity Strategy, as transmitted by the Committee of Ministers of the Council of Europe for adoption at this Conference, as a framework for the conservation of biological and landscape diversity. We welcome the readiness of the Council of Europe and UNEP, in co-operation with OECD and IUCN, to establish a Task Force or other appropriate mechanism in order to guide and co-ordinate the implementation and the further development of the Strategy. In this respect we request the widest possible consultation and collaboration in order to achieve its objectives with a view to reporting on progress at the next Conference."

The strategy has been prepared with the aim of supporting European implementation of the World Conservation Strategy, Agenda 21 and the Convention on Biological Diversity, the European Conservation Strategy and Helsinki Summit Declaration, Bern Convention, Bonn Convention and EU mechanisms principally under the 5th Environment Action Programme and Natura 2000. It has a working period of twenty years.

The operational framework is based on sustainability and integration of biological and landscape diversity into all economic and social sectors. The strategy aims to introduce sustainable management to viable areas of biological diversity, and to introduce ecological network elements such as corridors, buffer zones and stepping stones to increase viability of smaller areas. The Strategy is worked out into an Action Plan that is the basis for the implementation of the short term goals of the Strategy with actions for a five year period.

In the next 20 years, the Strategy seeks to introduce biological and landscape diversity considerations into all social and economic sectors by striving to integrate them into agriculture, forestry, hunting, fisheries, water management, energy and industry, transportation, tourism and recreation, defence, structural and regional policies and urban and rural planning. Main actors that would be involved in the implementation of the Strategy would include national authorities, bilateral donors, international organisations and financial institutions, organisations and associations active in the economic sector, private enterprises, the research community, information dissemination organisations, private and public landowners, non-governmental organisations, the public (grassroots and citizen groups), indigenous and local peoples of the regions of Europe.

The action themes can be divided into three groups, (a) organisational, (b) integrative actions and (c) ecosystem and species oriented actions. These are:
a   Organisation oriented: (0) Pan-European action to set up the Strategy process.
b   Integrative: (1) Establishing the Pan-European Ecological Network, (2) Integration of biological and landscape diversity considerations into sectors, (3) Raising awareness and support with policy makers and the public (4) Conservation of landscapes.

Box 2. Continued.

c   Ecosystem and species oriented: (5) Coastal and marine ecosystems, (6) River eco-
    systems and related wetlands, (7) Inland wetland ecosystems, (8) Grassland ecosys-
    tems, (9) Forest ecosystems, (10) Mountain ecosystems, (11) Action for threatened
    species.

The development of the Pan-European Ecological Network is the key action theme of the
strategy. Priority actions are designed to ensure that the Pan-European Ecological Network
can be implemented within 10 years:
1   Establish a development programme for the Pan-European Ecological Network.
    This programme will design the physical network of core areas, corridors, restora-
    tion areas and buffer zones.
2   Develop the first phase of an implementation programme for the Pan-European
    Ecological Network. This programme will be supported by the preparation of an
    implementation programme. The implementation programme will set out the
    actions that will be necessary to ensure that the Pan-European Ecological Network
    is created by 2005.
3   Stimulate the development of national ecological networks and their linkage with
    the Pan-European Ecological Network. Ecological networks are being developed in
    a large number of European countries. These networks can make an important con-
    tribution to both the design of the Pan-European Ecological Network and its imple-
    mentation at the national and regional level.
4   Promote awareness of the Pan-European Ecological Network. Provide opportunities
    for exchange of expertise between countries in Europe on effective education and
    communication policies, with emphasis on the Pan-European Ecological Network,
    national ecological networks and the integration policies.

At the conference of the European Ministers of the Environment in Sofia on
October, 25 1995 the Pan-European Biological and Landscape Diversity Strategy
has been discussed and a declaration was adopted in which the Ministers among
others called for a Pan-European approach to the conservation of biodiversity and
landscapes in Europe. They endorsed the Pan-European Biological and Landscape
Diversity Strategy as a framework for the conservation of biological and landscape
diversity (Box 2). This document strives towards a coherent ecological network consisting of core areas, corridors buffer zones and nature restoration zones. One of the
action themes explicitly mentions rivers and it has been decided by the executive
committee that this should be closely linked to the development of the European
ecological network because of its importance for the Pan-European Ecological
Network. The most important action in this theme is the development of an international programme of establishing and managing conservation areas and integrated
management plans for rivers and their floodplains to enhance buffering riparian
vegetation and their ecological corridor function.

The secretariat of the Ramsar convention together with Wetlands International
has taken the lead in this action theme. As important actions they have identified
the development of a Pan-European database and inventory of river sections and
associated wetlands that are of supranational importance for biological and landscape diversity and to undertake a detailed appraisal of the Rhine and the Danube
initiatives to learn lessons to be prevented or applied in other river systems.

5. Conclusions

Ecological principles such as the metapopulation concept have had an appealing impact on the development of land use planning. They have been used as a principle that can dealt with in a planning context. The principles are used and new ideas are translated into plans in many countries. Networks are developed consisting of core areas, buffer zones and ecological corridors.

It is important to distinguish between ecological relations in the sense of the metapopulation concept or the theory of island biogeography and between ecological corridors in the planning framework. The differences are that:

– in population dynamics ecological relations can be expressed as a probability that species disperse from one site to another, while in spatial planning an ecological relation is expressed as a natural or man made linkage in the landscape that can function for species;
– in research on ecological relations results are monofunctional while in planning ecological corridors are, although may be designed for an indicator species, in principle multifunctional.

Apparently in nature conservation plans rivers and streams often have a prominent place. The plans are developed on the basis of inventories of actual and potential important areas for nature conservation. In the most plans the concrete relation between ecological concepts and rivers have not been made explicit. However, river corridor functions are assumed implicitly. The development of insight of the planning and policy consequences of this relationship is, however, very important. On the one hand it is important to understand if metapopulation principles apply for natural and regulated rivers and on the other hand it is important to understand the ecological reasoning for rivers as ecological corridors as arguments in the political debate on the use and management of rivers and river floodplain areas.

References

Arts, G.H.P., Van Buuren, M., Jongman, R.H.G., Nowicki, P., Wascher, D. & Hoek, I.H.S. 1995. Editorial. Landschap, Special issue on ecological networks 12(3): 5-9.
Bischoff, N.T. & Jongman, R.H.G. 1993. Development of rural areas in Europe: The claim for nature. Netherlands Scientific Council for Government Policy, Preliminary and background studies, V79.
Brandt, J. 1995. Ecological networks in Danish planning. Landschap 12 (3): 63-76.
Council of Europe, UNEP, European Centre for Nature Conservation. 1996. The Pan European Biological and Landscape Diversity Strategy.
Council of the European Communities. 1979. Council Directive 79/409/EEC of 2 April 1979 on the conservation wild birds. Official Journal of the European Communities No 1 206: 1-18.
Council of the European Communities. 1992. Council Directive 92/43/EEC of 21 May 1992 on the conservation of natural habitats and of wild fauna and flora. Official Journal of the European Communities No 1 206: 7-50.
Den Boer, P.J. 1990. Isolatie en uitsterfkans. De gevolgen van isolatie voor het overleven van populaties van arthropoden. Landschap 7(2): 101-120 (in Dutch).
Florida Greenways Commission. 1994. Creating a statewide Greenways system, for people...for wildlife....for Florida. Report to the Governor. Tallahassee.
Foppen, R. & Reijnen, R. 1997. Ecological networks in riparian systems, examples for Dutch floodplain rivers. In Nienhuis, P.H., Leuven, R.S.E.W. & Ragas, A.M.J. (eds.). New concepts for sustainable management of river basins. p. 85-93. Backhuys Publishers Leiden.

Forman, R.T.T. 1983. Corridors in a landscape: their ecological structure and function. Ekologia 2: 375-387.

Forman R.T.T. & Godron, M. 1986. Landscape Ecology. John Wiley, New York.

Harris, L.D. 1984. The fragmented forest: Island biogeography Theory and the Preservation of Biotic Diversity. University of Chicago Press, Chicago.

Jongman, R.H.G. 1995. Ecological networks in Europe, congruent developments. Landschap 12(3): 123-130.

Jongman, R.H.G. & Troumbis, A.T. 1995. The wider landscape for nature conservation: ecological corridors and buffer zones. European Environmental Agency, project MN2.7.

Kavaliauskas, P. 1995. The Nature frame. Lithuanian experience. Landschap 12(3): 17-26.

Levins, R. 1970. Extinction. In: Gerstenhauber, M. (ed.), Some mathematical questions in biology (Vol 2). Lectures on Mathematics in the Life Sciences. American Mathematical Society, Providence, Rhode Island: 77-107.

Liro, A. (ed.). 1995. National Ecological Network EECONET-Poland. IUCN European Programme, Foundation IUCN Poland, Warsaw.

MacArthur, R.H. and Wilson, E.O. 1967. The Theory of Island biogeography. Monographs in Population biology 1. Princeton University Press , Princeton, New Jersey.

Mander, Ü., Jagomägi, J. & Külvik, M. 1988. Network of compensative areas as an ecological infra-structure of territories. In: Schreiber K-F. (ed.), Connectivity in Landscape Ecology. Proceedings of the 2nd International seminar of the International Association for Landscape Ecology, Münster (1987). p. 35-38. Münstersche Geographische Arbeiten 29.

Ministry of Agriculture, Nature Management and Fisheries. 1990. Nature Policy Plan of the Netherlands. The Hague.

Opdam, P.F.M. 1991. Metapopulation theory and habitat fragmentation: a review of holarctic breeding bird studies. Landscape Ecology 5(2): 93-106.

Simberloff, D. & Cox, J. 1987. Consequences and costs of conservation corridors. Conservation Biology 1: 63-71.

Van der Woud, A. 1987. Het lege land. De Ruimtelijke orde van Nederland 1789-1848. Meulenhof Informatief. Amsterdam (in Dutch).

Verboom, J., Schotman, A., Opdam, P. & Metz, J.A.J. 1991. European nuthatch metapopulations in a fragmented agricultural landscape. Oikos 61: 149-156.

NATURE REHABILITATION IN EUROPEAN RIVER ECOSYSTEMS: THREE CASES

G.B.M. Pedroli[1] & R. Postma[2]

[1] *River Basin Management, Delft Hydraulics, P.O. Box 177, 2600 MH Delft, The Netherlands (current affiliation Netherlands Institute for Forestry and Nature Research IBN-DLO, P.O. Box 23, 6700 AA Wageningen);* [2] *Institute for Inland Water Management and Waste Water Treatment (RIZA), P.O. Box 9072, 6800 ED Arnhem, The Netherlands (current affiliation Directorate General Rijkswaterstaat, P.O. Box 20901, 2500 EX 's Gravenhage)*

Abstract

Three cases of river restoration studies are described: middle Danube (southern Hungary), Lower Rhine (Netherlands) and Common Meuse (Belgium - Netherlands). Guiding principle in the definition of the rehabilitation goals is the intrinsic ecological potential. The intrinsic ecological potential of river and floodplain ecosystems deviates generally from the historical reference in that the boundary conditions for ecological development in the European lowland rivers have changed fundamentally in the last few centuries, and especially in the 20th century. Hydrodynamic and hydromorphological characteristics of the rivers under current conditions should be used as a starting point to determine which ecological development is possible, and subsequently which species may be expected within given water quality ranges. Not the species or vegetation types themselves are thus the target of river restoration, but the physical river processes that are prerequisite for the development of characteristic riverbound species and ecosystems. This guiding principle is illustrated with the three case studies.

1. Introduction

In the discussion on river restoration, an interesting change is gradually taking place in the way river ecologists and hydrologists are being consulted. Traditionally, ecologists were engaged mainly in the survey of remaining natural assets and in the prediction of environmental effects. This has greatly enhanced nature conservation. Currently, the question is often posed in a different way. Just rehabilitation of nature values known from any historical or earlier reference situation is generally impossible: because of river regulation, land use, deteriorated water quality, water quantity management and even climatic changes, conditions have changed too much to allow restoration of such a reference situation. Therefore, a purely historical reference for nature rehabilitation is seldom adequate. Although it is the task of policy makers to decide on the direction of nature and river management policy, researchers engaged in river restoration should offer alternative reference models based on objective studies.

In integrated river management (or total river management, cf. Van de Kamer *et*

New concepts for sustainable management of river basins, pp. 67–84
edited by P.H. Nienhuis, R.S.E.W. Leuven and A.M.J. Ragas
© *1998 Backhuys Publishers, Leiden, The Netherlands*

al. 1998), scientific, technological and political developments in Western Europe have lead to the understanding that the immense social chances and constraints related to river management should be approached in a systematic and interactive way. A clear delineation of nature rehabilitation targets should enhance unbiased public and scientific discussion of these chances and constraints.

Aim of this chapter is to report some recent examples of river restoration in Europe and to demonstrate the approaches used for defining nature targets. Guiding principle in these studies is that the intrinsic ecological potential of river stretches is a starting point for the definition of nature rehabilitation objectives. Main focus is on lowland rivers.

2. The intrinsic ecological potential

2.1. Reduced potential due to river management

It is widely acknowledged that virtually none of today's rivers in Europe is freely flowing any more. As far as human memory goes, man has modelled the rivers to his purposes by levees, dikes and other structures. The discharge regime of water and sediment has been changed drastically, and water quality characteristics have deteriorated. In Van der Kraats (1994) and Van Dijk *et al.* (1996), the consequences of such developments are well documented, especially for the Rhine. In most lowland rivers, as a result of flood levee construction, the active floodplain is reduced to a narrow zone along the river. Even a larger part of this narrow zone is rarely flooded, due to protection levees for agricultural lands in the active floodplain.

During the remaining rare flood events, large amounts of fine sediment have been deposited on the active floodplains, covering the original relief structure and increasing the floodplain level (Middelkoop 1997). As a result of these changes, the active floodplain and the main channel in most rivers have become narrower, more uniform and more intensely used. The width of the transition zones between aquatic and terrestrial ecosystems has accordingly diminished. The diversity in the characteristic pattern and processes of the fluvial landscape has decreased since the main motor of ecological differentiation, the flood pulse, has been reduced in most reaches of the river landscape (Bayley 1991).

The natural features of a river stretch are the result of physical and biotic processes and management activities. In a natural fluvial landscape, the abiotic processes, especially morphological and hydrological processes, determine the type of nature on the scale of a river section (Amoros *et al.* 1987). Therefore, to restore a natural situation in a certain river stretch, restoration of the morphological and hydrological processes is a prerequisite. In most cases, part of these processes can be restored relatively easily: e.g. the flooding frequency of the actual floodplains can be increased by removing protection levees or the sediment layer that covers the original relief structures. This may in many cases restore a more natural gradient between seldom and frequently inundated floodplain ecosystems. Restoration of other processes such as unimpeded erosion and sedimentation, however, can only be attained at the cost of often unacceptable social consequences, e.g. by giving up navigation opportunities or flood protection of urban areas. Finally, some processes might have changed irreversibly, e.g. changes of the sediment discharge as a result of sediment mining or increased incision of the river bed as a result of weirs.

2.2. On the search for a new reference for sustainable river nature

If the historical physical processes can not be restored, a historical reference for river and floodplain nature is not opportune and an alternative reference should be chosen. The best opportunities for sustainable, self-supporting nature are attained if nature is the result of dynamic fluvial processes, either historic or not (Petts 1990). First of all, the reference model should focus on the potential physical processes and then deduce the possible natural developments of vegetation and fauna from these processes.

To predict these potential physical processes, i.e. the morphological and hydrological development of a river provided human management ceases, requires the assessment of the dynamics of the river system under the boundary conditions of changed discharge, geometry and water quality characteristics. First steps on this way have been made by Wolfert (1992) and Middelkoop (1997). Main morphological developments, however, take place under high flood conditions, which intrinsically occur infrequently, and are difficult to study anyhow (Brakenridge 1988).

The natural development of nature and landscape in floodplains of lowland rivers is dependent on the variation in river processes (Theiling 1995). A certain geographical distribution in these processes can be recognised, for example over Western Europe (Billen *et al.* 1995), but the exact development in time and space is largely unpredictable. However, on the level of the landscape, the estimation of the ecological development potential of river systems appeared to be possible in certain cases (Dister *et al.* 1990, Postma *et al.* 1995).

2.3. State of the art

In many western and central European countries, attempts have been formulated and sometimes realised on the restoration of rivers (De Waal *et al.* 1995). Interestingly, most of those initiatives are being taken by local land owners or river managers, without much sophisticated methodology. The opportunity to buy out some land and to change the terrain management is often more decisive in the selection of locations for river restoration than well-defined and scientifically-based nature policies. This is reflected in the relative absence of good recent articles summarising those attempts. Still, small scale river restoration projects are known to be carried out in almost all European countries (see e.g. Dister *et al.* 1990, Large & Petts 1994, Milner 1994, Van der Kraats 1994, Hansen 1996).

Main constraints in river restoration are the traditional functions of the river for human society: navigation, water management, drinking water production, recreation, agriculture and housing on the active floodplains, etc. However, it appears that in many cases still large chances exist to make use of the remaining potential. In the following, three examples (i.e. middle Danube, Lower Rhine and Common Meuse) are given, in an international context (Fig. 1).

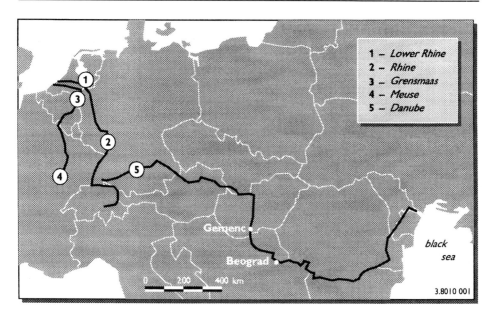

Fig. 1. Location of the river cases described.

3. Gemenc (Danube River)

3.1. The problem

International efforts recently stress the Danube's significance as an ecological corridor of the utmost importance for Central Europe. In 1992 the Hungarian Ministry
of Transport, Communication and Water and the Ministry of Environment and
Regional Policy, sponsored by the Netherlands Government, commissioned a combination of Dutch and Hungarian institutes to study possibilities for the rehabilitation of the Gemenc floodplain. It was agreed that the study would focus on the
water management of the area, but nevertheless take into account the wider scope
of other management areas and interests such as forestry, hunting, fisheries and recreation as well. The study used a policy analysis approach for formulating and analysing three different alternatives (Marchand 1993).

The Gemenc Landscape Protection Area, located in the Danube floodplain in
southern Hungary, is of outstanding natural beauty and represents important natural resources. In the Gemenc Floodplain, which is for the largest part under forest,
still remnants of the former natural alluvial forests are present. It is an important
game reserve and a unique habitat for several species of wild animals indicative for
relatively pristine ecosystems in the river floodplain, such as the predatory bird species White-tailed eagle (*Haliaeëtus albicilla*) and Black kite (*Milvus migrans*) and
also the Black stork (*Ciconia nigra*) and Night heron (*Nycticorax nycticorax*).

However, these natural resources are under an increasing pressure from a number of other interests. River training works since last century aimed at flood protection, better navigability of the main channel and prevention of ice-jams. Higher
stream velocities in the main channel led to its deepening and consequently to a

lowering of the ground water tables in the floodplain. Lower stream velocities in the abandoned side arms and cut-off meanders led to silting up and frequent occurrence of eutrophic conditions in these side arms. Hence the original ecological functions of the river have degraded substantially. Currently, the side arms and lateral channel habitats form a last refuge for many of the typical riverbound flora and fauna. Fore example, Little egret (*Egretta garzetta*) and Sand martin (*Riparia riparia*) breed in the area, and Waternut (*Trapa natans*) is an abundant water plant in the side-arms. Besides, the forestry and hunting practices in the Gemenc area have imposed pressure on the natural floodplain ecosystems and associated water management. Most recreational activities are water bound, such as angling, sailing and swimming. Along the river and the side channels many summer cottages have been built. Commercial fisheries are concentrated along the side arms which have a connection with the river.

These problems have led to the question how to create proper conditions for regeneration and restoration of the natural ecosystems of the Gemenc floodplain in such a way that the remaining functions of the area are not affected unduly. Because of the complexity of this question, and the different interests involved, it was decided to carry out a policy analysis, concentrating on the water management, to study the various options for the restoration of the Gemenc Floodplain.

3.2. The approach

The nature rehabilitation study used hydrodynamic and water quality models, a Geographic Information System of the Gemenc area and expertise from a range of disciplines. This made it possible to unravel the complex relations between the environment and human interventions, to define the intrinsic ecological potential of the various parts of the floodplain ecosystem. Crucial was the participation of local experts in the design and screening of measures, to guarantee that local knowledge on potential ecosystem development was used adequately. This resulted in the formulation of rehabilitation ideas, most of which had hitherto not been discussed (Marchand *et al.* 1992). The combination of creative solutions with practical possibilities and limitations has been worked out in a cyclic process from which three different alternatives emerged. These have been analysed on their feasibility with regard to the goals to be achieved in terms of dynamic boundary conditions, their costs and their impacts on other interests (Marchand 1993).

3.3. Alternative strategies

Alternative I entails the improvement of the side arms Grébeci (Ia), Rezéti (Ib) and Móric Duna (Id) by dredging, and of the Vén (Ic) and Kádár Duna (Ie) by enlarging the openings in the existing dams (Fig. 2). Alternative II involves the creation of a new lateral channel by connecting the old side arms. This alternative has been worked out for two variants which differ in length and location (IIa and IIb). For Alternative III, water from the Sió, a tributary to the Danube, will be directed to the nearby floodplain depressions (the Keselyüs area) during a period of 5 to 7 days in the flooding season (April – May).

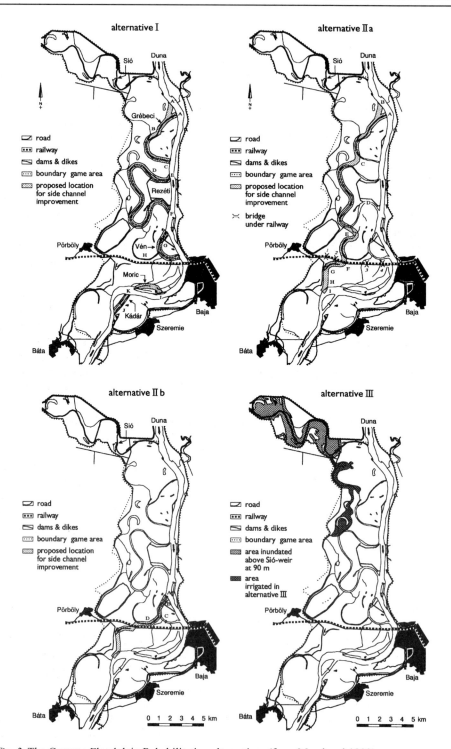

Fig. 2. The Gemenc Floodplain Rehabilitation alternatives (from Marchand 1993).

3.4. Results

The analysis results show that ecological rehabilitation can be attained at reasonable costs for the Vén, Móric and Kádár Duna (Alternatives Ic, Id and Ie). Improvement of the Grébeci Duna (Alternative Ia) will entail huge amounts of dredging and is therefore quite expensive. Due to the hydrological characteristics of the Rezéti Duna (Alternative Ib) here even major dredging does not seem to result in a significant improvement of the ecological situation. The intrinsic ecological potential is thus low here under current river management conditions.

Although for the long lateral channel (Alternative IIa) the initial investment costs are relatively high, the cost effectiveness of the alternative is favourable due to its length and low maintenance dredging costs. Hence, this alternative is also promising. The short lateral channel (Alternative IIb) shows some improvement of the ecological situation.

Alternative III is of quite a different nature compared to the other alternatives. It uses the discharge of the Sió tributary for a lateral supply of water to the northern ranges of the upper floodplain in periods when flooding from the Danube was normal but has largely ceased now. This alternative will have an effect on the terrestrial floodplain ecosystems in the northern part of the study area through the irrigation effect, rather than influence the aquatic habitats in the side arms. Especially the improvement of the ground water situation and thus mitigation of desiccation effects looks promising, but should be studied in more detail, also with reference to the intrinsic ecological potential for the dynamic floodplain ecosystem as a whole.

The impacts of the alternatives on the hydrology and morphology of the side channels and main channel and on the water quality within the side channels were assessed with one-dimensional mathematical models. None of the alternatives are expected to create problems with regard to the river management requirements, such as safety against flooding, ice dams and navigation. Improvements of the water quality which can be obtained with the different alternatives are variable. Alternative Ia (Grébeci), Ic (Vén) and Id (Móric) probably give the best results. The impacts on the forestry, as assessed by using a Geographical Information System developed for the Gemenc area, are limited (Pedroli 1993). For the fisheries, most alternatives show an improvement, while the recreation potential – especially fishing, boating and swimming – is enhanced.

3.5. Conclusion

The conclusion of the Gemenc Floodplain Rehabilitation Study is that by a sound water management the rehabilitation of the Gemenc floodplain in terms of increased natural fluvial dynamics, is promising (Marchand 1993). Taking into account the relatively high nature values still present in Gemenc, the intrinsic ecological potential implies the restoration of nationally and internationally acknowledged natural resources (Pedroli 1993). Gemenc could be used as an example for the restoration of similar floodplains elsewhere along the Danube and other Central European rivers, because of its large dimensions and characteristic ecosystems. A monitoring programme is recommended to improve the knowledge on the area and to be able to adjust the management plan whenever necessary.

4. Lower Rhine

4.1. The problem

Water quality of the Rhine has improved significantly after the Sandoz accident and the resulting international efforts as agreed upon in the Rhine Action Programme (IRC 1987). Several species have already recovered because of these efforts. However, for the return of many other indigenous species the lack of habitats is another major limiting factor (Van Dijk *et al.* 1995, Van den Brink *et al.* 1996). The Rhine is a strongly regulated river and natural river and floodplain habitats have disappeared as a result of the construction of numerous weirs, dams, groynes en dikes. In the "Ecological Master Plan for the Rhine" the participating members of the International Rhine Commission (IRC) have set targets for (1) the restoration of the main course as the "backbone of the ecosystem", especially for migratory fish, and (2) the preservation, protection, and rehabilitation of ecologically important areas (IRC 1992). The second target has started with an inventory of the actual nature areas, their state of protection and the plans for nature rehabilitation. Besides the international agreements made in the IRC, plans for protection as well as rehabilitation are being made in all the individual IRC-member states (e.g. Anonymous 1990, Vieser 1991, Anonymous 1994, Cals 1994, Voies Navigables de France 1995, Arbeitsgemeinschaft Renaturierung Hochrhein 1996).

In 1990, the Ministry of Agriculture, Nature Management and Fisheries have launched the Nature Policy Plan of the Netherlands (Anonymous 1990). The Nature Policy Plan is a long-term strategy for conservation, rehabilitation and development of nature and landscape. One of the main targets is the realisation of the National Ecological Network: a coherent network of areas, forming a sustainable basis for the ecosystems and species considered important in an (inter)national context. To reach this, the existing natural area in the Netherlands has to be enlarged. It has been agreed with agricultural organisations that 50,000 hectares of agriculture land can be integrated in the network as nature rehabilitation areas on a voluntary basis (Van Baalen 1995). Floodplains along the rivers form an important part of the National Ecological Network. The ministries of Agriculture Nature Management & Fisheries and of Transport & Water Management have agreed on buying 4,000 hectares of agriculture land in the actual floodplains for the development of new nature areas until the year 2000.

According to the Nature Policy Plan, nature in the active floodplains should be concentrated in large areas of several hundreds to thousands of hectares where – given certain management boundary conditions – unimpeded fluvial processes can freely landscape the area.

4.2. The approach

It is important to draw up hypotheses about the type of nature that can be expected to develop in the new nature areas of the national ecological network: hypotheses are needed to enable evaluation of policy results and to estimate potential risks for other functions, especially for flood protection and navigation.

Postma *et al.* (1995) describe a method to identify the type of nature that can develop under certain boundary conditions in floodplains (see also Pedroli *et al.* 1996).

The type of nature is expressed in areas [ha] of "ecotopes" in Postma *et al.* (1995). They define ecotopes as spatial ecological units with uniform morphodynamic and hydrodynamic characteristics and a certain vegetation structure as a result of land use (e.g. grazing or hay making) or natural developments (Rademakers & Wolfert 1994). Rademakers & Wolfert (1994) have developed a classification system of river ecotopes for the Dutch rivers. Originally, the classification counts 64 ecotopes; in this study they have been grouped to 14 ecotopes (Table 1).

Geomorphologic and hydrological processes determine the development of ecological units such as ecotopes (Amoros *et al.* 1987). The Rhine in the Netherlands can be divided into 12 river sections with more or less uniform geomorphologic characteristics (Wolfert 1992). For each of the river sections, a first estimate of feasible ecotopes was derived from the topographical atlas of 1850 (scale 1:50,000). Although physical processes in the Dutch rivers have changed radically during the past century as a result of human interaction, the analysis of historical patterns gives much insight in the river dynamics under varying conditions. Although the original processes could partly be restored, many changes must be regarded as irreversible. Combining information on the historical situation with recent features, it was analysed in a qualitative way ("expert judgement") which geomorphologic and hydrological processes and which ecotopes still have the intrinsic ecological potential to develop in the Rhine floodplains of the Netherlands (Fig. 3).

Table 1. Target ecotope types used in the Rhine study (Postma *et al.* 1995).

Ecotope groups	Target ecotopes
stream channel ecotopes	deep stream channel (> 1.5 m deep) shallow stream channel (< 1.5 m deep) natural river bank
woodland ecotopes	floodplain forest - softwood / pioneers floodplain forest - hardwood marsh woodland
shrubland ecotopes	river dune - natural levee floodplain shrubland marshland
natural grassland ecotopes (extensively grazed)	levee grassland floodplain grassland
aquatic ecotopes	oxbow - pond stagnant channel secondary (flowing) channel

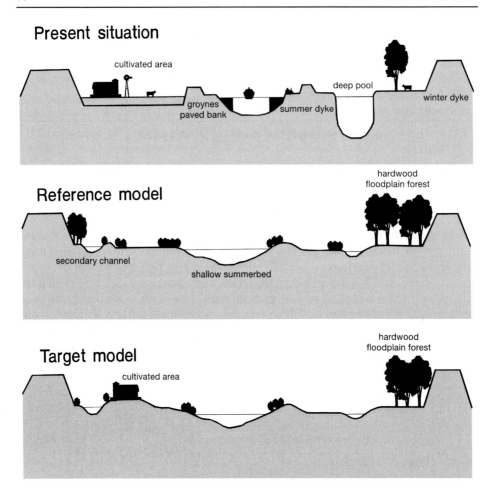

Fig. 3. Cross-sections of the river Rhine: present situation, reference model and rehabilitation target model (from Postma *et al.* 1996)

4.3. Alternative strategies

As a result of these analyses, it appeared that the larger parts of the active floodplains will turn into floodplain forests if a natural development under current conditions is allowed. Forests, however, tend to drive up water levels as they hinder fast run off of river water. To prevent trespassing of flood design levels, forests in active floodplains can not be allowed to develop on a large scale unless the increased hydraulic resistance is compensated, for example by restoring secondary channels. In "Landscaping the river Rhine" (Silva & Kok 1996) the effects of several landscaping alternatives on flood protection, navigation and nature have been analysed (see also Van de Kamer *et al.* 1998).

Given a certain configuration and distribution of ecotopes based on the intrinsic ecological potential of the particular river stretch, it is possible to apply a simple habitat evaluation procedure for selected plant and animal species. Based on the predicted ecotopes, the potential carrying capacity for characteristic riverbound species has been estimated (Postma *et al.* 1995). However, quantitative data with respect to species in a future situation should be regarded as merely indicative. The return of species is not only determined by the total area of ecotopes (cover types or habitats); also the distribution of the ecotopes over the length of the river should suit their ecological network demands. Reijnen *et al.* (1995; see also Foppen & Reijnen 1998) have developed an instrument to analyse the sustainability of species populations at different spatial patterns of ecotopes (cf. Lenders *et al.* 1998). It appeared that spatial patterns can determine to a large extent the suitability for species.

A first experiment of rehabilitation of a floodplain of the Rhine has been carried out in the "Duursche Waarden" in 1989. An isolated floodplain channel has been reconnected with the main channel by dredging activities and partial removal of a protection levee (Fig. 4).

4.4. Results

Since the rehabilitation activities, the water table in the floodplain channel and – at high discharges – the rest of the floodplain has followed the water table in the main channel. The morphological, hydrological and ecological developments have been monitored intensively (Cals 1994). Increased hydrological and morphological activity has resulted in the natural formation of new floodplain channels. Only a few years after the rehabilitation activities were finished, characteristic terrestrial flora species have returned in the floodplain. However, characteristic aquatic macrofauna and flora species have not yet returned (Van den Brink 1994). The reason is probably that the floodplain channel is connected to the main channel only at one point. The water is therefore flowing at high discharges only when the whole active floodplain is flooded, while at lower discharges the water remains stagnant. Most aquatic river species need permanent flow conditions. On the other hand, water quality in the floodplain channel has deteriorated after connection with the main channel. Thus, the conditions for the limnophilic species which were already present in the initial situation have deteriorated as well (Van den Brink *et al.* 1993). The example shows that field inventory before rehabilitation together with monitoring of results after nature rehabilitation is extremely important to improve insight in the intrinsic ecological potential of floodplain ecosystems.

4.5. Conclusion

In the International Rhine Commission, an inventory of remaining nature areas along the mainstream of the Rhine is being carried out. This inventory could provide an overview of the actual ecological network of the Rhine and its strong and weak points. The ecological potentials of the Rhine sections, should be the base for improvement of the ecological network through nature rehabilitation. For the Dutch Rhine-branches, nature rehabilitation targets have been deduced from physical processes that are attainable in the current situation and under current boundary conditions. The results of the first rehabilitation projects have to be monitored carefully, to be able to evaluate effects of rehabilitation measures and to intervene in undesired developments.

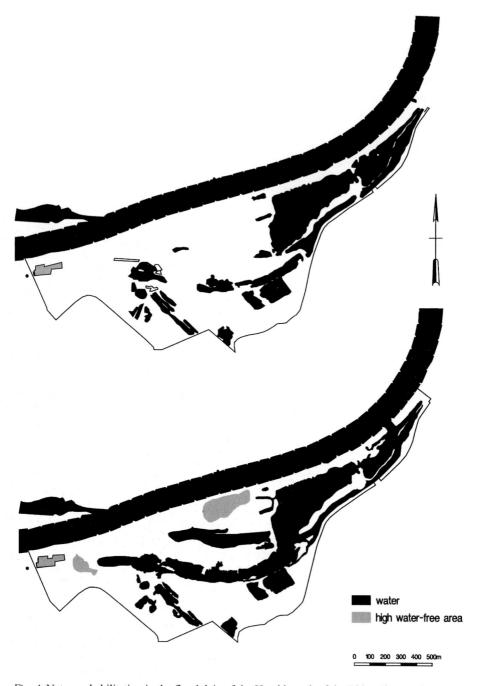

Fig. 4. Nature rehabilitation in the floodplain of the IJssel branch of the Rhine (from Cals 1994)

5. Grensmaas

5.1. The problem

The 40 km section of the River Meuse that forms the state boundary between Belgium and the Netherlands, the Grensmaas (Common Meuse), has lost much of its natural character because of gravel mining and regulation in the past 100 years. A deep-lying incised channel resulted, where hardly any river dynamics is still present (Dijkman & Pedroli 1994). Since no navigation takes place on this stretch, unique chances are present to rehabilitate the original river dynamics. To restore the natural processes, a plan was developed to widen the stream channel of the river, and lower the active floodplain (Fig. 5). This will cause the active river bed to be wider. In the same time, gravel will be produced which can be sold to the construction industry, and the design flood levels can considerably be lowered. Boundary conditions are the stability of the banks, especially at the Belgian side, and the river bed stability at those sections where fine sand is underneath. Since high floods caused considerable damage in 1993 and 1995, the Grensmaas study is part of an integrated flood protection study along the whole Meuse in the Netherlands (Roosjen & Lieshout 1998).

5.2. The approach

A large 60 x 40 m² physical scale model of part of the Grensmaas river was constructed as an experimental tool to model the complex processes of a gravel river with armoured bed (De Jong 1996). This allowed for one- and two-dimensional mathematical models to be tuned to the expected river processes. In an iterative procedure, the original layout of the plan was adapted to the extent that no unacceptable erosion of bed or banks would take place, and no adverse secondary effects would result for nature and landscape through lowered groundwater levels. For the latter, an impact assessment was carried out with the help of groundwater modelling. The intrinsic ecological potential of the river and floodplain ecosystems was thus determined on the basis of inundation characteristics and stream velocity pattern, given a realistic estimation of the expected developments in water and sediment quality.

5.3. Alternative strategies

Since the plan to be assessed was quite well defined in its preference for shallow gravel mining, and since the plan objectives deviated only little from the original plan, not much room existed for variation in layout of the plan. Main design differences laid in the amount of river morphological dynamics, where a balance should be sought between acceptability for river management (erosion control) and optimisation for restoration purposes. Therefore, besides the original plan an optimal river management alternative, an environmentally optimal alternative and a preferred alternative were developed. The resulting ecological potential was translated into the distribution of ecotopes.

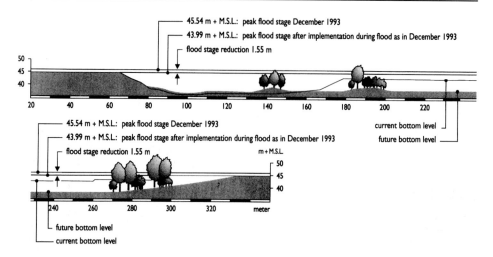

Fig. 5. Plan elements of the Grensmaas river restoration: widening the main stream channel and lowering the floodplain allow natural river dynamics to increase (after Dijkman & Pedroli 1994).

5.4. Results

It appeared that the original plan would result in unacceptable erosion of both bed and banks, developing deep erosion pits of more than 10 m deep. Also, unacceptable groundwater effects resulted. When reducing the amount of erosion by bed and bank protection, a rather sterile solution evolved, with suboptimal conditions for nature rehabilitation. In this optimal river management alternative, almost all river dynamics would disappear again from the river, but no uncertainty would remain for the river managers as to the erosion to be expected, and no significant groundwater lowering would take place. In this alternative, those elements were identified where river processes could be enhanced in an acceptable way. Therefore, the boundary condition that the place of the state boundary – by definition the line connecting the deepest points in the river – should be stable, was left. This allowed for more dynamics in the river bed (Fig. 6), increasing considerably the ecological potential in the sense of habitat characteristics for plant and animal species characteristic for dynamic gravel rivers, like Salmon (*Salmo salar*). This environmentally optimal alternative was further adapted only in a way to minimise noise emissions (gravel mining), and further optimise natural conditions (increasing connectivity between locations).

5.5. Conclusion

In the Grensmaas case it appeared possible to design with nature, although the result is a river which never has been existent in the same way. Originally it flowed several meters higher. But the original processes can be restored to a certain extent, leading to a considerable increase in the intrinsic ecological potential, and thus for the abundance and diversity of river and floodplain species, even if water quality does not yet allow very sensitive species to return.

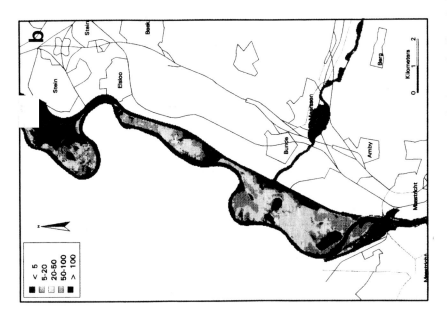

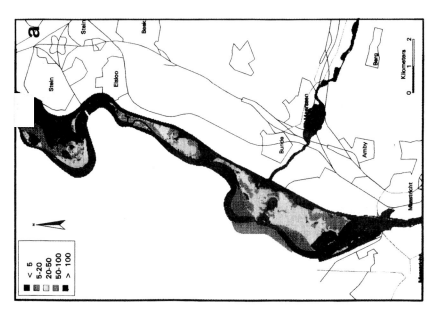

Fig. 6. Stream velocity pattern (in m/s at flood discharge level) before (a) and after (b) proposed realisation of rehabilitation works (from Pedroli 1994). The stream channel after rehabilitation will have chosen a new course, and the variation in stream velocity will increase, allowing for rehabilitation of dynamic river habitats.

6. Perspectives

In the three cases referred, no attempt was made to reconstruct the vegetation and ecosystem types considered to be typical for the particular river. Main guideline was to allow the river to create its own ecosystems, starting from the river dynamics still present or attainable under current conditions of river regulation upstream, water quality, etc. This confidence in the intrinsic ecological potential allows for combinations of efforts with third parties – in the Rhine and Meuse cases especially gravel, sand and clay mining, in the Danube case forestry, recreation and hunting – which gives the projects a sound economic and financial basis as well. Not much effort has been put in predicting the exact result of river rehabilitation in terms of numbers of plant and animal individuals. Concentrated is more on creating sound physical boundary conditions for ecosystem development, as expressed in terms of ecotopes (ha). Of course, also the development of ecotope types is included in the impact assessment, but the uncertainty of dynamic ecological processes only allows for general statements in the sense of percentage of nature area developed, balance in inundation characteristics and distribution of the various ecotope types.

It would be highly interesting to develop a European network of river corridors based on their intrinsic ecological potential, concentrating on those rivers with good opportunities for ecosystem development (cf. Jongman 1998). Since the river corridors are often less intensely used for other functions because of the flood risk, relatively modest investments will be required. Inland water transport networks should be tuned to the opportunities for ecosystem development. Moreover, rivers tend to connect areas far apart, allowing for migration routes of especially fish, birds and insects, but also some mammals, e.g. Beaver (*Castor fiber*) and Otter (*Lutra lutra*).

If the historical physical processes can not be restored, a historical reference for river and floodplain nature is not opportune and an alternative reference should be chosen, consciously inspired by historical or natural river dynamics. We would argue that the best opportunities for sustainable, self-supporting nature are attained when nature is the result of dynamic river processes, either historic or not. First the reference model should focus on the potential physical processes and then deduce the possible natural developments of flora and fauna from these processes.

References

Amoros, C., Rostan, J.C., Pautou, G. & Bravard, J.P. 1987. The reversible process concept applied to the environmental management of large river systems. Environ. Management 11: 607-617.
Anonymous 1990. Nature Policy Plan of the Netherlands. Ministry of Agriculture, Nature Management and Fisheries, The Hague.
Anonymous 1994. Natur 2000 in Nordrhein-Westfalen. Leitlinien und Leitbilder für Natur und Landschaft. Ministerium für Umwelt, Raumordnung und Landwirtschaft des Landes Nordrhein-Westfalen, Dortmund (in German).
Arbeitsgemeinschaft Renaturierung Hochrhein 1996. 1. Hochrhein Fachtagung "Lebendiger Hochrhein". Beiträge zur Umsetzung des Aktionsprogramms "Rhein 2000". Arbeitsgemeinschaft Renaturierung des Hochrheins, Basel (in German).
Bayley, P.B. 1991. The flood pulse advantage and the restoration of river-floodplain systems. Regulated Rivers, Research and Management 6: 75-86.

Billen, G., Décamps, H., Garnier, J., Boët, P., Meybeck, M. & Servais, P. 1995. Atlantic river systems of Europe. In: Cushing, C.E., Cummins, K.W. & Minshall, G.W. (eds.), River and Stream Ecosystems. Ecosystems of the world 22. pp. 389-418. Elsevier, Amsterdam.

Brakenridge, G.R. 1988. River flood regime and floodplain stratigraphy. In: Baker, V.R., Kochel & Patton, P.C. (eds.), Flood geomorphology. pp. 139-156. Wiley, New York.

Cals, M.J.R. (ed.), 1994. Evaluatie van de Duursche Waarden 1989 t/m 1993. Publicaties en rapporten van het project 'Ecologisch herstel Rijn en Maas'. Rapport EHR 60-1994. RIZA, Lelystad (in Dutch).

De Jong, R. 1996. River rehabilitation Grensmaas. Hydraulic aspects. Delft Hydraulics Report Q1969, Delft.

De Waal, L.C., Large, A.R.G., Gippel, C.J. & Wade P.M. 1995. River and floodplain rehabilitation in Western Europe: opportunities and constraints. Arch. Hydrobiol. Suppl. 101, (3/4): 679-693.

Dijkman, J.P.M & Pedroli, G.B.M. 1994. "De Maas Meester", Eindrapport Onderzoek Watersnood Maas. Waterloopkundig Laboratorium, Delft / Rijkswaterstaat, Den Haag (in Dutch).

Dister, E., Gomer, D., Obrdlik, P., Petermann, P. & Schneider, E. 1990. Water management and ecological perspectives of the Upper Rhine's floodplains. Regulated Rivers, Research and Management 5: 1-15.

Foppen, R.P.B. & Reijnen, R. 1998. Ecological networks in riparian systems. Examples for Dutch floodplain rivers. In: Nienhuis, P.H., Leuven, R.S.E.W. & Ragas, A.M.J. (eds.), New concepts for sustainable management of river basins. pp. 85-93. Backhuys Publishers, Leiden.

Hansen, H.O. 1996. River restoration - Danish experience and examples. Ministry of Environment and Energy, National Environmental Research Institute, Silkeborg.

IRC, 1987. Rhine Action Programme. Technisch-wissenschaftliches Sekretariat, International Rhine Commission, Koblenz.

IRC, 1992. Ecological Master Plan for the Rhine. "Salmon 2000". Technisch-wissenschaftliches Sekretariat, International Rhine Commission, Koblenz.

Jongman, R.H.G. 1998. Rivers: key elements in European ecological networks. In: Nienhuis, P.H., Leuven, R.S.E.W. & Ragas, A.M.J. (eds), New concepts for sustainable management of river basins. pp. 53-66. Backhuys Publishers, Leiden.

Large, A.R.G. & Petts, G.E. 1994. Rehabilitation of river margins. In: Calow, P. & Petts, G.E. (eds.), The Rivers Handbook. Hydrological and Ecological principles. Volume 2. pp. 401-418. Blackwell, Oxford.

Lenders, H.J.R., Leuven, R.S.E.W., Nienhuis, P.H., Oostinga, A.D. & Van den Heuvel, P.J.M. 1998. Ecological rehabilitation of floodplains along the middle reachof the Waal: a prosperous future for fauna target species? In: Nienhuis, P.H., Leuven, R.S.E.W. & Ragas, A.M.J. (eds) New concepts for sustainable management of river basins. pp. 115-130. Backhuys Publishers, Leiden.

Marchand, M. (ed.) 1993. Floodplain rehabilitation Gemenc. Final Report. Delft Hydraulics, RWS-RIZA, VITUKI, Delft.

Marchand, M., Pedroli, B., Marteijn, E. & Bakonyi, P. 1992. Policy analysis for the rehabilitation of the Gemenc Floodplain, Hungary. In: Contributions to the European Workshop Ecological Rehabilitation of Floodplains, 22-24 Sept 1992, Arnhem, The Netherlands. pp. 107-115. Report no. II-6 under the auspices of the CHR, Lelystad.

Middelkoop, H. 1997. Embanked floodplains in the Netherlands. Thesis, University Utrecht. Netherlands Geographical Studies 124.

Milner, A.M. 1994. System recovery. In: Calow, P. & G.E. Petts (eds.), The Rivers Handbook. Hydrological and Ecological principles. Volume 2. pp. 76-97. Blackwell, Oxford.

Pedroli, G.B.M. 1993. Vegetation Modelling. Working Document 5, Floodplain Rehabilitation Gemenc. Delft Hydraulics, Delft.

Pedroli, B. (ed.) 1994. Onderzoek Watersnood Maas. Deelrapport 8, Landschapsecologische aspecten. Waterloopkundig Laboratorium, Delft (in Dutch).

Pedroli, G.B.M., Postma, R., Rademakers, J.G.M. & Kerkhofs, M.J.J. 1996: Welke natuur hoort bij de rivier? Naar een natuurstreefbeeld afgeleid van karakteristieke fenomenen van het rivierlandschap. Landschap 13 (2): 43-61 (in Dutch).

Petts, G. 1990: Water, engineering and landscape: development, protection and restoration. In: Cosgrove, D. & Petts, G. (eds.), Water, engineering and landscape. Water control and landscape transformation in the modern period. pp. 188-208. Belhaven Press, London / New York.

Postma, R., Kerkhofs, M.J.J., Pedroli, G.B.M. & Rademakers, J.G.M. 1995. Een stroom natuur, Natuurstreefbeelden voor Rijn en Maas. Ministerie van Verkeer en Waterstaat, project Watersysteemverkenningen, RIZA nota 95.060, ISBN 9036945267, Arnhem (In Dutch with summary in English).

Rademakers, J.G.M. & H.P. Wolfert, 1994. Het Rivier-Ecotopen-Stelsel. Een indeling van ecologisch relevante ruimtelijke eenheden ten behoeve van ontwerp- en beleidsstudies in het buitendijkse rivierengebied. Lelystad, Rijkswaterstaat-RIZA, Publicaties en rapporten van het project "Ecologisch herstel Rijn en Maas", 61-1994 (in Dutch).

Reijnen, R., Harms, W.B., Foppen, R.P.B., de Visser, R. & Wolfert, H.P. 1995. Rhine Econet. Ecological networks in river rehabilitation scenario's: a case study for the Lower Rhine. Publications and reports of the project "Ecological rehabilitation of the rivers Rhine and Meuse", report nr. 58-1995. RIZA, Lelystad, 1995.

Roosjen, R. & Van Lieshout, M.C. 1998. Flood protection measures for the river Meuse ("Zandmaas"). In: Casale, R., Pedroli, G.B.M. & Samuels, P. (eds.), Ribamod, River basin modelling, management and flood mitigation, Concerted Action. Proceedings of the first workshop, Delft, 13 to 15 February 1997. pp. 371-380. European Commission Report EUR 18019 EN, DG Science, Research and Development, Brussels.

Silva, W. & Kok, M. 1996. Landscape planning of the River Rhine in the Netherlands. Main report: Towards a balance in River Management. Institute for Inland Water Management and Waste Water Treatment, Arnhem.

Theiling, C.H. 1995. Habitat rehabilitation on upper Mississippi river. Regulated Rivers: Research and Management 11: 227-238.

Van Baalen, J. 1995. Towards Nature development and the national ecological network for the Netherlands. In: Nature restoration in the European Union, proceedings of a seminar, Denmark 29-31 May 1995. Ministry of Environment, Roskilde.

Van Dijk, G.M., Marteijn, E.C.L., Schulte-Wülwer-Leidig, A. 1995. Ecological Rehabilitation of the River Rhine: Plans, progress and perspectives. Regulated Rivers: Research and Management 11: 377-388.

Van den Brink, F.W.B. 1994. Impact of hydrology on floodplain lake ecosystems along the lower Rhine and Meuse. Thesis, University of Nijmegen.

Van den Brink, F.W.B., Klink, A.G. & Van de Velde, G. 1993. Natuurontwikkeling in uiterwaarden door verhoging rivierdynamiek? De Levende Natuur 94: 59-64 (in Dutch).

Van den Brink, F.W.B., Van de Velde, G., Buijse, A.D. & Klink, A.G. 1996. Biodiversity in the lower Rhine and Meuse river-floodplains: its significance for ecological river management. Neth. J. Aquat. Ecol. 30: 129-149.

Van de Kamer, J.P.G., Postma, R., Marteijn, E.C.L. & Bakker, C. 1998. On the way towards total water management. In: Nienhuis, P.H., Leuven, R.S.E.W. & Ragas, A.M.J. (eds.), Concepts for sustainable management of river basins. pp. 291-307. Backhuys Publishers, Leiden.

Van der Kraats, J.A. (ed.), 1994: Rehabilitation of the River Rhine. Water Science & Technology, Special Issue: Proceedings of the International Conference on Rehabilitation of the River Rhine 15-19 March 1993, Arnhem.

Vieser, M., 1991. Flutungen der Polder Altenheim. Materialen zum integrierten Rheinprogramm, Band 3, Heft 1. Ministerium für Umwelt, Baden-Würtemberg (in German).

Voies Navigables de France, 1995. Der Polder Ernstein. Wie lassen sich Hochwasserschutz am Rhein und Wiederherstellung eines aussergewöhnlichen Auwaldes miteinander verbinden? Voies Navigables de France, Direction Régionale de Strassbourg (in German).

Wolfert, H.P. 1992. Geomorphological differences between river reaches: Differences in nature rehabilitation potentials. In: Contributions to the European Workshop Ecological Rehabilitation of Floodplains. Arnhem, Netherlands. 22-24 September 1992. pp. 137-144. Intern. Comm. Hydrol. Rhine, Report no II-6, Lelystad.

ECOLOGICAL NETWORKS IN RIPARIAN SYSTEMS: EXAMPLES FOR DUTCH FLOODPLAIN RIVERS

R.P.B. Foppen & R. Reijnen
Institute for Forestry and Nature Research (IBN-DLO), P.O. Box 23, 6700 AA Wageningen, The Netherlands

Abstract

In northwestern European rivers typical riparian ecosystems have become very fragmented: only small relics have remained and distances between these sites are sometimes very large. Since it is not possible to conserve viable populations in large continuous patches, populations have to meet the standards of sustainability by sufficiently large networks of suitable habitat. The networks function as a metapopulation and the configuration of the landscape determines the viability of these metapopulations. To preserve biodiversity not only viable populations of certain target species are important, but also the fact that a river can function as a nature corridor.

In this contribution some examples are shown of methods and instruments to evaluate population networks. Criteria are presented that select representative target species. Furthermore, two types of model are presented, a simple expert knowledge based model called LARCH, mainly consisting of guidelines and standards, and a complex mechanistic population model called METAPHOR simulating the population dynamics in a fragmented landscape. Both models are able to predict viability of fragmented populations. Results of both modelling approaches will be shown for a case study in the lower Rhine region. Three scenarios each with 10,000 ha of new nature are compared with the present situation. The results show that for many target species viability increases but that for an optimal viability for bird and mammal species also the area outside the river basin has to be taken into account. The models also calculate measures for ecological efficiency and for the corridor function. These measures can be used to discriminate between scenarios.

1. Introduction

Land and water management policies increasingly address the ecological rehabilitation of river floodplains (e.g. Harms & Roos-Klein Lankhorst 1994, Postma *et al.* 1995). Various action plans aim at protecting, improving, and developing habitats for plants and animal species. However, a high nature conservation value is only one of the functions of the river and its floodplains: shipping, recreation, agriculture, clay excavation are also of importance. Moreover, spatial planning aiming at large scale nature development scenarios have to meet the safety standards to prevent flooding. Therefore, the area of nature in the floodplains will be limited. The consequences of this limited size of nature areas is that for many particularly larger species like birds and mammals the size is under the threshold for a "minimum viable population", a population of an animal or plant species that, although isolated will not go extinct. Viability can only be obtained by linking the areas in a kind of network. In certain configurations, these networks can function as a so-called meta-

New concepts for sustainable management of river basins, pp. 85–93
edited by P.H. Nienhuis, R.S.E.W. Leuven and A.M.J. Ragas
© *1998 Backhuys Publishers, Leiden, The Netherlands*

population (Opdam 1991). A metapopulation is a set of subpopulations in a fragmented landscape linked by dispersal of individuals or e.g. seeds in case of plants. Subpopulations show independent dynamics. The small populations in a network are susceptible to stochastic processes (either caused by demographic or environmental fluctuations) and often go extinct. The viability of a metapopulation depends upon the balance between local extinction and recolonisation from other subpopulations. Not only total size of a network of subpopulations but also the spatial configuration is an important parameter for population viability.

In western Europe, the river and its floodplains have a high potential as nature corridors: chains of habitats offer animals and plants the possibility to exchange between areas in and contiguous to the floodplain areas. This is important because particularly in northwestern Europe, many habitats are highly fragmented and species will only survive in these landscapes if habitat units are linked in a network. The river and its floodplains can play an important role in connecting parts of these networks. Since the area of suitable habitat in the floodplains is limited, it is crucial that the spatial configuration of the habitat will guarantee an optimal corridor function. Corridor functioning can be expressed at different levels: a population and an individual level. A corridor at the individual level is a strip of habitat (either continuous or with breaks) acting as a dispersal route for individuals to go from one habitat patch to another. A corridor on the population level is a network of habitat patches along or in the river. For rivers particularly, the population corridors are of importance. In river systems with a well functioning population corridor, species are able to expand to newly rehabilitated nature areas or to recolonize existing ones. In this respect, the river acts as a corridor at different scale levels. For species with a low dispersal capacity (< 3 km), networks at the local scale are of importance and habitats are linked in a transversal direction, perpendicularly to the river. For species with an intermediate (3-10 km) and large dispersal capacity (>10 km), networks at the regional respectively national scale are of importance and rivers can act as longitudinal corridors as well.

For several river systems in the Netherlands, the ecological functioning has been evaluated for both viability and corridor function. The aim of this contribution is to show the importance of a network approach in river rehabilitation studies. Furthermore, some guidelines and tools will be proposed for use in network evaluation. Firstly, guidelines for the selection of target species will be presented and an example will be shown of target species in a transect of the river Meuse. Secondly, models will be presented that can be used to evaluate viability and corridor function. As an example some aspects of a nature rehabilitation evaluation in the river Rhine will be presented. Finally, the proposed methods and tools will be discussed.

2. Tools and methods

2.1. Defining the target species

To evaluate the network function of a river area it is necessary to define target species. Network analysis can only be carried out for a particular species and only by selecting the right target species it is possible to make a sound statement for the

whole system. These species must represent groups of organisms with similar ecological preconditions concerning network functioning. Within the framework of a study on ecological networks in the middle part of the river Meuse, criteria were formulated to select the (animal) target species of this particular strip of river (Foppen & Geilen 1997). The following criteria were established:
–   the species represent the most important habitat types of the system (e.g. riparian woodland, marshland, grassland and some aquatic habitat types);
–   the species represent different taxonomic groups (and thus dispersal strategies);
–   the species represent different scale levels, with emphasis on regional and national scale.
Not all combinations of criteria are represented by a species, mainly because taxonomic group and scale level are highly correlated (small animals usually have small dispersal distances and have to be treated on the local scale level).

An additional set of criteria appears to be more pragmatic: to use a species as a target species, sufficient ecological information must be available and furthermore species are preferred that are on target species lists for water management or on so-called red lists based on an international or European conservation status. As an example, we present the target species list chosen in the river Meuse study (Table 1).

2.2. Models as tools for evaluation

Models are extremely important for evaluation of ecological networks (Verboom 1996). Various types of model can be used for evaluation: simple expert knowledge based models, tactic mechanistic (e.g. individual based) models, strategic models, and regression models. They all have their advantages and disadvantages. Although the value of models in making absolute, quantitative predictions can be questioned, they are very useful for comparing scenarios. Differences between scenarios will be rather robust to the exact parameter values of the model.

The Department of Landscape Ecology of the Dutch Institute for Forestry an Nature Research (IBN-DLO) follows two model approaches.

Model approach 1: METAPHOR

The METAPHOR model is a complex mechanistic, individual based population model for a certain species. It can be used to simulate population dynamics of a species living in a fragmented landscape showing metapopulation characteristics. It is patch-based, this means that all individuals living in a certain patch of habitat are treated similarly. So rather than simulating the dynamics of individuals it simulates the dynamics of a spatially structured population (Verboom 1996, Foppen *et al.* 1998). Population dynamics are stochastic (i.e. chance plays a role). The three important components are birth, death, and dispersal. Input data are species specific parameters, death and birth rate, dispersal probabilities, and data on the size and configuration of habitat patches in a particular landscape. From the configuration data (e.g. distances between all patches) connectivity measures can be obtained for every patch and these are transformed to emi- and immigration rates.

The output of the model (averages over 100 runs) consists of predictions of numbers of individuals per patch and for the total metapopulation, extinction chances for the total metapopulation, and probabilities of occurrence in each patch.

Table 1. Target species list for the middle part of the river Meuse in The Netherlands.

| ECOTOPE TYPE | SCALE LEVEL | | |
	LOCAL	REGIONAL	NATIONAL
RIPARIAN WOODLAND		Night heron *Nycticorax nycticorax*	
		Middle spotted woodpecker *Dendrocopos medius*	
		Beaver *Castor fiber*	
HERBAGE/GRASSLAND	Water shrew *Neomys fodiens*	Corn bunting *Miliaria calandra*	
	Large marsh grasshopper *Stethophyma grossum*		
MARSHLAND		Bluethroat *Luscinia svecica*	Bittern *Botaurus stellaris*
		Otter *Lutra lutra*	
STAGNANT WATER	Tree frog *Hyla arborea*	Nortern pike *Esox lucius*	
FLOWING WATER		Bullhead *Cottis gobio*	
		Barbel *Barbus barbus*	
		"Dragonfly" *Gomphus flavipes*	
		"Caddisfly" *Tinodes waeneri*	
		"Water bug" *Aphelocheirus aestivalis*	

Model approach 2: LARCH

LARCH (Landscape ecological Rules for the Configuration of Habitat) is a decision support system based on simple guidelines for viability in (meta)populations in more or less fragmented landscapes (Reijnen *et al.* 1995, Bergers & Kalkhoven 1996, Kalkhoven *et al.* 1996, Verboom *et al.* 1997). As mentioned before, (meta)populations will be viable at a certain size, either expressed as total area suitable habitat, or the number of reproducing individuals. The threshold value depends upon the configuration of the habitat. This threshold will be lowest for one large population and highest for a highly fragmented metapopulation with many small patches. For instance for a Bittern *Botaurus stellaris* a non-fragmented area of 140 ha is needed, but in case of a highly fragmented network only an area 5 or 6 times as large will be viable. These guidelines are based on different models (both simple and complex, e.g. METAPHOR), field data, and experiments. Model input consists of size of habitat patches for a particular species and the configuration of surrounding habitat patches. Dispersal characteristics of a species are used to define network boundaries (distance between areas defines which areas belong to one metapopulation). Total area of suitable habitat within the network is tested against standards for viable populations.

With the model approaches both viability and corridor function can be assessed. Population viability is defined as the chance of a population surviving for a certain length of time, assessed qualitatively in the LARCH approach and expressed as extinction probability in the METAPHOR approach. Furthermore, also an efficiency measure of the network can be assessed: saturation. The degree of saturation determines to what extent the potentially suitable space is occupied by reproducing individuals. The closer this value approaches 1 (i.e. mean expected population size approaches the carrying capacity), the better the ecological efficiency.

3. An example: the Rhine-econet study

The use of models will be illustrated by examples from the Rhine-econet project (Reijnen *et al.* 1995). Three scenarios for parts of the Lower Rhine between Duisburg (Germany) and Gorinchem (The Netherlands) were evaluated on network function (Reijnen *et al.* 1995). The scenarios are inspired by the description of systems' natural situation in historical time and based on knowledge of the suitability for nature rehabilitation. The landscape structure was described by using ecotopes. An ecotope is a spatial unit combining the abiotic site conditions and the related plant and animal community. The ecotope patterns are related to differences in river dynamics and management activities. These differences are expected to be reflected in the network function. The scenarios are named after river systems that can be considered, entirely or partially, as a contemporary reference. In all scenarios, the total acreage at the disposal of nature rehabilitation is 10,000 ha (at present less than 1000 ha).
– The Rhine-Traditional scenario consists of relatively small forest and macrophyte marshes evenly spread throughout the study area. Hay production (by mowing) and clay extraction are allowed in order to maintain the macrophyte marshes and favour reed development. The present-day river management is continued.
– The Loire-River Dynamics scenario consists of medium-sized forest, macrophyte marsh, and water complexes and secondary channels. There is more room for dynamic river processes and low density grazing is an important management option.
– The Mississippi-Spillway scenario consists of large-scale macrophyte marshes outside the winterdikes and small forests in the floodplain area.
The two model approaches were used for evaluation of the expected ecotope configurations. Input for both models were habitat suitability assessments and a carry-

○ not viable ◐ marginally viable ● viable	Present situation	Rhine-Traditional	Loire-River dynamics	Mississippi-Spillway
Riverine forest				
Beaver	○	○	●	○
Middle spotted woodpecker	○	●	●	◐
Black kite	○	◐	◐	◐
Black stork	○	○	○	○
Macrophyte Marsh				
Great reed warbler	○	●	○	●
Bittern	●	●	●	●
Night heron	○	◐	○	◐
Secondary Channel				
Barbel	○	○	?	○
Riparian Landscape				
White-tailed eagle	○	○	○	○

Fig. 1. Viability (expected probability that a population will survive a long period) for the target species in three scenarios compared to the present situation (? = no viability estimation possible).

ing capacity figure (based on the area size) per ecotope for every target species. The output consists of measures for viability, ecological efficiency and the corridor function of the study area.

In Fig. 1 the viability is expressed in several classes, using the LARCH approach. The results permit to judge the three scenarios as compared to the present situation. In this case, all three scenarios provide better survival chances for most target species. Although the situation will improve for some species, even this large area of new nature is not enough to ensure viability for all target species. For these species viability is only possible when the habitat patches are linked into very large networks also outside the river basin.

In Fig. 2, saturation is calculated using METAPHOR and is used as a measure for ecological efficiency: the mean expected population size divided by the carrying capacity of the total network. Results are illustrated for the Middle spotted woodpecker *Dendrocopos medius*. The message from this picture is that an equal amount of nature does not always mean an equal number of woodpeckers. The Loire-River Dynamics scenario is the most efficient since 45% of the maximum number of pairs can be expected (against only 5% in the Mississippi Spillway scenario). This stresses the importance of an optimal spatial configuration of available habitat.

In Fig. 3 the corridor function is presented for the Middle spotted woodpecker, again using the METAPHOR model output. Corridor function is expressed as the network area with high probabilities of occurrence (>90%). As an example we compared the Rhine-Traditional scenario with the present situation. At present, corridor function is very low since no areas with high probability of occurrence are to be expected. In the scenarios, see the example for the Rhine-Traditional, the corridor function is strongly improved with regard to the present situation, although it cannot be considered optimal. The species will probably encounter problems in (re)colonising the westernmost parts of the study area.

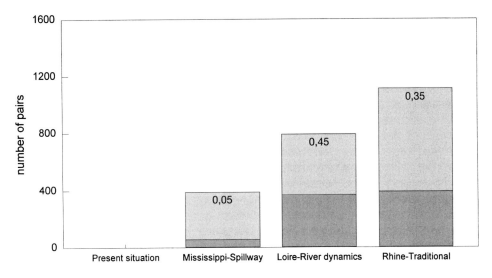

Fig. 2. Saturation, as a measure for ecological efficiency (see text) for the Middle spotted woodpecker in the three scenarios as compared to the present situation. The open bars indicate the maximum expected number (= carrying capacity), the blackbars indicate the predicted mean population size (also presented as datalabel which is expressed as fraction of the maximum number of pairs).

4. Discussion and conclusions

Linking patches in networks or linking different networks is probably a good strategy to maintain a high biodiversity in riparian systems. Evaluating such an ecological network can only be done on the species level. A good set of criteria is needed to select representative target species.

It can be concluded that the presented models are useful in evaluating the network function of different scenarios in floodplain rivers. Network function can be expressed in several measures, like viability, corridor function, and saturation. They all can be useful in helping to discriminate between scenarios. The models can be improved by adding an uncertainty interval based on a sensitivity analysis. At the moment, these improvements are being implemented in LARCH and METAPHOR. Spatial population models like METAPHOR require knowledge of the population biology of the species. Moreover, it is often difficult to obtain data for both calibration and validation. So, application will be possible for a small number of species only. To consider a wider range of species, as is required for representative results, the LARCH approach was developed. The results are less specific than obtained with METAPHOR. The output of both models is similar. In the LARCH model, currently new research results are being implemented and in future studies this will be the most powerful instrument that can be used to evaluate networks of animal or plant populations.

Although the Rhine-econet study was intended as an example to illustrate tools and methods to evaluate ecological networks, it can be concluded that at present viability of many target species of birds and mammals will be very low. Adding

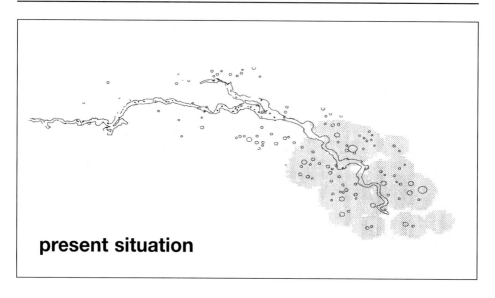

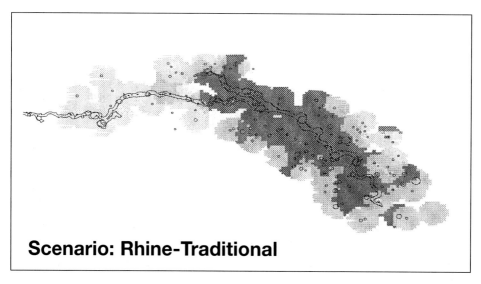

Fig. 3. Corridor function, visualized by showing the occupation probability for the Middle spotted woodpecker in the study area. Only the darkly hatched areas represent a good corridor function. The circles represent the habitat patches in and around the study area. Occupation probability<10%: no hatching, 10-40%: light hatch, 40-90%: medium hatch, >90%: dark hatch.

10,000 ha of new nature to the present area of about 1000 ha, certainly will improve the situation but even this quite large area is not enough to ensure persistence of all chosen target species.

A measure for the ecological efficiency of the network can be used to discriminate between the scenarios. The Loire-River Dynamics scenario proves to be the most efficient scenario for target species of riverine forest. Corridor function (expressed as areas with high occupation probabilities) will also increase in the three scenarios. The example shows that for the Middle spotted woodpecker, a species of riverine forest, the corridor function is not optimal in the Rhine-Traditional scenario. The westernmost parts probably will be the weakest parts of the network. The reason for that is that in this region the riverine forest is not supported by large forest areas outside the river basin. For many species, the areas outside the river basin play an important role for the sustainability of the population. Probably the Rhine river basin, as is the case for may other rivers, is too narrow to meet the area standards for viable populations, even if a large part of the basin will consist of nature.

The presented methods can be applied to other floodplains when an adequate description of (expected) ecotopes is available.

Acknowledgements

The Meuse and Rhine-econet study were commissioned by the Research Institute for Inland Water Management and Waste Water Treatment (RIZA). The authors wish to thank E. Marteijn, R. Postma and S. Kerkhofs of RIZA for their support.

References

Bergers, P.J.M. & Kalkhoven, J.T.R. 1996. Versnippering van de natuur in Nederland. De aard en de omvang van het probleem; de weg naar de oplossing (leaflet). Instituut voor Bos- en Natuuronderzoek (IBN-DLO), Wageningen (in Dutch).

Foppen, R.P.B. & Geilen , N. 1997. LARCH-RIVIER: methode voor het evalueren van ecologische netwerken in het Rivierengebied. Hoofdrapport. IBN-DLO/RIZA, Wageningen (in Dutch).

Foppen, R., Ter Braak, C.F., Verboom, J. & Reijnen, R. 1998. Sedge warblers (*Acrocephalus schoenobaenus*) and African rainfall, a low population resilience in fragmented marshlands. Ardea (in press).

Harms, W.B., Roos-Klein Lankhorst, J. 1994. Toekomst voor de natuur in de Gelderse Poort. Planvorming en evaluatie. Rapport 298.1. DLO-Staring Centrum, Wageningen / Grontmij, De Bilt (in Dutch).

Kalkhoven, J., Van Apeldoorn, R., Opdam, P. & Verboom, J. 1996. Worden onze natuurgebieden groot genoeg? Schatting van benodigde oppervlakte leefgebied voor kernpopulaties van een aantal diersoorten. Landschap 13: 5-15 (in Dutch).

Opdam, P. 1991. Metapopulation theory and habitat fragmentation: a review of holarctic breeding bird studies. Landscape Ecology 4: 93-106.

Postma, R., Kerkhofs, M.J.J., Pedroli, B.G.M. & Rademakers, J.G.M. 1995. Een stroom natuur. Natuurstreefbeelden voor Rijn en Maas. Ministerie van Verkeer en Waterstaat, project Watersysteemverkenningen, RIZA nota 95.060. Rijksinstituut voor Integraal Zoetwaterbeheer en Afvalwaterbehandeling, Lelystad (in Dutch).

Reijnen, R., Harms, W.B., Foppen, R.P.B., De Visser, R. & Wolfert, H.P. 1995. Rhine-econet: ecological networks in river rehabilitation scenarios: a case study for the lower Rhine. Publications and reports of the project Ecological rehabilitation of the Rivers Rhine and Meuse. Report 58. Research Institute for Inland Water Management and Waste Water Treatment (RIZA), Lelystad.

Verboom, J. 1996. Modelling fragmented populations: between theory and application in landscape planning. IBN Scientific Contributions 3, Institute for Forestry and Nature Research (IBN-DLO), Wageningen.

Verboom, J., Luttikhuizen, P.C. & Kalkhoven, J.T.R 1997. Minimumarealen voor dieren in duurzame populatienetwerken. IBN-rapport 259. Instituut voor Bos- en Natuuronderzoek (IBN-DLO), Wageningen (in Dutch).

NATURE REHABILITATION FOR THE RIVER RHINE: A SCENARIO APPROACH AT DIFFERENT SCALES

W.B. Harms and H.P. Wolfert
*DLO Winand Staring Centre for Integrated Land, Soil and Water Research,
P.O. Box 125, 6700 AC Wageningen, The Netherlands*

Abstract

Nature rehabilitation has become a major policy in river management in the Netherlands. A scenario approach combined with an expert system can support decision making. The methodology is illustrated by two case studies at different scales. In the Rhine-Econet study three scenarios for river management are presented and evaluated for the network function of some bird species. A second case concerns the Gelderse Poort area with two scenarios both aimed to enlarge the surface of the natural areas but in a different way. By means of the GIS-based landscape ecological decision support system LEDESS the ecological impact on vegetation and fauna has been assessed. Results are discussed. Although a lot of assumptions have to be made the results of both studies facilitate discussion and decision making about which nature policy targets are desirable and realistic.

1. Introduction

During the last decade the concept of river rehabilitation was introduced in river management in the Netherlands (Van Dijk *et al.* 1995). This policy is related to political issues such as sustainable exploitation of natural resources and biodiversity and has been enhanced by the need to reduce the total area of agricultural land, due to increasing production surpluses. In the past, river floodplains were predominately used by agriculture in spite seasonnal inundation. Nowadays, the same conditions give restricted use to agriculture, so that floodplain areas may be transformed into nature areas. Those floodplains are considered now as important areas for nature rehabilitation. Changes in land use, however, may have serious impact on other river functions which also have to be fulfilled. Situated within the most densely populated part of Europe, the River Rhine is intensively used for navigation. Extremely high discharges in 1993 and 1995 have stressed again the water discharge function and flood protection as high-priority issues (Silva & Kok 1996).

Thus, modern river management is confronted with conflicting interests and land use claims from various sectors. The outcome of the future developments in these sectors is uncertain. To cope with this uncertainty, scenario studies are believed to be useful tools in the decision making process. However, examples of scenario studies for nature policy are scarce. This paper will contribute to a methodology of scenario studies on nature policy for river systems.

First, the scenario approach will be introduced as well as the decision support instrument used for comparison of outcomes of the various scenarios for nature poli-

*New concepts for sustainable management of river basins, pp. 95–113
edited by P.H. Nienhuis, R.S.E.W. Leuven and A.M.J. Ragas*
© 1998 Backhuys Publishers, Leiden, The Netherlands

cy. Then, two studies are presented in which policies for nature rehabilitation are elaborated into various options for physical planning of nature areas along the River Rhine and in which the effectiveness of the various options is evaluated. Finally, the methodology presented is discussed with special emphasis on the perspectives for future usage.

2. The scenario approach

Forecasting and backcasting scenarios
For the purpose of analyzing future developments De Jong (1992) has presented a concept of identifiable domains of future (Fig. 1): what is possible, what is probable (located within the domain of what is possible), and what is desirable (overlapping with the other two domains). Predicting the future focuses on the 'probable' domain. What is possible must be explored by designing and inventing the future, whereas the desirable domain is correlated with what we now want to happen in the future, which is the domain of policy making. If the desirable future is also probable, one may state that 'there is no problem'. Problems arise, however, if the probable future is not desirable. Solutions must be sought in the overlap of possible and desirable domains.

Schoonenboom (1995) has introduced two scenarios: the projective or forecasting scenarios and the prospective or backcasting scenarios. In Fig. 1, the domains of future are combined with these two categories. Forecasting scenarios project present-day trends or expectations onto the domain of the probable future. Scenarios of this type vary mainly in that one particular parameter is expected to vary in the future. Environmental planning often involves this sort of scenarios: for example, what will be the probable impact on ecosystems by different rates of climatic change. As dose-effect relations play an important role, these scenarios can also be appointed as dose-effect scenarios. Predicting models are important tools in searching the most accurate impacts of changing factors.

Backcasting scenarios design possible alternatives and confront them with the present situation in order to determine the most desirable alternative. This procedure prevails in physical planning. In this sort of approach scenarios are not determined by the differences in a single factor. A complex of variables interrelated spatially is involved in the design of the prospective scenario alternatives. Whereas an analytical approach prevails in the projective scenario, a more holistic approach predominates in the prospective scenario. Decision-support systems rather than predictive models are the tools here. This paper is confined to this latter category: the backcasting scenarios. As a contribution to the planning of river rehabilitation, this scenario approach is presented here.

The cyclic planning procedure
As a contribution to the planning of nature rehabilitation, a backcasting scenario procedure is presented here. In the process of planning two stages are distinguished (Fig. 2):
– design: the making of the alternative futures;
– evaluation: the proper backcasting activity delineating the possible path from the present to the future.

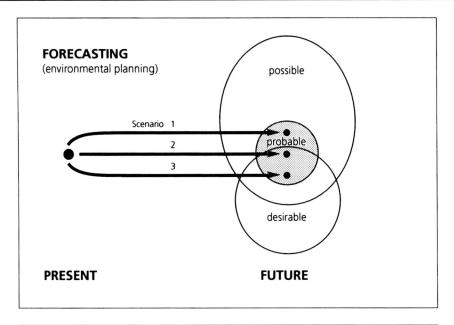

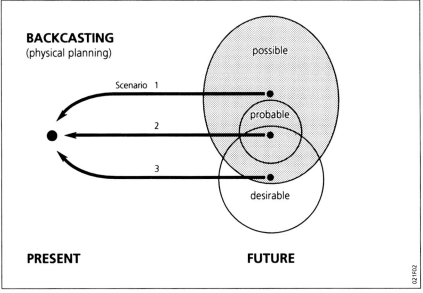

Fig. 1. Forecasting and backcasting scenarios.

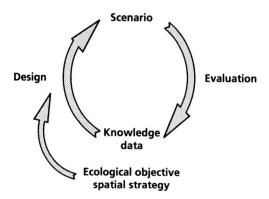

Fig. 2. The cyclic planning procedure.

In the design stage knowledge at the ecosystem or landscape level contributes to a creative solution to the problem. Concrete information about suitability for nature rehabilitation and spatial concepts related to different ecological objectives form the building blocks for the planner. In the plan evaluation, the scenarios are checked and assessed: is the alternative feasible and what are the ecological benefits of each plan? This means a validation of the scenarios at the species level concerning the target species. At this stage, expert systems are introduced as tools to assess as accurately as possible the impacts of the proposed future situations and to compare these with the present situation. Since the stages are not completed consecutively but may alternate cyclically in the planning process, the results of the evaluation are input to a new planning cycle in order to adjust the scenarios and to re-evaluate them. Ultimately, a more comprehensive plan can be developed. The procedure will be illustrated with the planning of scenarios for river rehabilitation at different scales.

Various nature rehabilitation policies in the Netherlands
To understand the basic strategies in nature rehabilitation, two questions are crucial: what is the ecological objective and what is the spatial strategy? The first question is related to the level of the ecosystem. Several ecosystems can develop on one site under different regimes of nature management. The choice of the system to be allowed to develop is a matter of nature policy. The second question is related to the landscape as a whole, the spatial order of ecosystems. It is taken into account that other activities, such as farming, recreation, water supply and quarrying, also require space. Nature management cannot be considered independently of those activities. Therefore, a spatial strategy is required.

   Four different policies for nature rehabilitation can be distinguished (Harms *et al.* 1991). Since the policies concern river dominated areas in the Netherlands each policy is given a motto referring to an animal species with a potential habitat in river landscapes and that could be favoured by realizing that policy (Fig. 3):
–   In the '**Godwit**' policy, a variety of ecosystems is obtained by integrating nature rehabilitation with other land use types, especially extensive agriculture, which often requires long-term agreements with farmers, or other multifunctional uses.

scenario	ecological objective	spatial strategy
"GODWIT"	variety of ecosystems	integration and zoning of land use
"OTTER"	improvement of dispersal	development of corridors and networks
"ELK"	self-sustaining ecosystems	segregation of land use
"HARRIER"	variety of ecosystems	segregation of land use optimal site selection

Fig. 3. Ecological objectives and spatial strategies of the four scenarios for nature rehabilitation (Harms *et al.* 1991).

This policy corresponds with the current trend in nature conservation policy in the Netherlands.
– The 'Otter' policy aims at improving the dispersal of endangered species that are sensitive to habitat fragmentation by a network of corridors and stepping stones connected with the source areas.
– The 'Elk' policy focuses on self-sustaining complete ecosystems with free play for natural processes without human interference. This kind of nature requires large tracts segregated from other land uses.
– In the '**Harrier**' policy, a variety of ecosystems in natural areas is planned also in large tracts. Various communities are controlled by different nature management techniques and located on optimal sites, such as transition zones and seepage areas.
The four policies must be understood as the abstract fields delineating the possibilities in nature rehabilitation in which only the corners have been surveyed. The consequences of implementing these extremes enable policy makers to choose a feasible and desirable compromise.

Landscape ecological decision support methodology
To evaluate the effects of the scenarios, the Landscape Ecological DEcision Support System (LEDESS) was used (Roos-Klein Lankhorst 1991, Harms *et al.* 1993). LEDESS is a deterministic knowledge-based system, which simulates the spatial and temporal development of vegetation and fauna. The two main operations of LEDESS are (Fig. 4):
– checking the ecological feasibility through confrontation with the abiotic site conditions;
– determining the final species composition of the vegetation, based on the expected vegetation development.

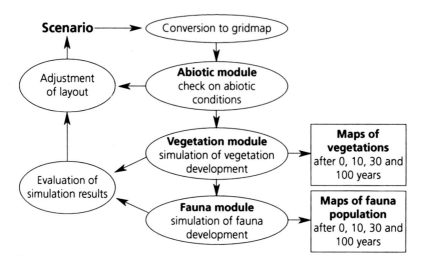

Fig. 4. Operation process of LEDESS.

Development of vegetation is determined by physiotope, target vegetation and man-agement. Physiotopes are spatial abiotic units characterized by a specific set of parameters on river morphodynamics and hydrodynamics (Knaapen & Rademakers 1990). The scenarios are formulated in terms of target vegetations, i.e. a set of the desirable vegetation types. Together, physiotopes and target vegetation determine the vegetation succession which may also be influenced by management. Land use and management can change the direction of vegetation development. The development of the vegetation determines the conditions for the fauna by changing the area suit-ed for breeding, foraging or refugal. Data on the actual situation and on the planned developments are stored in a grid-based geographical information system (GIS).

3. Two case studies at different scales

3.1. International level, scenarios for the 'Otter' policy: Rhine-econet

Aim
This section surveys the results of the case-study Rhine-Econet. In this case-study several scenarios are elaborated to assess the options for the 'Otter' policy, aiming at improving the dispersal of endangered animal species by means of creating a net-work of corridors and stepping stones connected with the source area. Improving existing habitats or re-creating former ones does not necessarily mean that animal species will become settled. The size of the habitat units might be too small to sup-port a viable population. Many species will only persist if habitat units are linked into a network system.

For this scenario study the part of the River Rhine system situated between the central mountains in Germany and the North Sea has been selected. The case-study focused on three habitat types: floodplain (riverine) forests, macrophyte marshes and secondary channels. Nature rehabilitation plans tend to focus on these habitat types, since these are very small and strongly fragmented at present. To evaluate the network function, vertebrate animal species were selected as indicator species characteristic for one or a combination of these habitat types, i.e. for riverine forest Beaver (*Castor fiber*), Middle spotted woodpecker (*Dendrocopus medius*), Black kite (*Milvus migrans*) and Black stork (*Ciconia nigra*), for macrophyte marshland Great reed warbler (*Acrocephalus arundinaceus*), Bittern (*Botaurus stellaris*) and Night heron (*Nycticorax nycticorax*), for side channel Barbel (*Barbus barbus*) and for the combination of all habitat types (the riverine landscape) White-tailed eagle (*Haliaeetus albicilla*).

The scenario approach was used to evaluate various options for spatial planning from a nature policy point of view. Based on an analysis at the ecosystem level, which provided knowledge on suitability for nature rehabilitation, scenarios have been designed that differed in spatial distribution of vegetations. To evaluate these scenarios in terms of their network function for species, models were used as tools to predict the impacts of the proposed future situations. A basis for the exploration of scenarios for nature rehabilitation as well as for modelling future situations has been provided by an analysis of the river landscape ecosystem, which has been performed on three hierarchical levels: drainage basin zones, river reaches and river ecosystems.

In the upstream half of the study area, the River Rhine flows in a wide valley, being part of the transport zone of the river system. It is characterized by fluvial terraces, indicating incision by a meandering river. Downstream, the depositional zone or Rhine delta, is characterized by a number of meander belts interspaced with large flood basins. Sediments have been deposited by meandering or low-sinuosity distributaries of the Rhine, that have changed their course repeatedly. Within both types of depositional styles mentioned, local differences in geological setting and river regime have caused a variable pattern of ecosystems at the river reach level.

The present geographical distribution of physiotopes within the study area was mapped, as well as the present distribution pattern of the vegetation types relevant to the study: softwood forest, hardwood forest and macrophyte marsh. To demonstrate the network approach it was also necessary to have some information on habitats outside the study area, but linked to the network. Based on foraging and home-range movements of the indicator species a special inventory of a zone of 10 km around the study area has been included as well. Macrophyte marshes were considered in a zone of 75 km around the study area.

Scenarios
Inspired by the description of the systems' natural situation in historical time and based on the knowledge on the suitability for nature rehabilitation, three scenarios have been chosen, which differ in spatial distribution of vegetations (Fig. 5). Fig. 6 gives a birds-eye view of the three scenarios. The patterns are related to different intensities of river dynamics and management activities. These differences are expected to be reflected in the network function. The scenarios are named after river systems that can be considered, entirely or partially, as a contemporary reference:

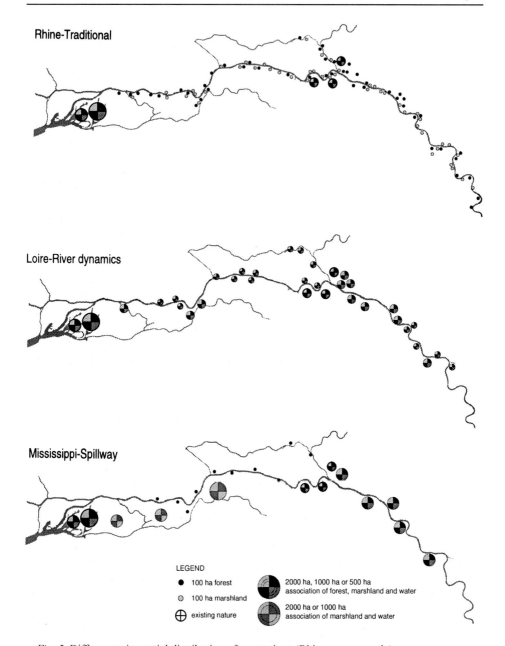

Fig. 5. Differences in spatial distribution of vegetations (Rhine-econet-study).

– **Rhine-Traditional Scenario**. Relatively small forests and macrophyte marshes will be spread evenly throughout the study area. Forests will be realized in the dry places. Sites for macrophyte marshes are only limited available at present, so excavations will have to be carried out to realize the scenario. This scenario allows mowing management and clay extraction in order to maintain the macrophyte marshes and favour Reed development. The present-day river management is continued.

– **Loire-River dynamics Scenario**. River dynamics will be given more room within the floodplains. This will result in forest-macrophyte marsh-water complexes, their relative proportions depending on local dynamics. Compared to the Rhine-traditional scenario larger units of nature areas will be the result, with larger distances in between. The forest component will often predominate. Mowing management is excluded in this scenario. However, extensive grazing, digging secondary channels or other excavation activities do fit in well. The secondary channels will have to be realized within river reaches that offer enough space and offer the appropriate river dynamics for maintaining open inflow points.

– **Mississippi-Spillway Scenario**. A chain of large-scale macrophyte marshes will be restored. Within the Rhine delta, the former flood basins are connected to the river system to restore them as spillways. This is only feasible in places without villages, main roads and railways, where large low-lying areas may be allowed to remain flooded nearly all year round. In the flood basins, the macrophyte marshes are to become as extensive as possible. This can be realized by river-water inlet during large winter discharges.

Evaluation

Automated processing of the scenarios has been enabled by using the LEDESS system. Elaborating the scenarios requires a typology that fits with the data processing. A distinction has been made between target vegetation and final vegetation. The scenarios are expressed in terms of target vegetation types: i.e. desirable vegetation types, which are influenced by a certain type of management and which can occur on a range of suitable physiotopes.

The vegetation that can be finally expected is the final vegetation. The final vegetation typology is correlated to the habitat requirements of the animal species involved of the study. Besides the desirable vegetation, other final vegetation types will develop. So, expressed in pecentages of the area each physiotope is covered by a set of final vegetation types which set is related to a particular target vegetation type. An example of the final dataset is given in Table 1. If a target vegetation cannot occur on a particular physiotope, one can take measures to improve the abiotic conditions, i.e. to change the physiotope. If measure taking makes no sense, this is also indicated in this expert system. All relationships are based on literature and expert knowledge.

The scenarios as expressed in terms of target vegetation types were transferred to the GIS map. The first evaluation concerns the suitability of the physiotopes for the objectives chosen. If a target vegetation type does not correspond with the prevailing present abiotic conditions, routines are included in the model LEDESS to propose measures to change the physiotope or to propose alternative target vegetations. The planner can choose either solution, or both. Consequently, vegetation development is simulated in accordance with the target vegetation and the present or adjusted physiotopes.

Rhine-Traditional

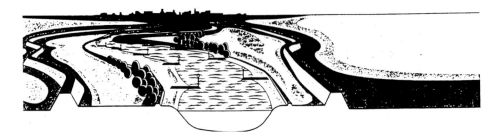

Loire-River dynamics

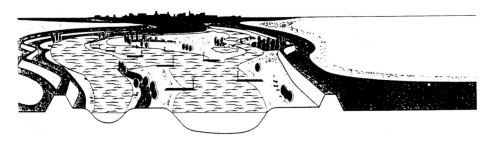

Mississippi-Spillway

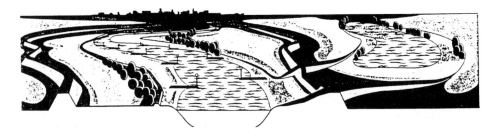

Fig. 6. A birds-eye view of the three Rhine-econet scenarios.

Table 1. Final vegetations for some selected combinations of target vegetation types and physiotopes, expressed in percentage of the physiotope area (selected physiotopes are protected against regular flooding by low summer dikes; M+ = measure has to be taken to change the physiotope in order to develop the final vegetation: i.e. lowering the soil surface by clay digging; M- = no measures can be taken possible).

Target vegetation type	Physiotope	Final vegetation type				
		Softwood forest	Hardwood forest	Macrophyte marsh	Open water vegetations	Grasslands
Softwood forest	Floodplain, natural	M+	M+	M+	M+	M+
	Stagnant floodplain channel/clay pits	40%	0%	10%	50%	0%
Hardwood forest	Floodplain, natural	0%	90%	0%	0%	10%
	Stagnant floodplain channel/clay pits	M-	M-	M-	M-	M-

In a second evaluation, the final vegetations of each scenario are checked. Although different in distribution patterns, all three scenarios must attain an equal total area of forests and macrophyte marshes (both 5000 ha) to be able to compare the relative impact of the habitat distributions on the network function for species. The total area of target vegetation types appeared to show an acceptable deviation of less than 10%. However, being dependent on the suitability of physiotopes, the specific terminal vegetation types can deviate from the expected target vegetation type:

- In the Rhine-Traditional Scenario many physiotopes proved to be unsuitable for vegetations with a high percentage of macrophyte marsh. Besides, the target vegetation type Macrophyte marsh (with winter mowing), turns out to develop softwood forest and isolated water as well. Consequently, the development of macrophyte marshes remains below the target area, whereas the development of softwood forests is beyond.
- According to the Loire-River dynamics Scenario the isolated waters are mainly transformed into waters connected with the river system, such as secondary channels and connected floodplain channels. The Scenario will develop a mosaic of bare soil, softwood and hardwood forests and, due to natural grazing management, grasslands. The area of macrophyte marshes remains far below the expected 5000 ha. The forest part of the scenario is almost such as was aimed at.
- The Mississippi-Spillway Scenario shows the largest contribution to the development of macrophyte marshes. However, caused by the natural manner of back swamp management chosen, the macrophyte marshes are only one third of the total inland areas designated for nature rehabilitation. Most part of this target vegetation type will develop into softwood forest or isolated waters.

As a third evaluation the network function for the target species in the three scenarios was evaluated. At first the habitat suitability and carrying capacity are estimated. Then the spatial dynamics of the populations are modelled by using the LAndscape ecological Rules for the Configuration of Habitat (LARCH) system or the METAPHOR model (METApopulation model FOR ecological impact assessment). The LARCH approach relies on expert knowledge. The METAPHOR model simulates the dynamics of a spatially structured population mathematically; of which the three major components are recruitment, mortality and dispersal. More details are given by Foppen & Reijnen (1998).

Results
The results of this study clearly show the importance of linking nature areas into a network system. They strongly support the growing attention for large scale approaches, such as river basin rehabilitation and transboundary river management. The network function is an important condition for successful strategies in terms of target species for nature policy.

Development of nature areas within 30% of the floodplains only results in viable network populations for species with small area demands. For all species the amount of habitat in the surrounding landscape largely determines the population viability. Thus, when developing strategies for nature rehabilitation these areas must be taken into account. However, some species, like the Black stork (*Ciconia nigra*) and the White-tailed eagle (*Haliaeetus albicilla*) which have very large area demands, will only persist if the nature areas within the river system are part of a network at sub-European scale.

Variations in the distribution patterns of new nature areas have large effects on the population saturation. Compared with the other distribution patterns, the best distribution pattern needs 40% less habitat to achieve a similar population size. However, there is not one single favourable pattern. Consequently, the success of the strategies will be raised considerably by choosing the optimal spatial pattern, especially where the available area to re-create former habitats is limited.

For some species the stepping stone function can become optimal, which means that they are able to expand to all parts of the river system. Other species, however, do not expand from one drainage basin zone into another. Here, the amount of habitat within the floodplains or the surrounding landscape is crucial. All three scenarios meet the forest target, but prove to be unable to produce sufficient macrophyte marsh. Suitable physiotopes for macrophyte marsh within the floodplains are only scarcely available, nor can they be developed within the transport zone of the river system. Attuning rehabilitation targets to the river landscape ecosystem characteristics reduces the risk of failure of strategies.

3.2. Regional level, scenarios for the 'Godwit', 'Harrier' and 'Elk' policies: The Gelderse Poort

Aim
On the regional scale a study was executed in the Gelderse Poort area, i.e. the gateway where the River Rhine enters the Netherlands (Harms & Roos-Klein Lankhorst 1994). The Gelderse Poort is an area of 12,000 hectares on the Dutch side of the

Dutch-German border. It extends to the same size in Germany. In the Gelderse Poort, the River Rhine bifurcates into Waal and Lower Rhine. The area can be divided into three parts: the river bed with floodplains between the dikes, the area south of the Waal and the area north of the Rhine. The last includes an important area of former Rhine channels. The proper gateway is formed by the two ice-pushed sandridges on both sides of the river. The project has been an initiative of the regional authorities of the Province of Gelderland. Since the area is part of the proposed national ecological network (LNV 1990), the 1000 ha of nature reserves in this area will have to be extended by approximately 3000 ha in the near future. The project was aimed at providing policy makers with rehabilitation scenarios as a basis for decisions on the future of this area.

Scenarios
Three policies for nature rehabilitation were combined into two scenarios (Fig. 7) and elaborated in detail as a part of an integrated study for landscape planning taking into account essential economic interests like outdoor-recreation, river management, agriculture and quarring of clay and sand.
– *Macrogradient Scenario.* This scenario is directed towards the sequence of ecological potentials inside and outside the dikes, coupled with specific nature management. This refers back to the richness of the biodiversity during the nineteenth century. This leads to a patterned spatial management, probably yielding results with less uncertainty, but often dependent on the sort of agriculture introduced, and labour-intensive nature management. Here, the 'Godwit' and 'Harrier' policies are actually combined (see section 2.1.).
– *River Dynamics Scenario.* In this scenario, the river processes are recognized as a driving force for nature rehabilitation. Human influence is minimal and limited to creating essential conditions. This concept allows uncertainty in space and time in developing communities, which, in turn, allows a rich variety of species and communities to evolve. This, however, will only occur when sufficient space is available. This scenario is related to the 'Elk' policy mentioned before (see also section 2.1.).
For the implementation of these two scenarios in the study area, 30% of the area was claimed for nature rehabilitation i.e. almost 3000 ha. The scenarios were elaborated now in spatial plans.

In the plan, based on the Macrogradient Scenario, the emphasis was on developing a pattern of nature in the old-Rhine-channel area inside the dikes. Here, a large reed marsh will be effected after most of the surface clay will have been removed. The water level control by the pumping station will be aimed at excluding the direct influence of the river. For an extended part of the plan the preference is to preserve and restore nature in the area, including the floodplains, as it was in former days when the landscape was dominated by tradional agricultural uses. This can only be realized nowadays by adapted farming and management agreements. The landscape remains open. Beside the 3000 ha for nature rehabilitation, modern agriculture remains in the less sensitive areas.

In the plan, based on the River Dynamics Scenario, the emphasis was on nature rehabilitation under the influence of the river in the floodplains and in the western part of the old Rhine channels. In the flood plains, parts of the clay layer will be

	ecological objective	management	spatial strategy
"Macrogradiënt"	biodiversity	nature management adjusted farming	integration / segregation of land uses
"Riverdynamics"	naturalness	non interference	segregation of land uses

Fig. 7. Two scenarios for the Gelderse Poort area (Harms & Roos-Klein Lankhorst 1994).

excavated, minor dikes removed and new channels dug, so that the river can have its own way again in some places, although within the constraints of river management. In the western part of the old-Rhine-channel area, the influence of the river will be considerable because water may flow freely in and out to a maximum level and the clay layer is excavated. Management will be kept to a minimum. In large parts, natural grazing throughout the year will be reintroduced, thus creating a small-scale landscape (Helmer *et al.* 1990). A control plan, based on the autonomous developments of the currently prevailing policy, has been made too. For comparison with the other alternatives, this plan is similar to the present situation.

Evaluation
To evaluate the effects of the two spatial plans on vegetation and fauna, the LEDESS-model was used (see Fig. 4). Data on the actual situation and on the planned developments were stored in a grid-based geographical information system (GIS), with 250 m x 250 m grids (6.25 ha). Landforms were mapped and a typology of physiotopes was developed simultaneously. Landforms characterized by the same developments in vegetation and fauna were combined into one type of physiotope, when situated next to each other. Information on site requirements and succession of vegetation communities and its impact on wildlife was derived from literature (Rademakers 1993).

Evaluation of the scenarios started with checking the suitability of physiotopes for the proposed development of the target vegetation types. From the model, alternative physiotopes can be deduced, if the development proposed does not correspond with the present situation. As a result several rehabilitation measures were planned to change the present abiotic circumstances. Subsequently, the vegetation and fauna developments were simulated, using the present or changed physiotopes as a basis. Developments were calculated for different periods. Results of the evaluation can be expressed as the area suited for vegetation and fauna populations considered. Results of the scenarios were compared with the present situation, and also with the situation that will exist when present developments in the area will continue.

Results
Some results are shown in Fig. 8 and 9. Fig. 8 shows the results of the computer simulation with the LEDESS-model for the Marsh-harrier (*Circus aeruginosus*). This species is the representative of a group of birds which need reed areas for

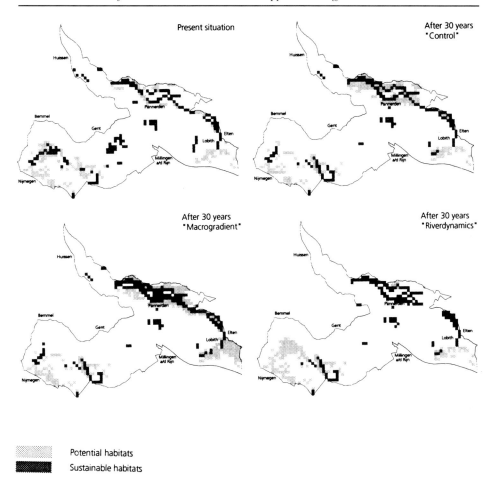

Potential habitats

Sustainable habitats

Fig. 8. Simulation of suitable habitats for the Marsh-harrier (*Circus aeruginosus*) in the Gelderse Poort area after thirty years, according to (a) the present situation, (b) the control plan, (c) plan "Macrogradient" and (d) plan "River Dynamics".

breeding and foraging and extensive agricultural land for foraging. The maps give the results for the present situation, the control plan, and both alternatives after thirty years. The control plan and plan "Macrogradient" both provide more suitable habitats than currently present, especially foraging areas contiguous to breeding areas within a radius of 4 km. In plan "River Dynamics" there are fewer foraging areas, because there is less extensively used agricultural land. Therefore, a lasting population is more guaranteed in "Macrogradient" than it is in "River Dynamics". For the beaver (*Castor fiber*) the maps show opposite results (Fig. 9). According to "River Dynamics" after thirty years there might be a suitable habitat for ten to twenty-five pairs of Beaver, a good opportunity to reintroduce this species, which became extinct in the Netherlands a century ago. Other plans and the present situation do not provide enough suitable habitats for a sustainable population.

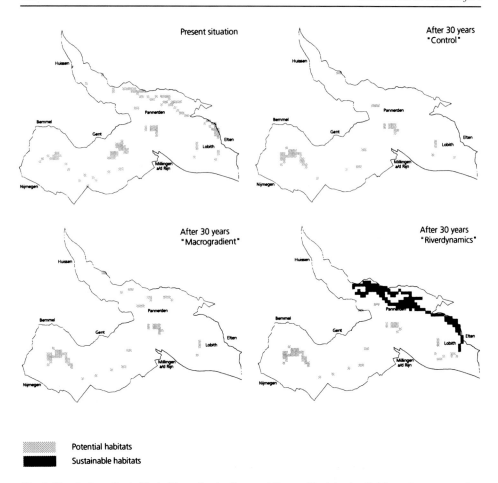

Potential habitats

Sustainable habitats

Fig. 9. Simulation of suitable habitats for the Beaver (*Castor fiber*) in the Gelderse Poort area after thirty years, according to (a) the present situation, (b) the control plan, (c) plan "Macrogradient" and (d) plan "River Dynamics".

To provide policy makers with a final evaluation, all the results of the Gelderse Poort study can be combined into one synoptic figure (Fig. 10). The horizontal line represents the total spectrum of possible fauna species in the Gelderse Poort area ranked in river-dependent species (left) and river-independent species (right); the vertical line delineates the area of suitable habitat with a species-specific threshold for sustainable population sizes. The figure shows that in the control plan only few of the considered species can develop a sustainable population. This is improved in plan "Macrogradient" for the whole range of species. In plan "River dynamics" the situation is improved only for part of the spectrum, but the improvement is considerable compared with the other plans, owing to the species dependent on river ecosystems. The options for policy makers are reduced now, but a difficult dilemma remains: is it preferable to develop good opportunities for species characteristic of river ecosystems only, or to improve biodiversity in the whole range, although with less suitable habitats for sustainable populations?

4. Discussion and perspectives

A large number of assumptions is incorporated in LEDESS. Knowledge of land-form development and developments of vegetation and fauna communities in many cases is far from detailed. Overall testing of the validity of LEDESS is therefore not possible yet. As a result the outcomes of this study should not be considered an accurate prediction. The importance to the planning process, however, is that different scenarios have been evaluated in exactly the same way, so that they are well comparable.

To explore and visualise the perspectives of future nature with varying efforts, the methodology elaborated in this study appears to be a successful tool. Its results facilitate discussion and decision making on nature policy targets are desirable and realistic.

The problem being studied is not specific for the River Rhine, but typical for lowland rivers in densely populated areas. Several demands for space within the river system have to be met: lost nature qualities are to be rehabilitated at the expense of the agricultural use of floodplains, whilst safety in case of flooding and in many cases a navigable river have to be guaranteed. As such, the study may well serve as an example of how to approach nature rehabilitation along other floodplain rivers.

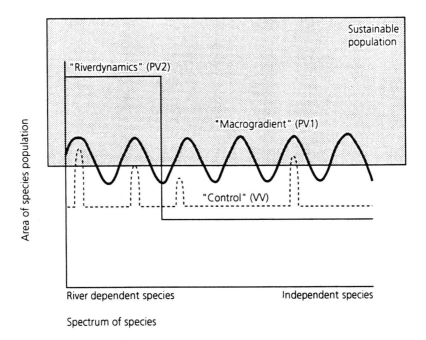

Fig. 10. Synoptic presentation of final results of the computer simulations for the Gelderse Poort area.

When applied to other floodplain rivers or other ecosystems, the selection of target species, the exploration of scenarios and the classifications and datasets used, must in the first place be adapted to the local circumstances. It may also be necessary to use a wider range of fauna species and possibly also plant species. The procedure itself, however, is considered usable for any other landscape ecological system.

Acknowledgements

The project Rhine-Econet was commissioned by the Dutch Research Institute for Inland Water Management and Waste Water Treatment (RIZA) and the Dutch Ministry of Agriculture, Nature Management and Fisheries (LNV). It was performed together with the DLO Institute for Forestry and Nature Research (IBN-DLO) and with the Consultancy for Environmental Planning, Landscape Architecture & Ecology (VISTA).

The project The Gelderse Poort was commissioned by the Province of Gelderland together with the Dutch Ministery of Housing, Spatial Planning and the Environment (VROM), Ministery of Transport, Public Works and Water Management (V&W) and Ministry of Agriculture, Nature Management and Fisheries (LNV). The study was performed together with Grontmij Consultancy.

References

De Jong, T.M. 1992. Kleine methodologie voor ontwerpend onderzoek. Boom. Meppel, Amsterdam (in Dutch).

Foppen, R.P.B. & Reijnen, R. 1998. Ecological networks in riparian systems: examples for Dutch floodplain rivers. In: Nienhuis, P.H., Leuven, R.S.E.W. & Ragas, A.M.J. (eds). New concepts for sustainable management of river basins. pp. 85-93. Backhuys Publishers, Leiden.

Harms, W.B., Knaapen, J.P. & Roos-Klein Lankhorst, J. (eds). 1991. Natuurontwikkeling in de Centrale Open Ruimte. SC-DLO Rapport 138. DLO-Staring Centrum, Wageningen (in Dutch).

Harms, W.B., Knaapen, J.P. & Rademakers, J.G.M. 1993. Landscape planning for nature restoration; comparing regional scenarios. In: Vos, C & P. Opdam (eds). Landscape ecology and management of a landscape under stress. IALE-studies 1. Chapman & Hall, London.

Harms, W.B. & Roos-Klein Lankhorst, J. (eds). 1994. Toekomst voor de natuur in de Gelderse Poort; planvorming en evaluatie. SC-DLO Rapport 298.1. DLO-Staring Centrum, Wageningen (in Dutch).

Helmer, W., Overmars, W. & Litjens, G. 1990. Rivierenpark Gelderse Poort. Stroming, adviesbureau voor natuur- en landschapsontwikkeling b.v., Laag-Keppel (in Dutch).

Knaapen, J.P. & Rademakers, J.G.M. 1990. Rivierdynamiek en vegetatie-ontwikkeling. Staring Centrum Rapport 82. Wageningen (in Dutch).

LNV. 1990. Natuurbeleidsplan; regeringsbeslissing. Ministerie van Landbouw, Natuurbeheer en Visserij. SDU. Den Haag (in Dutch).

Rademakers, J.G.M. 1993. Natuurontwikkeling uiterwaarden en ecologisch onderzoek; een verkennende studie. DLO-Instituut voor Bos- en Natuuronderzoek. NBP-onderzoeksrapport 2. (in Dutch).

Reijnen, R., Harms, W.B., Foppen, R.P.B., Visser, R. de, Wolfert, H.P. 1995. Rhine-Econet. Ecological networks in river rehabilitation scenarios: a case study for the Lower Rhine. Lelystad, RIZA, Institute for Inland Water Management and Waste Water Treatment. Publications and reports of the project 'Ecological Rehabilitation of the Rivers Rhine and Meuse' No. 58-1995.

Roos-Klein Lankhorst, J. 1991. Het COR-model. Een natuurontwikkelingsmodel voor de Centrale Open Ruimte. SC-DLO Rapport 170. DLO-Staring Centrum, Wageningen (in Dutch).

Schoonenboom, I.J.. 1995. Overview and state of the art of scenario studies fot the rural environment. In: Schoute, J.F.Th., Finke, P.A., Veeneklaas, F.R. & Wolfert, H.P. (eds). Scenario studies for the rural environment. Kluwer Academic Publishers. Amsterdam.

Silva, W. & Kok, M. 1996. Integrale Verkenning inrichting Rijntakken. Ministerie van Verkeer en Waterstaat, RIZA. Lelystad (in Dutch).

Van Dijk, G.M., Marteijn, E.C.L. & Schulte-Wülwer-Leidig, A. 1995. Ecological rehabilitation of the River Rhine: plans, progress and perspectives. Reg. Rivers Res. Managem. 11: 377-388.

ECOLOGICAL REHABILITATION OF FLOODPLAINS ALONG THE MIDDLE REACH OF THE RIVER WAAL: A PROSPEROUS FUTURE FOR FAUNA TARGET SPECIES?

H.J.R. Lenders[1], R.S.E.W. Leuven[1], P.H. Nienhuis[1, 2], K.D. Oostinga[1,2] & P.J.M. Van den Heuvel[2]
[1] Department of Environmental Studies; [2] University Centre of Environmental Sciences, University of Nijmegen, Toernooiveld 1, 6525 ED Nijmegen, The Netherlands

Abstract

This paper describes developments in the fragmentation of riverine ecotopes (e.g. side channels and sandy beaches) in floodplains along the middle reach of the river Waal, a Dutch branch of the river Rhine. The total and mean surface areas per ecotope type as well as the mean distance to the nearest similar ecotope were regarded as indicators for the degree of ecotope fragmentation. The values of these indicators in the present situation were compared to those at the end of the nineteenth century (reference period) and after the execution of floodplain rehabilitation projects as planned (target image period). The indicator values for the reference period could be calculated for three ecotope types. The analysis showed that the degree of fragmentation will decrease in the future. In order to determine whether this decreased ecotope fragmentation will also benefit so-called target species, the potential occupation of the ecotopes was assessed for eight selected fauna species. It was found that not all target species examined could be expected to be able to establish viable populations. Only three species, Cormorant (*Phalacrocorax carbo*), Night heron (*Nycticorax nycticorax*) and Water shrew (*Neomys fodiens*), may find patches of habitat large enough to establish core populations. Three other species, Bluethroat (*Luscinia svecica*), Little ringed plover (*Charadrius dubius*) and Spotted crake (*Porzana porzana*), might be able to establish reproductive units but no core populations. Finally, Great reed warbler (*Acrocephalus arundinaceus*) and Otter (*Lutra lutra*) are expected to be unable to establish even one single reproductive unit.

1. Introduction

The environmental problem of fragmentation refers to a lack of minimally required surface area and/or coherence for a particular desired function within a specific spatial unit. In a densely populated country like the Netherlands, several forms of fragmentation occur (e.g. with respect to cultural-historical, socio-economic, socio-psychological and hydrological characteristics; see RMNO 1990). Fragmentation problems facing nature can be defined at two levels: 1) fragmentation of *ecotopes*, defined in this context as landscape elements determined by specific abiotic and structural characteristics (landscape level), and 2) fragmentation of *habitat patches* (species level). Both types of fragmentation are closely related, since an ecotope that meets a species' requirements can be regarded as a habitat patch for that species. However, with respect to size and other characteristics, ecotopes are usually rather strictly deter-

New concepts for sustainable management of river basins, pp. 115–130
edited by P.H. Nienhuis, R.S.E.W. Leuven and A.M.J. Ragas
© *1998 Backhuys Publishers, Leiden, The Netherlands*

mined units, while the size and structure of habitat patches are species-dependent. Therefore, in some cases ecotopes coincide with habitats, while in other cases species only need a small part of a particular ecotope (e.g. forest edges), a combination of ecotopes (e.g. side channels *and* floodplain forests) or one specific feature that occurs in more than one ecotope type (e.g. merely the presence of surface water). This complicates a comparison of ecotope fragmentation with habitat patch fragmentation. The Dutch government, however, aims at solving fragmentation problems of both types by establishing the National Ecological Network (NEN; Ministerie van LNV 1990). According to the NEN, large (>250 ha) existing nature reserves (referred to as core areas) have to be consolidated, strengthened and enlarged, and new equally large nature areas are to be developed (nature development areas). With respect to habitat patch fragmentation in particular, core and nature development areas have to be connected by means of ecological corridors in order to allow an exchange between isolated populations (Reijnen *et al.* 1995, Wolfert *et al.* 1996, Foppen & Reijnen 1998, Jongman 1998). According to Foppen & Reijnen (1998), corridor functioning can be expressed at the level of the individual (strips of habitat, either continuous or discontinuous) or at the population level (a network of habitat patches).

The nature development areas Fort St. Andries (west of Tiel; Figure 1) and Gelderse Poort (east of Nijmegen; Figure 1) along the river Waal are considered to be spearhead links in the NEN (Anonymous 1995a, De Bakker *et al.* 1996). These areas are situated circa 30 km apart. In order to allow a dispersal flow between them, the twelve floodplains in the intermediate area (the Middle Waal region) have to function as an ecological corridor. From the above, however, it can be concluded that corridor functioning is species-specific. The minimum requirement in Dutch water management and riverine nature policies is that so-called (river-related) target species (cf. Bal *et al.* 1995, Postma *et al.* 1996) must be able to settle in the Fort St. Andries and Gelderse Poort areas. This implies that the Middle Waal region floodplains should not present unbridgeable barriers for these species. Furthermore, they must offer sufficient habitat for the settlement of, at least, small populations of species with intermediate dispersal capacities (3-30 km) and of large (core) populations of species with low dispersal capacities (<3 km). This would allow a species-specific corridor functioning at both the individual and the population levels to be achieved in the Middle Waal region.

Ecological rehabilitation plans have been drawn up for several of the twelve floodplains. These plans, however, were designed more or less independently from each other and from the plans for Fort St. Andries and Gelderse Poort. This raises the question to what extent the local rehabilitation plans contribute to defragmentation of ecotopes and habitat patches. In order to gain more insight into this issue, this paper compares the present degree of ecotope fragmentation with both the situation at the end of the nineteenth century and the expected situation after floodplain rehabilitation. Subsequently, the suitability of the floodplains for the settlement of (core) populations of eight fauna target species in the future is assessed.

2. Materials and methods

The study area is situated along the river Waal between the cities of Nijmegen and Tiel (Fig. 1). Table 1 lists the floodplains in this area and shows the status of the present

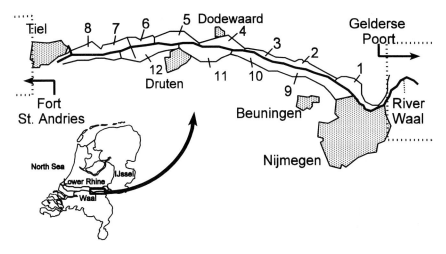

Fig. 1. Location of the twelve floodplains examined along the river Waal (the numbers of the flood-plains correspond to their listing in Table 1).

plans for floodplain rehabilitation. Official topographic river maps from the years 1870 and 1985, obtained from the Ministry of Transport, Public Works and Water Management, were used to analyse the historical and present situation. Maps from the rehabilitation plans showing predicted ecotopes were used to analyse the target image period 2025. The ecotopes (including non-natural ecotopes such as agricultural grounds) were classified according to the River Ecotope System (RES; Rademakers & Wolfert 1994). The poor level of detail of the 1870 maps, however, seriously hampered classification of some ecotopes. These historical maps did not even always allow a distinction to be made between marshes and floodplain forests. They often refer to both types of ecotopes as 'wasteland'. Eventually, only the following, rather crudely defined ecotope types could be distinguished: sandy beaches/river dunes, natural or semi-natural grasslands, floodplain forests, marshes (the latter two often combined), bodies of water resulting from excavations or breaches of the dikes, and side channels.

Table 1. The twelve floodplains examined in the Middle Waal region, with a list of present flood-plain rehabilitation plans and an assessment of the probability that these plans will be executed.

Floodplain	Floodplain rehabilitation plans	Execution probability
1. Oosterhoutsche waarden	–	-
2. Loenensche buitenpolder	Rademakers *et al.* (1993)	+
3. Wolferensche waard	Rademakers *et al.* (1993)	+
4. Hiensche uiterwaarden	Anonymous (1993)	+
5. Gouverneurse polder	Overkamp *et al.* (1995)	-
6. IJzendoornse waard	–	-
7. Willemspolder	–	-
8. Schipperswaard	Litjes *et al.* (1994)	+
9. Beuningse uiterwaarden	Overmars *et al.* (1994)	-
10. Winssensche waarden	–	-
11. Afferdensche en Deestse waarden	RWS (1993)	+
12. Drutensche waarden	Anonymous (1995b)	+

+: rehabilitation expected; -: no plan or execution of rehabilitation not expected.

According to current definitions of fragmentation (see Lenders *et al.* 1997), this environmental problem comprises both surface area and isolation aspects. Therefore, the surface area of each individual ecotope as well as the distance to the nearest similar ecotope in the Middle Waal region were calculated from the maps, as was the total surface area per type of ecotope. Subsequently, the relative change in the mean surface area per type of ecotope (ΔAm) and in the mean distance to the nearest similar ecotope (ΔDm) over the periods 1870-1985 and 1985-2025 were calculated by means of equations 1 and 2, respectively. Finally, an ecotope fragmentation decrease index (FDI) was calculated by means of equation 3.

$$\Delta Am_{(x,\ t=1\text{-}2)} = \frac{-\left(\dfrac{\sum_{i=1}^{n_{t1}} A_i}{n_{t1}} - \dfrac{\sum_{i=1}^{n_{t2}} A_i}{n_{t2}}\right) \times 100}{\dfrac{\sum_{i=1}^{n_{t1}} A_i}{n_{t1}}} \qquad \text{Equation (1)}$$

$\Delta Am_{(x,\ t=1\text{-}2)}$: relative decrease (-) or increase (+) in the mean surface area of ecotope type x over the period t=1 to t=2;

n_{t1} and n_{t2}: numbers of ecotopes belonging to type x at t=1 and t=2, respectively;

A_i: surface area of ecotope i, belonging to ecotope type x.

$$\Delta Dm_{(x,\ t=1\text{-}2)} = \frac{\left(\dfrac{\sum_{i=1}^{n_{t1}} D_i}{n_{t1}} - \dfrac{\sum_{i=1}^{n_{t2}} D_i}{n_{t2}}\right) \times 100}{\dfrac{\sum_{i=1}^{n_{t1}} D_i}{n_{t1}}} \qquad \text{Equation (2)}$$

$\Delta Dm_{(x,\ t=1\text{-}2)}$: relative increase (-) or decrease (+) in the mean distance of an ecotope belonging to ecotope type x to the nearest similar ecotope over the period t=1 to t=2;

n_{t1} and n_{t2}: numbers of ecotopes belonging to type x at t=1 and t=2, respectively;

D_i: distance of ecotope i, belonging to ecotope type x, to the nearest similar ecotope.

$$FDI_{(x,\ t=1\text{-}2)} = \frac{(\dfrac{\Delta Am_{(x,\ t=1\text{-}2)} + \Delta Dm_{(x,\ t=1\text{-}2)}}{2}) + \Delta Atot_{(x,\ t=1\text{-}2)}}{2} \qquad \text{Equation (3)}$$

$FDI_{(x,\ t=1\text{-}2)}$: fragmentation decrease index for ecotope type x over the period t=1 to t=2;

$\Delta Am_{(x,\ t=1\text{-}2)}$: relative decrease (-) or increase (+) in the mean surface area of ecotope type x over the period t=1 to t=2;

$\Delta Dm_{(x,\ t=1\text{-}2)}$: relative increase (-) or decrease (+) in the mean distance of an ecotope, belonging to ecotope type x, to the nearest similar ecotope over the period t=1 to t=2;

$\Delta Atot_{(x,\ t=1\text{-}2)}$: relative decrease (-) or increase (+) in the total surface area of ecotope type x over the period t=1 to t=2.

The future suitability of the floodplains as habitat patches was assessed for eight fauna target species. The selection of these species was carried out on the basis of 1) their status in nature or river management policies (Bal *et al.* 1995, Postma *et al.* 1996) and 2) availability of information on their habitat requirements and minimum numbers for core populations (Harms *et al.* 1991, Alieri & Fasola 1992, Kalkhoven *et al.* 1995). Using these criteria, the following species were selected: Cormorant (*Phalacrocorax carbo*), Bluethroat (*Luscinia svecica*), Great reed warbler (*Acrocephalus arundinaceus*), Little ringed plover (*Charadrius dubius*), Night heron (*Nycticorax nycticorax*), Spotted crake (*Porzana porzana*), Otter (*Lutra lutra*) and Water shrew (*Neomys fodiens*). The target species selected differ greatly with respect to reproduction strategy, type of habitat required, minimum habitat patch size and dispersal capacity, which ensured a more or less representative cross-section of relevant fauna target species for ecological rehabilitation of riverine ecosystems.

Subsequently, an assessment of the potential occupation of ecotopes by reproductive units or core populations was carried out for each species. A reproductive unit was defined as the minimum number of individuals required for successful reproduction (usually a pair). A core population was defined as the minimum number of individuals necessary to form a lasting (viable) population, relatively independent from other populations. The assessment was carried out in a two step procedure. The first step involved the calculation of the total surface area of the available habitat patches – i.e. species-specific ecotopes or combinations thereof – in the 2025 situation and subsequent confrontation of these figures with the required minimum surface area for a reproductive unit and a core population per species. The assumption was that, except as regards surface area, the available ecotopes represented an optimal habitat with respect to internal structure and environmental quality. This allowed us to determine whether the floodplain area as a whole could, at least in theory, harbour any reproductive units or core populations of the selected species at all. This approach, however, presumes an ideal spatial configuration of the total surface area of required ecotopes. Even in the 2025 situation, such an ideal configuration is not likely to occur. Some habitat patches will probably be situated too far from each other to allow dispersal or daily movements between them.

Furthermore, existing infrastructure might hamper such movements for some species. Therefore, a second approach was used: ecotopes located within distances that can be covered to satisfy daily needs (not dispersal) were clustered per species. A group of ecotopes was considered to be a cluster if the maximum distance between them did not exceed 1 kilometre for birds and large mammals and 40 metres for small mammals (cf. Verboom 1994). Since accurate figures on distances that can be covered for such purposes were lacking for the target species selected, we had to make do with these rather crude best professional judgements. For mammals, an additional demand was made on the nature of the area between two habitat patches: this area was not allowed to contain major infrastructure elements or large built-up sites. If this was the case, the intermediate area was considered an unbridgeable barrier to mammals (cf. Verboom 1994). Subsequently, the surface areas of the clusters were also confronted with the minimum surface areas for reproductive units and core populations. This allowed us to assess whether reproductive units or core populations of the eight species selected could settle in the planned ecotopes in each of the twelve floodplains, provided that the clusters would be accessible by means of dispersal and under otherwise optimal circumstances.

3. Results

Fig. 2 illustrates the development of the total surface area of the floodplains examined and the surface areas used for various functions (i.e. the main functions of agriculture and nature, and a residual category consisting of industry, infrastructure, habitation and recreation). Over the period 1870-1985, the total surface area of the floodplains increased by approximately 500 ha, due to a 20% decrease in the surface area of the river itself. The total area of agricultural land in the present situation is slightly smaller than that in the reference period and will decrease further in the future as a result of ecological rehabilitation of the floodplains. The surface area of nature (i.e. land not in agricultural, industrial, recreational or residential use) shows continual growth. In the period 1870-1985, this growth mainly resulted from excavation activities, which yielded many bodies of surface water at the expense of agricultural grounds. In the period 1985-2025, growth results from floodplain rehabilitation schemes. The surface area of the residual category has also grown over the period 1870-1985, mainly due to infrastructure facilities (e.g. harbours) and industrial developments (e.g. brick industries). In our study, the future surface area of the residual category was presumed to be roughly equal to that in the present situation. Expected or possible further growth of infrastructure, industry and recreational activities in the study area were not taken into account.

Fig. 3 shows the development of the natural ecotopes in the floodplains in more detail by indicating the surface areas of the different types of ecotopes. It indicates that it is especially the surface area of bodies of water, mainly resulting from excavation of sand and clay (referred to below as 'excavation waters') which has increased enormously over the last century. During the same period, side channels seem to have only slightly decreased in surface area. In the past, however, active side channels did not exist in the floodplains, but were an integral part of the river. Since our study focused on the floodplains only, these active side channels were

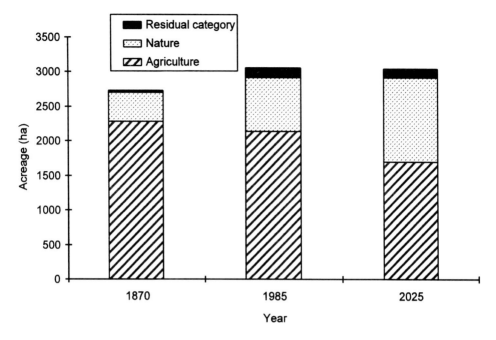

Fig. 2. Development of the total surface area and the acreage available for various functions (in ha) in twelve floodplains along the middle reach of the river Waal.

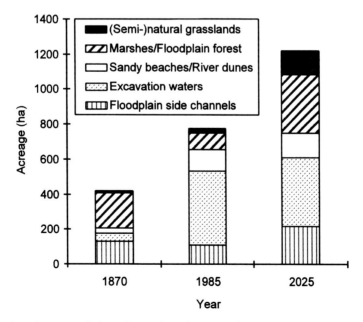

Fig. 3. Total surface areas (in ha) of a number of ecotopes in twelve floodplains along the middle reach of the river Waal in the years 1870, 1985 and the target situation 2025.

not taken into account. Due to river channelling, however, these river-integrated active side channels have disappeared completely in the present situation. The surface area of non-active side channels in the present situation has also decreased in comparison with the reference period. According to the floodplain rehabilitation plans, the surface area of both active (now situated in the floodplains themselves) and non-active side channels should greatly increase in the future.

The surface area of sandy beaches (including small river dunes) seems to have increased in comparison with the situation in the year 1870. However, their surface area in the past may have been underestimated, due to the poor level of detail of the reference maps (see also the Discussion section). On the other hand, this growth may also be partly realistic, since the groins constructed to channel the river have resulted in an increased surface area of sandy beaches between them. The surface area of sandy beaches, however, is not expected to grow much further in the future.

Compared to the 1870 situation, the (combined) surface areas of marshes and floodplain forests has decreased considerably (over 50%). In comparison with the present situation, these combined surface areas will greatly increase in the future. Marshes and floodplain forests will account for approximately 40% and 60%, respectively, of this growth. Natural and semi-natural grasslands seem to have grown in surface area as well. However, their historical surface area may have been greatly underestimated. Agricultural grasslands are believed to have been far less intensively used in the past than in the present situation. This can, however, not be derived from the topographical maps. For this reason, further analyses of natural and semi-natural grasslands were left out of consideration.

In expressing the decrease in fragmentation, it is not only the change in total surface area of particular ecotopes that is important, but also the changes in the mean surface area (ΔAm) and the mean distance to the nearest similar ecotope (ΔDm). Table 2 shows the developments in these parameters for five types of ecotopes over the periods 1870-1985 and 1985-2025. Conclusions drawn from the total surface area calculations (Fig. 3) do not necessarily have to match those of the fragmen-

Table 2. Development of the level of fragmentation of five riverine ecotopes in the floodplains along the middle reach of the river Waal, expressed as a percentage increase/decrease in the total (ΔAtot) and mean surface area (ΔAm), mean distance to the nearest similar ecotope (ΔDm) and fragmentation decrease index (FDI), calculated over the periods 1870-1985 and 1985-2025, assuming successful rehabilitation.

River ecotope	1870-1985				1985-2025			
	ΔAtot	ΔAm	ΔDm	FDI	ΔAtot	ΔAm	ΔDm	FDI
Excavation waters	833	301	23	498	-7	23	3	3
Side channels	-18	101	-4	15	103	-27	19	50
Sandy beaches	319	-64	92	167	14	22	2	13
Marshes	na	na	na	na	209	93	35	136
Floodplain forests	na	na	na	na	325	168	23	210

- represents decrease in total or mean surface area, increase in mean distance to nearest similar ecotope, increase in fragmentation; + represents increase in total or mean surface area, decrease in mean distance to nearest similar ecotope, decrease in fragmentation; na: not assessable because of insufficiently detailed data.

Table 3. Theoretical potential of the floodplains along the middle reach of the river Waal for the development of reproductive units or core populations of eight target species under the assumption that the planned surface areas of the required types of habitat are realised within one cluster.

Target species (1)	CP (2)	Ecotopes required (3)	C (4)	Assessed potentials (5)	
				Reproductive units	Core populations
Cormorant (a) *Phalacrocorax carbo*	+	FF (repr. only)	50	+++	++
Bluethroat (b) *Luscinia svecica*	±	M, FF	100	+++	-
Great reed warbler (b) *Acrocephalus arundinaceus*	±	M	100	+	-
Little ringed plover (b) *Charadrius dubius*	+	SB	40	+++	+
Night heron (a,b) *Nycticorax nycticorax*	±	FF (repr.)	50	+++	+
		FF (foraging)	50	+	-
Otter (a,b) *Lutra lutra*	-	SC, EW, MF (repr. only)	50	+	-
Spotted crake (b) *Porzana porzana*	+	SC, EW, M	40	+	-
Water shrew (b) *Neomys fodiens*	-	SC, EW, MF	100	+++	++

(1) Status of target species; a: target species according to Postma *et al.* 1996, b: target species according to Bal *et al.* 1995.
(2) CP: Current presence in study area (SOVON 1987, Broekhuizen *et al.* 1992); +: present in nearly all floodplains; ±: sporadically present; -: absent.
(3) Ecotope types; SC: Side channel; EW: Excavation water; FF: Floodplain forest; M: Marsh; MF: combination of marshes and floodplain forest; SB: Sandy beach; repr.: ecotopes needed for successful reproduction; foraging: ecotopes needed for gathering food.
(4) C: critical number of individuals to form a core population (derived from Harms *et al.* 1991, Alieri & Fasola 1992, Kalkhoven *et al.* 1995).
(5) Assessed potential: -, +, ++ and +++: none, 1 to 10, 10 to 20 and more than 20 reproductive units or core populations, respectively.

tation calculations. The floodplain side channels, for example, show a decrease in total surface area over the period 1870-1985, while over the same period, the mean surface area of this ecotope type increased by more than 100% and the mean distance to the nearest similar ecotope only increased by 4%. This results in a slight increase in the fragmentation decrease index (FDI = 15). From these figures it can be concluded that there are fewer, but relatively larger floodplain side channels, at shorter average distances from similar ecotopes. Table 2 furthermore shows a major decrease in the degree of fragmentation of excavation waters over the period 1870-1985, especially as a result of an increase of over 800% in the total surface area of

Little ringed plover

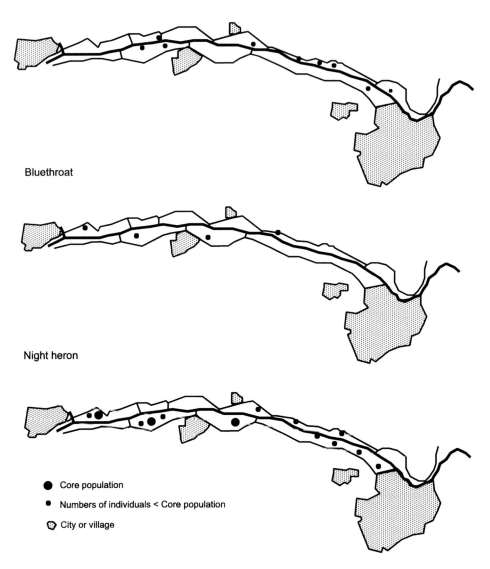

Bluethroat

Night heron

● Core population

• Numbers of individuals < Core population

⊕ City or village

Fig. 4. Potential locations for the settlement of reproductive units or core populations of six target species in floodplains along the middle reach of the river Waal, after execution of the floodplain rehabilitation plans.

Spotted crake

Cormorant

Water shrew

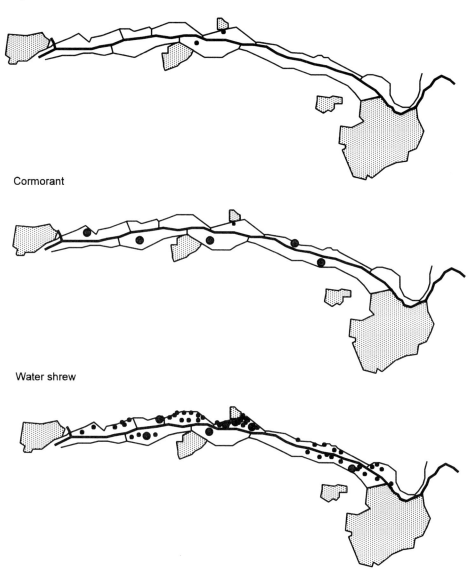

Fig. 4. Continued.

these ecotopes. Over the same period, the degree of fragmentation of sandy beaches also seems to have decreased, even though the mean surface area decreased by 64%. Due to the poor level of detail of the reference maps, small patches of sandy beach in particular may have been missed in the past. This may have resulted in an overestimation of the decrease in the distances between ecotopes of this type and an underestimation of the development of the mean surface area.

If floodplain rehabilitation plans are executed as planned, the level of fragmentation of all types of ecotopes will decrease, although large differences between them will occur. The degree of fragmentation of floodplain forests, for instance, will be greatly reduced, especially due to the increased mean and total surface area of this ecotope type, while the degree of fragmentation of excavation waters and sandy beaches will show little reduction.

Table 3 shows the carrying capacity of the entire study area for reproductive units or core populations of target species assuming that the surface areas of all required ecotopes (or combinations thereof) per species are realised within one cluster. The Cormorant, Night heron (regarding reproduction only), Little ringed plover and Water shrew would be able to establish core populations in the floodplains of the Middle Waal region, if the planned ecotopes are realised in one cluster. Under these circumstances, all species examined would be able to establish at least one reproductive unit. In comparison with the current presence of the target species in the study area, ecological rehabilitation of the floodplains is likely to enhance the opportunities for some species. Ecotope fragmentation, however, will restrict the opportunities for a number of species (Fig. 4). The Little ringed plover, for example, may be able to establish reproductive units in the floodplains, but the surface areas of habitat patches are too small to enable the settlement of any core populations. As regards the availability of sufficiently large habitat patches, the Cormorant, Night heron and Water shrew might be able to establish 5, 3 and 7 core populations, respectively, provided that the potential habitat patches will be accessible by means of dispersal. Species that require a large surface area of marshes (Bluethroat, Great reed warbler, Spotted crake and Otter) will find it particularly difficult to form core populations, even if ecotope configuration is not taken into account (Table 3). If the spatial configuration of ecotopes is taken into account (Fig. 4), only the Bluethroat and Spotted crake might be able to establish a small number of reproductive units. Great reed warbler and Otter will not be able to establish even one single reproductive unit in the Middle Waal region. Hence, these species are not included in Fig. 4. From Table 3 it can be concluded that this problem cannot be solved by merely connecting or concentrating the planned surface areas of marshes, but only by enlarging the total surface areas of interconnected patches of marshland, either in the floodplains or in areas on the landside of the dikes (see also the Discussion section). Both Table 3 and Fig. 4 illustrate that the floodplain rehabilitation plans in the Middle Waal region do not contribute to an equal decrease in habitat patch fragmentation at the population level for all species.

4. Discussion

In determining trends in ecotope fragmentation, the use of developments in total surface areas per ecotope type, combined with developments in mean surface area and mean distance to a similar ecotope, was found to be a convenient and accurate method. A major restriction in applying this method concerns the level of detail of the maps used. In our study, the poor level of detail of especially the historical maps was insufficient to accurately describe developments of ecotope fragmentation in natural or semi-natural grasslands, sandy beaches, marshes and floodplain forests. The method used to determine settlement opportunities for core populations or reproductive units also proved to be easy to use. This method, however, can only be used to gain insight into area size aspects of habitat patches fragmentation under several preconditions (e.g. good environmental quality of the habitat patches, optimal habitat patch structure and optimal ratio between habitat patches needed for feeding and reproduction within one cluster). Other methods (e.g. Foppen & Reijnen 1998) are without doubt more subtle, taking into account the dispersal capacity of the examined species. The input requirements of such approaches, however, are much higher, which means they are far more labour-intensive than our method.

Taking into account additional species demands would undoubtedly lead to more accurate predictions of possibilities for the settlement of target species populations. This would, however, require more detailed input of species-specific parameters as well as of target situation landscape parameters (as it does in other methods for assessing the effects of floodplain rehabilitation). Knowledge on the first type of input (e.g. species-specific dispersal capacity) appears to be lacking for many (target) species, while data necessary for the second type of input can in most cases not be derived from ecological rehabilitation plans. The floodplain rehabilitation plans used in our study, for example, did not always state clearly which areas were eventually expected to develop into marshes and which into floodplain forests. This can be partly ascribed to the fact that dynamic processes (i.e. flooding, erosion and sedimentation) are supposed to be the driving forces for ecological rehabilitation and their effects are not always clear in advance. Hence, the predictability of the development, exact location and surface area of riverine ecotopes is limited (see also Lenders *et al.* 1998). Furthermore, because of agricultural interests, water control aspects or limited finances, there is as yet not always consensus about the ultimate surface areas of particular ecotopes to be realised. As long as clear descriptions of ecotope qualities, exact surface areas and their spatial configuration are lacking, the use of relatively crude methods like ours suffices for an assessment of the effects of floodplain rehabilitation plans on target species settlement.

In applying the method, existing nature reserves on the landside of the dikes were not taken into account. Suitable habitat patches which are large enough to harbour (core) populations for the target species examined (for instance large reed marshes in old river arms for the Bluethroat) hardly seem to be available on the landside of the dikes in the present situation, and ecological rehabilitation plans that might provide such habitat patches in these areas, do not exist. Therefore, it would seem justified not to take into account the surface areas of ecotopes on the landside of the dikes.

From our calculations it can be concluded that the total surface area of most types of ecotopes will probably increase in comparison to the present situation. In some cases, the total surface area of a particular type of ecotope might even exceed the 1870 surface area (e.g. floodplain side channels). However, the degree to which ecotope fragmentation will decrease differs greatly per ecotope type. For sandy beaches, for instance, the mean surface area of the patches as well as the mean distance to the nearest sandy beach patch, will improve only slightly. Clear improvements concerning both total surface area and fragmentation decrease index will be attained especially for marshes and floodplain forests.

These developments in ecotope characteristics affect the opportunities of the target species to establish reproductive units and, especially, core populations. Species that are highly dependent on sandy beaches for habitat patches (such as the Little ringed plover) are not expected to be able to form core populations in the study area after execution of the floodplain rehabilitation plans. The surface area increase of this ecotope type (expressed in both total surface area and mean surface area) proves to be too small to enable the Little ringed plover to establish populations larger than 40 individuals. Other species that will encounter difficulties in establishing core populations or even reproductive units include Bluethroat, Great reed warbler, Spotted crake and Otter, species that are highly dependent on the availability of large areas of marshland. This is remarkable, since the fragmentation indicators show that major improvements will be achieved concerning defragmentation of this type of ecotope. This will, however, prove insufficient to solve the problems encountered by marsh-dependent target species. Reijnen et al. (1995) used a scenario approach to illustrate various options for planning nature areas along the Dutch parts of the river Rhine (the so-called Rhine-Econet study). Their evaluation of three scenarios (i.e. Rhine-Traditional, Loire-River Dynamics and Mississippi-Spillway) showed that variations in the total acreage and distribution patterns of new nature areas have large (positive) effects on the viability of ecological networks for many species. In accordance to our findings, however, all three scenarios proved unable to produce sufficient macrophyte marsh to enable the settlement of core populations of many marshland dependent fauna species.

At present, the execution of ecological rehabilitation plans is expected to be feasible in only six of the twelve floodplains in the study area. For the remaining floodplains, plans are lacking or execution is not likely (Table 1). Enlargement of the total surface area of nature, especially marshlands, in the Middle Waal region could be achieved by means of two strategies, involving additional acreage of nature in 1) areas on the landside of the dikes or 2) the remaining six floodplains. For areas on the landside of the dikes, however, no ecological rehabilitation plans have so far been drawn up. In fact, it is even to be expected that agriculture in these areas will be intensified as a result of a trade-off with agricultural grounds in the floodplains (Stuurgroep NURG 1990), which may even result in a further decrease in the ecological significance of these areas. Therefore, efforts to improve ecological functioning in the Middle Waal region can best be directed towards enlarging the surface areas of nature reserves in those floodplains for which no ecological rehabilitation plans have so far been drawn up or for which execution of existing plans is not foreseen.

The rehabilitation plans examined have been designed more or less independently from each other and from the plans for Fort St. Andries and Gelderse Poort and the Rhine-Econet study. The elaboration of the NEN (Ministerie van LNV 1990) in the Middle Waal region seems, for the greater part, to be aiming at ecotope defragmentation, and does not sufficiently take into account habitat patches defragmentation. Moreover, planned infrastructure facilities in the Middle Waal region have not been taken into account. These developments may seriously hamper dispersal possibilities for target species, especially for poor dispersers such as the Water shrew.

In the above, the use of the floodplains in the Middle Waal region as an ecological corridor at the population level was discussed. For some species (e.g. Cormorant and Little ringed plover) it might not be necessary to establish core populations or even reproductive units to connect the nature development areas of the Gelderse Poort and Fort St. Andries, since they are able to cover the distance between these areas by means of dispersal. Other species, however, are not able to do so (especially Bluethroat and Water shrew). For these species, the floodplains of the Middle Waal region must offer sufficient suitable habitats and opportunities to colonise these habitats. Our study showed that this will not be the case for all species.

In order to solve these problems, a master plan for ecological rehabilitation of the study area as a whole should be developed, in which plans for individual floodplains are attuned and the effects of planned infrastructure facilities are taken into account. Such a master plan should provide conditions that might result in both a higher degree of defragmentation of ecotopes and better opportunities for the settlement of (target) species. It is only under this precondition that ecological rehabilitation of floodplains may prove to offer a prosperous future for more fauna target species.

Acknowledgements

The authors are greatly indebted to Mr. J. Klerkx and Mr. A.M.J. Ragas for critical remarks and to the Geometrical Service of the Directorate-General for Public Works and Water Management (Ministry of Transport, Public Works and Water Management) in Arnhem and the Province of Gelderland for putting at our disposal topographic maps and rehabilitation plans.

References

Alieri, A. & Fasola, M. 1992. Breeding site requirements for Herons. In: Finlayson, M., T. Hollis & T. Davies (Eds.) Managing Mediterranean wetlands and their birds. pp. 206-209. Proceedings of an IWRB International Symposium. Grado, Italy.

Anonymous. 1993. Integrale herinrichting van de Hiense waard. LB&P Ecologisch Advies BV/ Heidemij Advies, Den Bosch/Arnhem (in Dutch).

Anonymous. 1995a. Ontwikkelingsvisie de Gelderse Poort. Stuurgroep de Gelderse Poort, Provincie Gelderland, Arnhem (in Dutch).

Anonymous. 1995b. Waaier van Geulen; Leeuwense en westelijke Drutense waard. Delgromij/Wereld Natuur Fonds, Arnhem/Zeist (in Dutch).

Bal, D., Beije, H.M., Hoogeveen, Y.R., Jansen, S.R.J. & Van der Reest, P.J. 1995. Handboek natuurdoeltypen in Nederland. Rapport IKC-Natuurbeheer nr. 11, Wageningen (in Dutch).

Broekhuizen, S., Hoekstra, B., Van Laar, V., Smeenk, C. & Thissen, J.B.M. 1992. Atlas van de Nederlandse zoogdieren. KNNV, Utrecht (in Dutch).

De Bakker, J., Van Nieuwenhuijze, L. & De Koning, R. 1996. Visie Fort Sint Andries; een toekomstvisie op het natuurontwikkelingsgebied waar Maas en Waal elkaar ontmoeten. DHV/H+N+S, Amersfoort/Utrecht (in Dutch).

Jongman, R. 1998. The role of rivers in the European ecological network. In: Nienhuis, P.H., Leuven, R.S.E.W. & Ragas, A.M.J. (Eds.). New concepts for sustainable management of river basins. pp. 53-66. Backhuys Publishers, Leiden.

Foppen, R.P.B. & Reijnen, R. 1998. Ecological networks in riparian systems, examples for Dutch floodplain rivers. In: Nienhuis, P.H., Leuven, R.S.E.W. & Ragas, A.M.J. (Eds.). New concepts for sustainable management of river basins. pp. 85-93. Backhuys Publishers, Leiden.

Harms, W.B., Knaapen, J.P. & Roos-Klein Lankhorst, J. 1991. Natuurontwikkeling in de Centrale Open Ruimte. SC-DLO, Wageningen (in Dutch).

Kalkhoven, J.T.R., Van Apeldoorn, R.C. & Foppen, R.P.B. 1995. Fauna en natuurdoeltypen; minimumoppervlakte voor kernpopulaties van doelsoorten zoogdieren en vogels. IBN-DLO, Wageningen (in Dutch).

Lenders, H.J.R., Leuven, R.S.E.W., Nienhuis, P.H. & Schoof, D.J.W. 1997. Natuurbeheer en –ontwikkeling. Handboeken Milieukunde 2. Boom, Amsterdam (in Dutch).

Lenders, H.J.R., Aarts, B.G.W., Strijbosch, H. & Van der Velde, G. 1998. The role of reference and target images in ecological recovery of river systems. Lines of thought in the Netherlands. In: Nienhuis, P.H., Leuven, R.S.E.W. & Ragas, A.M.J. (Eds.). New concepts for sustainable management of river basins. pp. 35-52. Backhuys Publishers, Leiden.

Litjens, G. Overmars, W. & Helmer, W. 1994. Natuur in de Schipperswaard; steenfabrieken Korevaar, Steenfabriek Schipperswaard. Stroming BV, Laag Keppel (in Dutch).

Ministerie van LNV 1990. Natuurbeleidsplan. SDU, Den Haag (in Dutch).

Overkamp, E.T.M., Spanjers, A.T. & Jonkers, J. 1995. Ontwikkelingsvisie en inrichtingsschets Gouverneurse polder. LB&P Ecologisch Advies BV, Den Bosch (in Dutch).

Overmars, W., Helmer, W., Litjens, G., Bosman, W., & Kurstjens, G. 1994. Beuningse uiterwaarden; natuurontwikkeling langs de Waal. Stroming BV, Laag Keppel (in Dutch).

Postma, R., Kerkhofs, M.J.J., Pedroli, G.B.M. & Rademakers, J.G.M. 1996. Een stroom natuur: natuurstreefbeelden voor Rijn en Maas. Watersysteemverkenningen 1996: een analyse van de problematiek in aquatisch milieu. Rijksinstituut voor Integraal Zoetwaterbeheer en Afvalwaterbehandeling, Waterloopkundig Laboratorium en Grondmij, Arnhem (in Dutch).

Rademakers, J.G.M. & Wolfert, H.P. 1994. Het Rivier-Ecotopen-Stelsel; een indeling van ecologisch relevante ruimtelijke eenheden ten behoeve van ontwerp- en beleidsstudies in het buitendijkse rivierengebied. Publicaties en Rapporten van het project 'Ecologisch herstel Rijn en Maas', nr. 61-1994. Rijksinstituut voor Integraal Zoetwaterbeheer en Afvalwaterbehandeling, Lelystad (in Dutch).

Rademakers, J.G.M., Voorwinden, A., Van der Meulen, E., Schepers, M. & Litjens, G. 1993. Inrichtingsplan Wolferensche Waard. Grondmij/Stroming BV, Zeist/Laag Keppel (in Dutch).

Reijnen, R., Harms, W.B., Foppen, R.P.B., De Visser, R. & Wolfert, H.P. 1995. Rhine-econet. Ecological networks in river rehabilitation scenarios: a case study for the Lower Rhine. Publications and reports of the project 'Ecological Rehabilitation of the Rivers Rhine and Meuse', no 58-1995. Research Institute for Inland Water Management and Waste Water Treatment (RIZA), Lelystad.

RMNO. 1990. De versnippering van het Nederlandse landschap. Onderzoeksprogrammering vanuit zes disciplinaire benaderingen. RMNO-publikatie nr. 45. Raad voor het Milieu- en Natuuronderzoek, Rijswijk (in Dutch).

RWS. 1993. Projectplan Natuurontwikkelingsproject Afferdense en Deestse Waarden. Rijkswaterstaat-Directie Flevoland, Lelystad (in Dutch).

SOVON. 1987. Atlas van de Nederlandse vogels. SOVON, Beek (in Dutch).

Stuurgroep NURG. 1990. Nadere Uitwerking Rivierengebied. Stuurgroep NURG, Arnhem (in Dutch).

Verboom, J. 1994. Een modelstudie naar de effecten van infrastructuur op dispersiebewegingen van dieren. Rapport 23, Project Versnippering. Instituut voor Bos- en Natuuronderzoek, Wageningen (in Dutch).

Wolfert, H.P., Harms, W.B., Marteijn, E.C.L. & Reijnen, R. 1996. Ecological networks in river rehabilitation scenarios: Rhine-Econet summary report. RIZA-report 96008. Research Institute for Inland Water Management and Waste Water Treatment (RIZA), Lelystad.

IMPACT OF HYDROLOGY ON FLOODPLAIN VEGETATION IN THE LOWER RHINE SYSTEM: IMPLICATIONS FOR NATURE CONSERVATION AND NATURE DEVELOPMENT

H. M. Van de Steeg & C.W.P.M. Blom
Department of Ecology, University of Nijmegen, P.O. Box 9010, 6500 GL Nijmegen, The Netherlands.

Abstract

Observations on floodplains of the Lower Rhine system in the Netherlands clearly indicate that summer flooding in particular has a large impact on flora and vegetation. A large group of floodplain species is very sensitive to flooding. The majority of these species are characteristic of species-rich grassland types and species-rich variants of hardwood forest, both occupying the highest levees in the floodplain.

Observations also show that many aquatic and riparian species of well-isolated floodplain waters are extremely sensitive to incidental deep summer flooding.

The serious threat of vast inundations during extremely high Rhine water levels, like those which occurred in the winters of 1993/1994 and 1995, has necessitated extensive efforts to secure future safety. This time, safety will be promoted by measures increasing the river's discharge capacity, rather than by raising dyke levels again. Artificial embankments will be removed, floodplain levels lowered and silted-up floodplain channels reopened.

It has been stated that maintaining of the present range of flora elements and vegetation types will only be possible if sufficiently high levees and sufficiently isolated floodplain waters can successfully be incorporated in the rearranged floodplains.

1. Introduction

Opportunities for nature restoration in floodplains of the large rivers in the Netherlands have only recently improved greatly (Van Dijk *et al.* 1995, MTPW 1996). Until the 1980s, ecosystems in the Lower Rhine system dramatically deteriorated, first by reclamation and embanking of the river valley, and during the last and present century by river regulation, water pollution and optimisation of agricultural production. Extensive reclamation of the fertile river valley for agricultural purposes was started in the Late Iron Age, continued in Roman times, and completed in the Middle Ages. The genuine floodplain hardwood forest was completely eliminated (after Teunissen in Willems 1984, p. 267). Natural riparian softwood forest was also largely absent, as a result of extensive grazing of the river banks or the planting of willow shrubs to promote sediment deposition. At present, the Netherlands has only small remnants of floodplain hardwood forests on steep slopes bordering the river valley. Such floodplain hardwood forests are also extremely rare elsewhere in Europe. Only a few large floodplain hardwood forests have been saved, thanks to their former significance as royal or feudal game reserves.

New concepts for sustainable management of river basins, pp. 131–144
edited by P.H. Nienhuis, R.S.E.W. Leuven and A.M.J. Ragas
© *1998 Backhuys Publishers, Leiden, The Netherlands*

The constriction of the river valley by dyke building in the Late Middle Ages has greatly changed river water levels and river and floodplain morphology. Within the much narrower floodplains, the river's erosional power and water levels greatly increased, resulting in the formation of more sandy and higher natural levees. The drier conditions on the higher levees presented a new habitat to a large group of grassland species and grassland communities. In the first half of the present century, the species-diversity of grassland on levees in the floodplain largely disappeared as a result of the promotion of grassland productivity by manuring and subsequent intensification of grassland use. The last remnants of species-rich grassland were lost by dyke improvement in the final decades of this century.

At present, the only well-preserved ecosystems in the Rhine floodplains in the Netherlands are isolated former river channels with luxuriant aquatic and amphibian vegetation (see Van Donselaar 1961). These ecosystems are, however, also increasingly affected and threatened by the ever rising river water levels which are due to a large range of human activities, increasing catchment run-off (Van de Steeg 1984, Brock *et al.* 1987, Jongman 1992).

Recently, measures taken by the European Union to counteract agricultural over-production have resulted in good opportunities for nature development in the Netherlands. Arguments in favour of large-scale nature development in floodplains (De Bruin *et al.* 1987) were supported by recent extremely high winter floods in 1993/1994 and 1995. During the 1995-winter flood, 200,000 inhabitants and a large number of cattle were evacuated from threatened polders in the central part of the Netherlands. The goverment's dyke improvement programme has been accelerated and adjusted by the Flood Protection Act of 1996, which stipulates that the dyke improvement programme is to be completed in 2001.

Extensive measures in the floodplain should contribute to the safety of the impounded river valley by reduction of river water levels. Large-scale dyke improvement and nature development in floodplains are now being combined by excavating clay for dyke improvement and brick making, creating large areas of floodplain wetland. Nature development in floodplains mainly consists of: (a) lowering the floodplain level by excavating clay, (b) reopening former, silted-up floodplain channels, (c) removing embankments obstructing the stream, and (d) preventing excessive development of softwood forest through grazing by cattle in low numbers. An impression of the new floodplain landscape is shown in Fig. 1.

The objective of this paper is to show the impact of river water levels on the vegetation composition of the Lower Rhine system in the Netherlands. Section 2 describes the pattern and zonation of floodplain vegetation in relation to hydrology and management. Section 3 then discusses the impact of specific flooding events on the diversity of the flora and on particular flora elements. Opportunities and restrictions developing characteristic vegetation types will be discussed.

Fig. 1. A semi-natural river landscape showing the river with groynes, a grazed mid- level levee and an isolated floodplain channel.

2. River and floodplain vegetation of the Lower Rhine system

2.1. Main vegetation pattern in Lower Rhine floodplains

The natural floodplain vegetation of rivers which freeze only occasionally in winter is completely dominated by woodland, as it was in Northern America until the arrival of the European settlers (Mitsch & Gosselink 1986). It is only at the mouth of large rivers that this woodland is replaced by marshland as a consequence of the permanently wet conditions due to delta formation or tidal water level fluctuation.

In large parts of the Eurasian continent, however, man has long since changed the floodplain vegetation. The most profitable form of land use was developed in the floodplains of the Lower Rhine. In floodplains with seasonal flooding concentrated in winter and spring, the form of land use was strongly related to the floodplain elevation. Land use started with the planting of willow to promote sediment accumulation, and was followed by grazing. After embanking, the grassland was used for haymaking. The highest parts on natural levees were eventually turned into arable land.

In the freshwater tidal area of the combined Rhine-Meuse estuary, the original marsh vegetation has in the end been transformed completely by planting, ditching and embanking. Semi-natural bulrush and reed cultures were succeeded by a planted willow culture within low embankments (Table 1). Detailed information on floodplain forest zonation is provided by Dister (1980), on floodplain grassland zonation by Sykora *et al.* (1988), and on freshwater tidal vegetation by Zonneveld (1960).

Table 1. Main natural and man-made vegetation types in floodplains of the Lower Rhine system.

	Upper (non-tidal) river		**Lower, tidal river**	
Hydrological regime: flooding period:	seasonal, very irregular days to months		tidal, extremely regular 2 times daily	
Land use: occurrence:	natural rare	man-made common	natural rare	man-made common
Levee (high-level):	species-rich hardwood forest	flood-sensitive grassland		
Backswamp (mid-level):	species-poor hardwood forest	flood-tolerant grassland		
River bank (low-level):	softwood forest	open vegetation with annuals		
Intertidal area:			reed marsh sea club-rush marsh	willow culture reed culture bulrush culture

2.1.1. Forest development and zonation

In natural as well as in managed floodplains, a distinct vegetation pattern occurs in relation to floodplain elevation and flooding intensity. In the upper part of the Lower Rhine system, with seasonal flooding of the floodplain concentrated in winter and spring, the forest starts on the river bank as a softwood forest with *Salix alba*. Softwood forests of *Populus nigra* are restricted to river banks with coarse sand. Under natural conditions, accumulation of ever finer sediment raises the soil level and makes the site suitable for the establishment of tree species of the floodplain hardwood forest (Barnes 1985). In the Lower Rhine system, these species are *Quercus robur*, *Ulmus minor*, *Acer pseudoplatanus* and *Fraxinus excelsior* (see also Siebel 1998). A prerequisite for the development of a hardwood forest from a softwood forest is the availability of abundant seeds brought in by the stream from hardwood forests upstream (*Ulmus*, *Acer*, *Fraxinus*), or by birds from adjacent hardwood forests (*Quercus*).

Within the floodplain, two types of hardwood forest can be distinguished. In mid-level floodplains the hardwood forest consists of only a few tree and field layer species due to frequent and prolonged flooding. At high floodplain levels the hardwood forest is well structured and rich in tree, shrub and field layer species (see Carbiener 1970, Dister 1980).

2.1.2. Grassland zonation

The zonation of grassland types in the floodplain is similar to that of the hardwood forest. Grassland types of mid-level floodplains with frequent and prolonged flooding are poor in species, while grassland types of high, occasionally flooded sites are rich in species. Common grasses of intermittently dry and wet mid-level sites are *Elymus repens*, *Alopecurus pratensis* and *Agrostis stolonifera*. Characteristic herbaceous species are *Potentilla reptans*, *Inula britannica*, *Achillea ptarmica*, *Ranunculus repens* and *Rumex crispus*. *Alopecurus geniculatus* and *Rorippa sylvestris* are in most years restricted to permanently wet parts of the floodplain. In wet years, with flooding in summer, it is especially *Rorippa sylvestris* which dominates large parts of the floodplain.

At high elevations in the floodplain, the flood-tolerant species are largely suppressed by species that have been shown to be flood-intolerant (Blom *et al.* 1994). Characteristic species for high-level hayfields on clay are the grasses *Arrhenatherum elatius* and *Trisetum flavescens*, umbelliferous species such as *Peucedanum carvifolia*, *Pimpinella major*, *Carum carvi* and *Heracleum sphondylium* and biennial species such as *Crepis biennis* and *Tragopogon pratense*. In grazed situations hayfield species disappear and species with a low stature such as *Lolium perenne*, *Poa trivialis*, *Trifolium repens* and *Bellis perennis* become more prominent. Common appearances in grazed grassland are unpalatable species such as *Ranunculus acris* and *Cirsium arvense*. Characteristic high-level species on sand are *Festuca rubra*, *Eryngium campestre*, *Medicago falcata*, *Salvia pratensis*, *Rumex thyrsiflorus* and *Ranunculus bulbosus* (Blom *et al.* 1996).

Grazing, even in very low densities, prevents the establishment of softwood forest species on river banks through trampling. Steep, eroded parts of the river bank support an open vegetation of the geophytes *Cirsium arvense*, *Equisetum arvense* and *Rorippa sylvestris*, sprouting from rhizomes. After recession of the water level in summer a pioneer vegetation dominated by *Chenopodium* species develops on the flat, lower part of the river bank.

2.2. River vegetation and water level fluctuation

In a large part of the Lower Rhine system, *Polygonum amphibium* is the only aquatic wetland species on the river bank, and *Phalaris arundinacea* the only emergent wetland species. Additional wetland species are found in the downstream parts, near te mouths of the branches. In the IJssel branch, the pondweeds *Potamogeton pectinatus* and *P. nodosus* first occur near Zwolle. It is also near Zwolle that the first stands of *Phragmites australis* are found on the river bank. Further downstream, near Kampen, stands of *Scirpus lacustris* and *Typha angustifolia* are present on the river bank.

There is a striking relationship between the aquatic and emergent vegetation of river banks and the degree of water level fluctuation. In the upper parts, characterised by large fluctuations, the scattered aquatic and extent emergent vegetation consists of species, that are able to cope with the wet and rather dry conditions of alternately submerged and exposed river banks. The aquatic and emergent bank vegetation in the lower parts of the Dutch Rhine system consists of species restricted to permanently wet conditions. In the upper parts of the Lower Rhine branches, permanently wet conditions on the river bank coincide with far deeper and more prolonged submergence with turbid water than in the lower parts. Expressed as the 80%-data frequency for the decade 1981-1990 (MVW 1994), water level amplitudes on the Lower IJssel are 0.72 m at Kampen and 1.39 m at Zwolle, supporting a well-developed aquatic and riparian vegetation on the river bank. More upstream, the water level amplitude at 80% of the data is 2.04-2.71m on the Middle and Upper IJssel and 3.79-3.19 m on the Upper Rhine and Waal. In large parts of the Lower Rhine system, the deeper and longer flooding, in combination with more extreme stream and soil conditions, seems to result in conditions which are too severe for most aquatic and emergent species. The occurrence of *Polygonum amphibium* and *Phalaris arundinacea* in the hydrologically highly dynamic part of the Lower Rhine system may be based on their relative drought-resistance.

2.3. Impact of hydrology on the vegetation patterns of floodplain channels

The vegetation of the various floodplain channels differs greatly. Based on the vegetation types present, three groups can be distinguished (Table 2). Only the aquatic and emergent vegetation will be described here; the pioneer vegetations of mudflats and vegetation types of grazed channel banks have been omitted.

The first group of floodplain channels, connected with the river and characterised by an ever-fluctuating water level, lacks nearly all aquatic vegetation. The bank vegetation at ungrazed sites consists of *Phalaris arundinacea*, while locally scattered clumps of *Carex acuta* may be present. Below the closed belt of *Phalaris*, patches of *Polygonum amphibium* are present on regularly exposed parts of the lower bank.

The second group of floodplain channels, situated in unembanked floodplains and experiencing occasional summer flooding, is characterised by large patches of the aquatic species *Nymphoides peltata*. At ungrazed banks, a wide belt of *Phalaris arundinacea* is followed by a belt of *Carex acuta* on the lower parts. Locally, stands of *Scirpus maritimus* may be present.

The third group of floodplain channels, in large parts of the Lower Rhine system confined to embanked floodplains, possesses a well-developed aquatic and emergent vegetation. The aquatic vegetation is dominated by *Nuphar lutea* or *Nymphaea alba*. *Nymphoides peltata* may be abundant. In most years, submerged species are rather scarce or entirely absent. The emergent vegetation consists of several, in most years almost monospecific belts of *Phragmites australis*, *Typha angustifolia* and *Scirpus lacustris*. The *Phragmites* belt is situated on the higher, regularly exposed part of the channel bank, while *Typha* and *Scirpus* are restricted to the part of the bank undergoing more prolonged flooding. If present, the lowest belt is formed by *Scirpus lacustris*. The entire *Phragmites* belt and the upper part of the *Typha* belt are very susceptible to grazing, which leads to *Phragmites* soon being replaced by *Glyceria maxima*. After cessation of the grazing, *Phragmites* is hardly able to recover.

Table 2. Wetland vegetation of floodplain channels in the highly dynamic part of the Dutch Lower Rhine system. Vegetation types in parentheses occur only locally. Vegetation types are named after the best-adapted, dominant species. Several of these vegetation types are difficult to classify in accordance with existing phytosociological literature.

channel types and characteristics		
Connected channel	Moderately isolated channel	Well-isolated channel
unembanked floodplain large summer fluctuation	unembanked floodplain moderate summer fluctuation	embanked floodplain small summer fluctuation
emergent vegetation		
Phalaridetum arundinaceae	Phalaridetum arundinaceae Caricetum acutae (Scirpetum maritimae)	Phragmitetum communis Typhetum angustifoliae Scirpetum lacustris
aquatic vegetation		
Polygonetum amphibiae (Potametum pectinatis)	Polygonetum amphibiae Nymphoidetum peltatae	Nupharetum luteae

3. Impact of flooding events on the floodplain flora and vegetation

The distinct zonation of plant species and vegetation types in floodplains strongly suggests that flooding has a large impact on their distribution. In most years, changes are rather small and only detectable after detailed and long-term research. However, after a spell of years with low spring and summer water levels or in years with extremely high summer water levels, changes in the distribution of species are large enough to be easily detected. Some clear examples of the impact of flooding, showing the sensitivity to flooding of particular species and groups of species, will be discussed below.

3.1. Impact of flooding on terrestrial flora

A constant supply of diaspores by the river, in combination with an open vegetation, offers opportunities for the establishment of a multitude of plant species. In 1974, after a spell of years without flooding during the growing season and with ample flooding in winter, 275 plant species were found on a 1300 m long and up to 100 m wide natural levee along the Waal branch near Boven-Leeuwen (Table 3). In 1975, only 199 of these species were found again on this levee. A considerable proportion of the missing species were pioneer species of open vegetation on sand and grassland species of dry substrate, characteristic of high natural levees near the river bank. Since the highest part of the natural levee, supporting the specific high-level species, had only been flooded in winter, and no signs of mechanical interference like soil erosion or sand deposition could be seen, it was concluded, that the absence of this species group had been caused by the winter flooding. After the exceptionally late and high summer flood peak in July 1980, only 113 species were found in 1981. The species group of the high-level floodplain had been virtually decimated.

Table 3. Impact of flooding on the floristic diversity of a mid-level natural levee (the part with a concentration of species characteristic of high floodplain levels corresponds with a Lobith level of 12.90 m above sea level). The levee was unmanaged in 1970-1975 and 1980-1981.

Year	Flooding characteristics		Number of species present	
	flooding duration (days) /flooding depth (m) winter (Nov.-Apr.)	summer (May-Oct.)	total species number	number of high-level species
1972	0	0		
1973	4 / 0.71	0		
1974	0	0	275	88
1975	32 / 1.38	0	199	54
1980	24 / 2.78	18 / 1.50		
1981	15 / 1.60	0	113	24

The floristic data allowed the conclusion that many of the high-level floodplain species are very sensitive to flooding.

In most years, high-level floodplain species are absent from groynes in the Lower Rhine branches. After a number of consecutive years with low spring and summer water levels, high-level woodland species such as *Clematis vitalba* and *Sambucus nigra*, as well as high-level grassland species such as *Arrhenatherum elatius*, *Galium mollugo* and *Heracleum sphondylium*, have been able to establish themselves on these stone dams, which are perpendicular to the river bank (Table 4). Observations since at least 1991 indicate that these species are able to survive several winter floods. However, in a year with high spring water levels flooding the groynes in April and May, the high-level species are eliminated from the groynes, not the mid- and low-level species. It appears, that tree species such as *Fraxinus excelsior* and *Acer pseudoplatanus* are less sensitive to flooding in April than high-level woodland and grassland species (see also Siebel 1998).

Both sets of field data (Tables 3, 4) indicate that early spring flooding and even winter flooding are decisive for the position or even survival of flood-intolerant species in the floodplain.

3.2. Impact of summer flooding on aquatic and emergent wetland species

High river water levels in the summers of 1970, 1978, 1980 and 1983 caused major changes in the aquatic and riparian flora and vegetation of floodplain channels in embanked floodplains which had hardly ever been flooded in summer before (Van de Steeg 1984, Brock *et al.* 1987). The main cause of these high water levels was the increasing coincidence of the discharge peak of the Upper Rhine with those of the Neckar and Main as a consequence of the canalization of the Upper Rhine.

In 1970, a flood peak in May had already washed away *Stratiotes aloides* from an abandoned river channel in an embanked floodplain near Nijmegen. In the same year, *Ranunculus lingua* and *Sparganium erectum* were lost here by drowning. After the May/June flood peak of 1978, a substantial upward shift was observed in the

Table 4. Impact of flooding during the winter and spring of 1994 on some woodland and grassland species established on groynes during a preceding five-year period with low spring and summer water levels. Figures indicate the number of groynes with the species in 1993 and 1994. For woody species, the total number of plants is given in parentheses. The Lobith-level of the groynes at Kekerdom (Ke) is 10.90 m above sea level, at Waardenburg (Wa) 11.60 m above sea level.

		1990-1992		1993		1994	
		Ke	Wa	Ke	Wa	Ke	Wa
Flooding data (days)							
	winter (Nov.-March)	21-39	13-25	41	36	78	60
	April	0-3	0	0	0	25	16
	summer (May-Oct.)	0	0	0	0	25	5
Botanical data							
	number of groynes inspected			6	5	6	5
High-level species							
woodland:	*Clematis vitalba*			6(13)	4(23)	0	0
	Sambucus nigra			1(1)	5(29)	0	0
grassland:	*Arrhenatherum elatius*			1	1	0	0
	Galium mollugo			4	1	0	0
	Heracleum sphondylium			2	2	0	0
Tree species:							
	Tilia platyphyllos			1(1)		0	
	Acer pseudoplatanus			1(1)		1(1)	
	Fraxinus excelsior				1(3)		1(3)
Mid- and low-level species							
woodland:	*Rubus caesius*			4	5	4	5
	Solanum dulcamara			5		5	
	Lysimachia vulgaris			5		5	

lower borders of the *Typha angustifolia* and *Phragmites australis* belts. Very dramatic was the impact of the exceptionally high flood peak in July 1980. Stands of *Scirpus lacustris* on muddy soil were uprooted and washed away. *Typha angustifolia* was completely submerged and died back over vast areas. At the end of the summer, new shoots from surviving rhizomes were formed only very locally. Nymphaeid species tended to survive the summer floods by quickly making new leaves on longer petioles than normal, allowing them to reach the water surface again.

Comparing 1954/1955 data (Van der Voo & Westhoff 1961) with 1988/1989 data (Maenen 1989, Van den Brink 1990) for eight floodplain channels within embankments shows the impact of summer flooding on aquatic and emergent species in those channels which are normally only flooded in winter (Table 5).

The aquatic species group shows a highly differentiated response. The non-anchored species *Stratiotes aloides* disappeared from all stations. The three nymphaeids, anchored by rhizomes and roots in the soil, managed to survive at all (*Nymphaea* and *Nuphar*) or most (*Nymphoides*) of the stations. The differences in survival rate between the three nymphaeids, 100% for *Nymphaea* and *Nuphar* and 63% for *Nymphoides*, may be the result of differences between the species in the amount of food reserves.

Table 5. Comparison of two data sets indicating the impact of summer flooding in 1970, 1978, 1980 and 1983 on aquatic and emergent plant species of former river channels in embanked floodplains. The table lists the frequency (%) and abundancy (s = sparse, f = frequent, a = abundant) of the species present. After data in Van der Voo & Westhoff (1961), Maenen (1989) and Van den Brink (1990).

| | Frequency | | Abundancy | | | | | |
	1954	1988	1954/55			1988/89		
Number of floodplain channels	8	8	8			8		
	%	%	s	f	a	s	f	a
Aquatic species								
Stratiotes aloides	50	0	2	2				
Nymphaea alba	50	50		1	3		2	2
Nuphar lutea	100	100	3	2	3	1	2	5
Nymphoides peltata	88	50	2	2	3	1	1	2
Emergent species								
Equisetum fluviatile	88	0		5	2			
Sparganium erectum	75	25	1	2	3	2		
Typha angustifolia	88	63	1		6	1	3	1

All three emergent species suffered severely from summer flooding. *Equisetum fluviatile* has disappeared completely and will probably not be able to re-establish itself. The low frequency and abundancy figures for *Sparganium erectum* indicate complete disappearance followed by only local initial re-establishment from seed. The large shift in abundancy of *Typha angustifolia* reveals the rather small regrowth capacity of the species. It can be concluded from these data that characteristic aquatic and emergent wetland species of formerly well-isolated floodplain channels in embanked floodplains are extremely sensitive to flooding during the growing season. In contrast, *Nuphar lutea* and *Nymphaea alba* are very tolerant.

4. Discussion

Hydrological conditions in most of the Lower Rhine system are highly dynamic and characterized by frequent water level fluctuations with large amplitudes, especially in winter and spring. Water level fluctuations in the Waal branch are of almost the same magnitude as those in the narrow Middle Rhine valley between Bingen and Bonn. Only at the lower end of the IJssel branch are fluctuations in water level small enough to permit well-developed aquatic and amphibious vegetation in and along the river. Good conditions for emergent vegetation types also occur in the tidal part of the interconnected branches of Rhine and Meuse in the western part of the Netherlands.

The highly dynamic hydrological conditions at lower and middle elevations of floodplains in a large part of the Lower Rhine branches are only suitable for flood-tolerant vegetation types like softwood forest and flood-tolerant grassland types. The combination of high spring water levels with low summer water levels eliminates competitive amphibious species, leaving bare soil for the germination of summer annuals, which survive major flooding periods as seed. Due to the large variety of habitats, species diversity in the floodplains can be very high. However, most of these species are flood-sensitive. Continuous occurrence of these species is restricted to the higher parts of the floodplains.

Floodplain rehabilitation by digging new channels and lowering floodplain levels is a suitable method for restoring the most dynamic ecosystems of floodplains, such as connected channels with flowing water, recreating the lost habitat of characteristic river fish species. In ungrazed situations, the softwood forest will benefit. Restoration of more complex or less dynamic floodplain ecosystems is far more difficult or almost impossible under the hydrological conditions of unembanked floodplains along a large part of the Lower Rhine system (Table 6).

In most part of the Lower Rhine system, survival of the luxuriant aquatic and riparian vegetation of isolated floodplain channels within embankments and its highly diverse fauna (Van den Brink & Van der Velde 1991) is only possible by preserving the embankments to a sufficient extent. When isolated channels are connected to the deeply incised river, the floodplain channels frequently run dry. The well-developed aquatic and riparian ecosystems disappear completely by drying out during prolonged low river water levels and by drowning during high summer water levels. They are replaced on the banks by a pioneer vegetation of annuals (Fig. 2 and Fig. 3).

Current research on flooding tolerance and developmental restrictions of hardwood tree species strongly suggests that in large parts of the floodplains in the Lower Rhine system re-establishment of hardwood forest is not a hydrological but a developmental problem. Lack of seed in the system, high predation pressure on seeds, seedlings and juveniles, and competition by a highly productive field layer vegetation of tall herbs or grasses prevents a successful establishment of hardwood tree species in the floodplains of the Lower Rhine system.

Table 6. Opportunities and restrictions for the development of vegetation types in rearranged floodplains in hydrologically highly dynamic parts of the Lower Rhine system.

Level	Vegetation types	Opportunities	Restrictions
	natural types (unmanaged)		
high	species-rich hardwood forest	low	developmental
middle	species-poor hardwood forest	low	developmental
low	softwood forest	good	
	annual pioneer vegetation	good	
water	aquatic vegetation	low	hydrological
	man-made types (grazed)		
high	flood-sensitive grassland	good	acreage
	shrubland	moderate	developmental
middle	flood-tolerant grassland	good	
low	marshland	no	hydrological
	pioneer vegetation	good	
water	aquatic vegetation	low	hydrological

Fig. 2. A well isolated floodplain channel with luxuriant aquatic and riparian vegetation.

Fig. 3. The downstream part of the floodplain channel in Figure 2 after removal of the embankment and connection to the river: aquatic vegetation was lost by drying out, marshland vegetation by drowning.

5. Conclusions

The severe flooding conditions in a large part of the Lower Rhine system have a strong impact on the river and floodplain vegetation. At the lower and middle levels of the floodplain, it is only the submergence-tolerant plant species which can survive. Characteristic vegetation types are the softwood forest on ungrazed river and channel banks and flood-tolerant grassland types in grazed mid-level floodplains. In much of the Lower Rhine system flooding conditions in unembanked floodplains are too severe for most aquatic and riparian wetland species. In the present Lower Rhine system, these species and the corresponding ecosystems of abondened channels can only be maintained by conservation of the embankments.

Most species of species-rich grassland and of species-rich hardwood forest are also rather intolerant to flooding. The acreage of these vegetation types will be restricted by the presence of floodplain levels of a sufficient height.

References

Barnes, W.J. 1985. Population dynamics of woody plants on a river island. Canadian Journal of Botany 63: 647-655.

Blom, C.W.P.M., Voesenek, L.A.C.J., Banga, M., Engelaar, W.M.H.G., Rijnders, J.H.G.M., Van de Steeg, H.M. & Visser, E.J.W. 1994. Physiological ecology of riverside species: adaptive responses of plants to submergence. Annals of Botany 74: 253-263.

Blom, C.W.P.M., Van de Steeg, H.M. & Voesenek, L.A.C.J. 1996. Adaptive mechanisms of plants occurring in wetland gradients. In: Mulamoottil, G., Warner, B.G. & McBean, E.A. (eds.): Wetlands, Environmental Gradients, Boundaries, and Buffers, pp. 91-112. CRC Press Inc./Lewis Publishers, Boca Raton.

Brock, Th. C.M., Van der Velde, G. & Van de Steeg, H.M. 1987. The effects of extreme water level fluctuations on the wetland vegetation of a nymphaeid-dominated oxbow-lake in The Netherlands. Archiv für Hydrobiologie, Beiheft Ergebnisse der Limnologie 27: 57-73.

Carbiener, R. 1970. Un exemple de type forestier exceptionnel pour l'Europe occidentale: la forêt du lit majeur du Rhin au niveau du fossé rhénan. Intérêt écologique et biogéographique. Comparaisons à d'autres forêts thermohygrophiles. Vegetatio 20: 97-148 (in French).

De Bruin, D., Hamhuis, D., Van Nieuwenhuijze, L., Overmars, W., Sijmons, D. & Vera, F. 1987. Ooievaar, de toekomst van het rivierengebied. Stichting Gelderse Milieufederatie, Arnhem (in Dutch).

Dister, E. 1980. Geobotanische Untersuchungen in der hessischen Rheinaue als grundlage für die Naturschutzarbeit. Dissertation Universität Göttingen (in German).

Jongman, R.H.G. 1992. Vegetation, river management and land use in the Dutch Rhine floodplains. Regulated Rivers: Research and Management 7: 279-289.

Maenen, M.M.J. 1989. Water- en oeverplanten in het zomerbed van de Nederlandse grote rivieren in 1988. Hun voorkomen en relatie met algemene fysische en chemische parameters. Rapport Ecologisch Herstel Rijn 13 (in Dutch).

Mitsch, M.J. & Gosselink, J.G. 1986. Wetlands. Van Nostrand Reinhold, New York.

MTPW. 1996. Landscape planning of the river Rhine in the Netherlands. Towards a balance in river management. Brochure, Ministry of Transport, Public Works and Water Management, The Hague.

MVW. 1994. Tienjarig overzicht 1981-1990: presentatie van afvoeren, waterstanden, watertemperaturen, golven en kustmetingen. Ministerie van Verkeer en Waterstaat, Den Haag (in Dutch).

Siebel, H.N. 1998. Floodplain forest restoration: tree seedling establishment and tall herb interference in relation to flooding and shading. PhD Thesis, University of Nijmegen.

Sykora, K.V., Scheper, E. & Van der Zee, F. 1988. Inundation and distribution of plant communities on Dutch river dikes. Acta Botanica Neerlandica 37: 279-290.

Van de Steeg, H.M. 1984. Effects of summer inundation on flora and vegetation of river foreland in the Rhine area. Acta Botanica Neerlandica 33: 365-366.

Van den Brink, F.W.B. 1990. Typologie en waardering van stagnante wateren langs de grote rivieren in Nederland, op grond van waterplanten, plankton en macrofauna, in relatie tot fysischchemische parameters. Rapport Ecologisch Herstel Rijn 25 (in Dutch).

Van den Brink, F.W.B. & Van der Velde, G. 1991. Macrozoobenthos of floodplain waters of the rivers Rhine and Meuse in The Netherlands: a structural and functional analysis in relation to hydrology. Regulated Rivers: Research and Management 6: 265-277.

Van der Voo, E.E. & Westhoff, V. 1961. An autecological study of some limnophytes and helophytes in the area of the large rivers. Wentia 5: 163-258.

Van Dijk, G.M., Marteijn, E.C.L. & Schulte-Wülwer-Leidig, A. 1995. Ecological rehabilitation of the River Rhine: plans, progress and perspectives. Regulated Rivers: Research and Management 11: 377-388.

Van Donselaar, J. 1961. On the vegetation of former river beds in the Netherlands. Wentia 5: 1-85.

Willems, W.J.H. 1984. Romans and Batavians. A regional study in the Dutch Eastern River Area, II. Berichten van de Rijksdienst voor het Oudheidkundig Bodemonderzoek 34: 39-331.

Zonneveld, I.S. 1960. De Brabantse Biesbosch. Een studie van bodem en vegetatie van een zoetwatergetijdendelta. Dissertatie Landbouwhogeschool Wageningen (in Dutch).

'HABITAT SYSTEMS' AS QUALITY INDICATOR IN LARGE RIVERS; A FIRST STEP TO CONSTRUCT AN INSTRUMENT FOR RIVER NATURE MANAGEMENT

R.C. Nijboer[1], P.F.M. Verdonschot[1] & C.M. Bisseling[2]

[1] Institute for Forestry and Nature Research, Department of Aquatic Ecology, P.O. Box 23, 6700 AA Wageningen, The Netherlands; [2] National Reference Centre for Nature Management, P.O. Box 30, 6700 AA Wageningen, The Netherlands.

Abstract

The quality of the aquatic nature in large Dutch rivers was studied. Therefore, 'habitat systems', based on macro-invertebrate communities were used as quality indicators. 'Habitat systems' are defined as the combination of habitat variables, for example substratum in relation to the species assemblage. Changes in habitat variables will lead to changes in the species assemblage and conversely.

With multivariate techniques, the present 'habitat systems' in the Rhine and their developmental directions were described. The 'habitat systems' were mutually related by the main habitat variables. These variables were connected to management measures. The 'habitat systems' and their relationships were placed in a web. A web is a coherent system of stages of ecosystem development. Different related 'habitat systems' reflected developmental stages. Thus, the web is composed of developmental directions towards an optimal or natural stage. The web informs about the quality of the aquatic nature. 'Habitat systems' are suited as an instrument for ecological assessment and nature management in large rivers.

In the near future, some problems must be tackled. Through inconsistency of the present data sets, which all differ and lack important habitat variables, the web approach is still limited. The first step to be taken is to compile a consistent data set with which it becomes possible to describe the 'habitat systems' more precisely for daily management practice.

1. Introduction

The pristine aquatic nature in rivers was very diverse. The relationships between different groups of plants and animals composed a complex structured web of communities in river bed and riparian zone as well as between them. Physical habitat diversity is important for the variety of communities in rivers. In a natural river a continuous shift of habitats occurs. As water moves downstream, materials in the river channel and the flood plains are transported and rearranged (Fittkau & Reiss 1983). The construction of weirs and dams, and the regulation of the stream bed caused dramatic morphological and hydrological changes; many riverine habitats got lost.

Together with the habitats, the characteristic river communities disappeared. Already in the beginning of this century, when regulation and embankment were finished (De Bruin 1982) most of the characteristic riverine fauna in the Dutch rivers was lost (Smit 1985). Also, the dense vegetation in the standing sections of the

New concepts for sustainable management of river basins, pp. 145–157
edited by P.H. Nienhuis, R.S.E.W. Leuven and A.M.J. Ragas
© 1998 Backhuys Publishers, Leiden, The Netherlands

rivers had disappeared. Biota in rivers are not only affected by the loss of habitats but also by the degradation of water and habitat quality. Around the seventies, the aquatic nature in the Dutch rivers was very poor. Later on, water quality slowly improved and density and species number of macro-invertebrates again increased (Van Urk 1981, Van den Brink *et al.* 1990). Even, some of the original riverine species returned (Van Urk 1984, Bij de Vaate *et al.* 1992). Recently, this recovery does not progress anymore, probably because of the lack of sufficient suitable habitats.

1.1. River nature management

To assess and develop the quality of aquatic natural elements in a river, adequate management methods are required. First, a suitable method for assessment or valuation is needed. This method must discriminate between quality states of aquatic nature in rivers, must detect recent trends, must indicate possible developmental directions (target and reference stages), and must indicate the most suitable measures to be taken that initiate improvement. For regional waters such methodology was already developed (Verdonschot 1990a,b, Verdonschot *et al.* 1998). This method, the web approach, is based on an ecological typology of waters. Different water types (represented by their macrofauna community and related environmental variables) and their developmental stages are presented in a web. The stages and types in the web are connected by environmental factors indicative for the main processes functioning between them. Measures related to these factors are included in such a way that the water manager is able to manage the water into the direction of the desired (improved) condition. The web approach represents reality but reduces the complexity of relationships between environmental variables and community characteristics to a limited set of parameters.

In the Dutch stretches of the rivers Rhine and Meuse, a web approach based on water types is too simple. Under the present conditions, these only two Dutch river sections are both quite uniform. A more discriminating typology was needed. Such typology was therefore based on 'habitat systems'.

1.2. 'Habitat systems'

Habitats compose important elements in a river. A habitat is a combination of abiotic variables, which can be physical (including vegetation as structural factor) as well as chemical. These environmental variables are named habitat variables, e.g.; substratum, current velocity and salinity. Theoretically, a number of combinations of habitat variables are possible within a river stretch. A pristine river is structured by many habitats. The differences in habitat variables become manifest in specific species assemblages which inhabit the habitats. Species assemblages are characterised by parameters like, species diversity, dominant and characteristic species, and by the information extracted from knowledge on the autecology of species, like preference for low or high current velocity, substrate type or oxygen requirements.

The habitat and its species assemblage together compose a 'habitat system'. The word 'system' emphasise the existence of mutual relationships, which implies that habitat variables and species assemblage affect each other (Fig. 1).

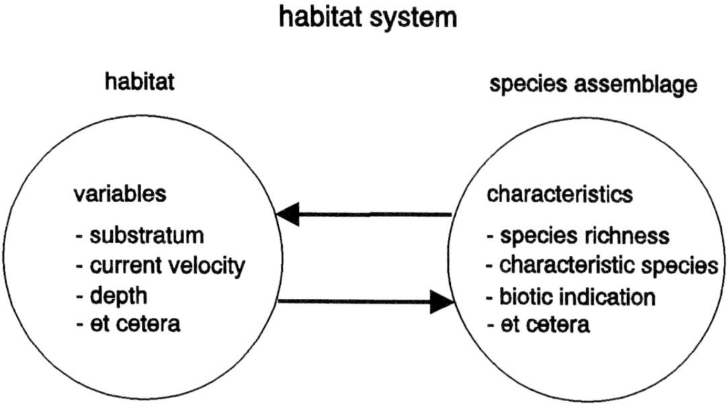

habitat system

Fig. 1. Compartments and mutual relationships in a 'habitat system'.

1.3. Objective

This study is part of the project 'Nature Foresight 1997'. Object of the project was constructing a characterisation of the present and future condition of the quality of aquatic nature in the Dutch rivers. Firstly, a web of river 'habitat systems' was constructed. Secondly, this web was used to evaluate the rivers' nature quality (Nijboer & Verdonschot 1998). This study focuses on 'habitat systems', based on macrofauna assemblages in the river Rhine.

2. Methods

The first and most important step in constructing a web based on 'habitat systems', is extracting and characterising the present 'habitat systems'. Fig. 2 illustrates a flow chart, which presents the methods included.

2.1. Distinguishing 'habitat systems'

To delimit 'habitat systems' in the river Rhine two data sets were used. The first one consists of data collected in the years 1988 and 1990, the second one contains data collected in 1995. In each data set, sample sites from different sections in the river Rhine, are present. At each sampling site, a macrofauna sample was taken and habitat variables (depth, substratum) were measured. Because of differences in sampling methods, habitat variables as well as taxon identification levels, different data sets could not be analysed as one whole data set. Detailed information about sampling sites and methods is given by Bij de Vaate & Greijdanus-Klaas 1991, Bij de Vaate & Greijdanus-Klaas 1993 and De la Haye 1996.

Each data set consisted of two sub-sets, one with macrofauna abundances, the other with habitat variables (Fig. 2, step 1). The macrofauna abundances were transformed into Preston classes (Verdonschot 1990a), all abiotic parameters were transformed into logarithmic values ($\ln(x+1)$).

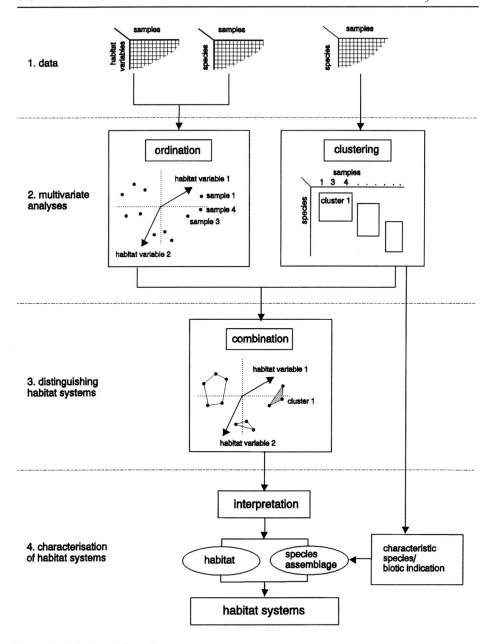

Fig. 2. Methodological flow chart.

The data were analysed with two multivariate techniques (Fig. 2, step 2). The first technique, clustering, was done with the program FLEXCLUS (Van Tongeren 1986) using the macrofauna data. The program clusters samples that resemble in species composition and abundance.

With CANOCO, an ordination program, the habitat variables are related to the biotic samples (Ter Braak 1987). For this direct analysis both, macrofauna and habitat variables were analysed together. Detrended Canonical Correspondence Analysis (DCCA) ordinates similar samples close to each other in a resulting ordination diagram. The habitat variables are presented in this diagram by arrows. The longer the arrow the more such variables adds to the explanation of the pattern between samples in the diagram, especially to those samples that are positioned near the point of the arrow or the perpendicular projection to it. The clusters were indicated in the ordination diagram, by drawing a contour line that connects the outer samples of one cluster. Clusters of sampling sites and habitat variables, that are related to the position of the clusters in the diagram, informed about potential 'habitat systems' (Fig. 2, step 3).

2.2. Characterisation of 'habitat systems'

A 'habitat system' is characterised by the habitat variables that result from the ordination analysis and by the macrofauna assemblage derived from all samples from the respective cluster (Fig. 2, step 4). The assemblage is described by three parameters:
– species richness;
– characteristic species;
– autecological information of the species.
Species richness is expressed by the number of species that occur within each habitat system. The characteristic species are determined by calculation of the indicator weight of each species. This is done by the program NODES (Verdonschot 1990b), which assigns an indicator weight (from 0 (= no indicative value) to 12 (= a high indicative value)) to each species in a habitat system, based on three factors:
– constancy; amount of samples in which a species occurs;
– fidelity; the ratio between the frequency of occurrence in the 'habitat system'compared with the frequency in the whole data set;
– relative abundance; the ratio between the average abundance in the 'habitat system' compared with the average abundance in the whole data set.
The indicator weights of all 'habitat systems' (from both data sets) were extracted from the whole data set.

The biotic characterisation of each 'habitat system' included autecological information on habitat preference, preference for high, low or medium current velocity, and functional feeding group. Biotic characterisation is determined on the basis of the characteristic species (species with a indicative weight higher than 3) only. Autecological information is based on literature research (Klink & Moller Pillot 1982, Van Dessel 1989, Van der Hoek & Verdonschot 1994).

3. 'Habitat systems' in the river Rhine

Table 1 presents the 'habitat systems' in the permanently aquatic part of the river Rhine. The site clusters resulted from the FLEXCLUS analysis, the important habitat variables from the ordination analysis. For biotic characterisation (habitat preference, current preference and functional feeding group) the most striking features were given. Each 'habitat system' was named after its abiotic condition.

Table 1. 'Habitat systems' in the river Rhine based on macro-invertebrate communities.

Major habitat variables	Sample year	Number of species	Number of characteristic species	Habitat preference of char. species	Current velocity preference of char. species	Functional feeding group of char. species	Name of the 'habitat system
stones shallow	1988	55	0	-	-	-	stones in shallow polluted stagnant water
stones shallow	1990	66	4	stones/silt/sand with silt layer	stagnant water	scraper/predator	stones with silt in polluted shallow water
stones shallow	1995	127	11	stones/vegetation	slowly running water	filter feeder/collector/shredder	stones with silt in shallow slowly running water
gravel shallow	1988	30	8	stones (in current)	running water	gatherer	gravel in shallow running water
bottom deep	1988	29	8	silt/sand with silt layer	stagnant water	gatherer	polluted deep silt bottom
bottom deep	1990	53	16	silt/sand with silt layer	generalist	filter feeder/scraper	deep silt bottom
bottom deep	1995	34	5	sand	slowly running water	filter feeder/gatherer/scraper	deep sand bottom
bottom shallow	1995	127	25	silt/sand	stagnant water	collector/scraper	shallow silt-sand bottom in stagnant water
bottom shallow	1995	33	3	stones	stagnant water	shredder/gatherer	shallow bottom in fresh-brackish water
bottom/stones shallow	1995	14	7	stones	slowly running water	filter feeder/scraper/shredder	bottom/stones in shallow brackish-marine water

Over the sampling years 1988, 1990 and 1995, in total ten 'habitat systems' were distinguished, five of which occurred in 1995. The 'habitat systems' of the river Rhine were grouped into three main categories: 'hard substrate-systems' (cluster 3, 4, 5, 6), 'soft substrate-systems' (cluster 1, 2, 7, 8) and 'brackish water-systems' (cluster 9, 10). The brackish water-systems' were characterised by brackish water species, like *Balanus improvisus* and *Crangon crangon*. Although salinity was not included in the analyses, this variable was indirectly established on basis of the autecology of the indicative species and on general knowledge of the sampling sites (sites in the river sections 'Nieuwe Waterweg' and 'Oude Maas').

The stony 'habitat systems' within the category of 'hard substrate-systems' occurred in each of the analysis. However, the species assemblages were different over the two data sets. From 1988 till 1995, an increase in species diversity and amount of characteristic species was found. This increase was most probably caused by an improvement of water quality. The three stony 'habitat systems' represent three quality stages of one 'habitat system' (cluster 3, 4 and 6, respectively). Because of the lack on chemical data, this conclusions could not be confirmed.

The gravel 'habitat system' (cluster 5) within the category of 'hard substrate-systems' was different. It was characterised by a high current velocity in contrast with all stony 'habitat systems', which occurred in stagnant water. Also, the functional feeding groups indicated a difference with the stony ones. Gatherers were more abundant, they collect their food between the gravel. In the stony 'habitat systems', especially filter feeders and scrapers were found. The filter feeders filter organic particles from the water, while they are attached to the stones. The scrapers scrape algae, which grow on the stone surface.

It is obvious that the more shallow 'habitat system' (cluster 7) within the category of 'soft substrate-systems' was richer in species with more characteristic species than the deeper 'habitat systems' (cluster 1, 2 and 9). The deep bottom is dynamic and therefore for many species difficult to inhabit. Table 1 indicates that silt and sand bottoms were inhabited by a different species assemblage. The silt bottom was slightly richer in species, probably because it contained more food. In 1988 the silt bottom was very poor in species, probably as a result of bad water quality (toxic substances and organic load).

4. Constructing a web of 'habitat systems'

A 'habitat system' can develop from a species poor system towards a more optimally developed, species rich system. This development was extracted from the category of stony 'hard substrate systems' in the river Rhine. From 1988 until 1995 an increase in species richness and amount of characteristic species was observed (see column 3 and 4 in Table 1).

To make the web approach suitable for biological assessment and management, it is necessary to value the different developmental stages. In Fig. 3 a general valuation scale is illustrated.

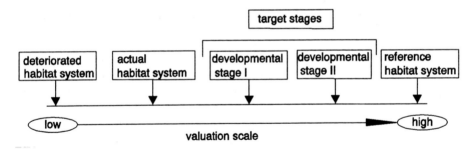

Fig. 3. A valuation scale along a development series of 'habitat systems'.

The most recent stony 'habitat system', the one observed in1995, was considered as the present state. The others were situated somewhere between a degraded stage and the present state (Fig. 4). The reference 'habitat system' is a system which represents an optimal ecological state under the present general system conditions. The distances between different developmental stages is not quantified. Fig. 4, only shows one developmental direction. But states can develop in several directions, following different changes in the environment. To include these possibilities, a

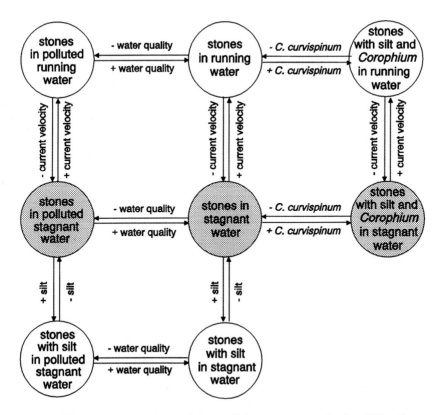

Fig. 4. A web of former, present and potential stony 'habitat systems' in the river Rhine. Former and present systems are indicated by shaded circles, potential 'habitat systems' by open circles.

more complex web of development stages was constructed in which the stony 'habitat systems' in the river Rhine were included. A stony 'habitat system' in polluted stagnant river sections can develop towards:
– a stony 'habitat system' in less polluted stagnant water river sections;
– a stony 'habitat system' in running water sections of bad or good quality;
– a stony 'habitat system' in stagnant water sections of bad or good water quality but which is silted.

Factors that influence the direction of development of stony 'habitat systems' (master factors) connect the different states. These factors also point towards management measures, such as reduction of nutrients or improvement of current profile diversity. Thus, these factors are related to the web and can be used to steer the 'habitat system' from one to another state.

The stony 'habitat system' in stagnant, polluted river sections can be managed towards a stony 'habitat system' in river sections with unpolluted water. Management measures can lead to a reduction in nutrients and toxic substances and to an increase of oxygen content. To improve the stony 'habitat system' in running water sections, the current velocity must be increased. This can be attained by hydrological and morphological improvement of the river section. Re-meandering will cause current velocity patterns to vary and will provide riffles with running water where these stony 'habitat systems' thus develop.

5. Valuation of 'habitat systems'

The combination of ordination and clustering is a suitable method for defining 'habitat systems'. Ordination and clustering together have been used in a number of typological studies and have proved to be suitable for analysing large data sets. The 'habitat systems' are made operational by assigning indicator weights to characteristic species per habitat system.

The web approach, based on 'habitat systems' may be a suitable tool for river management. 'Habitat systems' are real spatial parts of a river section and are therefore suitable objects for management measures and quality valuation. Changes in environmental conditions, represented by the habitat variables, will be followed by changes in the species assemblages. This also offers a practical tool for biological monitoring and assessment.

From this study the following questions arose:
1. Can aquatic nature be valued by macrofauna only?
2. How to deal with inconsistent and incomplete data sets?
3. How to characterise a habitat system?

5.1. Can aquatic nature be valued by macrofauna only?

In this study macro-invertebrates were used because:
– it is a species rich group in Dutch rivers;
– macrofauna has an important ecological role and stands between plankton and fishes in the food chain (Cummins 1992);

- macrofauna assemblages respond unambiguous and relatively fast at environmental changes and therefore serve as sensitive indicators (Hellawell 1986);
- macrofauna depends on and is bounded to habitats, in contrast to for example some fish species (Smit & Van Urk 1987);
- much information about this species group is already available.

The results showed that macrofauna is suited for the chosen approach. Because of their high species diversity over a small area, a fine-scaled variation between habitats is detectable. The analyses resulted in clear recognisable 'habitat systems'. However, it is advisable also to take other groups (for example macrophytes, fishes, zooplankton, and algae) into account. When all groups are included in a research, a more complete picture of the community is gathered. This provides a more complete description of all present aquatic natural values. If the Dutch rivers would develop towards a more natural state with a higher number of species and a greater variation within river stretches, differentiation between 'habitat systems' distinguish more precise when based on knowledge of the larger part of the community. On the other hand, this would involve higher costs for water and nature management.

5.2. How to deal with inconsistent and incomplete data sets?

Many data are already available. However, because of differences in identification level of macrofauna, sampling method and restricted number of measured environmental variables, the analyses were more complicated. Coupling different and incomparable data sets, asked for a very careful approach. Finally, we decided to analyse the different data sets one by one. Only in the end they were mutually related; when the 'habitat systems' from each data set were already identified.

A complete and consistent data set will improve the results. Therefore, concerning the biotic data, it is important that sampling methods and identification levels of biota will be standardised. The following criteria must be taken into account:

- identification of species to species level;
- including as many groups as possible (for example, *Oligochaeta* are often left out because they are too small to be collected with the sieves used, although they are very abundant, especially in bottom samples);
- sampling of as many different habitats as possible, this means different substrates at different depths and from localities with different current velocities. Even within one substrate type different 'habitat systems' can be distinguished (for example, the top, sides and underside of stones are inhabited by different species);
- standardisation of sampling method (size of the sample, materials used for sampling, sieving and sorting).

Concerning the habitat variables comparable problems were met. Often many important habitat variables were lacking. Sometimes depth and substrate (stones or bottom) were the only measured variables. Thus, little was known about the abiotic habitat. In many situations only the species assemblage explained differences between habitats. In future, this can be prevented by including the measurement of more environmental factors in a monitoring program. For macrofauna, current velocity, temperature, oxygen content, grain size distribution, salinity, toxic substances and (secondary) organic matter are known to be important variables, which should be measured at the scale of the habitat.

5.3. How to characterise a habitat system?

The species with their known autecology offer much additional information on the environment. When certain important habitat variables are not measured, species still tell a lot about the environment they prefer. But only when their ecological requirements are known. The brackish water 'habitat systems' illustrate this importance (see paragraph 3).

Also the total number of species and the number of characteristic species inform about environmental conditions. The quality gradient between the stony 'habitat systems' show this (paragraph 3). Groups of samples resulting from different ordination analyses were compared mutually on the basis of their species assemblages. The comparison of the stony 'habitat systems' showed the higher diversity and higher number of characteristic species in the samples from the year 1995.

The ecological condition of a certain 'habitat system' is based on the autecology of the more important species only. Especially, these characteristic species determine the differences between 'habitat systems'. Thus, the information they present about the environment is crucial.

Dominant species play an important role in 'habitat systems'. In contrast with characteristic species, they do not necessarily characterise specific 'habitat systems'. Dominant species are often generalists, they also occur in other 'habitat systems'. Because of their high abundance, dominant species can strongly influence the conditions within a 'habitat system'. Thus, it is necessary to identify dominant species and include them into the biotic characterisation. An example of a dominant species is *Corophium curvispinum*. The mass explosion of this exotic species led to changes in habitat conditions and species assemblages (Van den Brink *et al.* 1993, Nijboer & Verdonschot 1998, Van der Velde *et al.* 1998).

Biotic characterisation of a 'habitat system' on the basis of all species present is most promising. This would result in a complete description of all environmental conditions and biotic interactions, relevant. The more variables which are taken into account, the more accurate the 'habitat system' will be described. But it takes a lot of knowledge to compile all information for each species in the habitat system.

6. Future needs

The following steps are necessary to construct a web suited to assess and manage aquatic nature in large rivers:
1. Compiling a consistent data set.
2. Analysing this data set by means of multivariate techniques.
3. Describing the present 'habitat systems' in terms of habitat variables and community characteristics.
4. Constructing a web of 'habitat systems', mutually connected by main habitat variables.
5. Defining target and reference stages (Verdonschot *et al.* 1993).
   This step needs more research, because there is only little information available on more natural communities in the Dutch rivers in former times (Nijboer & Verdonschot 1998). Other sources of information can be provided by results

from paleo-limnological research (Klink 1989) and research of present 'habitat systems' in comparable foreign rivers, which still are in a more natural state.

6. Including mathematical techniques into the web to make it possible to assign a new sample to one of the 'habitat systems' or stages in the web (Nijboer 1996).

7. Including a valuation technique based on criteria that are used in nature management: diversity, naturalness and uniqueness.

8. Relating main habitat variables to practical management measures by developing and using expert systems.

7. Conclusions

Constructing a web based on 'habitat systems' asks for a thorough investment. It is expected to be a practical instrument to assess and manage aquatic nature in large rivers. A new macrofauna sample taken from any site in a river must be assigned to the web easily. When the present state is known, the possible developmental directions and the main habitat variables are read from the web. When these habitat variables are related to management measures, a management advice can be given. In time, this prevents management mistakes.

Acknowledgements

We thank the Dutch Institute for Inland Water Management and Waste Water Treatment (RIZA) for the allowance to let us use their data sets as well as for their active co-operation.

References

Bij de Vaate, A., Klink, A. & Oosterbroek, F. 1992. The mayfly, *Ephoron virgo* (Olivier), back in the Dutch parts of the rivers Rhine and Meuse. Hydrobiol. Bull. 25 (3): 237-240.

Cummins, K.W. 1992. Invertebrates. In: Calow P. & Petts G.E. (eds.). The Rivers Handbook. Volume 1: 234-250.

De Bruin, D. 1982. Rivierbeheer op de Nederlandse Rijntakken. Rijkswaterstaat, Dir. Bovenrivieren (in Dutch).

Fittkau, E.J. & Reiss, F. 1983. Versuch einer Rekonstruktion der Fauna Europäischer Strömer und ihrer Auen. Arch. Hydrobiol. 97 (1): 1-6 (in German).

Hellawell, J.M. 1986. Biological indicators of freshwater pollution and environmental management. Elsevier Publ., Barking, U.K..

Klink, A. 1989. The lower Rhine: Palaeoecological Analysis. In: Petts, G.E. (ed.). Historical change of large alluvial rivers: Western Europe. John Wiley & Sons Ltd. p183-201.

Klink, A. & Moller Pillot, H. 1982. Onderzoek aan de makro-evertebraten in de grote Nederlandse rivieren. Hydrologisch Adviesburo Klink, Wageningen, Oekologisch Advies Bureau Moller Pillot (in Dutch).

Nijboer, R.C. 1996. Ecologische karakterisering van oppervlaktewateren in Overijssel; toetsing van een expertsysteem voor regionaal waterbeheer. Verslagen Milieukunde nr. 128. Vakgroep Milieukunde, Faculteit der Natuurwetenschappen, Katholieke Universiteit Nijmegen & DLO-Instituut voor Bos- en Natuuronderzoek, Wageningen (in Dutch).

Nijboer, R.C. & Verdonschot, P.F.M. 1998. Habitatsystemen als graadmeter voor natuur in de zoete rijkswateren. Achtergronddocument Natuurverkenningen '97. DLO-Instituut voor Bos- en Natuuronderzoek, Wageningen (in Dutch).

Smit, H. 1985. Het ecosysteem van de Nederlandse grote rivieren. De Levende Natuur 86 (5):162-167 (in Dutch).

Smit, H. & Van Urk, G. 1987. Het herstel van de ecologische waarden van de Rijn: over de zalm en ecologische doelstellingen. H_2O 20 (17): 427-430 (in Dutch).

Ter Braak, C.J.F. 1987. CANOCO -A FORTRAN program for canonical community ordination by [partial] [detrended] [canonical] correspondence analysis, principal component analysis and redundancy analysis (version 2.1). TNO Institute of Applied Computer Science, Wageningen.

Van den Brink, F.W.B., Van der Velde, G. & Cazemier, W. 1990. The faunistic composition of the freshwater section of the River Rhine in The Netherlands: present state and changes since 1990. In: Friedrich, G. & R. Kinzelbach (eds.) Biologie des Rheins. Limnologie aktuell 1: 191-216. Gustav Fischer Verlag, Stuttgart, New York.

Van den Brink, F.W.B., Van der Velde, G. & Bij de Vaate, A. 1993. Ecological aspects, explosive range extension and impact of a mass invader, *Corophium curvispinum* Sars, 1895 (*Crustacea: Amphipoda*), in the Lower Rhine (The Netherlands). Oecologia, 93: 224-232.

Van der Hoek, W.F. & Verdonschot, P.F.M. 1994. Functionele karakterisering van aquatische eco-tooptypen. IBN-rapport 072. Instituut voor Bos- en Natuuronderzoek, Wageningen (in Dutch).

Van der Velde, G., Rajagopal, S., Van den Brink, F.W.B., Kelleher, B., Paffen, B.G.P., Kempers, A.J. & Bij de Vaate, A. 1998. Ecological impact of exotic amphipod invasions in the river Rhine. In: Nienhuis, P.H., Leuven, R.S.E.W. & Ragas, A.M.J. New concepts for sustainable management of river basins. pp. 159-169. Backhuys Publishers, Leiden.

Van Dessel, B. 1989. Ecologisch herstel van de Rijnmacrofauna. Publicaties en rapporten 1989-14 van het project "Ecologisch Herstel Rijn" (in Dutch).

Van Tongeren, O. 1986. FLEXCLUS, an interactive flexible cluster program. Acta Bot. Neerl. 35: 137-142.

Van Urk, G. 1981. Verandering in de macroinvertebratenfauna van de IJssel. H_2O 14: 494-499 (in Dutch).

Van Urk, G. 1984. Lower Rhine-Meuse. In: Whitton, B.A. (ed.). Ecology of European Rivers, Blackwell, Oxford, 437-468.

Verdonschot, P.F.M. 1990a. Ecological characterization of surface waters in the province of Overijssel (The Netherlands). Thesis. Institute for Forestry and Nature Research, Wageningen, the Netherlands.

Verdonschot, P.F.M. 1990b. Ecologische karakterisering van oppervlaktewateren in Overijssel. Het netwerk van cenotypen als instrument voor ecologisch beheer, inrichting en beoordeling van oppervlaktewateren. Rapport, DLO-Instituut voor Bos- en Natuuronderzoek, Wageningen (in Dutch).

Verdonschot, P.F.M, Schot, J.A. & Scheffers, M.R. 1993. Potentiële ecologische ontwikkelingen in het aquatisch deel van het Dinkelsysteem; onderdeel van het NBP-project 'Ecologisch onderzoek Dinkelsysteem. IBN-rapport 004. DLO-Instituut voor Bos- en Natuuronderzoek, Wageningen (in Dutch).

Verdonschot, P.F.M., Peeters, E.H.T.M., Schot, J.A., Arts, G., Van der Straaten, J. & Van den Hoorn, M. 1998. Waternatuur in de regionale blauwruimte; gemeenschappen in regionale oppervlaktewateren. Achtergronddocument Natuurverkenningen '97, concept. DLO-Instituut voor Bos- en Natuuronderzoek, Wageningen (in Dutch).

ECOLOGICAL IMPACT OF AN EXOTIC AMPHIPOD INVASION IN THE RIVER RHINE

G. Van der Velde[1], S. Rajagopal[1], F.W.B. Van den Brink[2], B. Kelleher[1], B.G.P. Paffen[1], A.J. Kempers[1] & A. Bij de Vaate[3]
[1]Department of Ecology, Laboratory of Aquatic Ecology, University of Nijmegen, Toernooiveld 1, 6525 ED Nijmegen, The Netherlands; [2]Department of Water Management, Province of Limburg, P.O. Box 5700, 6202 MA Maastricht, The Netherlands; [3]Institute for Inland Water Management and Waste Water Treatment, P.O. Box 17, 8200 AA Lelystad, The Netherlands.

Abstract

Ecological impact of an exotic amphipod, *Corophium curvispinum* was studied in the River Rhine and its branches by sampling stones from groynes and by the diet of eel, *Anguilla anguilla*. A maximum *C. curvispinum* density of 642,000 individuals m^{-2} was recorded at De Steeg in the River IJssel. *C. curvispinum* numbers in the River Rhine branches (River Waal, R. Nederrijn/Lek and R. IJssel) showed a clear positive correlation with average stream velocities. The amount of mud material including all macroinvertebrates fixed on the stone surface varied between 38 and 1044 g m^{-2} (dry weight). A correlation was established between population densities of *C. curvispinum* and mud material fixed on stones. The mass colonisation of *C. curvispinum* in the River Rhine has resulted in a drastic decline of zebra mussels, *Dreissena polymorpha*. The possible reasons are discussed by comparing population densities of *D. polymorpha* before (September 1989) and after (September 1993) the explosive population growth of *C. curvispinum* along the River Rhine. The diet of eel was dominated by *C. curvispinum* and indicates its significant role in the food supply of fish in the River Rhine.

1. Introduction

The River Rhine has long been exposed to human activities which have drastically altered its physical and chemical characteristics (Van der Weijden & Middelburg 1989; Van Urk & Smit 1989; Van den Brink *et al.* 1990; Den Hartog *et al.* 1992). Canalization measures, together with organic, inorganic and thermal pollution, have contributed to the loss of many native macrozoobenthic species and facilitated the success of several invading exotic species over the last century (Van den Brink *et al.* 1990, 1991; Van der Velde *et al.* 1990; Pinkster *et al.* 1992). The euryhaline and often thermophilous nature of these invaders is well suited to the present physical and chemical conditions of the Rhine (Den Hartog *et al.* 1989, 1992; Van den Brink 1995).

Crustacea make up the largest and most successful portion of this exotic element. The amphipods *Gammarus tigrinus* Sexton and *Corophium curvispinum* Sars have been the most successful invaders (Van den Brink *et al.* 1993a), currently occurring in very high densities in the main channel's littoral zone. *G. tigrinus* is an

New concepts for sustainable management of river basins, pp. 159–169
edited by P.H. Nienhuis, R.S.E.W. Leuven and A.M.J. Ragas
© 1998 Backhuys Publishers, Leiden, The Netherlands

introduced species, originating from North-America, and was first found in the Rhine in significant numbers during 1983 (Van Urk & Bij de Vaate 1990). Currently it reaches densities of thousands of individuals per m². However, in the last decade, Ponto-Caspic amphipods have been the most frequent invaders (see Van den Brink *et al.* 1989, 1993b; Bij de Vaate & Klink 1995). This influx has been aided by an increase in the connectivity of Europe's major rivers, such as the Danube and Rhine, by means of trade-route canals and shipping. *C. curvispinum*, is a tubiculous corophiid and was first noticed in the Rhine in 1987 (Van den Brink *et al.* 1991).

Through their dominance, these new species may well have played a large role in restructuring the Rhine ecosystem in the last decade. Exotic invaders can cause many disruptions to ecosystem functioning (Drake *et al.* 1989), particularly if such species are abundant and untypical for the ecosystem. Unlike the change in gammarid composition, *C. curvispinum* is not an example of generic alteration, but is the first tubiculous amphipod to occur in the Rhine (Pinkster *et al.* 1992). Thus, the impact of this corophiid on the biotic composition, energy flows and food web structure of the stressed Rhine ecosystem has probably been the greatest of all the invaders. This paper outlines the results of our research on *C. curvispinum* carried out in response to the urgent need to understand their impact on the Rhine's ecology.

2. Materials and methods

2.1. Population densities

In order to determine the population densities of *C. curvispinum* and the relative densities of the other important macroinvertebrates, stones from groynes in the River Meuse and Rhine (Fig. 1) were sampled (at depth of 1 m) from a ship by means of a polyp-grab operated with a hydraulic crane. The collected stones were sampled by carefully brushing them for various macroinvertebrates. Per locality, three to five stones were taken for each month. The surface area of the stones and population densities of macroinvertebrates were estimated by following equation (Bij de Vaate & Greijdanus-Klaas 1991; Bij de Vaate *et al.* 1992):

$$D = (\Sigma N / \Sigma A) * 10,000$$

where, D = the number of animals m⁻², ΣA = the sum of mean surfaces (in cm²) of all sides of stones, ΣN = the sum of animals on all sides of stones and 10,000 = the conversion factor.

All materials collected from stones were preserved in 70% ethanol for further analysis. In the laboratory, the number of specimens in each sample was counted and calculated for the average numbers per square metre of stone surface from three to five stone samples.

2.2. Mud-fixation by C. curvispinum

In order to estimate the amount of fixed muddy material on stones, an extra stone was sampled each month at a constant depth of 4 – 5 m following the above men-

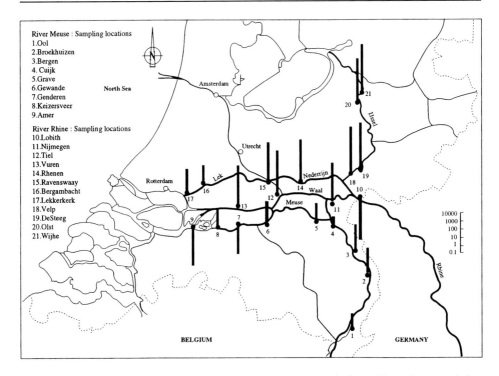

Fig. 1. Map showing the sampling locations in the River Meuse and River Rhine. Mean population densities of *Corophium curvispinum* (individuals m^{-2} stone surface at 1 m depth) at different sampling locations in the River Meuse and River Rhine during September 1993.

tioned procedure. The stones surface was carefully brushed clean and the resulting materials were collected in plastic containers. In the laboratory, this material, including macroinvertebrates, was dried for 24 hours at 105°C and weighed with a Mettler Balance for constant weight (dry weight).

2.3. Food web changes

In order to assess the importance of exotic amphipods in the Rhine food web, the diet of eel was studied. Eel, *Anguilla anguilla* (L.), is a common and commercially important fish in The Netherlands and its generalist feeding habit was considered likely to yield important dietary information indicative of many other fish species. Specimens were collected in the summer of 1994 from breakwater biotopes along the river IJssel using electrofishing equipment. To measure the extent of any possible diet shift following the invasion of these exotics, data of 1994 were compared against data collected in 1989 (see Bergers 1991) just prior to the population explosion of *C. curvispinum*. The same sampling method and location was used in both sampling years. Comparison of diets from the two sample years are illustrated by histograms of percentage frequency of prey types. The degree of similarity was measured by

Percentage Similarity (PS) and these values were tested for significance by a One-tailed Spearman's Rank (r_s) correlation test where a significant positive correlation between the two sample years indicated no shift in diet composition.

3. Results

3.1. Continuous domination throughout the year

Since it was first noted in the Lower Rhine in 1987, C. curvispinum has undergone a population explosion which has seen average densities reach more than 100,000 individuals m^{-2} at many sampling locations during September 1993 (Fig. 1). The maximum C. curvispinum density of about 642,000 individuals m^{-2} was recorded at De Steeg in the R. IJssel (Fig. 1). The population densities of C. curvispinum in the Rhine branches viz., R. Nederrijn/Lek (log y = -9.39 + 52.51x, r = 0.75, P<0.001; y = population densities of C. curvispinum in individuals m^{-2}; x = average stream velocities in m sec^{-1}), R. Waal (log y = 3.95 – 0.84x, r = 0.87, P<0.001) and R. IJssel (log y = 2.82 + 3.50x, r = 0.93, P<0.001) showed a positive correlation with the average stream velocities (Fig. 2).

The average densities of C. curvispinum in the Rhine decreased in a downstream direction. Average C. curvispinum densities were lower in the R. Nederrijn/Lek branch (varied from 13 individuals m^{-2} at Bergambacht to 47,463 individuals m^{-2} at Rhenen), which is dammed by weirs, than in the weir-free R. Waal (varied from 33,011 individuals m^{-2} at Vuren to 111,915 individuals m^{-2} at Tiel) and R. IJssel (varied from 70,870 individuals m^{-2} at Olst to 642,022 individuals m^{-2} at De Steeg). However, C. curvispinum numbers (ranged from 2 individuals m^{-2} at Cuijk to 31,430 individuals m^{-2} at Amer) showed no clear correlation with average stream velocities (which ranged from 0.10 to 0.15 m sec^{-1}) in the River Meuse. The impact of C. curvispinum population expansion and its tubiculous settlement strategy on the other previously dominant macrofauna has been noted with a simultaneous decrease in the densities of Dreissena polymorpha (Pallas) (Table 1).

3.2. Mud fixation

Mud-material, including macroinvertebrates, fixed by the tube building activity of C. curvispinum on the stones ranged from 38 to 1044 g m^{-2} (dry weight) in Nijmegen during July 1992 – February 1994 (Fig. 3). A highly significant correlation was established between population densities of C. curvispinum and dry weight of muddy material present on the stones (y = 160.01 + 0.004x, r = 0.86, P<0.001; y = dry weight of mud material on stone surface in g m^{-2}; x = densities of C. curvispinum in individuals m^{-2} stone area).

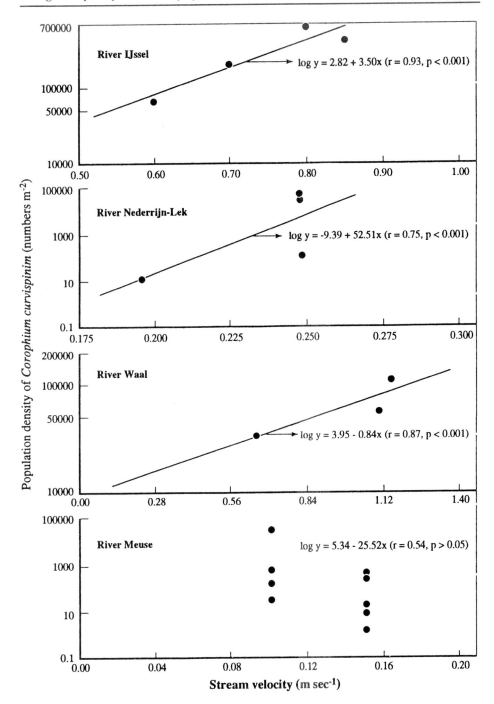

Fig. 2. Population densities of *C. curvispinum* (individuals m⁻² stone surface) and average stream velocities (m sec⁻¹) along the three major branches of River Rhine (R. IJssel, R. Nederrijn/Lek and R. Waal) and River Meuse during September 1993.

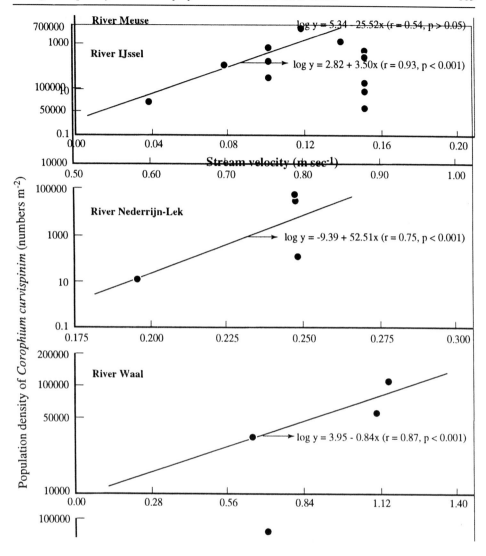

Fig. 2. Population densities of *C. curvispinum* (individuals m^{-2} stone surface) and average stream velocities (m sec^{-1}) along the three major branches of River Rhine (R. IJssel, R. Nederrijn/Lek and R. Waal) and River Meuse during September 1993.

Table 1. Mean population densities (individuals m⁻² stone surface at 1 m depth) of zebra mussel, *Dreissena polymorpha* on the different sampling locations in the River Rhine before (September 1989) and after (September 1992 and September 1993) the population explosion of *Corophium curvispinum.*

Sampling location	International River distance (km)[a]	Population density of *Dreissena polymorpha* (numbers m⁻²)		
		September 1989[b]	September 1992[c]	September 1993[c]
Lobith	859	1700	39**	48**
Nijmegen	891	2800	17**	154**
Tiel	917	21000	210**	125**
Vuren	951	18000	37**	237**
Rhenen	910	13000	330**	2285**
Ravenswaay	930	9100	1008**	27856**
Bergambacht	971	1200	70**	221**
Lekkerkerk	980	2500	5050**	5**
Velp	885	100	30**	–
De Steeg	896	300	250*	–
Olst	957	95	600**	–
Wijhe	966	2500	1050**	–

[a] the difference between sampling locations are ±2 km in 1992 and 1993 from 1989.
[b] Bij de Vaate *et al.* 1992.
[c] the differences between before (September 1989) and after (September 1992 and September 1993) the population explosion of *Corophium curvispinum* are compared by student's t-tests. Significant levels: *$P<0.05$; **$P<0.001$.
– data not available.

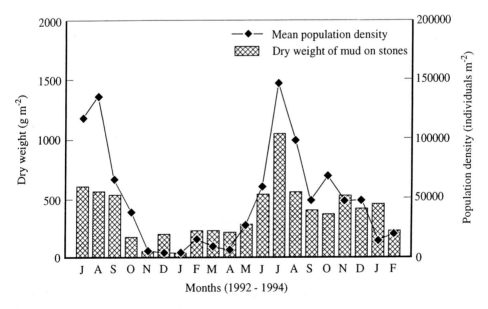

Fig. 3. Population densities of *Corophium curvispinum* and dry weight of mud material m⁻² stone surface at 4 – 5 m depth (including macroinvertebrates) in Nijmegen during July 1992 – February 1994.

3.3. Changes in the food web (e.g. food of eel, Anguilla anguilla)

The impact of the population explosion of *C. curvispinum* on the densities of other macroinvertebrates has also resulted in a shift in the diet of *A. anguilla* (Fig. 4). *C. curvispinum* now dominates the dietary composition of *A. anguilla* whilst the contribution of other prey types, *G. tigrinus* and *D. polymorpha*, has decreased significantly since 1989. The abundance of these formerly important prey species has been reduced by roughly the amount recently contributed by *C. curvispinum*. *C. curvispinum* occurred in 80% of the eels sampled in 1994 and *G. tigrinus* decreased in percentage occurrence from 32% in 1989 to 4% in 1994. The decline of another exotic filter-feeder, *D. polymorpha*, was also noted. In 1994, it was eaten to a far lesser extent, and by fewer fish, than in 1989. As a result of these changes, a very low PS (18%) in diet composition between the two sample years was measured. Statistical comparison of the two sampling years showed a negative correlation in diet composition ($r_s = 0.607$, P<0.01), indicating a significant shift in diet.

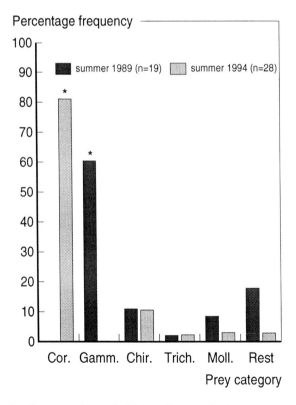

Fig. 4. Changes in the diet composition of eel (*Anguilla anguilla*) in the River Rhine following mass invasion of amphipod *Corophium curvispinum* (Cor – *Corophium curvispinum*; Gamm – *Gammarus tigrinus*; Chir – Chironomidae; Trich – Trichoptera; Moll – Mollusca; Rest – other species). * indicates a complete diet switch from *Gammarus* to *Corophium* from 1989 to 1994.

4. Discussion

The success of *C. curvispinum* makes it one of the most important biotic factors in the functioning of the Rhine ecosystem. In the River Rhine, *C. curvispinum* was found both on stones in the littoral zone and in the sandy sediments at the bottom. However, heaviest settlement occurs on hard substrates which are widespread in the river's littoral areas. The highest densities of *C. curvispinum* were recorded in the upstream parts of the River Rhine branches (*viz.*, R. Waal and R. IJssel), which have higher average river flow and stream velocities (between 0.65 m sec^{-1} at Vuren and 1.15 m sec^{-1} at Tiel) than the wider parts and the weired R. Nederrijn/Lek (between 0.1 and 0.15 m sec^{-1}). Despite explosive range extension of *C. curvispinum* in River Rhine, the species density was comparatively very less in River Meuse. The maximum density of 31,430 individuals m^{-2} was observed at Amer, which is the connecting point of River Meuse with River Rhine. Excluding Amer, the population densities of *C. curvispinum* varied from 2 individuals m^{-2} at Cuijk to 731 individuals m^{-2} at Genderen. This is possibly due to the lower chloride values (Cl$^-$) and higher pollution (e.g. Cd) in the River Meuse (for the year 1993; Cl: mean = 53 mg l^{-1}, range = 16 - 136 mg l^{-1}; Cd: mean = 0.4 μg l^{-1}, range = 0.1 - 4.0 μg l^{-1}, RIWA 1993) than in the River Rhine (for the year 1993; Cl: mean = 151 mg l^{-1}, range = 47 – 236 mg l^{-1}; Cd: mean = <0.1 μg l^{-1}, range = <0.1 - 0.1 μg l^{-1}, RIWA 1993). Moreover, stream velocities were also lower in River Meuse (maximum of 0.15 m sec^{-1}) than River Rhine (maximum of 1.12 m sec^{-1}). For a filter feeding species like *C. curvispinum* food can be most easily collected at sites where the flow is strong enough for a continuous supply of food.

The population density of *C. curvispinum* in the Rhine is one of the highest ever reported in the literature. The nearest density value of 100,000 individuals m^{-2} was reported by Schöll (1990) from the River Rhine in Germany. The differences in population densities of *C. curvispinum* from different waters might be related to differences in the amount of available food, salinity, flow velocity, pollution etc. Food conditions in the heavily eutrophicated River Rhine may be relatively better because of a continuous supply of phytoplankton and suspended organic material provided by the flow of the river to this filter feeding amphipod (Van den Brink *et al.* 1993a).

The highest values of mud-material including macroinvertebrates fixed by *C. curvispinum* were generally observed during summer months (Fig. 3). There was no significant difference observed in percentage of organic matter between mud materials including macroinvertebrates (mean percentage = 16 ± 2, range = 13 – 20) and mud material excluding macroinvertebrates (mean percentage = 21 ± 4, range = 11 – 29). The higher population densities of *C. curvispinum* were also observed during summer (June to September) when favourable hydrographic conditions such as higher water temperatures (17 – 20°C, RIWA 1993), high availability of food etc. existed in the River Rhine. The lowest values of fixed mud-material coincided with lower temperatures (6 – 9°C, RIWA 1993) during the winter months (November to February). Moreover, the dry weight of mud material present on the stones was highly correlated with the population densities of *C. curvispinum* in the River Rhine.

D. polymorpha requires a solid substrate for their settlement with its byssus threads. However, the filter-feeding *C. curvispinum* builds muddy tubes made of mud particles, sand and spinning secretions. In the River Rhine, nearly all stones have been covered by a 1 to 4 cm thick layer of muddy materials laid down by *C. curvispinum*. Therefore, a decline of *D. polymorpha* has occurred in the River Rhine since 1989 (Bij de Vaate *et al.* 1992; Van der Velde *et al.* 1994), after the explosive invasion of *C. curvispinum* (Table 1). Similar observations were made by Schöll (1993) and Jantz (1996) from the German part of River Rhine between Emmerich (Rh-km 861) and Basel (Rh-km 168). Schöll (1993) observed that the thick layers of muddy tubes of *C. curvispinum* reduced the *D. polymorpha* abundance and shifted the size distribution towards smaller shell length in comparison to contiguous mussel stocks without settlement of *C. curvispinum*. Jantz (1996) also reported that the populations of *D. polymorpha* covered with the muddy layers of *C. curvispinum* showed a higher proportion of dead individuals and a shifted size distribution towards smaller specimens. The mortality of *D. polymorpha* completely covered with muddy tubes of *C. curvispinum* possibly resulted from the isolation of mussels from the flowing water. Several incidents of reduced shell growth rates and numerous interruption lines on the shell surfaces of *D. polymorpha* in relation to presence of *C. curvispinum* have been reported (Jantz 1996). The impact of *C. curvispinum* on other macroinvertebrate species is under study.

Despite the importance of the population explosion of *C. curvispinum* in the River Rhine (Van den Brink *et al.* 1993a), very little is known about the fundamental features of filtration rate and tube building activity of this species. The present large populations of *C. curvispinum* in the Rhine may have a capacity to remove seston and clarify water. Such an increase in water clarity will result in an increase in the magnitude of the euphotic zone and thus transfer nutrient and energy to the benthos, thereby increasing benthic production.

The high abundance of *C. curvispinum* on groynes and the diet of eel suggests that it dominates the food supply of fish and thus plays a significant role in the feeding relationship between the fish fauna and lower trophic groups (Van den Brink *et al.* 1993; Marguillier *et al.* 1997). It is the first tubiculous amphipod to occur in the Rhine and its high consumption by one of the Rhine's dominant macrozoobenthivores can therefore be viewed as a predator diet switch due to the mixing of faunal associations occurring in the Rhine today. While it is difficult to argue that the Rhine food web has acquired non-westeuropean characteristics as a result of the key position held by this non-indigenous species, the fact that there has never been a generic equivalent for the corophiid suggests that the Rhine food web has been significantly altered from its natural state. To a large extent, the numbers and masses of populations in a community/food web are determined by the amount and quality of the respective food sources of each assemblage/trophic group and the degree of competition and predation each population experiences and exerts (Nikolskii 1969). Exotic amphipods now dominate the macroinvertebrate community and form the largest energy source for fish in the Lower Rhine (Marguillier *et al.* 1997). Considering this, the great importance of *C. curvispinum* for the Rhine ecosystem and its components is certain and this, in turn, has large-scale implications for its future ecological management and restoration.

5. Conclusion

At present, in the River Rhine, the epilithic macroinvertebrate community is dominated by exotic amphipods. The community consists of euryhaline, filter and deposit feeding macro-invertebrates. This composition is a reflection of the changed conditions of the river due to increased salinization and eutrophication over the years as well by connection to other rivers such as the Danube and Rhône by canals, for shipping activity. Our results indicate that exotic species like *C. curvispinum* have the capacity to change the species composition of the whole community and energy flows of the ecosystem.

Acknowledgements

Thanks are due to M.J.E. Orbons, M.G. Versteeg and students for their assistance in the field and laboratory. This project was financially supported by Ministry of Transport and Public Works (RIZA, The Netherlands), Ministry of Housing, Physical Planning and Environment (The Netherlands), Netherlands Organization of the Advancement of Pure Research (BION) and Beijerinck-Popping Foundation (The Netherlands).

References

Bergers, P.J.M. 1991. Voedselecologie van vissen in de Nederlandse Rijntakken. Report No. 28-1991 of the project Ecological Rehabilitation of the river Rhine. pp. 1-119. Institute for Inland Water Management and Waste Water Treatment, Lelystad (in Dutch).
Bij de Vaate, A. & Greijdanus-Klaas, M. 1991. Monitoring macroinvertebrates in the River Rhine. Ecological Rehabilitation of the River Rhine 27: 1-39.
Bij de Vaate, A., Greijdanus-Klaas, M. & Smit, H. 1991. Densities and biomass of zebra mussels in the Dutch part of the Lower Rhine. In: Neumann, D. & Jenner, H.A. (eds), The zebra mussel *Dreissena polymorpha*: ecology, biological monitoring and first applications in the water quality management. pp. 67-77. Gustav Fischer Verlag, Stuttgart.
Bij de Vaate, A. & Klink, A.G. 1995. *Dikerogammarus villosus* Sowinsky (Crustacea: Gammaridae) a new immigrant in the Dutch part of the Lower Rhine. Lauterbornia 20: 51-54.
Den Hartog, C., Van den Brink, F.W.B. & Van der Velde, G. 1989. Brackish water invaders in the River Rhine. A bioindication for increased salinity level over the years. Naturwissenschaften 76: 80-81.
Den Hartog, C., Van den Brink, F.W.B. & Van der Velde, G. 1992. Why was the invasion of the River Rhine by *Corophium curvispinum* and *Corbicula* species so successful?. J. Nat. Hist. 26: 1121-1129.
Drake, J.A., Mooney, H.A., Di Castri, F., Groves, R.H., Kruger, F.J., Rejmánek, M. & Williamson, M. (eds) 1989. Biological invasions. A global perspective. J. Wiley & Sons, Chichester.
Jantz, B. 1996. Wachstum, Reproduktion, Populationsentwicklung und Beeinträchtigung der Zebramuschel (*Dreissena polymorpha*) in einem Grossgewässer, dem Rhein. pp. 1-141. Ph.D thesis, Universität zu Köln, Germany.
Marguillier, S., Dehairs, F., van der Velde, G., Kelleher, B. & Rajagopal, S. 1998. Initial results on the trophic relationships based on *Corophium curvispinum* in the Rhine traced by stable isotopes. In: Nienhuis, P.H., Leuven, R.S.E.W. & Ragas, A.M.J. (eds), New concepts for sustainable management of river basins, pp. 171-177. Backhuys Publishers, Leiden.
Nikolskii, G.V. 1969. Theory of fish population dynamics as the biological background for the rational explanation and management of fishery resources. Oliver & Boyd, Edinburgh.
Pinkster, S., Scheepmaker, M., Platvoet, D. & Broodbakker, N. 1992. Drastic changes in the amphipod fauna (Crustacea) of Dutch inland waters during the last 25 years. Bijdr. Dierk. 61: 193-204.
RIWA, 1993. Samenwerkende Rijn- en Maas- waterleidingbedrijven. RIWA, Amsterdam (in Dutch).
Schöll, F. 1990. Zur Bestandssituation von *Corophium curvispinum* Sars im Rheingebiet. Lauterbornia 5: 67-70.

Schöll, F. 1993. Der Schlickkrebs (*Corophium curvispinum*) und die Augustfliege (*Ephoron virgo*): zwei Arten mit rezenter Massenentwicklung im Rhein. In: Ministerium für Umwelt Rheinland-Pfalz (Hg.): Die Biozönose des Rheins im Wandel-lachs 2000? Beiträge zur Fachtagung März 1992 in Mainz, S. pp. 89-94 (in German).

Van den Brink, F.W.B. 1994. Impact of hydrology on floodplain lake ecosystems along the lower Rhine and Meuse. pp. 1-196. Ph.D. thesis, University of Nijmegen, The Netherlands.

Van den Brink, F.W.B. 1995. Biodiversity as affected by invader species. Econieuws 26: 17-18.

Van den Brink, F.W.B., Paffen, B.G.P., Oosterbroek, F.M.J. & Van der Velde, G. 1993b. Immigration of *Echinogammarus ischnus* (Stebbing, 1906) (Crustacea: Amphipoda) into The Netherlands via the Lower Rhine. Bull. zool. Museum Univ. Amsterdam 13: 167-170.

Van den Brink, F.W.B., Van der Velde, G. & Bij de Vaate, A. 1989. A note on the immigration of *Corophium curvispinum* Sars, 1895 (Crustacea: Amphipoda) into The Netherlands via the River Rhine. Bull. zool. Museum Univ. Amsterdam 11: 211-213.

Van den Brink, F.W.B., Van der Velde, G. & Bij de Vaate, A. 1991. Amphipod invasion on the Rhine. Nature 352: 576.

Van den Brink, F.W.B., Van der Velde, G. & Bij de Vaate, A. 1993a. Ecological aspects, explosive range extension and impact of a mass invader, *Corophium curvispinum* Sars, 1895 (Crustacea: Amphipoda), in the lower Rhine (The Netherlands). Oecologia 93: 224-232.

Van den Brink F.W.B., Van der Velde, G. & Cazemier, W.G. 1990. The faunistic composition of the freshwater section of the river Rhine in The Netherlands: present state and changes since 1900. In: Friedrich, G. & Kinzelbach, R. (eds), Die Biologie des Rheins. Limnologie aktuell 1: 191-216.

Van der Velde, G., Paffen, B.G.P., Van den Brink, F.W.B., Bij de Vaate, A. & Jenner, H.A. 1994. Decline of Zebra mussel populations in the Rhine. Competition between two mass invaders (*Dreissena polymorpha* and *Corophium curvispinum*). Naturwissenschaften 81: 32-34.

Van der Velde, G., Van den Brink, F.W.B., Van der Gaag, M. & Bergers, P.J.M. 1990. Changes in the numbers of mobile macroinvertebrates and fish in the River Waal in 1987, studied by sampling in the cooling-water intakes of a power plant: first results of a Rhine biomonitoring project. In: Friedrich, G. & Kinzelbach, R. (eds), Die Biologie des Rheins. Limnologie aktuell 1: 325-343.

Van der Weijden, C.H. & Middelburg, J.J. 1989. Hydrogeochemistry of the River Rhine: longterm and seasonal variability, elemental budgets, base levels and pollution. Wat. Res. 23: 1247-1266.

Van Urk, G. & Bij de Vaate, A. 1990. Ecological studies in the lower Rhine in The Netherlands. Limnologie aktuell 1: 131-145.

Van Urk, G. & Smit, H. 1989. The Lower Rhine. Geomorphological changes. In: Petts, G.E. (ed), Historical change of large alluvial rivers, Western Europe. pp. 167-182. J. Wiley & Sons, Chichester.

Walz, N. 1978. The energy balance of the fresh water mussel *Dreissena polymorpha* Pallas in laboratory experiments and in Lake Constance. I. Pattern of activity, feeding and assimilation efficiency. Arch. Hydrobiol. 55: 81-105.

INITIAL RESULTS ON THE TROPHIC RELATIONSHIPS BASED ON *COROPHIUM CURVISPINUM* IN THE RHINE TRACED BY STABLE ISOTOPES

S. Marguillier[1], F. Dehairs[1], G. Van der Velde[2], B. Kelleher[2] & S. Rajagopal[2]
[1]Department of Analytical Chemistry, Vrije Universiteit Brussel, Pleinlaan 2, 1050 Brussels, Belgium; [2]Department of Ecology, Laboratory of Aquatic Ecology, University of Nijmegen, P.O. Box 9010, 6500 GL Nijmegen, The Netherlands

Abstract

Stable isotope techniques were used to assess the energy pathways and the role of an exotic amphipod species in the altered food web of the river Rhine. The exotic tube-building amphipod, *C. curvispinum* invaded the river Rhine in 1987 and has reached average densities of 100,000 individuals m^{-2} stone area. Therefore, it is assumed to be extremely important in river Rhine food web. *C. curvispinum* and its tube material and several fish species, each taken to represent different compartments of the food web, were collected for analysis. $\delta^{13}C$ values ranged from -27.7 (tube material of *C. curvispinum*) to -30.1‰ (*Anguilla anguilla*). $\delta^{15}N$ values ranged from +9.3 (tube material of *C. curvispinum*) to +20‰ (*Perca fluviatilis*). Cluster analysis conducted on the isotope data separated the material into five distinct groupings reflecting trophic status. Graphical depiction of ratio values plotted against each other showed that tubes of *C. curvispinum* are formed partly by material at the base of the food web, followed by *C. curvispinum* and benthivorous as well as filter-feeding cyprinids. The median cluster was made up of a number of fish species employing a generalist diet based either on benthivory, omnivory or piscivory. Cluster four was made up of benthic feeding fish. The fifth cluster consisted of piscivores, high $\delta^{15}N$ values reflected their high position in the food web. The high importance of exotic species at the base of food chain in the mediation of energy flow through the food web is clear. The usefulness of isotope signatures for river management in the identification of nutrient sources and effects of ecological change are discussed.

1. Introduction

Natural stable carbon and nitrogen isotope ratios can be used as a tool to trace source and pathway of carbon and nitrogen matter through ecosystems. Stable isotopes abundance of carbon and nitrogen in animals are set by the isotope composition of their diet and the selective excretion or respiration of the lighter isotopes. Isotope fractionation across trophic levels is relatively small for carbon (0 to +1‰ per trophic level) but is larger for nitrogen (+3 to +4‰ per trophic level). Thus, $\delta^{13}C$ has the potential to trace the carbon source, while $\delta^{15}N$ has the potential to identify the trophic level.

The river Rhine is a dramatic example of an ecosystem under anthropogenic stress (Admiraal *et al.* 1993). Following these disturbances, the number of invader species like the tubicolous amphipod *Corophium curvispinum* Sars, the bivalves *Corbicula fluminea* (Müller) and *C. fluminalis* (Müller), and the American crayfish

New concepts for sustainable management of river basins, pp. 171–177
edited by P.H. Nienhuis, R.S.E.W. Leuven and A.M.J. Ragas
© 1998 Backhuys Publishers, Leiden, The Netherlands

Orconectes limosus (Rafinesque) in the Rhine has increased and they have occupied niches left empty by the decline of native macrozoobenthos (Den Hartog *et al.* 1992). In 1987, *C. curvispinum* was first observed in the Lower Rhine, the Netherlands (Van den Brink *et al.* 1989). The maximum density (750,000 individuals m^{-2}) of *C. curvispinum* in the Lower Rhine is one of the highest ever reported in the literature (Van den Brink *et al.* 1993). By virtue of its high densities and construction of tubes nearly all stones are covered by a 1-4 cm layer (38-1044 g m^{-2} dry weight of muddy material including macroinvertebrates). The percentage of organic matter in this mud layer, including macroinvertebrates ranged from 9% to 23% with the mean value of 16% (Van der Velde *et al.* 1994). As a filter feeder, its high densities are thought resposible for decline in the amount of total organic carbon and suspended matter since its invasion (Van den Brink *et al.* 1993).

The objective of this study is to identify the present role of the invading amphipod *C. curvispinum* in the food web dynamics of the river Rhine by means of stable carbon and nitrogen isotope ratios of different fish species and *C. curvispinum* and its tube material.

2. Materials and methods

2.1. Sampling sites

Materials for stable isotope analysis were collected from the main channel of the Rhine branches IJssel and Waal in the Netherlands during 1994.

2.1.1. Fish
Fish were collected with electrofishing equipment and stored on ice during transport to the laboratory. Subsequently, each specimen's total length was measured and its total weight was recorded to the nearest gram using an electronic balance. Only muscle tissue, carefully excised from each specimen with a clean scalpel, was used for the analysis of isotopic composition. This is because the slow turnover rate of muscle results in integrating diet effects over months, and thus allows the exclusion of short-term variability effects (Gearing 1991). Samples were wrapped individually and freeze-dried for 24 hours.

2.1.2. *C. curvispinum* and tube material
Eleven samples (10 x 10 cm quadrates) of sediment fixed to groyne stones on the breakwater were taken. Materials were transported to the laboratory and subsequently deep-frozen (-20°C). *C. curvispinum* and its tube material were removed from the thawed material. Specimens of *C. curvispinum* in the water column were also collected with a hand held drift net (mouth diameter: 30 cm; depth: 1 m; mesh: 1 mm; handle length: 1.8 m). The net's position in the stream was maintained by suspending a 1 kg weight from its circular mouth. Collected specimens of *C. curvispinum* were freeze-dried for 24 hours. Tube material was dried at 60°C for several hours and then ground to a fine powder using a pestle and mortar.

2.2. Isotopic analysis

Mass spectrometric measurements were performed using a Delta E, Finnigan Mat isotope ratio mass spectrometer. For carbon isotopic ratios, the organic material was combusted in an Elemental Analyzer (Carlo Erba NA 1500). The CO_2 generated during the combustion was automatically trapped in an on-line Finnigan Mat trapping box for cryopurification before injection into the mass spectrometer. For the nitrogen isotopic ratios, the N_2 gas produced during combustion was cryogenically trapped in stainless steel tubes fitted with a molecular sieve, and samples were manually introduced into the mass spectrometer. A graphite reference material (USG-24) was used as a standard for carbon isotopic ratio measurement. Values are expressed relative to the VPDB (Vienna Peedee Belemnite) standard (Coplen, 1996). High-purity tank nitrogen gas was used as working standard for nitrogen isotope. This working standard was calibrated against N1 and N2 ammonium sulphate (IAEA, Vienna). $\delta^{15}N$ values are reported relative to nitrogen in air. Stable carbon and nitrogen isotopic ratios are presented as d values.

$$\delta R = [(X_{sample} - X_{standard})/X_{standard}] \times 10^3 \ (\text{‰})$$

where R = ^{13}C or ^{15}N and X = $^{13}C/^{12}C$ or $^{15}N/^{14}N$
Reproducibility for the analysis of different aliquots of the same tissue sample was generally better than 0.2‰ for both isotopes.

3. Results

Cluster analysis (Statistica version 5) was conducted on the data of $\delta^{13}C$ and $\delta^{15}N$ from fish, *C. curvispinum* and its tube material. The species type and total length of each fish analyzed is given in Table 1. For a cluster analysis of the results, euclidean distances and complete linkage were chosen (Fig. 1). Five clusters were selected by setting an arbitrarily linkage distance of four.

The $\delta^{13}C$ values of the measured samples ranged from -24.7‰ (tube material of *C. curvispinum*) to -30.1‰ (*Anguilla anguilla*) and $\delta^{15}N$ values ranged from +9.3‰ (tube material of *C. curvispinum*) to +20‰ (*Perca fluviatilis*). Cluster 1, with the lowest range in $\delta^{15}N$ (from +9.3 to 12.7‰) was made up of tube material from *C. curvispinum* ($\delta^{13}C$ = -24.7 to -27.6 ‰). This material consists of mud filtered out of the water column and excretory products from the amphipod. In the second cluster (range $\delta^{15}N$ = 13.7 to 16.0‰ ; $\delta^{13}C$ = -27.2 to -28.6‰), *C. curvispinum* was grouped together with the benthic feeder *Abramis brama* and also with *Rutilus rutilus*. *R. rutilus* can feed on a variety of food items but individual specimens can more or less specialise on molluscs, crustaceans, algae and detritus. Cluster three (range $\delta^{15}N$ = 16.5 to 19.2‰; $\delta^{13}C$ = -25.7 to -28.6‰) had a more diverse array of feeding guilds, consisting of benthic feeders, omnivores and piscivores, represented by *Pleuronectes flesus*, *R. rutilus*, *A. anguilla* and *P. fluviatilis*, respectively. Cluster four (range $\delta^{15}N$ = 16.5 to 18.3‰; $\delta^{13}C$ = -27.9 to -30.1‰) consisted of benthic feeders, represented by *A. anguilla*, *Gobio gobio* and *P. flesus*. Finally, cluster five (range $\delta^{15}N$ = 19.8 to 20.0‰; $\delta^{13}C$ = -27.8 to -29.0‰) with the highest values in $\delta^{15}N$ was made up of piscivorous *P. fluviatilis*, the top predator (Fig. 2).

Linkage Distance

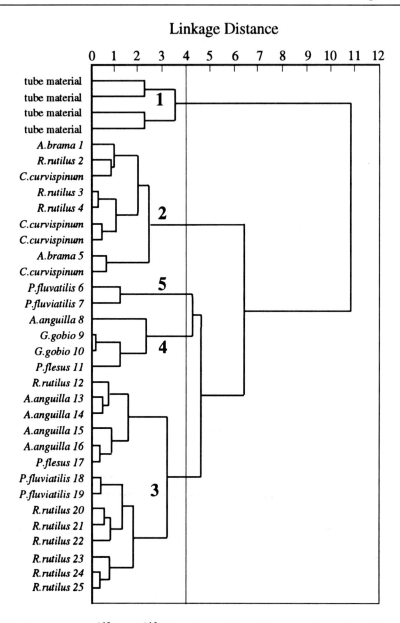

Fig. 1. Cluster analyses on δ¹³C and δ¹⁵N data by euclidean distances and complete linkage from fishes, *C. curvispinum* and its tube material in the rivers Waal and IJssel.

Table 1. Total length of fish specimens shown in Figure 1.

River Waal			River IJssel		
Fish species	**Sample number in Fig.1**	**Total length (cm)**	**Fish species**	**Sample number in Fig.1**	**Total length (cm)**
Rutilus rutilus (L.)	4	29	*Rutilus rutilus* (L.)	25	29
	2	26		21	20
	12	20		20	17
	23	20	*Pleuronectes flesus* (L.)	11	25
	3	19		17	18
	24	14	*Anguilla anguilla* (L.)	15	34
Abramis brama L.	5	19		13	32
	1	17		8	21
				16	17
				14	14
			Gobio gobio (L.)	9	13
				10	12
			Perca fluviatilis L.	18	18
				19	18
				7	9
				6	9

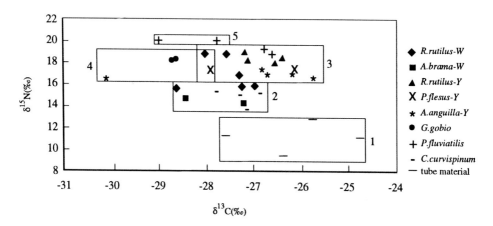

Fig. 2. δ^{13}C versus δ^{15}N values from fishes, *C. curvispinum* and its tube material in the rivers Waal (W) and IJssel (Y). 1 – 5 indicate the clusters obtained from the cluster analysis as shown in Fig. 1.

4. Discussion and conclusion

The isotope techniques give information which is useful in the understanding of ecological processes operating within the Rhine. The $\delta^{13}C$ range of this food web (from -24.7 to -30.1‰) coincides with the $\delta^{13}C$ range of the C3 plants (-24 to -30‰ ; Fry & Sherr 1984), indicating that the organic carbon pool in the Rhine is derived to a large extent from terrestrial organic carbon. Furthermore, this particular food web is characterised by high $\delta^{15}N$ values. *C. curvispinum* tube material, which can be taken to reflect the suspended matter, and thus a lower trophic level, already shows quite positive $\delta^{15}N$ values (up to +12.7‰). $\delta^{15}N$ values of *C. curvispinum* appeared to be intermediate between their potential fish predators and their tube material, indicating that *C. curvispinum* forms the food base of the fish assemblage. Another study, in which stomach contents are examined, will assess how far fish species have made a diet shift towards *C. curvispinum* after its invasion (Kelleher *et al.* 1998). The diet shift study and present study identify *C. curvispinum* as an important resource for consumers in the Rhine food web, and clearly show that a significant amount of energy flows through this non-native component.

The highest $\delta^{15}N$ value for fish (+20‰ for *Perca fluviatilis*) exceeds the values generally observed for other piscivores in other ecosystems (Hobson & Welch 1992; Rau *et al.* 1992; Newell *et al.* 1995; Marguillier *et al.* 1997) i.e. *Perca flavescens* (Mitchill) (12‰) (Cabana & Rasmussen 1996). The observed high $\delta^{15}N$ values for the Rhine may be the result of the significant anthropogenic influence over the river's nitrogen input, for example, due to enhanced mineralisation of soil organic matter through agricultural practices (like using fertilizers) and disposal of animal or sewage wastes (Macko & Ostrom 1994; Cabana & Rasmussen 1996). Cabana & Rasmussen (1996) present data on $\delta^{15}N$ contents of primary consumers related to increased human population densities in water sheds. They reported a enrichment of 8‰ $\delta^{15}N$ at the highest population densities. This is in accordance with the very high $\delta^{15}N$ values found in the river Rhine. The observed $\delta^{13}C$ and $\delta^{15}N$ values are some of the highest ever reported in an aquatic ecosystem and stongly indicate that the Rhine's carbon pool is largely derived from terrestrial sources and a significant input of nitrogen by anthropogenic sources. The results of this study show that measuring $\delta^{15}N$ signatures at the base of food chain can provide useful tool in the assessment of human nutrient inputs which has been identified as an important contributor to the nitrogen budget of a aquatic system (Cabana & Rasmussen 1996).

Acknowledgements

We thank Prof. Dr. E. Keppens for access to mass spectrometer facilities. We also thank F. Koomen, P.H. van Avesaath and M.G. Versteeg for collection of samples. Help rendered during the laboratory work by M.J.E. Orbons, is greatly acknowledged.

References

Admiraal, W., Van der Velde, G., Smit, H. & Cazemier, W.G. 1993. The rivers Rhine and Meuse in The Netherlands: present state and signs of ecological recovery. Hydrobiologia 295: 97-128.

Cabana, G. & Rasmussen, J.B. 1996. Comparison of aquatic food chains using nitrogen isotopes. Proc. Natl. Acad. Sci. USA 93: 10844-10847.

Coplen, T.B. 1996. New guide lines for reporting stable hydrogen, carbon, and oxygen isotope-ratio data. Geochim. Cosmochim. Acta 60: 3359-3360.

Den Hartog, C., Van den Brink, F.W.B. & Van der Velde, G. 1992. Why was the invasion of the river Rhine by *Corophium curvispinum* and *Corbicula* species so successful?. J. Nat. Hist. 26: 1121-1129.

Fry, B. & Sherr, E.B. 1984. $\delta^{13}C$ measurements as indicators of carbon flow in marine and freshwater ecosystems. Contrib. Mar. Biol. 27: 13-47.

Gearing, J.N. 1991. The study of diet and trophic relationships through natural abundance ^{13}C. In: Coleman, D.C. & Fry, B. (eds), Carbon isotope techniques. pp. 201-218. Academic Press, London, UK.

Hobson, K.A. & Welch, H.E. 1992. Determination of trophic relationship within a high Artic marine food web using $\delta^{13}C$ and $\delta^{15}N$ analysis. Mar. Ecol. Prog. Ser. 84: 9-18.

Kelleher, B., Bergers, P.J.M., Van den Brink, F.W.B., Giller, P.S., Van der Velde, G. & Bij de Vaate, A. 1998. Effects of exotic amphipod invasions on fish diet in the Lower Rhine. Arch. Hydrobiol. (Accepted).

Macko, S.A. & Ostrom, N.E. 1994. Pollution studies using stable isotopes. In: Lajtha, K. & Michener, R.H. (eds), Stable isotopes in ecology and environmental science. pp. 45-62. Blackwell Science Inc., Oxford, UK.

Marguillier, S., Van der Velde, G., Dehairs, F., Hemminga, M.A. & Rajagopal, S. 1997. Trophic relationships in an interlinked mangrove seagrass ecosystem as traced by $\delta^{13}C$ and $\delta^{15}N$. Mar. Ecol. Prog. Ser. 151: 115-121.

Newell, R.I.E., Marshall, N., Sasekumar, A. & Chong, V.C. 1995. Relative importance of benthic microalgae, phytoplankton, and mangroves as sources of nutrition for penaeid prawns and other coastal invertebrates from Malaysia. Mar. Biol. 123: 595-606.

Rau, G., Ainley, D.G., Bengtson, J.L., Torres, J.J. & Hopkins, T.L. 1992. $^{15}N/^{14}N$ and $^{13}C/^{12}C$ in Weddell sea birds, seals, and fish: implications for diet and trophic structure. Mar. Ecol. Prog. Ser. 84: 1-8.

Van den Brink, F.W.B., Van der Velde, G. & Bij de Vaate, A. 1989. A note on the immigration of *Corophium curvispinum* Sars, 1895 (Crustacea: Amphipoda) into The Netherlands via the River Rhine. Bull. zool. Museum Univ. Amsterdam 11: 211-213.

Van den Brink, F.W.B., Van der Velde, G. & Bij de Vaate, A. 1993. Ecological aspects, explosive range extension and impact of a mass invader, *Corophium curvispinum* Sars, 1895 (Crustacea: Amphipoda), in the lower Rhine (The Netherlands). Oecologia 93: 224-232.

Van der Velde, G., Paffen, B.G.P., Van den Brink, F.W.B., Bij de Vaate, A. & Jenner, H.A. 1994. Decline of Zebra mussel populations in the Rhine. Competition between two mass invaders (*Dreissena polymorpha* and *Corophium curvispinum*). Naturwissenschaften 81: 32-34.

IMMISSION ASSESSMENT PROCEDURES FOR DISCHARGE PERMITTING

J.L.M. Haans, R.S.E.W. Leuven & A.M.J. Ragas
Department of Environmental Studies, Faculty of Science, University of Nijmegen, P.O.Box 9010, 6500 GL Nijmegen, The Netherlands

Abstract

The main objective of this paper is to present a generalised overview of the current status of immission assessment procedures for discharge permitting in four countries: Germany, the Netherlands, the United Kingdom (notably England and Wales) and the USA. Information was gathered through a literature search and interviews with various experts. The procedures are assessed by focusing on distinguishing features of immission assessment, such as the applied sets and types of environmental quality criteria, the derived permit requirements, the allocation of procedural responsibilities, operational aspects of immission assessment (including preconditions for application, types of water quality models and their selection) and the degree of elaboration. All countries more or less combine immission assessment with technology-based requirements when permitting discharges. If the EU intends to introduce a scientifically sound, practical, transparent and harmonised immission assessment procedure for discharge permitting, various options are available. The most important issues to be solved when harmonising immission assessment procedures are identified. The procedure of the USA is worth evaluating as a reference for ideas on how to tackle the identified issues.

1. Introduction

Water policies in the Netherlands involve two basic and complementary approaches for deriving emission limit values (ELVs) for waste water discharge permits. The emission-based or technology-based approach (also called Best Available Technology or BAT-approach) centres on cleaning at source level, using the best technical or practical means available. The immission-based or water quality-based approach (also called Environmental Quality or EQ-approach) focuses on the impact of the discharge on the quality of the receiving water body. The term 'immission' is used for the part of an emission or discharge that actually reaches the receiving water.

Dutch water boards generally concentrate on the well-established and extensively elaborated BAT-approach. Although Dutch national legislation does provide for the application of the EQ-approach on a case-by-case basis, it is in practice poorly and ambiguously elaborated (De Bont *et al.* 1996).

At the request of the national Institute for Inland Water Management and Waste Water Treatment (RIZA) of the Dutch Ministry of Transport, Public Works and Water Management, an inventory was made of the basic assumptions, water quality models and immission assessment procedures in the Netherlands and abroad, in order to gain insight into the necessary choices and options for elaboration of the

EQ-approach. Moreover, the relation between the BAT- and EQ-approaches is a subject of international debate in the European Union (EU), in view of the collective revision of European water quality Directives, embodied in the forthcoming Water Framework Directive (Kraemer 1996). Although all EU Member States apply both approaches simultaneously, there are differences with regard to the degree of elaboration and the relation between the two (OECD 1996). An important goal of the new EU Water Framework Directive will be the harmonisation of these different procedures, to achieve greater efficiency through uniformity of regulations, and equality of law for countries and companies within the EU. In the continuing discussion about this subject, a tendency can be discerned to regard the two approaches as complementary, rather than alternative. The relation between the BAT- and EQ-approaches in discharge permitting is outlined by Ragas *et al.* (1998) elsewhere in this book.

The aim of this paper is to provide a generalised overview of the current status of immission assessment procedures for discharge permitting in four countries: Germany, the Netherlands, the United Kingdom (UK; notably England and Wales) and the United States of America (USA). It focuses on distinguishing features of immission assessment, which include:

1. the sets and types of environmental quality objectives (EQOs) used in immission assessment;
2. characteristics of these sets of EQOs;
3. permit requirements within the framework of immission assessment;
4. allocation of responsibilities within the discharge permitting procedure;
5. operational aspects of immission assessment, including preconditions for application, types of water quality models used and model selection;
6. the degree of elaboration of the immission-based approach for discharge permitting.

2. Materials and methods

The information used was gathered by conducting a literature search. Among the databases consulted were the UNCOVER database of the CARL organisation (http://uncweb.carl.org), the Online Library System (OLS) of the United States Environmental Protection Agency (US-EPA; telnet://epaibm.rtpnc.epa.gov), the Universities Water Information Network (UWIN; http://www2.uwin.siu.edu/databases/wrsic/index.html) and the CD-ROM database Polltox II-3/95 (Elseviers Science Publishers). Key words used were "water", "quality", "objectives", "standards", "criteria", "discharge", "effluent", "model", "permit", "consent", "allocation" and "mixing zone". In addition, 51 water managers, policy makers and scientists in England, Wales, Germany and the USA were contacted and asked to provide supplementary information. Data on the German situation was collected mainly from LWA (1991) and Höhne & Irmer (1995). The most important document on the UK was NRA (1996). Information on the Dutch situation was mainly obtained from De Bont *et al.* (1996) and Voeten (1996). The most important document for the USA data was US-EPA (1991). Data on European aspects were principally obtained from OECD (1996) and Kraemer (1996). Information on all countries exept the Netherlands was also taken from Ragas & Leuven (1996).

Generalisation and loss of detail are unavoidable in this type of comparative study. This implies that the information outlined in this paper does not necessarily apply to each individual discharge permit issued in the respective countries.

3. Results

3.1. Environmental quality objectives in immission assessment

Table 1 gives an overview of the sets and types of environmental quality objectives used by the respective countries in immission assessment. The federal states of Germany use sets of function-oriented EQOs of the EU (such as those for drinking water, bathing waters, fish and shellfish-sustaining waters; Höhne & Irmer 1995) and state-specific AGA-objectives. The AGA-objectives are soon to be replaced by new objectives (with an ecotoxicological basis) for the protection of inland surface waters against hazardous substances, based on the so-called BLAK-QZ (BLAK-QZ 1993). This water quality targets derivation concept, developed jointly by the federal government and the federal states, enables the formulation of quality objectives which are termed *Zielvorgaben* (water quality targets), in order to make it clear that the derived values are orientational ones, rather than legally binding limit values (Irmer *et al.* 1997). Impairment of functional uses, such as supply of drinking water or the protection of aquatic communities, is not expected if the water quality targets are complied with. Violation of these water quality targets indicates the need to explore the causes, thus allowing a more appropriate fine-tuning of water pollution control and priority-setting of sanitation projects and the analytical methods to be optimised (Irmer *et al.* 1995). Based on the BLAK-QZ a water quality classification system is being developed (Irmer *et al.* 1997). The water quality objectives of the International Rhine Committee (IRC) are applied in states in the Rhine catchment area. The use of EQOs in the immission assessment procedure differs per federal state (Höhne & Irmer 1995).

The Netherlands applies function-oriented EQOs of the EU and national AMK-objectives, which are chemical-specific objectives, intended to prevent chronic effects. The IRC-objectives apply for the Rhine catchment area (VROM 1992).

In their immission assessment procedure, England and Wales use the function-oriented EU water quality objectives, chemical-specific EU water quality objectives for list I substances, national water quality objectives for list II and red list substances, and a set of objectives for the protection of river ecosystems (RQOs; NRA 1994). With regard to novel substances, the various regions of the UK Environment Agency (EA) are allowed to develop and apply their own intermediary objectives, if national ones are lacking. However, where a substance of concern is novel, toxicological data are sought so that an appropriate EQ-criterion can be derived. This proces is undertaken centrally by the EA and a database is maintained to ensure that the same substance is dealt with in a consistent manner by all EA-regions. The EA has recently undertaken consultation with industry concerning the introduction of toxicity based controls. A specific National Centre has been established to take this enterprise forward.

Table 1. Sets and types of environmental quality objectives (EQOs) used in immission assessment.

	Germany	The Netherlands	UK (Eng. & Wales)	USA
Sets of EQOs	EU/AGA/ BLAK-QZ/IRC	EU/AMK/IRC	EU/RQO/II/RL Environment Agency regions	US-EPA (federal)/ states
Sediment quality	-	-	-	±
Chemical-specific	+	+	+	+
Whole effluent toxicity	-	-	-	+
Biological water quality[1]	-	-	-	±
Acute toxicity	-	-	-	+
Chronic toxicity	+	+	+	+

1 = parameters indicating presence or abundance of biota; EU = function-oriented water quality objectives of the European Union; AGA = *Allgemeine Güteanforderungen für Fliessgewässer* (general quality objectives of the federal state of Nordrhein-Westfalen); BLAK-QZ = *Bund/Länder Arbeitskreis (Wasser) Qualitätsziele* (federal objectives developed by the *Bund/Länder Arbeitskreis gefährliche Stoffen Qualitätsziele für oberirdische Gewässer*); IRC = objectives developed by the International Rhine Committee; AMK = *Algemene milieukwaliteitsnormen* (general objectives for environmental quality); RQO = *River Quality Objectives*; II = national objectives for *List II Substances*; RL = national objectives for *Red List Substances*; - = not applied; + = applied; ± = underdevelopment

The USA has federal water quality objectives (for which the American term is water quality *criteria*), developed by the United States Environmental Protection Agency (US-EPA), which may be adopted by the states. However, each state is allowed to develop and use its own objectives, which must be at least as stringent as the national US-EPA objectives. To this end, US-EPA has formulated guidelines, and the state EQOs and their application have to be approved by US-EPA.

In general, all countries use chemical-specific objectives to avoid chronic effects. No country actively uses sediment criteria or biological water quality parameters (in the USA also known as biological criteria) in immission assessment, although the USA is working on both. The USA is the only country which uses water quality objectives based on (effluent) toxicity in immission assessment, as well as objectives to avoid acute effects. Germany also uses a whole effluent toxicity (WET) test, but it is applied within the framework of the BAT-approach (Höhne & Irmer 1995). The Netherlands and the UK are considering a WET-approach (Tonkes & Botterweg 1995, Crawshaw 1993).

3.2. Characteristics of the sets of EQOs

Table 2 shows that the USA is the only country to use spatial specifications in its EQOs, a feature of the mixing zone approach. This approach is used by US-EPA for situations in which complete mixing does not occur near the discharge point. The European countries studied all use percentile scores as temporal specification of their national EQOs. The time specifications of EQOs used in the USA take the form of a maximum allowable excursion frequency and duration. The European function-oriented EQOs lack temporal (and spatial) specifications. All countries apply sets of objectives that, in combination, cover the three main groups of pollution categories. For a large number of pollutants, however, EQOs do not (yet) exist.

Table 2. Characteristics of the sets of environmental quality objectives (EQOs) used in immission assessment.

Sets of EQOs*	European Union					Germany			NL	UK (England & Wales)			USA	
	D	B	F	Sh	I	BLAK-QZ	IRC	AGA	AMK	RQO	II	RL	Aq	Hh
Temporal specification														
percentile score	-	-	-	-	-	+	+	+	+	+	+	+	-	-
duration of excursion	-	-	-	-	-	-	-	-	-	-	-	-	+	+
frequency of excursion	-	-	-	-	-	-	-	-	-	-	-	-	+	+
Spatial specification	-	-	-	-	-	-	-	-	-	-	-	-	+	+
Pollution categories														
conventional	+	+	+	+	-	-	±	+	+	+	-	-	±[1]	±[1]
metals	+	-	±	-	+	+	+	+	+	±	+	-	+	+
toxic agents	+	-	-	±	+	+	+	-	+	-	+	+	+	+

*D = EQOs for drinking water; B = EQOs for bathing water;; F = EQOs for fish-sustaining water; Sh = EQOs for shellfish-sustaining water; I = EQOs for *List I Substances*; BLAKQZ = federal objectives developed by the *Bund/Länder Arbeitskreis gefährliche Stoffen Qualitätsziele für oberirdische Gewässer*; IRC = objectives developed by the International Rhine Committee; AGA = *Allgemeine Güteanforderungen für Fliessgewässer* (general quality objectives of the federal state of Nordrhein-Westfalen); NL = the Netherlands; AMK = *Algemene milieukwaliteitsnormen* (general objectives for environmental quality); RQO = *River Quality Objectives*; II = national objectives for *List II Substances*; RL = national objectives for *Red List Substances*; Aq = objectives for the protection of aquatic life; Hh = objectives for the protection of human health; - not elaborated; ± = partially elaborated; + elaborated; 1 = not all conventional pollutants have Aq and Hh objectives, and some are not directly the subject of a criterion; instead a related parameter is specified.

3.3. Permit requirements

Table 3 lists permit requirements recorded in discharge permits within the framework of immission assessment. All countries more or less combine the immission-based approach and the BAT-approach in their discharge permits (Stortelder & Van de Guchte 1995, OECD 1996). In Germany, the Netherlands and the USA the emission limit values resulting from immission assessment are supplementary to the discharge limits derived from the BAT-approach (LAWA 1990, Blumenschein 1992). In the UK, the same goes for permits within the framework of the Environmental Protection Act (EPA), which mainly regulates the BAT-approach. Permits covered by the Water Resources Act (WRA), however, are only based on immission assessment.

Table 3. Permit requirements recorded in discharge permits within the framework of immission assessment.

	Germany	The Netherlands	UK (Eng. & Wales)	USA
Effluent concentration	+	+	+	+
Waste load	+	+	+	+
Seasonal effluent criteria	-	-	+	+

- = not applied; + = applied

3.4. Permitting procedure

The allocation of responsibilities within the discharge permitting procedure is shown in Table 4. In all countries, the applicant is responsible for supplying the effluent-related data and for effluent monitoring. In the UK, the applicant also performs the immission assessment.

Table 4. Allocation of responsibilities within the discharge permitting procedure.

	Germany	The Netherlands	UK (Eng. & Wales)	USA
Permit issued by	Federal state/ regional authority	Water Boards/regional or national authority	Environment Agency	US-EPA/ state[1]
Required effluent-related data supplied by	applicant	applicant	applicant	applicant[2]
Effluent monitoring	applicant	applicant	applicant	applicant
Immission assessment	p. authority	p. authority	applicant	p. authority

p. authority = permitting authority; 1 = In general, permitting is carried out by US-EPA nationally. Many states are delegated, i.e. they are allowed to do the permitting instead of US-EPA. However, they must follow US-EPA rules and regulations on permitting. US-EPA can rescind this delegation if they do not believe the state is carrying out its responsibilities. 2 = This concerns information related to plant operations, discharged chemicals and effluent quantities. Data on the receiving water are usually provided by the permitting authority. However, in case of disputes over these data, the applicants can gather their own data and provide them to US-EPA.

3.5. Operational aspects of immission assessment

Table 5 shows some application characteristics of immission assessment at the operational level. In the UK, immission assessment is performed for each permit, while in the USA, immission assessment is carried out if effluent data and calculations (or estimates) indicate that future water quality might fail to comply with water quality criteria. In Germany, the individual states have their own qualitative screening criteria to determine the need for immission assessment. The Netherlands lacks detailed guidelines on when immission assessment should be performed.

Table 5. Operational aspects of immission assessment.

	Germany	The Netherlands	UK (England & Wales)	USA
Application of immission assessment				
always	-	-	+	-
screening test[1]	±[2]	±	-	+
Types of water quality models applied				
mass balances	+	±	+	+
mixing zone models	-	±	±	+
system models	-	±	+	+
Types of models according to input definition				
steady-state	+	±	-	+
stochastic	-	-	+	+
dynamic	-	±	+	+
Model selection				
water body specific	-	±	+	+
data-dependent	-	±	+	+
guidelines	-	-	+	+

1 = based on a prediction of the future water quality, effluent and/or dilution data, a decision is made regarding the necessity of immission assessment; 2 = this applies to the situation in the federal state of Nordrhein-Westfalen; - = not applied; ± = occasionally applied; + = applied.

As outlined by Ragas *et al.* (1998), different types of models can be applied for immission assessment: mass balances, mixing zone models and system models (including catchment scale models). These models can either be steady-state (deterministic input values), stochastic (probability distributions as input values) or dynamic (time series as input values). Since detailed guidelines on immission assessment are lacking in the Netherlands, it is difficult to draw a clear picture of model application in this country. All kinds of models are available, but in practice they are rarely applied (De Bont *et al.* 1996, Ragas *et al.* 1997). Germany applies a steady-state mass balance, while the UK predominantly applies stochastic mass balances and stochastic or dynamic system models. Steady-state mixing zone models are rarely applied in the UK; where receiving water use dictates, such a model may be developed to establish spatial/temporal variation in the effluent plume. This might then be used to determine necessary changes in outlet design or location, or otherwise to determine the appropriate limit value for the discharge permit. The USA uses all of the above types of models for immission assessment, although the most common models used in water quality-based permitting are steady-state mass balances. The more sophisticated models usually only come into play when the cost of pollution reduction gets very high, and the permitted facility begins to question the accuracy of the simple model. The USA is the only country with well-elaborated recommendations in several guidance publications for the construction of mixing zones and the use of mixing zone models, although these are not required. Consequently, state implementations of mixing zones vary greatly, from using sophisticated mixing zone models to just calculating a dilution factor.

Both in the UK and the USA, model selection is associated with the type of water body and the available data. In both countries the opinion prevails that one general water quality model would not be compatible with the existing diversity of locations and situations.

3.6. The degree of elaboration of the immission-based approach

Table 6 lists a set of criteria relevant for policy decisions, such as costs, data requirement, user support and guaranteed level of protection. The guaranteed level of protection indicates the level of certainty associated with EQ-criterion compliance. A low level does not automatically indicate insufficient protection: it is very well possible that discharge limits based on the BAT-approach offer (more than) enough protection. However, this cannot be guaranteed without immission assessment (Ragas & Leuven 1996).

In Germany and the Netherlands, elaboration of the immission-based approach is limited. This leads to low costs and low data requirement, but also to a low guaranteed level of protection.

In the UK, the approach is reasonably well-elaborated, with ample documentation, support and scientific argumentation, a high data requirement and high costs. The guaranteed level of protection is high for substances for which quality objectives apply, but it is limited in the absence of toxicity objectives and a formalised mixing zone approach.

The immission-based approach has been elaborated most extensively in the USA. The procedure has been worked out for specific chemicals and for whole effluent toxicity. The approach has extensive documentation and user support, and a high level of scientific support. The data requirement generally seems (very) high, as are the estimated costs. This is rewarded by a high guaranteed level of protection.

Table 6. Degree of elaboration of the immission-based approach for discharge permitting.

	Germany	The Netherlands	UK (Eng. & Wales)	USA
Elaboration	+	±	++	+++
Documentation	+	-	++	+++
Support for users	-	+	++	+++
Scientific argumentation	-	-	++	+++
Data requirement	low	low	high	(very) high
Estimated costs	low	low	high	(very) high
Guaranteed level of protection	low	low	reasonable	high

- = not elaborated; ± = in proces of development; + = limited elaboration; ++ = reasonably elaborated; +++ = extensively elaborated.

4. Discussion

The immission assessment procedures of the various countries differ in numerous respects. Obviously, there are many ways to elaborate the immission-based approach. The European Commission is reviewing the collective European water quality Directives, in order to replace them with the forthcoming Water Framework Directive. In this respect, harmonisation of discharge permitting procedures (including the BAT- and EQ-approaches) may be worth considering, since it leads to equality of law for countries and companies in the EU, and improved efficiency through uniformity of regulations. If the EU intends to introduce a scientifically sound, practical, transparent and harmonised immission assessment procedure for discharge permitting, various options are available for its design. The present study shows that various decisions can be made. A number of important issues should be solved when harmonising the European immission assessment procedures (and the discharge permitting procedures in general). The most important questions that should be answered are:

- How should the immission-based approach be combined with the BAT-approach?
- What are the preconditions for application of the immission-based approach?
- How is the allocation of responsibilities between authorities and dischargers regulated in the discharge permitting procedure?
- For which substances does the immission-based approach apply?
- How should substances for which no EQOs apply be dealt with?
- How should EQOs be specified in space and time?
- Which environmental compartments should be considered during immission assessment?
- How should acute and chronic toxic effects be dealt with?
- Which models should be used to predict future water quality and derive additional ELVs through immission limits?
- How should discharge permit requirements be formulated or specified in the actual permit?

The answers to these questions may have major consequences for the ELVs in discharge permits. To achieve harmonisation at EU level, more research should be done on the consequences of different immission assessment procedures and assumptions (for a comparison of model predictions, see Ragas *et al.* (1998)), allowing the conclusion that a harmonised European immission assessment procedure is still a long way off. The well-elaborated design of the American immission-based approach, their concept of EQOs, and modelling expertise, are worth evaluating as a reference for ideas on how to tackle various issues in the decision making process regarding the development of a scientifically sound, transparent and harmonised immission assessment procedure.

5. Conclusions

1. All countries more or less combine the immission-based approach with the BAT-approach when permitting waste water discharges. The immission assessment procedures of the various countries differ in numerous respects, which shows that there are many ways to elaborate the immission-based approach.
2. The sets and types of objectives used in immission assessment vary between countries. Those in Germany, the Netherlands and the UK are rather similar, mainly due to EU regulations. Only the USA uses water quality objectives based on (effluent) toxicity in immission assessment, as well as objectives to avoid acute toxic effects.
3. The European countries included in the present study all use percentile scores as temporal specification of their EQOs. The USA uses a maximum allowable excursion frequency and duration for temporal specification of its EQOs. The USA is the only country to use spatial specifications in its EQOs. The European function-oriented EQOs lack temporal and spatial specifications.
4. The USA is the only country with well-elaborated recommendations for constructing mixing zones and the use of mixing zone models. However, these recommendations are not required and consequently state implementations of mixing zones vary greatly.
5. All countries apply an immission assessment procedure in discharge permitting, but the level of elaboration of the immission-based approach differs per country, ranging from highly detailed in the USA to very limited in the Netherlands.
6. The questions pertaining to the discussion are the most important issues to be solved in the development of a scientifically sound, transparent and harmonised immission assessment procedure. In this respect, the well-elaborated procedure of the USA is worth evaluating as a reference for ideas on how to tackle the important issues. Insight into the consequences of different options to elaborate these issues is vital, because of their possible impact on the actual ELVs in the discharge permit. Therefore, more research should be done on the consequences of different immission assessment procedures and assumptions. Consequently, a harmonised European immission assessment procedure seems still a long way off.

Acknowledgements

Part of this research has been financed by the Dutch national Institute for Inland Water Management and Waste Water Treatment (RIZA) of the Ministry of Transport, Public Works and Water Management (project RI-1772). The authors wish to extend their gratitude to Mr. C. Chubb, Mr. U. Irmer, Mr. J.H.H.M. Klerkx, Mr. G. LaVeck and Dr. W. Rocker for critical remarks on the manuscript.

References

Blumenschein, C. 1992. New regulations on water quality permitting. Pollution Engineering 25 (15): 68-72.

BLAK-QZ. 1993. Konzeption zur Ableitung von Zielvorgaben zum Schutz oberirdischer Binnengewässer vor gefährlichen Stoffen. Bund/Länder Arbeitskreis gefährliche Stoffen Qualitätsziele für oberirdische Gewässer, Berlin, Deutschland (in German).

Crawshaw, T. 1993. National Rivers Authority (NRA), UK. Pre-congress workshop, SETAC Effluent Toxicity Program: Implementation, Compliance and Enforcement, March 28, 1993. SETAC, Lisbon, Portugal.

De Bont, L.A.C., Leuven, R.S.E.W. & Ragas, A.M.J. 1996. Toepassing van waterkwaliteitsnormen in lozingsvergunningen van speerpuntbedrijven in het Rijnstroomgebied. H$_2$O 29 (11): 318-320, 325 (in Dutch, with English summary).

Höhne, I. & Irmer, U. 1995. Beurteilung der stofflichen Beschaffenheit von Fliessgewässern in der Bundesrepublik Deutschland: Kriterien und Klassifikationsschemata. Landesumweltamt Brandenburg & Umweltbundesamt Berlin, Deutschland (in German).

Irmer, U., Markard, Chr., Blondzik, K., Gottschalk, Chr., Kussatz, C., Rechenberg, B. & Schudoma, D. 1995. Quality targets for concentrations of hazardous substances in surface waters in Germany. Ecotoxicology and Environmental Safety 32: 233-243.

Irmer, U., Rocker, W. & Blondzik, K. 1997. Qualitätsanforderungen an Oberflächengewässer: Zielvorgaben, Qualitätsziele und chemische Gewässergüteklassifizierung. Acta Hydrochimica Hydrobiologica 25 (2): 62-70 (in German, with English summary).

Kraemer, R.A. (ed). 1996. Approaches to pollution control and the protection of the aquatic environment. Report of the Environment Agency and LAWA joint technical workshop. 25-26 April 1996, Brussels, Belgium.

LAWA. 1990. Forderungen der Wasserwirtschaft für eine fortschrittliche Gewässerschutzpolitik: LAWA 2000. Länderarbeitsgemeinschaft Wasser (LAWA), Deutschland (in German).

LWA. 1991. Allgemeine Güteanforderungen für Fliessgewässer (AGA): Entscheidungshilfe für die Wasserbehörden in wasserrechtlichen Erlaubnisverfahren. Landesamt für Wasser und Abfall Nordrhein-Westfalen, LWA-Merkblätter 7, Deutschland (in German).

NRA. 1994. Water quality objectives: Procedures used by the National Rivers Authority for the purpose of Surface Waters (River Ecosystem) (Classification) Regulations 1994. National Rivers Authority / Environment Agency, Bristol, UK.

NRA. 1996. National Rivers Authority discharge consents manual. Volume 24A/B, Pollution control. National Rivers Authority / Environment Agency, Bristol, UK.

OECD. 1996. Workshop on environmental requirements for industrial permitting. Reference guide. 9-11 May 1996, Paris, France.

Ragas, A.M.J. & Leuven, R.S.E.W. 1996. Immissiebeoordeling van afvalwaterlozingen. Een inventarisatie van uitgangspunten, procedures en modellen in het buitenlandse waterbeheer. Verslagen Milieukunde nr. 120, Vakgroep Milieukunde, Katholieke Universiteit Nijmegen, Nederland (in Dutch, with English summary).

Ragas, A.M.J., Haans, J.L.M. & Leuven, R.S.E.W. 1997. Selecting water quality models for discharge permitting. European Water Pollution Control 7 (5): 59-67.

Ragas, A.M.J., Van de Laar, B.J., Van Schijndel, A.M.J., Stortelder, P.B.M. & Klapwijk, S.P. 1998. The water quality-based approach in water pollution control: possibilities and restrictions. In: Nienhuis, P.H., Leuven, R.S.E.W. & Ragas, A.M.J. (eds). New concepts for sustainable management of river basins. pp 191-209. Backhuys Publishers, Leiden, The Netherlands.

Stortelder, P.B.M. & Van de Guchte, C. 1995. Hazard assessment and monitoring of discharges to water: concepts and trends. European Water Pollution Control 5 (4): 41-47.

Tonkes, M. & Botterweg, J. 1995. Totaal Effluent Milieubezwaarlijkheid. Ministerie van Verkeer en Waterstaat, RIZA document 94.020, Rijksinstituut voor Integraal Waterbeheer en Afvalwaterbehandeling (RIZA), Lelystad, Nederland (in Dutch).

US-EPA. 1991. Technical support document for water quality based toxics control. Office of Water, Environmental Protection Agency, Report No. EPA 505/2-90-001, Washington DC, USA.

Voeten, J.C.A.M. 1996. Inventarisatie van uitgangspunten en instrumenten bij emissie-immissiebeoordelingen door Nederlandse waterkwaliteitsbeheerders. Ministerie van Verkeer en Waterstaat, RIZA document 96.053X, Rijksinstituut voor Integraal Waterbeheer en Afvalwaterbehandeling (RIZA), Dordrecht, Nederland (in Dutch).

VROM. 1992. Milieukwaliteitsdoelstellingen bodem en water / Derde Nota Waterhuishouding. Ministerie van Volkshuisvesting, Ruimtelijke Ordening en Milieubeheer, Tweede Kamer, vergaderjaar 1991-1992, 21.990 / 21.250, nr.3, SDU-uitgeverij, Den Haag, Nederland (in Dutch).

APPLICATION OF THE WATER QUALITY-BASED APPROACH IN WATER POLLUTION CONTROL: POSSIBILITIES AND RESTRICTIONS

A.M.J. Ragas[1], B.J. Van de Laar[1], A.M.J. Van Schijndel[1], S.P. Klapwijk[2] &
P.B.M. Stortelder[3]
*[1] Department of Environmental Studies, University of Nijmegen, P.O. Box 9010,
6500 GL Nijmegen, The Netherlands; [2] Foundation for Applied Water Research
(STOWA), P.O. Box 8090, 3503 RB Utrecht, The Netherlands;
[3] Institute for Inland Water Management and Waste Water Treatment (RIZA),
P.O. Box 17, 8200 AA Lelystad, The Netherlands*

Abstract

The relation between the technology- and water quality-based approaches in water pollution control is a subject of international debate. At present, this is particularly true in the European Union, where both approaches are used in different ways by the various Member States, and where a new Water Framework Directive is forthcoming. It is within this scope that the present paper outlines the possibilities and restrictions of the water quality-based approach. It concentrates on discharge permitting and outlines the procedures followed by Germany, the Netherlands, the United Kingdom (UK) and the United States of America (USA). To illustrate the possible consequences of differences in discharge permitting procedures, four pollutant load case studies are presented which allow the conclusion that a combined technology- and water quality-based approach is the best option for setting emission limits. It prevents avoidable pollution, as well as violations of environmental quality objectives (EQOs). The results of the water quality-based approach strongly depend on what type of water quality model, input data and EQOs are being used. Harmonisation of these ingredients is necessary to prevent widely divergent pollutant loads and unequal treatment of dischargers under comparable conditions.

1. Introduction

One of the goals of sustainable water management is to control pollution sources in order to achieve good water quality. Two basic principles can be distinguished in pollution control: a pollution prevention principle and a carrying capacity principle (Fig. 1). The former is based on the idea that any form of pollution may have an adverse impact on water quality, and should therefore be prevented. Within this framework, source-oriented measures depend on the technological possibilities for emission reduction and their economic and social consequences. This results in technological standards, like the Best Practical Means (BPM), the Best Available Technology (BAT) and the Best Available Technique not Exceeding Excessive Cost (BATNEEC). This method of establishing source-oriented measures is referred to as the technology-based approach.

New concepts for sustainable management of river basins, pp. 191–209
edited by P.H. Nienhuis, R.S.E.W. Leuven and A.M.J. Ragas
© *1998 Backhuys Publishers, Leiden, The Netherlands*

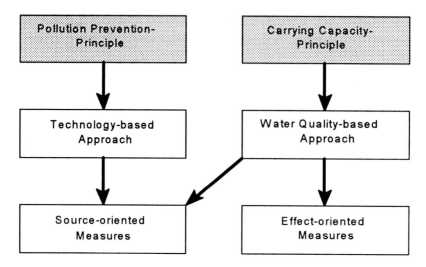

Fig. 1. Relations between the pollution prevention and carrying capacity principles, and the related technology- and water quality-based approaches in sustainable water management.

The carrying capacity principle is based on the idea that the environment can cope with certain pollutant loads: as long as the carrying capacity of a water system is not exceeded, no adverse effects will follow. In most cases, the carrying capacity is not established as an acceptable load, but laid down in environmental quality objectives (EQOs). If the actual environmental quality is worse than the EQO, effect-oriented measures should be taken, e.g. strewing of chalk in acidified lakes or remediation of contaminated soil. Source-oriented measures depend on whether or not EQOs are expected to be violated. This method of establishing source-oriented measures is referred to as the water quality-based approach.

The relation between the technology- and water quality-based approaches in water management is currently the subject of international debate, especially within the European Union (EU), where a new Water Framework Directive is forthcoming (Commission of the European Communities 1997, Kraemer 1996). Although all EU Member States apply both approaches to control water pollution, the degree of elaboration and the relation between the two differs (OECD 1996). One of the goals of the new EU Directive will be to harmonise these different procedures, improving uniformity of regulations and legal equality within the EU.

The proposed EU Water Framework Directive contains a combined approach in which the source-oriented measures of the water quality-based approach are additional to those of the technology-based approach. Such a combined approach has already been adopted for industrial facilities covered by the recent EU directive on Integrated Pollution Prevention and Control (96/61/EU) which comes into effect in 1999 for new discharges and in 2007 for existing discharges. In the USA, a combined technology- and water quality-based approach is already put into practice (Blumenschein 1992).

The goal of the present paper is to outline the possibilities and restrictions of implementing a water quality-based approach as a supplement to the technology-based approach. It concentrates on discharge permitting procedures for point sources. The first section outlines some of the theoretical backgrounds to the use of water quality models and EQOs in discharge permitting. This is followed by a survey of the application of the water quality-based approach in discharge permitting procedures of four countries (Germany, the Netherlands, the UK and the USA). To illustrate the consequences of differences in these procedures, six water quality models were selected and applied to four discharge situations, comparing the calculated pollutant loads. Also, a comparison was made with pollutant loads resulting from the technology-based approach. Based on these comparisons, conclusions are drawn concerning the possibilities and restrictions of the water quality-based approach in water pollution control.

2. Water quality models and EQOs in discharge permitting

The water quality-based approach in discharge permitting comes down to predicting future water quality, comparing it with EQOs and, if they are expected to be exceeded, deriving water quality-based emission limits. The basic ingredients of this procedure are a water quality model, input data and EQOs (Fig. 2). A comparison of the input data, models and EQOs used in Germany, the Netherlands, the UK and the USA, shows that they vary greatly (Ragas *et al.* 1997, Haans *et al.* 1998). The consequences of these differences for permitting requirements can only be assessed by understanding their interrelations. Therefore, these ingredients and their interrelations are discussed in more detail below. First, the relation between model types and EQOs is discussed, followed by the compatibility of model output and EQOs.

2.1. Model types and EQOs

The core of the water quality-based approach is a model which is used to predict future water quality and to derive emission limits which comply with EQOs. Basically, three types of water quality models can be distinguished:
- *Simple mass balances*, which are equations based on the principle of mass conservation (Warn & Brew 1980). It is assumed that complete mixing between discharge and ambient water takes place instantaneously. As a consequence, possible mixing zone effects near the outfall are neglected. EQOs used in combination with mass balances generally lack a spatial specification: they apply to the entire water system.
- *Mixing zone models*, which simulate the mixing process between discharge and ambient water. If the discharge does not meet EQOs inside the discharge pipe, violation of EQOs in the ambient water is inevitable. The area in which EQOs are exceeded is called the formal mixing zone. To ensure the integrity of the water system, the size of the formal mixing zone should be limited. EQOs used in combination with mixing zone models must include a spatial specification, e.g. the maximum length, width or surface area of the mixing zone.
- *Water system models*, which are complex model frameworks simulating water quality in an entire water system, e.g. a river basin. Water system modelling makes it possible to account for the interactions between multiple dischargers.

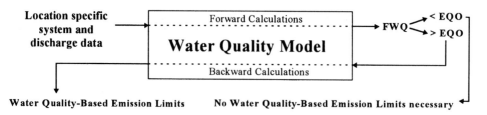

Fig. 2. The water quality-based approach in discharge permitting (FWQ = future water quality).

If these interactions are not accounted for, downstream dischargers depend on the performance of upstream dischargers. Application of system models does not have direct consequences for the type of EQOs used, but it necessitates permitting authorities to formulate schemes to allocate waste loads efficiently and fairly among dischargers.

2.2. Compatibility of model output and EQOs

An essential element of the water quality-based approach to discharge permitting is the comparison between predicted environmental quality and EQO. It is a prerequisite for this comparison that the time specifications of model output and EQO are compatible (Table 1). These time specifications depend on the way the EQO and the model account for variations in time. Most EQOs are specified as percentile scores, allowing the EQO to be exceeded during a limited period of time. It is also possible to specify the maximum allowable frequency and duration of excursions separately. Model output can be a single value, a probability distribution or a function of time, depending on the model used:

– *Steady-state models* use single values for all input variables and, consequently, model output is also a single value. The input values should reflect a system condition in which water quality must equal the EQO. The output of a steady-state model can be compared with both types of EQOs (a percentile score or an excursion frequency in combination with an excursion duration), provided the incidence of the simulated system condition corresponds to the time specifications of the EQO (US-EPA 1988a). To ensure this compatibility, the derivation of suitable input values should include a detailed analysis of the variability in system and discharge characteristics. In practice, this detailed analysis is often refrained from, resulting in incompatibility of model output and EQOs.

– *Stochastic models* define (some) variable parameters as probability distributions. This results in an output probability distribution, which can be used to check EQOs specified as percentile scores. EQOs with a maximum allowable excursion frequency and duration cannot be checked since the output probability distribution does not differentiate between these time characteristics. A 90-percentile score may imply one excursion for 10% of the period, as well as 10 excursions for 1% of the period.

– *Dynamic or continuous models* define (some) variable parameters as functions of time. Input data are time series, e.g. successive measurements of pollutant concentrations and flow. The output is a time series, which makes it possible to

Table 1. Compatibility between different types of model output and EQOs.

EQO specifications	Steady-state models	Stochastic models	Dynamic models
Percentile score	yes[1]	yes	yes
Excursion frequency and duration	yes[1]	no	yes

1 = provided the incidence of the system condition reflected by the input values corresponds to the time specifications of the EQO

check the excursion frequency and duration of EQOs. Percentile scores can also be checked, provided a frequency distribution is constructed from the output time series.

3. National application of the water quality-based approach

A detailed comparison of discharge permitting procedures in Germany, the Netherlands, the UK and the USA is presented elsewhere in this book (Haans *et al.* 1998). The following survey concentrates on the relation between the technology- and water quality-based approaches. Furthermore, the models and EQOs used by the various countries are placed within the theoretical framework presented in the previous paragraph.

Information on the various discharge permitting procedures was gathered by conducting a literature search. Furthermore, 51 water managers and scientists in Germany, the UK and the USA were contacted and asked to provide supplementary information (Ragas & Leuven 1996). Information on Dutch permitting procedures resulted from a study of the application of EQOs in discharge permits (De Bont *et al.* 1996), or was taken from Voeten (1996).

3.1. Germany

In German discharge permitting, priority is given to the technology-based approach. Emission limits result from branch-specific *"Minimum requirements for waste water discharges"*, which are established at federal level (Bundesanzeiger 233b 1992). If it is deemed necessary for the protection of the water system or specific water functions, the competent authorities may impose additional emission limits. The procedure for setting these limits varies among the federal States. Most States lack a detailed procedure and only provide indicative guidelines, as is the case in Baden-Württemberg (UMBS 1991). Nordrhein-Westfalen has relatively detailed guidelines on the setting of additional emission limits (MUNW 1991). It prescribes the application of a steady-state mass balance to predict future water quality. Officially, EQOs are specified as 90 percentile scores, but this specification is rather devoid of meaning within the context of discharge permitting, because the incidence of the system condition reflected by the prescribed input values is incompatible with this percentile score (Table 2). German EQOs do not include a spatial dimension. System models are not applied on a regular basis in German discharge permitting, and waste load allocation schemes are consequently lacking.

3.2. The Netherlands

The Netherlands, like most other European countries, predominantly uses a generic technology-based approach to set emission limits in discharge permits. Emissions of so-called Black Substances are limited by prescribing the Best Available Technology (BAT), while the Best Practicable Means (BPM) apply for other substances. An exception is made for relatively non-noxious substances, which are exclusively regulated through a water quality-based approach (MVW 1986).

National guidelines on elaboration and application of the water quality-based approach are lacking. In practice, this approach is elaborated and applied on a case-by-case basis, which makes it difficult to present a general picture of the water quality-based approach in Dutch permitting. The EQOs used are 90 percentile scores with no spatial dimensions. Application of system models and waste load allocation schemes is rare.

De Bont *et al.* (1996) examined the application of EQOs in 22 Dutch permits of major dischargers in the river Rhine basin. The permits were compared with a model of reference, reflecting the application of EQOs prescribed by Dutch legislation. Points were allocated for each permit provision that corresponded with the model of reference, with a maximum of 100 points. The results of the study are shown in Fig. 3. Only two permits scored over 50 points, and the average score was 30 points, allowing the conclusion that the water quality-based approach has been poorly and ambiguously elaborated in Dutch discharge permits.

The water quality-based approach in Dutch discharge permits was also examined by Voeten (1996), who interviewed 12 water managers involved in discharge permitting. He concluded that the principles and instruments used in deriving additional emission limits vary greatly and are sometimes mutually inconsistent.

3.3. The United Kingdom

The UK has a long tradition of applying the water quality-based approach. It predominantly uses stochastic mass balances like MCARLO and WARNB to predict future water quality. Stochastic system models like SIMCAT and TOMCAT are used for conventional water quality variables, such as oxygen, nitrogen and Biological Oxygen Demand (BOD). For some complex systems and discharges, dynamic system models like MIKE11 and QUESTS are used (NRA 1996).

The EQOs used in the UK are specified as percentile scores with no spatial dimensions. Besides EQOs, the UK also applies a "no deterioration" principle, which states that no change of more than 10% in the mean and 95 percentile concentrations of key determinants in the receiving water is allowed, unless there is insignificant environmental change as a consequence. Although system models are being applied, guidelines on the allocation of waste loads among multiple dischagers are lacking.

Since the introduction of the *Environmental Protection Act* in 1990, discharges of toxic substances are also controlled through a technology-based approach. This approach is considered more suitable to deal with relatively dangerous and stable pollutants, whereas a water quality-based approach is preferred for degradable pollutants. The UK has formulated branch-specific guidelines for emission control of so-called Schedule-A Processes (see e.g. HMIP 1993). Emission limits for individual

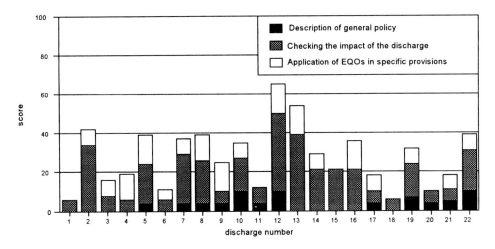

Fig. 3. Scores for the application of EQOs in 22 Dutch permits of dischargers in the river Rhine basin (De Bont *et al.* 1996). The allocation of points is divided over three categories: (1) description of general policy principles (maximum score 10 points), (2) checking the impact of the discharge (maximum score 60 points) and (3) application of EQOs in specific permit provisions (maximum score 30 points). A score of 100 points indicates a perfect match with the model of reference.

dischargers are based on these guidelines, taking into account the site-specific economic and social consequences of emission reduction. This is referred to as the Best Available Technique Not Entailing Excessive Cost (BATNEEC). The emission limits resulting from the water quality-based approach are considered minimum requirements, while those of the technology-based approach are considered additional.

3.4. The United States of America

The USA uses a combined technology- and water quality-based approach to determine discharge emission limits. Technology-based standards are considered minimum acceptable standards, without regard to the quality of the receiving waters. The Best Conventional Technology (BCT) is prescribed for conventional pollutants, e.g. BOD and Total Suspended Solids (TSS), while the Best Available Technology (BAT) that is economically feasible is used for other pollutants. Additional emission limits may follow from the water quality-based approach.

Deriving additional emission limits is a State competence in the USA. To facilitate this process, US-EPA has formulated guidelines (US-EPA 1991). Steady-state mixing zone models are recommended if adverse impacts within the mixing zone are expected. Otherwise, steady-state or stochastic mass balances will suffice. To assess the influence of multiple discharges US-EPA recommends to use steady-state, stochastic or dynamic system models.

Deriving EQOs is also a State competence in the USA. US-EPA recommends to use three types of EQOs: a Criterion Maximum Concentration (CMC) to prevent acute toxic effects on aquatic life, a Criterion Continuous Concentration (CCC) to prevent chronic toxic effects on aquatic life and a Reference Ambient Concentration (RAC) to protect human health (Fig. 4). The toxic dilution zone is limited by the

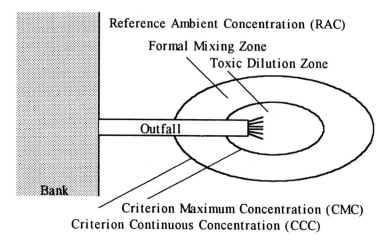

Fig. 4. The mixing zone concept of US-EPA (1991). The Criterion Maximum Concentration (CMC) is set to prevent acute toxicity and applies at the border of the toxic dilution zone. The Criterion Continuous Concentration (CCC) is set to prevent chronic toxicity and applies at the border of and outside the formal mixing zone. The Reference Ambient Concentration (RAC) is set to protect human health and applies outside the formal mixing zone.

CMC. The formal mixing zone is limited by the CCC. Outside the formal mixing zone the CCC and RAC apply. The EQOs include a maximum excursion frequency and duration. To allocate pollutant loads among multiple dischargers, several types of allocation schemes are being used (Chadderton *et al.* 1981).

4. Pollutant load case studies

The differences in discharge permitting procedures outlined in the previous paragraph may have consequences for the permitted pollutant loads. As far as the water quality-based approach is concerned, permitted loads depend on the model used to predict future water quality, the input data and the EQO. To illustrate the influence of those ingredients, six water quality models used in Germany, the Netherlands, the UK and the USA were selected and applied to four discharge situations. Each model is applied to each discharge situation for two different system conditions. First, pollutant loads were calculated with comparable input data and EQOs, allowing conclusions on the influence of model selection (scenario A). This was followed by a calculation of pollutant loads with input data and EQOs as prescribed or suggested by national guidelines, allowing an international comparison of permitted pollutant loads resulting from the water quality-based approach (scenario B). Finally, pollutant loads resulting from the technology-based approach were derived, allowing conclusions on the possible surplus value of the water quality-based approach in discharge permitting.

Table 2. Equations and input characteristics of the six models selected.

	Model equation	MB/ MZ	SS/ ST	Q_u	Q_e	C_u	EQO	Model specific parameters
NWMB	$P_L = f_1 (EQO \cdot [Q_u + Q_e] - Q_u \cdot C_u)$	MB	SS	MLF	mean	90p	90p	$f_1 = 1.0$
MCARLO	$C_e = \dfrac{EQO \cdot [Q_u + Q_e] - Q_u \cdot C_u}{Q_e}$	MB	ST	mean/5p	mean/SD	mean/SD	opt.	none
DMZ model	$P_L = f_x \cdot EQO \cdot (1.45 \cdot \sqrt[3]{f_{sa}} \cdot Q_u + Q_e)$	MZ	SS	LFNY	mean	mean	90p	$f_x = 0.1$ $f_{sa} = 0.1$
PSF model	$P_L = 2.07 \cdot f_{fl} \cdot (EQO - C_u) \cdot (Q_u + Q_e)$	MZ	SS	7Q10	mean	mean	4d10y	$f_{fl} = 0.25$
CORMIX	various equations[1]	MZ	SS	7Q10	mean	mean	4d10y	$L = 10W$
STREAMIX	$P_L = f_{mz} \cdot (EQO - C_u) \cdot (Q_u + Q_e) + Q_e \cdot C_u$	MZ	SS	7Q10	mean	mean	4d10y	$L = 10W$

$$f_{mz} = \frac{\sqrt{(2\frac{Y}{W}+1)^2 \cdot \pi \cdot D_y \cdot d \cdot \sqrt{g \cdot d \cdot S} \cdot \frac{L}{u}}}{W}$$

MB= mass balance; MZ = mixing zone model; SS = steady-state model; ST = stochastic model; Q_u = upstream flow; Q_e = effluent flow; C_u = upstream concentration; P_L= pollutant load; C_e = effluent concentration; f_1 = effluent variability correction factor; f_x = pollutant load allocation fraction; f_{sa} = mixing zone surface area fraction; f_{fl} = downstream flow fraction; f_{mz} = mixing zone fraction; Y = distance between discharge and nearest bank; W = water body width; d = water body depth; D_y = dimensionless lateral dispersion coefficient; g = acceleration constant; S = channel slope; L = maximum mixing zone length; u = flow velocity; SD = standard deviation; p = percentile; opt. = optional; MLF = mean low flow; LFNY = lowest flow in a normal year; 7Q10 = lowest 7 day average flow in 10 years; 4d10y = 4 day average concentration with a maximum excursion frequency of once every 10 years; 1 = Jirka *et al.* 1996

4.1. Model selection

The six models selected and the characteristics of their input values as prescribed or suggested by national guidelines are listed in Table 2. System models were not considered for selection, because of their complexity and large data need. The six models selected are:

– The *Nordrhein-Westfalen mass balance* (NWMB), a simple steady-state mass balance with a correction factor (f_1) to account for effluent variability (MUNW 1991). The factor is used to translate operational emission limits in emission limits which are monitored. State authorities suggest a value for f_1 between 1.7 and 4.0. Since the present paper aims at comparing annual average pollutant loads, the factor f_1 was neglected (i.e. set at 1.0).

– *MCARLO*, a stochastic mass balance applied in the UK (NRA 1996). Specification of a characteristic system condition to be modelled is unnecessary because of the stochastic nature of the model. The input probability distributions are defined by a mean value and a variability parameter, i.e. the standard deviation or 5 percentile score.

– The *Dutch Mixing Zone model* (DMZ model), a steady-state mixing zone model that has not yet actually been used in discharge permitting procedures. The model was developed by the Institute for Inland Water Management and Waste Water Treatment (RIZA) for an exploratory study on immission assessment of discharges (Voortman 1994). The steady-state model allows excursion of EQOs in a fraction of the surface area of the physical mixing zone. This surface area fraction is represented by the input parameter f_{sa}, which is set at 10%. The physical mixing zone is defined as the zone in which the concentration variation over the lateral direction of the water body exceeds 5%. To account for multiple discharges, the permitted pollutant load is only a fraction of the allowable pollutant load, represented by the input parameter f_x. If the upstream concentration lies below the EQO, this parameter is set at 10%, while it is set at 1% if it exceeds the EQO.

- The *Partial Stream Flow model* (PSF model), a steady-state mixing zone model suggested by Hutcheson (1992) for use in USA discharge permitting procedures. The basic assumption of the model is that a fraction of the downstream flow may be polluted up to EQO level. This fraction is represented by the input parameter f_{fl}, which was set at 25% in the calculations presented here.
- The *Cornell Mixing Zone Expert System* (CORMIX), a set of steady-state mixing zone models. CORMIX classifies a discharge, selects the proper simulation equations and predicts the size of the mixing zone. For easy reference, Table 2 does not contain the CORMIX model equations, and only the major input parameters are presented. Detailed information can be found in the CORMIX Users Manual (Jirka *et al.* 1996) and in Van Schijndel (1996). CORMIX was used in this study to calculate the pollutant load that corresponds with a mixing zone length of ten times the water body width.
- The *Stream Mixing Zone Model* (STREAMIX), a steady-state mixing zone model developed by US-EPA Region VIII (US-EPA 1995). The STREAMIX equation can be used to calculate a pollutant load that corresponds with a maximum mixing zone length. As in CORMIX, this length is set at ten times the water body width.

Note that the compatibility of prescribed input values and EQOs is questionable for the five steady-state models (NWMB, DMZ, PSF, CORMIX and STREAMIX). For example, the mean low upstream flow (MLF), the mean effluent flow and the 90 percentile upstream pollutant concentration prescribed for the German NWMB model, are unlikely to be compatible with the 90 percentile EQO. Although the prescribed input values of the other steady-state models are more in line with the applicable EQOs, compatibility can not be guaranteed since it depends on location specific discharge and ambient characteristics.

4.2. Input values and EQOs

The six selected models were applied to four discharge situations:
- a small copper discharge (Cu discharge) into a large river with a relatively stable flow;
- a large nitrogen discharge (N discharge) into a large river with a highly variable flow;
- a small cadmium discharge (Cd discharge) into a canal with a stable moderate flow;
- a large phosphate discharge (P discharge) into a canal with a stable small flow.

Table 3 lists the input data used to simulate the discharge situations. Data were obtained from the Institute for Inland Water Management and Waste Water Treatment (RIZA), the Province of Groningen and the Water Board Dollardzijlvest, all in the Netherlands. The data represent real-life discharge situations. Upstream pollutant concentrations (C_u) have been altered, because actual pollutant concentrations were in some cases higher than the EQO. The mean upstream concentrations were assumed to equal one fourth of the Dutch EQO. The standard deviation was derived from the original data assuming a constant coefficient of variation. Data on the variation in effluent flow (Q_e) and in effluent pollutant concentration (C_e), which were needed for MCARLO, were lacking. For all discharges, the coefficient of variation for the effluent flow was assumed to equal 0.3 and for the effluent pollutant concentration 1.0.

Table 3: Input data used to calculate pollutant loads for the four discharge situations. Legend: [a] = derived from the available data, based on the assumption of a lognormal distribution; [b] = assumed, based on personal judgement by the authors; [c] = default values used in CORMIX (0.25 for regular channels and 0.5 for moderately winding channels).

	Cu discharge	N discharge	Cd discharge	P discharge	Units
Upstream flow (Q_u)					
mean	350.0	271.00	15.00	0.0750	m^3s^{-1}
standard deviation	97.5[a]	463.00[a]	5.35[a]	0.0365	m^3s^{-1}
10 percentile	237.0[a]	30.60[a]	9.07[a]	0.0374[a]	m^3s^{-1}
5 percentile (MLF)	215.0	20.00	8.00	0.0316[a]	m^3s^{-1}
LFNY (2 percentile)	200.0	10.00	6.94[a]	0.0262[a]	m^3s^{-1}
7Q10 (0.2 percentile)	153.0[a]	4.72[a]	5.22[a]	0.0179[a]	m^3s^{-1}
Effluent flow (Q_e)					
mean	100.0	2000.0	10.0	403.0	$l\,s^{-1}$
standard deviation	30.0[b]	600.0[b]	3.0[b]	121.0[b]	$l\,s^{-1}$
Upstream concentration (C_u)					
mean	0.75	550.0	0.0500	37.50	µg l[-1]
standard deviation	0.25	94.0	0.0190	9.48	µg l[-1]
90 percentile	1.08[a]	674.0[a]	0.0748[a]	50.00[a]	µg l[-1]
Effluent concentration (C_e)					
coefficient of variation	1.0[b]	1.0[b]	1.0[b]	1.0[b]	none
Miscellaneous parameters					
flow velocity (u)					
10 percentile	0.91[a]	0.46[a]	0.121[a]	0.00320[a]	m s[-1]
7Q10	0.79[a]	0.21[a]	0.070[a]	0.00153[a]	m s[-1]
water body depth (d)					
10 percentile	2.60	0.89	2.50	1.80	m
7Q10	1.94	0.30	2.50	1.80	m
water body width (W)	100.0	75.0	30.0	6.5	m
distance nearest bank (Y)	5.0[b]	0.0[b]	5.0[b]	0.0[b]	m
channel slope (S)	0.00013	0.00050	0.00050[b]	0.00050[b]	none
dispersion coefficient (D_y)	0.5[c]	0.5[c]	0.25[c]	0.25[c]	none
Manning's n	0.025[b]	0.04[b]	0.02[b]	0.02[b]	none

The EQO is an important factor in determining the permitted pollutant load. The EQOs used and their characteristics are presented in Table 4, including the sources from which the EQOs originate. The German EQOs were taken from an overview of EQOs applied in the federal States (Höhne & Irmer 1995). If States applied diverging EQOs, the most stringent applicable EQO was chosen. In the UK, EQOs for total nitrogen and phosphate are lacking, while several EQOs apply for copper and cadmium. For copper, a water hardness below 10 mg/L $CaCO_3$ was assumed, resulting in a 95 percentile of 5 μg/L (NRA 1994). For cadmium, the EQO for potable abstraction was used (NRA 1996). The principle of "no deterioration" applicable in the UK was not considered in the case studies because it contains several ambiguously defined statements, like "insignificant" and "key determinants". Of the CMC, CCC and RAC values applicable in the USA, only the CCC values were considered (CFR 1992). American EQOs for total nitrogen and phosphate were not considered because they vary widely between States (total nitrogen: 1.5-10 mg/L; phosphate: 50-1,000 μg/L; US-EPA 1988b).

In scenario A, the input data of the five steady-state models consisted of the 90 percentile upstream flow (Q_u), the mean effluent flow (Q_e) and the mean upstream pollutant concentration (C_u). The input probability distributions of MCARLO were defined by the characteristics listed in Table 2. The 90 percentile Dutch EQO was used as a standard for environmental quality in all calculations of scenario A.

In scenario B, the input data and EQOs prescribed or suggested by national guidelines were used. The characteristics of these parameters are listed in Tables 2 and 4. The NWMB model requires the mean low upstream flow (MLF) as an input value. Since this parameter was not available for the case studies presented here, it was assumed to equal the 5 percentile flow. The DMZ model requires the lowest upstream flow in a normal year (LFNY). This input value was lacking for the Cd discharge and was therefore estimated on the assumption that it equals the 2 percentile flow. The 7Q10 flow used in the USA was assumed to equal the 0.2 percentile flow.

Table 4. EQOs used in model calculations (all in μg/L; p = percentile; 4d10y = the 4 day average concentration with a maximum excursion frequency of once every 10 years; NA = not available; NC = not considered).

	Cu	N(total)	Cd	P	Time Specification	Source
Germany	3.0	4,000	0.07	100	90p	Höhne & Irmer 1995
Netherlands	3.0	2,200	0.20	150	90p	VRO 1992
UK	5.0	NA	5.00	NA	95p	NRA 1994, 1996
USA	12.0	NC	1.10	NC	4d10y	CFR 1992

MCARLO calculations result in an effluent pollutant concentration (C_e), expressed in a 95 percentile value and a standard deviation (Table 2). To compare this outcome with the other model outcomes, an annual pollutant load (P_L) was derived. A lognormal distribution was assumed for effluent pollutant concentration (C_e) and effluent flow (Q_e), and both distributions were multiplied, using the Monte Carlo simulation technique. The software package Excel 5.0© (Microsoft Inc. 1994) was used in combination with Crystal Ball 3.0© (Decisioneering Inc. 1993) to perform these simulations. The mean value of the resulting pollutant load distribution was assumed to represent the annual pollutant load and used for comparison with the other model outcomes.

4.3. Model results

Table 5 lists the calculated pollutant loads using comparable input data and EQOs in all discharge situations (scenario A). The mass balances NWMB and MCARLO tend to result in the least stringent loads, while the DMZ model results in the most stringent loads. The ratio between these pollutant loads equals about a factor 10.

Table 6 lists the calculated pollutant loads using input values and EQOs prescribed or suggested by national guidelines (scenario B). The loads show a more irregular pattern than those in Table 5.

Table 5. Calculated pollutant loads (in kg/year) for the four discharges using comparable input data and Dutch EQOs (scenario A).

	Cu discharge	N discharge	Cd discharge	P discharge
NWMB	16,800	1,730,000	43.00	2,040
MCARLO	11,200	1,900,000	31.60	1,020
DMZ	1,510	157,000	3.86	202
PSF	8,710	878,00	22.20	809
CORMIX	2,480	608,000	26.80	2,110
STREAMIX	2,980	312,000	43.10	2,040

Table 6. Calculated pollutant loads (in kg/year) for the four discharges using the input data and EQOs as prescribed or suggested by national guidelines (scenario B).

	Cu discharge	N discharge	Cd discharge	P discharge
NWMB (Germany)	13,000	2,350,000	0.00	1,320
MCARLO (UK)	15,300	–	740.00	–
DMZ (Netherlands)	1,270	60,600	2.95	196
PSF (USA)	28,100	–	89.60	–
CORMIX (USA)	7,320	–	55.80	–
STREAMIX (USA)	8,260	–	174.00	–

4.4. Technology-based pollutant loads

Table 7 lists the pollutant loads resulting from the technology-based approach in Germany (Bundesanzeiger 233b 1992), the UK (HMIP 1993), the European Union (EU; Directive 85/513/EC) and the USA (Clean Water Act, Parts 415, 421 and 468). Since the Netherlands determine technology-based permit requirements on a case-by-case basis and lack general emission limitation guidelines, they are not listed in Table 7. EU directives apply in Germany, the Netherlands and the UK. However, the EU directives on toxic substances allow Member States to choose between the application of technology-based emission limits and the enforcement of EQOs. Member States are also allowed to set more stringent national emission limits and EQOs, as is the case in Germany and the UK (Table 7). It should be emphasised that most loads presented in Table 7 are minimum requirements. If economically feasible, authorities are likely to prescribe more stringent effluent limitations. To illustrate this, Table 7 also lists the currently permitted pollutant loads for three of the four discharges.

Table 7. Overview of the pollutant loads (in kg/year) for the four discharges, resulting from the technology-based approach. The loads listed for Germany, the European Union and the USA are minimum requirements. Stricter requirements are likely if they are economically feasible. The UK load for cadmium is a guideline instead of a minimum requirement (NA = not available).

	Cu discharge	N discharge	Cd discharge	P discharge
Germany	400	1,140,000	150.0	25,400
UK	NA	NA	15.8	NA
European Union	NA	NA	300.0	NA
USA	95	NA	26.0	NA
Current permit	73	2,370,000	NA	12,000

5. Discussion

5.1. Pollutant load case studies

The pollutant loads calculated in scenario A (Table 5) illustrate that the results of the water quality-based approach vary with the type of model used and the discharge situation simulated. The four mixing zone models resulted in pollutant loads which are a factor 2-12 more stringent than those produced by mass balances. This is logical since mass balances are based on the assumption of instantaneous complete mixing, resulting in a relatively large absorption capacity for pollutants.

Both mass balances (NWMB and MCARLO) produced comparable results. The differences between both models are due to the divergent methods for dealing with parameter variability (Warn & Brew 1980). MCARLO resulted in more stringent loads for the Cu, Cd and P discharges, because the large variability in effluent flow (Q_e) and pollutant concentration (C_e) results in a high variability in downstream river quality, which is not accounted for by the NWMB model. The NWMB model produced more stringent loads for the N discharge due to the relatively large variability in upstream flow (Q_u), resulting in an extreme 90 percentile input value. In MCARLO, this variability is "flattened" by the lesser variability in effluent flow (Q_e) and pollutant concentration (C_e).

The DMZ model produced the most stringent pollutant loads for all discharges. These stringent loads can almost entirely be attributed to the use of the pollutant allocation fraction (f_x). If this factor is omitted, the loads would be a tenfold higher. From this, it can be concluded that a regulatory mixing zone surface area equalling ten percent of the physical mixing zone results in only slightly stricter loads than mass balances assuming complete mixing.

The ratio between the loads produced by the NWMB, DMZ and PSF models is more or less constant. Apparently, limitation of the mixing zone surface area (DMZ model) is proportional to limitation of water flow (NWMB and PSF models). A comparison of the model equations (Table 2) confirms this thesis. All models allow a fixed part of the water flow to be polluted up to EQO level. The major differences between the models are the amount of water flow allowed to be polluted and the way the upstream pollutant concentration is dealt with.

The loads produced by CORMIX and STREAMIX are not proportional to the loads produced by the other models. This can be explained by comparing the model equations of STREAMIX with those of the other models (Table 2). In contrast with the other models, the fraction of water flow which is allowed to be polluted up to EQO level is not constant for STREAMIX. It depends on discharge and system specific parameters like the distance of the discharge to the nearest bank (Y), the water body width (W) and depth (d), the flow velocity (u) and the channel slope (S). Together these parameters determine the length of the mixing zone. A deeper water body, for example, will tend to result in a larger allowable pollutant load. So the load calculated by STREAMIX is determined by discharge and system specific parameters which do not influence the other models. Although the model equations of CORMIX are not listed in Table 2, CORMIX uses a comparable, but more sophisticated, procedure to calculate the maximum allowable pollutant loads (Jirka *et al.* 1996).

Remarkable are the differences in pollutant loads produced by CORMIX and STREAMIX. Both models calculate loads corresponding with a mixing zone length of ten times the water body width. Nonetheless, the differences amount up to a factor 2 for the N discharge. The differences are caused by the fact that CORMIX accounts for several mixing processes for which STREAMIX does not account, e.g. discharge-induced mixing, bottom attachment of the discharge plume and buoyancy. Accounting for discharge-induced mixing will tend to result in higher pollutant loads (e.g. for the N discharge), but buoyancy and bottom attachment will tend to result in smaller loads (e.g. for the Cd discharge).

The differences between the loads calculated in scenario B (Table 6) and those calculated in scenario A (Table 5) are mainly due to differences in the applicable

EQOs (Table 4), and to some extent to differences in input parameters (Table 2). The zero pollutant load for cadmium in the German situation (NWMB model) is due to a stringent EQO (Table 4) and a relatively high upstream cadmium concentration (Table 3). The large pollutant load for cadmium in the UK situation (MCAR-LO) is almost entirely caused by the lenient EQO. The Dutch pollutant loads (DMZ model) are more stringent because the lowest flow in a normal year (LFNY) is used, instead of the 10 percentile flow used for the calculations in Table 5. Although the USA (PSF model, CORMIX and STREAMIX) also applies more critical flow conditions (the 7Q10 flow), the resulting pollutant loads are less stringent due to lenient EQOs. Remarkable are the large differences in calculated cadmium loads between CORMIX and STREAMIX. Apparently, CORMIX produces more stringent loads under extremely critical flow conditions, like the 7Q10 flow.

Comparison of the pollutant loads of the water quality-based approach (Tables 5 and 6) with those of the technology-based approach (Table 7) leads to the conclusion that water quality-based considerations may result in additional emission limits. This is not the case for the Cu discharge, which can easily be understood if one realises that effluent dilution is high due to a large and stable river flow, resulting in a relatively large pollutant absorption capacity. For the N discharge, the results in Tables 5, 6 and 7 indicate that a water quality-based approach may result in additional emission limits. This can be explained by the relatively small dilution under critical conditions, resulting in a low pollutant absorption capacity. The same picture arises for the Cd discharge. For the P discharge, the results of the water quality-based approach are in all cases more stringent than those of the technology-based approach. This can be explained by the large effluent flow, which is much larger than the upstream flow under critical conditions, resulting in an almost negligible dilution.

5.2. Applicability of the water quality-based approach in water management

The case studies demonstrate that exclusive application of a technology-based approach in discharge permitting may result in pollutant loads which are inconsistent with EQOs, and which are likely to result in EQO violations. Exclusive application of a water quality-based approach does not result in EQO violations, but it may result in avoidable pollution which is inconsistent with the pollution prevention principle. It can therefore be concluded that a combined technology- and water quality-based approach is the best option to prevent both avoidable pollution and EQO violations. Such a combined approach does justice to the pollution prevention and carrying capacity principles, two basics of environmental management.

If a general combined technology- and water quality-based approach is to be introduced in European discharge permitting, it is clear that a great deal of harmonisation remains to be done. This applies to the technology-based approach, but even more so to the water quality-based approach. Differences in water quality models, input data and particularly EQOs may result in widely divergent pollutant loads. The first step to overcome these differences is to harmonise EQOs and to specify them in more detail. It is especially the temporal and spatial dimensions of EQOs which deserve more attention, i.e. where and when the EQOs apply in a water system. The EQO system advocated by US-EPA can serve as an example (US-EPA 1991). The second step is to harmonise and validate the models used to predict future water quality. Furthermore, successful implementation of a combined technology- and water quality-based approach calls for transparent guidelines, an extensive users support system for permitting authorities and easily accessible water quality data (Haans *et al.* 1998).

It should be noted that the case studies presented in this paper are rather theoretical exercises in which practical implications have not been considered. In practice, a water manager may be confronted with situations in which it is difficult to impose additional emission limits resulting from the water quality-based approach, for example in case of an existing discharge with acquired rights, or in case of a treatment plant for which additional emission limits are unfeasible. Therefore, it seems reasonable to distinguish between existing and new discharges. For existing discharges, the surplus value of the water quality-based approach lies in revealing water quality problems. Permits of discharges resulting in EQO violations should be revised with priority. This may result in adjustment of the production process, additional treatment of effluent, moving the discharge or redesigning the outfall. For new discharges, the emission limits resulting from the water quality-based approach should be considered a precondition for obtaining a permit.

Another practical problem of the water quality-based approach may be the enforcement of permit requirements. The monitoring and assessment of effects of individual discharges at field sites are often quite difficult because of interference with other point and non-point discharges (Stortelder & Van de Guchte 1995). This problem might be solved by translating the pollutant loads resulting from the water quality-based approach in technological requirements for effluent treatment and adopting these requirements in the actual permit. In such a situation, enforcement of permit requirements can be restricted to checking the actual performance of the effluent treatment units.

The case studies presented in this paper deal with pollution from point sources. However, the water quality-based approach may also be useful when dealing with other sources of pollution, e.g. intermittent discharges or non-point sources. As regards intermittent discharges, the approach can be applied to determine the capacity and location of overflow basins. With regard to non-point sources, the water quality-based approach can be used to reveal the contribution of these sources to the total pollutant load in a water system. An example of this application is outlined elsewhere in this book (Dogterom *et al.* 1998).

6. Conclusions

Compared to the exclusive application of a technology-based approach, additional application of a water quality-based approach may have a surplus value for water pollution control. In particular it may prevent EQO violations in discharge situations with low effluent dilution. However, the results of a water quality-based approach strongly depend on the water quality models, the input data and the EQOs used. If a water quality-based approach is to be applied within a legal context, e.g. for discharge permitting, it is important that these aspects are harmonised. Otherwise, it may result in widely divergent pollutant loads and unequal treatment of dischargers under comparable conditions. Furthermore, preconditions for the introduction of a water quality-based approach are the formulation of transparent guidelines, an extensive users support system for permitting authorities and easily accessible water quality data.

Acknowledgements

Part of this study has been financed by the Dutch Institute for Inland Water Management and Waste Water Treatment (RIZA; project RI-1772). The authors are greatly indebted to RIZA Dordrecht, the Province of Groningen and the Water Board Dollardzijlvest for providing data. The authors are grateful to J.H.H.M. Klerkx (Translation Bureau Bèta, Maastricht), G. LaVeck (US-EPA, Watershed Modeling Section, Washington), R.S.E.W. Leuven (University of Nijmegen, Department of Environmental Studies) and A.E. Warn (UK Environment Agency, Anglian Office, Peterborough) for critical comments and suggestions for improvement on an earlier version of this paper.

References

Blumenschein, C. 1992. New regulations on water quality permitting. Pollution Engineering 24 (15): 68-75.
Bundesanzeiger 233b. 1992. Bekanntmachung der Neufassung der Allgemeinen Rahmen-Verwaltungsvorschrift über Mindestanforderungen an das Einleiten von Abwasser in Gewässer. Rahmen-AbwasserVwV vom 25. november 1992, Bonn, Germany (in German).
CFR. 1992. Water quality standards; Establishment of numeric criteria for priority toxic pollutants; States' compliance; Final rule. Federal Register, Part II, 40 CFR Part 131, United States Environmental Protection Agency, Report EPA/823/Z-92-001, Washington DC, USA.
Chadderton, R.A., Miller, A.C. & McDonnell, A.J. 1981. Analyses of waste load allocation procedures. Water Resources Bulletin 17: 760-766.
Commission of the European Communities 1997. Proposal for a counsel directive establishing a framework for Community action in the field of water policy. COM(97) 47 final, Brussels.
De Bont, L.A.C., Leuven, R.S.E.W. & Ragas, A.M.J. 1996. Toepassing van waterkwaliteitsnormen in lozingsvergunningen van speerpuntbedrijven in het Rijnstroomgebied. H₂O 29 (11): 318-320 & 325 (in Dutch).
Dogterom, J., Van der Wiele, P.J. & Buijs, P.H.L. 1998. Diffuse loadings as a yet unsolved problem for receiving water bodies (rivers). In: Nienhuis, P.H., Leuven, R.S.E.W. & Ragas, A.M.J. (eds), New concepts for sustainable management of river basins. pp 211-228. Backhuys Publishers, Leiden, The Netherlands.
Haans, J.L.M., Leuven, R.S.E.W. & Ragas, A.M.J. 1998. Immission assessment procedures for discharge permitting. In: Nienhuis, P.H., Leuven, R.S.E.W. & Ragas, A.M.J. (eds), New concepts for sustainable management of river basins. pp 179-189. Backhuys Publishers, Leiden, The Netherlands.
HMIP. 1993. Chief inspector's guidance to inspectors. Environmental protection act 1990. Process guidance note IPR 4/23. Processes involving the use or release of cadmium or any compounds of cadmium. Her Majesty's Inspectorate of Pollution (HMIP), Department of the Environment, Bristol. HMSO publications, London, UK.
Höhne, I. & Irmer, U. 1995. Beurteilung der stofflichen Beschaffenheit von Fliessgewässern in der Bundesrepublik Deutschland: Kriterien und Klassifikationsschemata. Landesumweltamt Brandenburg / Umweltbundesamt Berlin, Germany (in German).
Hutcheson, M.R. 1992. Waste load allocation for conservative substances to protect aquatic organisms. Water Resources Research 28: 215-220.
Jirka, G.H., Doneker, R.L. & Hinton, S.W. 1996. User's manual for CORMIX: A hydrodynamic mixing zone model and decision support system for pollutant discharges into surface waters. Technical Report, DeFrees Hydraulics Laboratory, School of Civil and Environmental Engineering, Cornell University, Ithaca, New York, USA.

Kraemer, R.A. 1996. Approaches to pollution control and the protection of the aquatic environment. Environment Agency and LAWA Joint Technical Workshop, Brussels, 25 & 26 april 1996. Environment Agency, Bristol, UK.

MUNW. 1991. Allgemeine Güteanforderungen für Fliessgewässer (AGA): Entscheidungshilfe für die Wasserbehörden in wasserrechtlichen Erlaubnisverfahren. Ministerium für Umwelt, Raumordnung und Landwirtschaft des Landes Nordrhein-Westfalen, Ministerialblatt für das Land Nordrhein-Westfalen 42: 863-874, Köln, Germany (in German).

MVW. 1986. De waterkwaliteit van Nederland. Indicatief meerjarenprogramma water 1985-1989. Ministerie van Verkeer & Waterstaat (MVW), Tweede Kamer 1984-1985, 19153, nrs. 1-2, SDU-uitgeverij, Den Haag, The Netherlands (in Dutch).

NRA. 1994. Water quality objectives: procedures used by the National Rivers Authority for the purpose of the Surface Waters (River Ecosystem) (Classification) Regulations 1994. National Rivers Authority (NRA), Bristol, UK.

NRA. 1997. Discharge consents manual. Volume 024 A/B. Pollution Control. National Rivers Authority / Environment Agency, Bristol, UK.

OECD. 1996. Workshop on environmental requirements for industrial permitting. Reference guide. 9-11 may 1996, Paris, France.

Ragas, A.M.J. & Leuven, R.S.E.W. 1996. Immissiebeoordeling van afvalwaterlozingen. Vakgroep Milieukunde, Verslagen Milieukunde nr 120, Katholieke Univerisiteit Nijmegen, The Netherlands (in Dutch).

Ragas, A.M.J., Haans, J.L.M. & Leuven, R.S.E.W. 1997. Selecting water quality models for discharge permitting. European Water Pollution Control 7 (5): 59-67.

Stortelder, P.B.M. & Van de Guchte, C. 1995. Hazard assessment and monitoring of discharges to water: concepts and trends. European Water Pollution Control 5(4): 41-47.

UMBS. 1991. Verwaltungsvorschrift des Umweltministeriums zur Durchführung des §7a Wasserhaushaltgesetz (WHG) und des Abwasserabgabengesetzes (AbwAG). Umweltministerium des Landes Baden-Württemberg, Gemeinsames Amtblatt des Landes Baden-Württemberg S.946, Staatsanzeiger für Baden-Württemberg GmbH, Stuttgart, Germany (in German).

US-EPA. 1988a. Technical guidance on supplementary stream design conditions for steady-state modeling. United States Environmental Protection Agency, Office of Water, Report EPA/440/4-88-091, Washington DC, USA.

US-EPA. 1988b. Water quality standards summaries. United States Environmental Protection Agency, Office of Water, Reports EPA/440/5-88/032 – EPA/440/5-88/088, Washington DC, USA.

US-EPA. 1991. Technical support document for water quality-based toxics control. United States Environmental Protection Agency, Office of Water, Report EPA/505/2-90-001, Washington DC, USA.

US-EPA. 1995. Stream mixing zone model STREAMIX I (Version 2). User's Guide. United States Environmental Protection Agency, Region VIII, Denver, Colorado, USA.

Van Schijndel, A.M.J. 1996. Immissietoetsing van afvalwaterlozingen: een vergelijking van waterkwaliteitsmodellen en -normen. Vakgroep Milieukunde, Verslagen Milieukunde nr 137, Katholieke Universiteit Nijmegen, The Netherlands (in Dutch).

Voeten, J.C.A.M. 1996. Inventarisatie van uitgangspunten en instrumenten bij emissie-immissie-beoordelingen door Nederlandse waterkwaliteitsbeheerders. Rijksinstituut voor Integraal Zoetwaterbeheer en Afvalwaterbehandeling (RIZA), Werkdocument nr 96.053X, Lelystad, The Netherlands (in Dutch).

Voortman, A.J. 1994. De invloed van een mengzone benadering op lozingseisen: Rivieren en kanalen. Rijksinstituut voor Integraal Zoetwaterbeheer en Afvalwaterbehandeling (RIZA), Werkdocument nr 94.112X, Lelystad, The Netherlands (in Dutch).

VROM. 1992. Milieukwaliteitsdoelstellingen bodem en water / Derde nota waterhuishouding. Ministerie van Volkshuisvesting, Ruimtelijke Ordening en Milieubeheer, Tweede Kamer, Vergaderjaar 1991-1992, 21.990 / 21.250, nr. 3, SDU-uitgeverij, Den Haag, The Netherlands (in Dutch).

Warn, A.E. & Brew, J.S. 1980. Mass balance. Water Research 14: 1427-1434.

DIFFUSE LOADINGS AS A YET UNSOLVED PROBLEM FOR RECEIVING WATER BODIES

J. Dogterom, P.J. Van der Wiele & P.H.L. Buijs
International Centre of Water Studies (ICWS BV), P.O.Box 1399, 3800 BJ Amersfoort, The Netherlands

Abstract

This paper briefly describes the main types of diffuse loadings that presently and in the future pose problems to achieve internationally agreed water quality objectives for the basins of the rivers Rhine and Meuse. The main problems are emissions of nutrients (mainly from agricultural sources), emission of enteropathogens, like *Giardia* and *Cryptosporidium* from untreated sewage and run off of manure, and run off of polar pesticides as a result of application by municipalities and farmers.

Reduction of non-point pollution is expected for nutrients and the enteropathogens by reducing the discharges of untreated sewage, in particular in the Meuse river basin, and by extending nutrient removal capacity in existing sewage treatment plants. Agricultural run off of nutrients and polar pesticides will be reduced by introducing good agricultural practices based on EU-directives.

Scenario studies show that water quality objectives will not be realized, however, without taking extra measures. A case study is reported that shows that technical possibilities exist to address non-point source pollution at the source by identification of specific user groups of pesticides and quantification of emissions by these groups with the help of specific problem oriented monitoring programmes.

1. Introduction

The issue of diffuse or non-point sources is at present one of the greatest challenges in water resources management. The pollution from non-point sources is relevant to groundwater resources as well as surface water resources, including rivers, lakes and small standing waters. The main pollutants are nutrients, in particular nitrogen compounds, and polar pesticides.

In polluted river basins with a very high density of population and industries, like the Rhine and Meuse, clean-up efforts have been targeted between 1960 and 1985 on point sources, being an easily to identify target group. The non-point sources, like agriculture and traffic, being the more difficult groups to address, have got wider attention only the last 10 years, in particular in relation to the eutrophication risks for coastal seas. The North Sea Action Plan in 1987 can be regarded as the start of the breakthrough to address non-point sources of nutrients. At the same time, the shift in agricultural use from mostly non-polar chlorinated pesticides to more polar pesticides, like atrazin, bentazon and diuron, has introduced the problem of groundwater pollution. Since polar pesticides do hardly adsorb to soil, they percolate into groundwater.

New concepts for sustainable management of river basins, pp. 211–228
edited by P.H. Nienhuis, R.S.E.W. Leuven and A.M.J. Ragas
© *1998 Backhuys Publishers, Leiden, The Netherlands*

A problem receiving increased attention is the contamination of drinking water resources with parasitic protozoa *Cryptosporidium* and *Giardia*. Rivers with discharges of untreated sewage and/or high agricultural run-off usually contain such numbers of these protozoa, that a significant health risk exists.

Different approaches are applied to address non-point sources. These approaches are incorporated in policy documents, usually adopted at EU level. These depend to a great extent on the voluntary cooperation of in particular the agricultural sectors in the EU member states and are therefore difficult to enforce. Some recent technical developments reveal approaches to address non-point sources, which are similar to the approach to address point sources. A recent case study on the agricultural and municipal run off of pesticides in a Dutch small river catchment area shows promising results.

This paper briefly summarizes the problem of pollution from non-point sources with nutrients, *Cryptosporidium* and *Giardia*, and toxic compounds, in particular polar pesticides, in the Meuse and Rhine river basins.

2. Nutrients

After bacteriological pollution, eutrophication is probably the most wide spread problem world wide in water resources management. Growing populations and bio-industry cause high emissions of nitrogen and phosphorous compounds. The technology to remove these compounds from sewage is, though available, very expensive. Untreated sewage and agricultural run-off from manure and fertilizer application cause uncontrolled emissions. Cleaning up of river basins usually starts with the point sources, putting non-point sources lower on the agenda. The history of cleaning the rivers Rhine and Meuse is illustrative in this respect. While loads of heavy metals and other potentially toxic anthropogenic compounds have been reduced with often more then 80% in the last 20 years, loads of nitrogen compounds have been reduced with less then 30% in the Rhine and have stayed at the same level in the river Meuse (Buijs 1995). For phosphorous compounds the figures for the Rhine are better: 75% reduction in 20 years. Again for the Meuse no changes. Governments in the Rhine basin had committed themselves to reduce riverine discharge of total-nitrogen (N_{tot}) and total-phosphorous (P_{tot}) with 50% between 1985 and 1995 (Buijs 1995). For N_{tot}, this objective clearly has not been achieved. A set of new measures has been defined based on EU directive 91/271/EC concerning urban waste water treatment and on directive 91/676/EC, the nitrate directive on agricultural run off, which should lead to a further reduction. Based on these measures, a prognosis has been made for the transboundary loads of N_{tot} in the rivers Rhine and Meuse (Buijs 1995). The results are shown in Fig. 1 (Rhine) and Fig. 2 (Meuse).

These figures show that without additional measures the 50% reduction objective set for 1995, will even in 2015 not be achieved. Further measures are necessary and will be most effective if they are directed towards the agricultural run off and urban waste water.

For P_{tot}, similar prognoses have been made (Buijs 1995), which are presented in Fig. 3 (Rhine) and Fig. 4 (Meuse).

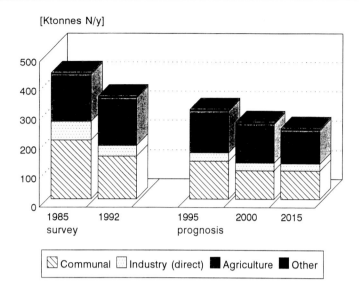

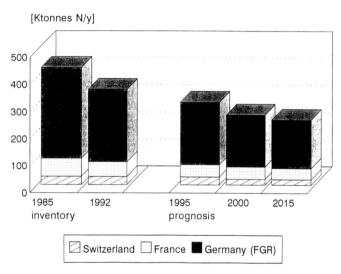

Fig. 1. Rhine: foreign contributions to total N emissions: per country and per category (natural background loads not included; Buijs 1995).

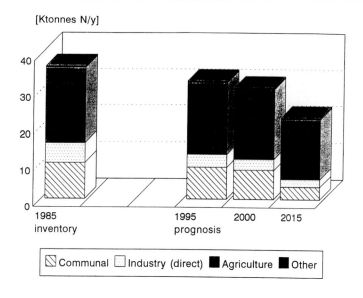

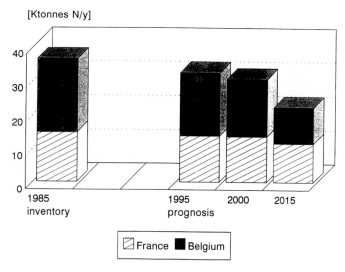

Fig. 2. Meuse: foreign contributions to total N emissions: per country and per category (natural background loads not included; Buijs 1995).

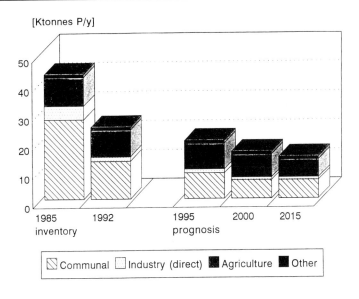

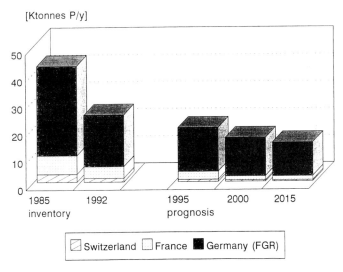

Fig. 3. Rhine: foreign contributions to total P emissions: per category and per country (natural background loads not included; Buijs 1995).

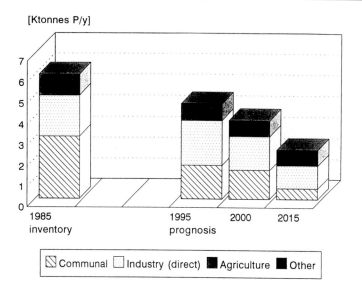

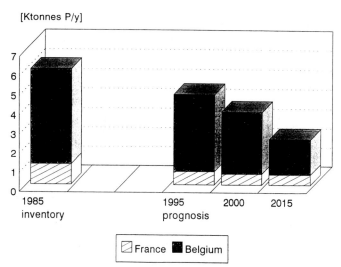

Fig. 4. Meuse: foreign contributions to total P emissions: per category and per country (natural background loads not included; Buijs 1995).

The P_{tot} prognoses are better then for N_{tot}, in particular for the Rhine. It is expected, that in 2015, P_{tot} concentrations in the river Rhine will be at the target value of 0.15 mg/l. For the Meuse, substantial improvements are expected after 2000, assuming that by then many new municipal sewage treatment plants will be constructed.

Figs. 5 and 6 show the development of emissions of N_{tot} and P_{tot} from different emission categories for the Netherlands, compared to transboundary import. This development is based on the current policy scenario. For N_{tot}, objectives for 1995 at the national level have not been achieved and will probably not be achieved by 2015. For P_{tot} the results in 1995 are practically on track.

3. *Cryptosporidia* and *Giardia*

It is estimated that enteropathogens world wide cause over 1 billion cases of infection and more than 1.000.000 deaths per year (Girdwood 1995). The majority of these infections occurs in non-industrialised countries. However, infection with *Cryptosporidium* and *Giardia* also impose a risk in industrialised countries. These enteropathogens can be lethal for specific groups like AIDS patients, while in healthy persons infections cause among others diarrhoea and loss of weight. Infections occur through the faecal-oral route from animals to humans and vice versa. The main vector is water, and infections occur in particular through bathing in open water.

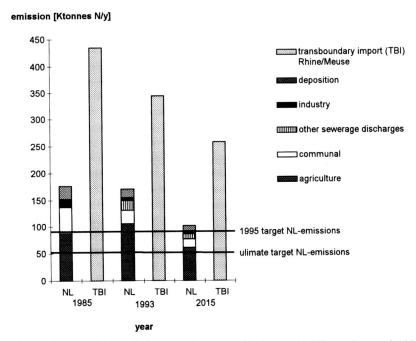

Fig. 5. Changes in the emission of nitrogen – 'current policy' scenario (Wagemaker *et al.* 1997).

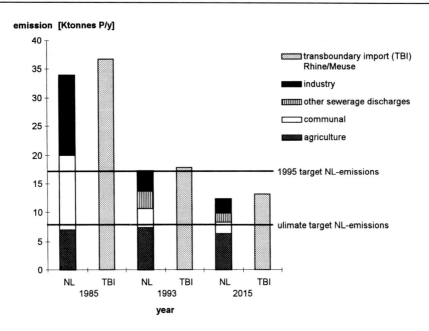

Fig. 6. Changes in the emission of phosphorous – 'current policy' scenario (Wagemaker *et al.* 1997).

Epidemic infections have been reported in the USA and the UK (Medema & Ketelaars 1995). Since the production of drinking water in the Netherlands will gradually shift from mainly groundwater resources to more surface water, this type of contamination is getting more attention. Research in a number of industrialised countries has revealed that *Giardia* and *Cryptosporidium* usually occur in surface water in which treated or untreated sewage water is discharged (Exner & Gornik 1991, Le Chevallier *et al.* 1991, Rose *et al.* 1991, Ketelaars *et al.* in prep).

Contamination with enteropathogens can be drastically reduced by proper treatment of surface water in particular by extensive treatment with coagulation, flocculation, filtering and disinfection. However, even with such treatment, infection risk cannot be completely ruled out. Infection can even occur in situations where the quality of drinking water meets all bacteriological quality standards. Because of these risks, there is a growing interest to determine the occurrence frequency of the pathogens in drinking water and in rivers used to produce drinking water. Since the pathogens are related to faecal contamination, in particular from untreated sewage and manure from livestock, they typically originate from non-point sources.

The Dutch drinking water companies have investigated the occurrence of *Cryptosporidia* and *Giardia* in the Rhine and Meuse rivers, which both are sources of raw surface water. Densities of *Cryptosporidia* and *Giardia* have been determined at intakes of river water for drinking water production in the Rhine and Meuse and at monitoring stations at the borders with Germany and Belgium. An inventory was made of potential non-point sources. The results have been reported recently (Medema *et al.* 1996). Table 1 shows the results of density measurements at 3 locations in each river. Samples were taken in the autumn of 1995. Earlier research revealed that densities are higher in the winter season. For *Cryptosporidium*, 87% of the samples were positive and densities varied from 0.6-100 per litre, for *Giardia* 100% of the samples were positive and densities varied form 0.8-100 per litre.

With these findings, the contamination of the Rhine and Meuse appears to be of the same order as in rivers in other industrialised countries. Based on these densities and the flow of both rivers, the protozoa loads are 4-9 x 10^{11}/day for *Cryptosporidium* and 2-4 x 10^{12}/day for *Giardia* in the river Rhine at the Dutch-German border at Lobith and 5-45 x 10^9/day for *Cryptosporidia* and 1-8 x 10^{11}/day for *Giardia* in the river Meuse at the Dutch-Belgian border at Eijsden. Based on these densities, it is concluded that highly effective treatment techniques have to be applied in order to achieve an acceptable infection risk, which is set at 1 per 10,000 consumers per year (Medema *et al.* 1996).

Table 1. Densities in sampling locations at the river Rhine (week 40-48, 1995) and Meuse (week 41-47, 1995) corrected for recovery of analysis (Medema *et al.* 1996).

Cryptosporidium

	number of samples	number positive	density mean	density min	density max
Meuse					
Tailfer	4	4	34	1,3	100
Eijsden	4	4	5,3	1,9	13
Keijzersveer	4	4	4,1	0,6	10
Rhine					
Lobith	5	5	4,5	0,6	9,4
Zwolle	5	3	4,3	<0,1	19
Nieuwegein	5	3	12	<0,1	32

Giardia

	number of samples	number positive	density mean	density min	density max
Meuse					
Tailfer	4	4	94	29	180
Eijsden	4	4	95	38	210
Keijzersveer	4	4	19	0,8	35
Rhine					
Lobith	5	5	22	7,5	33
Zwolle	5	5	24	12	57
Nieuwegein	5	5	13	0,8	19

In order to prepare proposals for additional measures to reduce this type of contamination, as a first step an inventory of potential sources of the protozoa in the river Meuse basin was made, which could then be followed by a monitoring campaign at these sources (Niederländer 1996). Discharges of untreated sewage and agricultural run off after application of manure, are expected to contribute largely to this contamination. The inventory revealed that in particular in the Belgian part of the river Meuse catchment, discharge of untreated sewage is common practice. More than 50% of sewage water is not treated. Fig. 7 shows the results.

The catchment was split in 6 subcatchments: no I is mainly situated in France, no II and III mainly in Belgium, no V in Germany and no IV and VI in the Netherlands. Since agricultural run off after manuring is expected to be an important source, an inventory of live-stock numbers in the same subcatchments was made as well. Fig. 8 shows the results.

Fig. 8 shows that numbers of live stock are the highest in the Dutch part of the Meuse catchment. A direct link between these live stock numbers and the contamination of surface water could not be demonstrated.

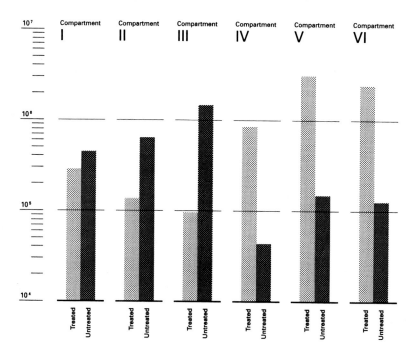

Fig. 7. Total amount of sewage water per subcatchment in the Meuse catchment: discharged treated or untreated (per 100,000 i.e.; Medema *et al.* 1996).

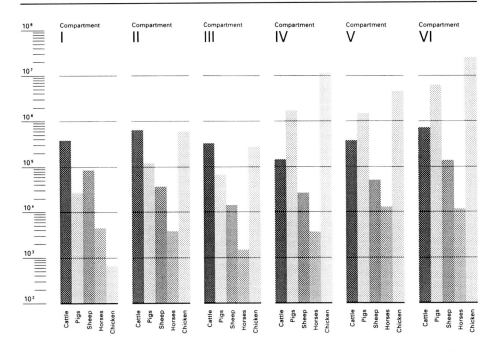

Fig. 8. Numbers of live stock per subcatchment in the Meuse catchment (Medema *et al.* 1996).

4. Pesticides

Recently, the Netherlands Institute for Inland Water Management and Waste Water Treatment (RIZA) has published an extensive review on the use of pesticides, emission routes and a prognosis for 2015 of use and emission of pesticides in the Netherlands (Wagemaker *et al.* 1997). The use of pesticides in active compound as kg/hectare in the Netherlands is by far the highest in the world. As a consequence, extensive research has been done on emission routes and loads. In 1985, the agricultural sector used 21.000 ton active compound, which is 20 kg/hectare. For some cultures like bulb growing, 100 kg active compound per hectare has been applied. In 1995, total use had been reduced with 40%, nevertheless the Netherlands has the highest use of all neighbouring countries. It is not only the agricultural sector that uses these high amounts. Park services of municipalities use significant amounts, and the army and the railway company as well. For some pesticides, municipal use equals or exceeds the agricultural use as shown in the case study in paragraph 5. During application, pesticides can be emitted along a number of routes. Fig. 9 shows the result of an analysis of emission routes to surface water for 5 different pesticides.

Atmospheric deposition, run off and wash-out are the most important transport routes for pesticides. It is clear, that to influence these emission routes, good agricultural practices during the application process by individual farmers are crucial. Programmes for education, stimulation and, sometimes, financial incentives are needed to influence this behaviour. Present measures are directed towards admission per-

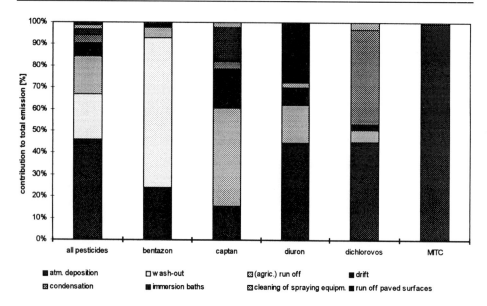

Fig. 9. Importance of various emission routes for all and some individual pesticides in 1993 (Wagemaker *et al.* 1997).

mits for a smaller number of different compounds and technical measures to reduce emission during application, like careful cleaning of equipment, discharge permits for green houses, special protecting measures in fruit farms, limitation for application in bulb cultures and a few others. This has resulted in an average reduction of emissions of 11% for 20 different compounds between 1985 and 1993 (Wagemaker *et al.* 1997).

Figs. 10 and 11 show the result of a scenario study by Wagemaker *et al.* (1997) on the development of use and emission until 2015 of these 20 compounds, when additional measures would be implemented.

This scenario, called 'SYSTEEM', is based on a set of extra measures that can be categorised as follows:
– environmentally sound procedures for filling, cleaning and storage of spraying equipment;
– introduction of physical barrier between receiving water body and fields;
– technologically controlled emission routes (recirculation of drain water and condense water; prevention of losses from immersion baths).

This results in about 16 different and specific measures, a selection of which can be applied for different types of compounds and cultures. The total emission reduction that can be achieved by implementation of these measures is more than 50% for 18 of the 20 compounds studied (for 2 it is less than 50%). The emission via air to surface water will be reduced with 90% in 2015. Implementation of these measures brings considerable costs to the agricultural sector. This is estimated at 600 million Dutch guilders a year, which equals about 300 million EURO (Wagemaker *et al.* 1997).

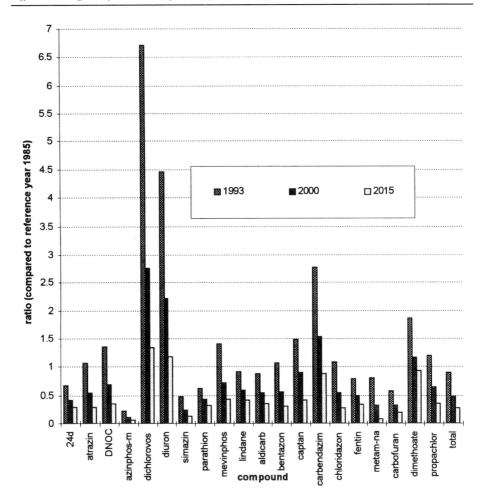

Fig. 10. Changes in the consumption of pesticides – 'SYSTEEM' scenario (Wagemaker *et al.* 1997).

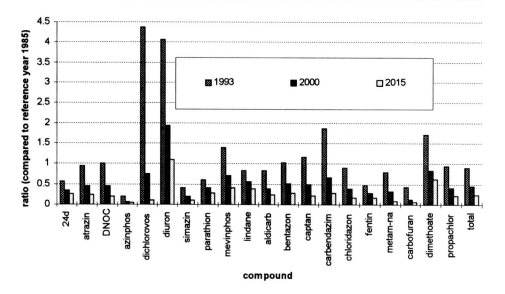

Fig. 11. Changes in the emission of pesticides – 'SYSTEEM' scenario (Wagemaker et al. 1997).

5. Case study – How to proof a direct relationship between use of pesticides, run off and damage to other water users

5.1. The problem

Drinking water companies in the western part of the Netherlands use rivers, like the river Meuse, as a resource for drinking water production. These rivers are contaminated with (polar) pesticides, making high investments in additional purification techniques necessary. Accordingly it is in the interest of the drinking water companies to reduce this pollution as much as possible for reasons of reducing health risks and costs. Since pesticide pollution originates from non-point sources, this problem cannot (easily) be ascribed to individual polluters. In general, the agricultural sector and municipalities are considered to be the main polluters. Proving a direct relationship between the use of pesticides in agriculture and municipalities and the pollution of surface waters with these substances would enable the companies to formulate and take directed measures. A problem solving oriented monitoring programme was therefore designed and implemented.

5.2. Problem oriented monitoring

Because of the presence of pesticides in raw drinking water, water companies suffer considerable financial damage. To link this damage to various groups of users of pesticides, a field survey has been conducted in 1994 on the run off of pesticides in a number of selected areas in the Meuse catchment (Van der Wiele 1995).

In the survey most attention was given to the pesticides that currently threaten drinking water production in the Meuse catchment (compounds belonging to the triazines and fenylureaherbicides), but also other substances of interest, such as gly-fosate and its major metabolic product aminomethyl-fosfonylic acid, were included in the study.

Proving the aforementioned relationship in large, complex catchment areas, like the river Meuse, is rather difficult. By focusing on relatively small areas – to be defined as hydrological subcatchments and with limited numbers of users and types of crops, this relationship is much easier to establish.

In the province of Noord-Brabant, four subcatchments were selected. Two regions can be considered as urban areas (the cities of Eindhoven and of Hilvarenbeek); the other two regions are typically agricultural areas (tributaries of the Achterste Stroom and the Bakelse Aa). The urban emission of pesticides was assessed by collecting quality and flow data of the effluent of the corresponding sewage treatment works (STW). In the agricultural areas, the surface water was monitored at the single outflow point of the subcatchment, thus being a representative sampling point for the subcatchment. In order to anticipate varying flow rates and to calculate loads, 'state of the art' sampling devices (flow-proportionate continuous sampling) were installed in all cases. Samples were collected and analysed throughout the growing season (April-October) at regular intervals and analysed. Flow data (daily rates) were received from the regional water authorities.

Data on crop type and crop size were collected for the agricultural areas, to associate emissions of pesticides with various groups of users. In addition, an inventory was made of pesticides that were most likely to be applied on the crops at hand, since no data on actual pesticide use was available. Doses (per ha) for crop specific applications have been estimated from literature data. Using all of the abovementioned information, crop specific emission loads were calculated with the help of a run off model (Van der Wiele 1995). Total loads from the field survey were used as a reference.

5.3. Results

The following groups of users appeared to be responsible for the presence of the four priority compounds (diuron, atrazin, simazin and isoproturon) in surface water:
- agriculture (especially the production of maize, asparagus, trees & shrubs, fruit and leek);
- local authorities (maintenance of paved surfaces – weed control).

The most important sources for each of these compounds are:
- the STW of the city of Eindhoven: the most important source of all four compounds, particularly of diuron;
- the STW of the city of Hilvarenbeek: a major source of diuron, atrazin and simazin;
- maize: the only agricultural source of atrazin (both areas);
- trees & shrubs/fruit: most important agricultural source of simazin (Achterste Stroom tributary);
- asparagus: agricultural source of simazin (especially Achterste Stroom tributary) and diuron (Bakelse Aa tributary);
- leek: agricultural source of simazin (both areas).

After having extrapolated the results obtained for the four different areas to the scale of the Dutch part of the Meuse catchment, and after having calculated the upriver load and the total load near the mouth of the river, it appeared that the urban areas (i.e. the STWs) contribute significantly to the pollution of the river Meuse. In the Netherlands, isoproturon and diuron are almost completely originating from STWs. On a small scale, diuron is also applied in the production of asparagus. Urban and agricultural areas contribute equally to the emission of atrazin and simazin. 'Agricultural' atrazin could be unambiguously attributed to the production of maize. Simazin has wide application: asparagus, leek, trees & shrubs and fruit. The Dutch contribution to the pollution of the river Meuse amounts to 36-40% for diuron, atrazin and simazin. The Dutch contribution to the total isoproturon load is estimated at about 1%.

5.4. Actions

The results indicate a direct relationship between the pollution of surface waters with pesticides and the use of these substances by cities and farmers i.c. growers of specific crops. The representatives of the drinking water companies were thus able to start negotiations to reduce pesticide pollution in these regions, aiming at establishing agreements with the polluters on the reduction of pesticide emissions.

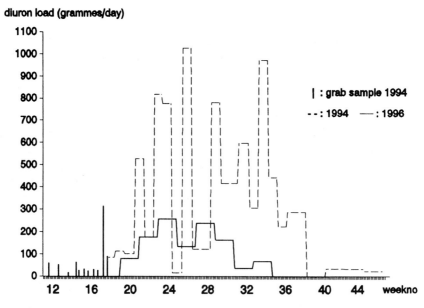

Fig. 12. Diuron emission loads of the STW of the city of Eindhoven in 1996 and in the reference year 1994 (Van der Wiele 1996).

Table 2. Assessment of diuron application reduction (versus 1994: -90% in 1996) on paved surfaces by the city of Eindhoven (Van der Wiele 1996).

	1994	**1996**
Municipal use of diuron at concrete surface:	480 kg	22,5 kg
Application period:	throughout year	wk 24 and 25
Highest effluent concentration in growing season:	6,7 $\mu g/l$	1,9 $\mu g/l$
Date:	wk 25	wk 23-25
Highest calculated daily load at STW outlet:	1026 gr	257 gr
Total load in growing season:	67,2 kg	16,2 kg
Achieved load reduction at STW outlet:		appr. 75%

The results of the negotiations were confirmed in 1996. The monitoring programme of 1994 was repeated at the STW of the city of Eindhoven (Van der Wiele 1996). The monitoring results of 1994 and 1996 at the outlet of the STW are shown in Fig. 12 and Table 2. The strongly reduced diuron use by the city (minus 90%) resulted in a significant reduction of the diuron load at the outlet of the STW (minus 75%).

6. Conclusions

From the abovementioned examples on nutrients, microorganisms and pesticides it is clear that indeed many yet unresolved problems exist with non-point sources. Scenario studies show that even in the next 20 years water quality objectives for the rivers Rhine and Meuse for nutrients, in particular nitrogen compounds, and for polar pesticides will not be implemented.

Diffuse pollution is not so hard to investigate as sometimes suggested. The case study presented in this paper clearly shows that (in flowing surface waters) diffuse pollution can be assessed in a way comparable to point sources. By focusing on small, surveyable and hydrological well-defined areas, representative measuring points can be chosen in such a way that these points can be treated as discharge points (=point sources). By doing so, the diffuse pollution can be assessed by means of relatively simple calculations and attributed to specific (groups of) sources.

References

Buijs, P.H.L. 1995. Watersysteemverkenningen 1996: prognose grensoverschrijdende belasting via Rijn en Maas 1995-2015. International Centre for Water Studies (ICWS). Ministerie van Verkeer en Waterstaat, Directoraat-Generaal Rijkswaterstaat, Den Haag (in Dutch).

Exner, M. & Gornik, V. 1991. Cryptosporidiosis. Characterization of a new infection with special respect to water as source of infection. Zbl.Hyg. 190: 13-25.

Girdwoord, R.W.A. 1995. Some clinical perspectives on waterborne parasitic protozoa. In: Betts, W.B. (ed.). Protozoan parasites and water. pp. 3-9. The Royal Society of Chemistry, Cambridge.

Ketelaars, H.A.M., Medema, G.J., Pikaar-Schoonen, C.P.R. In prep. Het voorkomen van *Cryptosporidium* en *Giardia* in de Maas, correlaties met waterkwaliteitsparameters en verwijdering in de Biesbosch spaarbekkens. Report Waterwinningbedrijf Brabantse Biesbosch, Werkendam (in Dutch).

LeChevallier, M.W., Norton, W.D. & Lee, R.G. 1991. Occurrence of *Giardia* and *Cryptosporidium* spp. in surface water supplies. Appl.Environ.Microbiol. 57: 2610-2616.

Medema, G.J. & Ketelaars, H.A.M. 1995. Betekenis van *Cryptosporidium* en *Giardia* voor de drinkwatervoorziening. H_2O 23: 699-704, 709 (in Dutch).

Medema, G.J., Ketelaars, G.J. & Hoogenboezem, W. 1996. *Cryptosporidium* en *Giardia* in Rijn en Maas en inventarisatie van potentiële bronnen in de Maas. Rijks Instituut voor Volksgezondheid en Milieu (RIVM), Bilthoven (in Dutch).

Niederländer, H.A.G. 1996. Inventarisatie van potentiële bronnen van *Cryptosporidium*, respectievelijk *Giardia* in het Maastroomgebied. Reportnr. 95.07, International Centre for Water Studies (ICWS), Amersfoort (in Dutch).

Rose, J.B., Gerba, C.P. & Jakubowski, W. 1991. Survey of potable water supplies for *Cryptosporidium* and *Giardia*. Environ.Sci.Technol. 25: 1393-1400.

Van der Wiele, P.J. 1995. Project Onderzoek Maas: Meetcampagne Bestrijdingsmiddelen 1994. Report 94.07, International Centre for Water Studies (ICWS), Amersfoort (in Dutch).

Van der Wiele, P.J. 1996. Diuronvrachtbepaling rwzi-Eindhoven – groeiseizoen 1996. VEWIN Milieuplan, Rijswijk (in Dutch).

Wagemaker, F.H., Reus, J.A.W.A, Boers, P.C.M. & Arnold, G.E. 1997. Doelgroepstudie landbouw: verslag van de beleidsanalyse voor de doelgroep landbouw. Watersysteemverkenningen, Ministerie van Verkeer en Waterstaat, Directoraat-Generaal Rijkswaterstaat, Den Haag (in Dutch).

INITIAL ESTIMATES OF NUTRIENT-RELATED PROCESS RATES IN FLOODPLAINS ALONG MODIFIED RIVERS IN THE NETHERLANDS

J.T.A. Verhoeven, H. Bogaards, R.S.P. Van Logtestijn & A. Spink
Department of Plant Ecology and Evolutionary Biology, Utrecht University, P.O. Box 80084, 3508 TB Utrecht, The Netherlands

Abstract

Floodplain ecosystems in the lower reaches of large rivers in The Netherlands are only rarely being flooded due to the protection provided by summer dykes immediately bordering the river channel. Restoration projects are underway to restore the connection with the river by cutting the summer dykes and creating side channels in the floodplain areas. This study focused on some basic characteristics of the nitrogen and phosphorus dynamics in these systems, to evaluate the possible effects of the plans on plant productivity and community structure. Nutrient-related process rates (nitrogen mineralization, phosphorus release, denitrification) were measured during spring in a number of grassland and wetland sites in the floodplains of the Rhine, and in tidal wetlands along the Oude Maas and Scheldt rivers. Data on process rates were related to a series of nutrient-related soil variables, and to the standing crop of the vegetation.

The floodplain sites studied were found to be enriched with phosphorus, in particular the freshwater tidal wetlands with their high frequency of flooding. The rates of phosphorus release, nitrogen mineralization and denitrification were all primarily correlated with soil phosphorus richness. Plant biomass in the grasslands was just below 700 g m^{-2}, which is already too high to permit a high species richness. As plant nutrient concentrations indicated N-limited plant growth and the more frequent flooding after the restoration measures will result in enrichment with N as well as P, the potential for high plant diversity in the grasslands will remain low, unless nutrient outputs would be increased through harvesting the vegetation for hay.

1. Introduction

River-floodplain ecosystems have been altered drastically by human activities in most parts of the world. The channels of the lower reaches of most large rivers have been embanked by artificial levees in order to prevent flooding of the major part of the original floodplain which is in use for agriculture or urban developments. These alterations have resulted in the destruction of the major driving forces determining the functional characteristics of river ecosystems, i.e. the natural processes of erosion and sedimentation, which result normally in meandering and floodplain formation (Sparks *et al.* 1990; Sparks 1992, 1995).

River ecology has traditionally focused more on small rivers than on large river-floodplain systems and has emphasized primarily the processes in the river channel itself (Vannote 1981). Only recently, the importance of the integrity of the river-floodplain connection for the functioning of large river ecosystems has been fully

New concepts for sustainable management of river basins, pp. 229–240
edited by P.H. Nienhuis, R.S.E.W. Leuven and A.M.J. Ragas
© *1998 Backhuys Publishers, Leiden, The Netherlands*

recognized. The 'flood pulse concept' (Junk *et al.* 1989) emphasizes the overriding effects of seasonal floods on the functioning of the floodplain as well as the river channel. Floodplains receive sediment inputs through each flooding event and have long been recognized as nutrient-rich, fertile environments.

The lower reaches of the large rivers Rhine, Meuse, and Scheldt in the Netherlands and Belgium have been modified strongly in several respects. These rivers have been 'tamed' by dyke constructions; the river channel itself has been fixed by so-called summer dykes, whereas higher winter dykes (1-3 km apart) protect the hinterland from flooding. The area between the summer dykes and winter dykes floods for short periods at very high river discharge, and is mostly in use as grassland for dairy production (see Fig. 1; WWF 1993). As is pointed out in several chapters in this volume, these floodplain grasslands are currently subject to restoration activities, in which the agricultural activities are ended, the summer dykes are removed and the development of side channels is promoted. The purpose of these activities is to restore part of the forests and riverine grasslands which normally would characterize an active floodplain.

Although river floodplains are known to be nutrient-rich, there are surprisingly few studies which have actually addressed the nutrient dynamics of the floodplain ecosystem, and most of them focused specifically on floodplain lakes (Forsberg *et al.* 1988, Van den Brink *et al.* 1993). Still, the availability of nutrients, and particularly of nitrogen and phosphorus, is a very important soil characteristic which has direct influence on primary productivity, plant species composition and food chain support of wetland ecosystems (Maltby *et al.* 1994, 1996; Verhoeven *et al.* 1996a). Knowledge on the nutrient status of the floodplains to be restored, and on the possible effects of the restoration on their nutrient dynamics, is essential to evaluate the potential for restoration of typical floodplain plant communities.

The floodplains along the Rhine in the Netherlands have become enriched with nutrients during the past decades. This has been due to intensification of the agricultural use of the grasslands (fertilization, increase of the grazing pressure). Further, the N and P loads of the rivers were very high, which resulted in enhanced nutrient inputs in association with flooding events, although these were rather infrequent (less than once in two years for most areas) because of the presence of the summer dykes.

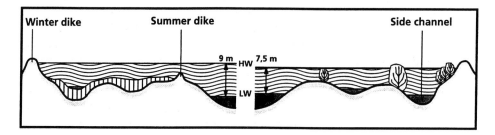

Fig. 1. Cross section of the Waal River showing the present situation in the left part of the diagram, and the situation after restoration of the floodplain in the right part. HW, high water level; LW, low water level. Vertical hatching, clay layer. In the present situation, the river channel is protected by a summer dyke which leads to low flooding frequency (less that once per year). The restoration will involve the removal of the clay layer and the summer dyke, so that flooding frequency will increase. Redrawn after WWF (1993).

The partial restoration of the connection with the river in the floodplain areas between the winter dykes in the Netherlands will result in more frequent flooding and the enhancement of sediment deposition. Although the water quality of the Rhine river has improved in recent years, the nitrogen and phosphorus levels in the river water are still higher than natural background values (Van Dijk *et al.* 1994, 1995). For the parts of the floodplain which have not been heavily fertilized for agricultural purposes, these higher nutrient inputs may lead to higher nutrient-related process rates in the floodplain soil.

The purpose of this study was to determine some basic features of the nitrogen and phosphorus dynamics of the present floodplain areas along the Rhine river in the Netherlands and to evaluate the effects of enrichment on their vegetation. The approach chosen was to measure nutrient-related process rates (i.e. nitrogen and phosphorus mineralization, denitrification), soil and water variables and vegetation characteristics in a relatively short field period in spring in a range of floodplain habitats (see also Verhoeven *et al.* 1994, 1996a). The floodplain habitats investigated were riverine grasslands, *Phragmites* marshes and *Salix* forests in several Rhine branches. For comparison, freshwater tidal wetlands along the Oude Maas and the Scheldt rivers were also studied.

We expected that the freshwater tidal systems, which are subject to a regime of daily flooding, would have higher soil nitrogen and phosphorus levels than the riverine grasslands and claypits, which have been flooded only rarely because of the protection provided by the summer dykes. Further, we expected that the process rates studied would be correlated with the N and P richness of the soil.

2. Site description

The main study areas were the river forelands ('uiterwaarden') in the Millinger-waard and the Blauwe Kamer. We also studied freshwater tidal wetlands along the Oude Maas between Rotterdam and Spijkenisse, and along the Scheldt near St. Niklaas, Belgium.

The Millingerwaard is located along the Waal River, just downstream of the divergence of the Waal and the Nederrijn. The 700 ha floodplain is being managed by WWF and Staatsbosbeheer (the Dutch Forest Service), and a connection of the floodplain with the river will be restored by removing part of the summer dyke within the next five years. The Waal River has no dams so that the river stage is allowed to follow natural fluctuations. The river forelands consist of meadows, marshes and alluvial forest. The Blauwe Kamer is a river forelands area located along the Nederrijn near Rhenen; this river has weirs to ensure a minimum flow in the river channel during the low-flow season (Admiraal *et al.* 1993), and the river therefore has a more stable discharge over the seasons. A 120 ha floodplain area is being managed by the 'Utrechts Landschap'. Since 1993, the connection between river and floodplain has been restored by removing part of the summer dyke. The area consists mainly of wet meadows, but alluvial forests are forming rapidly.

In both study areas, comparable grasslands on elevational gradients from ridges to swales were identified, and four sampling stations were established, of which the driest station was at the foot of a sandy river dune and grassland stations 1, 2 and

3, were on the dry, intermediate and wet end of the gradient (approximately 300 m), respectively. The site codes for the sampling stations along these gradients are WRD, WFG1, WFG2, and WFG3 for the Millingerwaard, and RRD, RFG1, RFG2, and RFG3 for the Blauwe Kamer (see also Table 1). The vegetation in these grasslands can be characterized as Arrhenaterion elatioris communities (Westhoff & Den Held 1969), with moisture-indicating species such as *Phalaris arundinacea* and *Eleocharis palustris* at the lower part of the gradients. In the Millingerwaard, sampling stations were also installed in a *Phragmites* marsh (WFM) and a *Salix* forest (WFF) in old claypits (shallow depressions originating from clay extraction). The Millingerwaard sites are only flooded by river water at very high river discharge, which happens about every other year. The Blauwe Kamer sites are more subject to river flooding since the opening up of the summer dykes in 1993.

Along the southern bank of the Oude Maas, sampling stations were established in a herbaceous tidal wetland dominated by *Scirpus maritimus, Cardamine amara* and *Bidens cernua* (OTM) and a wetland shrub dominated by *Alnus glutinosa* and *Salix spp* (OTF). Tidal amplitude was about 1 m in the marsh, whereas the shrub was a little more protected from inundations. Finally, a sampling station was located in the Scheldt river near Hingene, Belgium, in a tidal *Phragmites* marsh (STM) with a tidal amplitude of about 4 m.

All sampling stations had 5 replicate sampling points located at least 15 m apart on a line parallel to the river. All measurements were carried out at each of the sampling points.

Table 1. Soil characteristics and plant biomass of 13 riverine wetland sites. Values are means of 5 replicates. Values followed by the same letter are not significantly different (ANOVA, Tukey test, p<0.05). LOI, Loss on ignition (organic matter content) –, biomass not estimated (forested site).
Key to the site codes:
S, Scheldt (Hingene, Belgium); O, Oude Maas (east of Spijkenisse); W, Waal (Millingerwaard); R, Nederrijn (Blauwe Kamer).
T, freshwater tidal; F, floodplain; RD river dune.
M, marsh; F, forest; G, grassland; 1,2,3 elevational gradient from dune to swale.

Site	Total N g kg⁻¹	Total P g kg⁻¹	Bulk density g cm⁻³	LOI %	Water content g cm⁻³	pH	C/N	C/P	Plant biomass g m⁻²	Type
STM	6.99[b]	7.01[a]	0.39[fg]	22.3[b]	0.66[b]	7.28[bc]	16.9	16.9	1821[a]	clay
OTF	13.52[a]	5.00[b]	0.22[g]	34.7[a]	0.80[a]	7.09[c]	13.6	36.8	–	clay
OTM	0.66[f]	0.47[cd]	1.13[e]	6.0[def]	0.27[gh]	6.67[d]	48	68.1	568[b]	clay
WFF	5.25[cd]	1.40[c]	0.45[f]	15.3[bc]	0.45[de]	7.15[bc]	15.4	57.8	–	clay
WFM	5.69[bc]	1.25[cd]	0.44[f]	16.1[bc]	0.55[c]	6.99[cd]	15	68.2	1158[a]	clay
WRD	0.07[f]	0.28[d]	1.75[a]	0.9[f]	0.01[j]	8.57[a]	64.2	15.9	297[b]	sand
WFG1	3.52[e]	1.18[cd]	1.48[bc]	11.1[cde]	0.28[gh]	7.17[bc]	16.8	50	185[c]	sand/clay
WFG2	4.41[cde]	1.45[c]	1.44[cd]	12.9[cd]	0.34[fg]	7.34[bc]	15.5	46.9	597[b]	sand/clay
WFG3	5.00[cde]	1.47[c]	1.26[de]	13.5[cd]	0.39[ef]	7.33[bc]	14.3	48.5	723[b]	sand/clay
RRD	0.80[f]	0.93[cd]	1.68[ab]	3.4[ef]	0.14[i]	7.53[b]	22.4	19.2	325[b]	sand
RFG1	3.93[de]	0.88[cd]	1.49[bc]	12.8[cd]	0.25[h]	5.21[f]	17.2	77.1	656[b]	sand/clay
RFG2	5.15[cde]	1.26[cd]	1.32[cde]	17.8[bc]	0.43[e]	5.69[e]	18.3	75.1	617[b]	sand/clay
RFG3	5.90[bc]	1.36[c]	1.18[e]	12.3[cd]	0.52[cd]	6.01[e]	11.1	47.9	645[b]	sand/clay

3. Methods

All sampling points were laid out in May 1995 and sampled from May-July. In the second half of May, at the start of a 6-week field period, soil samples of the upper 10-cm layer were taken at all sampling points for determination of total nitrogen and phosphorus, extractable nitrogen and phosphorus, organic matter, bulk density, water content, and soil pH. For extractable N, 12 g of fresh soil sample was extracted with 50 ml of 0.2 M KCl; ammonium and nitrate in the extracts were measured with a Skalar continuous-flow analyzer (Verhoeven *et al.* 1990). Extractable P was measured after extraction of 12 g of fresh soil with 50 ml of 0.1 M HCl in combination with 0.03 M NH_4F (Bray-II method) by determining the extinction of the phospho-molybdenum-blue complex.

Nitrogen and phosphorus mineralization were estimated by incubating soil material *in situ* during a field period of 6 weeks in capped PVC tubes (diameter 4 cm; length 12 cm), as the difference between extractable N and P of incubated samples and fresh soil samples taken at the start of the field period. Denitrification was determined at the start and at the end of the field period by using the acetylene blockage technique as described by De Klein & Van Logtestijn (1994). Soil cores were incubated in 1-l glass jars for 24 h at field temperatures. The jars were flushed with N_2 gas prior to the incubation to create anaerobic conditions. In the herbaceous sites, aboveground plant biomass was determined by clipping the plant shoots in 40 x 40 cm squares at the beginning of July (1 sample per station), and drying (48h, 70C) and weighing the samples which had previously been sorted into living and dead parts. Plant N and P content was measured by grinding the dry samples and determining N and P concentrations after acid digestion of the dry, ground plant material according to a salicylic acid thiosulphate modification of the Kjeldahl method (Page *et al.* 1982). In the forested sites, samples of leaf tissue of trees, shrubs and herbaceous plants were pooled to obtain a representative sample for each sampling station; these samples were treated as described for the sites with herbaceous vegetation.

For a complete description of the techniques used, the reader is referred to Verhoeven *et al.* (1994, 1996a). Data were tested for unequal variances and logarithmically transformed if necessary. The data were analyzed using ANOVA. Differences between mean values were tested for significance by using the Tukey-Cramer test. Principle Components of soil variables were determined using the Factor Analysis procedure in SAS (Sokal & Rohlf 1981; SAS 1985). Process rates were correlated with the Principal Components by using stepwise multiple regression.

4. Results

Two out of the three tidal wetlands studied, i.e. the *Phragmites* marsh along the Scheldt and the forest along the Oude Maas, have very high soil N and P, organic matter and water content compared to all of the other sites (Table 1). Extractable P was very high in all three tidal wetlands (Fig. 2). The three sites with low organic matter, i.e., the tidal *Scirpus* marsh and the two river dune sites, had low values for total N and water content, and high values for C/N ratio. The soils of the two dune grassland sites contrast with those of the grassland sites further down the gradients

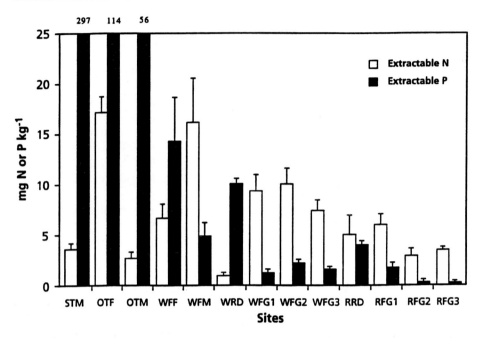

Fig. 2. Extractable nitrogen and phosphorus in the sampling stations studied. Site codes as in Table 1. Error bars indicate SE.

in having lower organic matter, total N, water content, clay content, and C/P ratio, and higher C/N ratio. The grasslands in the Blauwe Kamer area had lower soil pH than those of the Millingerwaard (Table 1).

The Factor Analysis (Table 2) resulted in three Principal Components (i.e., reduced the number of soil variables to three by combining variables which are strongly mutually correlated). The first Principal Component (or 'Factor') was closely associated with the nitrogen richness of the soil (total soil N as well as extractable ammonium), soil organic matter, bulk density and soil water content, and explained 40% of the variance in the soil variables. The P richness (total soil P and extractable phosphate) was the second Factor, which explained 27% of the variance. The third Factor combined soil pH and extractable nitrate, which explained 14% of the variance.

Nitrogen mineralization showed distinct gradients along both transects, with high values on the dunes, low values (net immobilization in the Millingerwaard) on the neighbouring (highest) grassland stations, and increasing values further down (Fig. 3). Phosphorus release was, however, very low on the dunes, and did not show a consistent picture along the gradients. Phosphorus release was high in the three tidal sites with an exceptionally high value for the Scheldt site in Belgium. It is remarkable that P release is higher than N mineralization in all tidal and claypit sites, but the reverse is true for the dunes and grassland sites (except for WFG1).

Table 2. Principal components of the soil variables

	FACTOR1	FACTOR2	FACTOR3
total soil N	0.88964	0.31712	-0.06889
soil organic matter	0.86151	0.33557	-0.08392
soil water content	0.83455	0.43665	-0.19345
extractable NH_4	0.68184	-0.12280	0.16372
bulk density	-0.71764	-0.49593	0.09155
extractable PO_4	0.17263	0.92872	-0.03395
total soil P	0.46178	0.83748	0.03308
soil pH	-0.27923	0.32737	0.77486
extractable NO_3	0.16166	-0.27106	0.76776
% variance explained	40	27	14

Denitrification was high in the Scheldt reed marsh and the *Salix* forest in the Millingerwaard (Fig. 4). Intermediate values for this process were found along the grassland gradients, whereas all other sites had low values. Above-ground plant biomass (Table 1) was distinctly higher in both *Phragmites* marshes (STM and WFM) than in the other herbaceous sites. Biomass was generally intermediate (around 650 g m⁻²) in the grassland sites and low on the dunes, as well as the grassland site bordering the dune in the Millingerwaard. Plant N concentration and plant P concentration showed similar patterns of variation (Fig. 5).

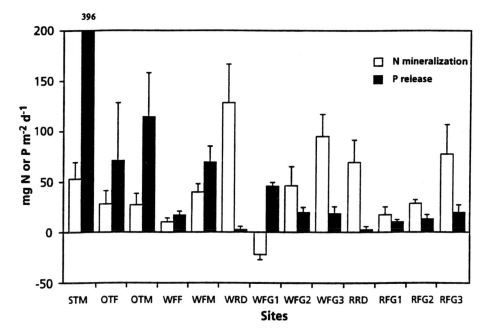

Fig. 3. Nitrogen mineralization and phosphorus release, as measured during a 6-week field period in spring. Site codes as in Table 1. Error bars indicate SE.

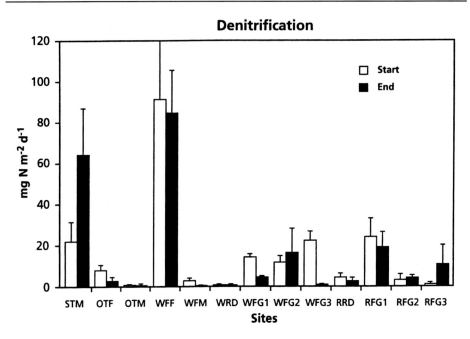

Fig. 4. Denitrification at the start (May) and at the end (June) of the 6-week field period.Site codes as in Table 1. Error bars indicate SE.

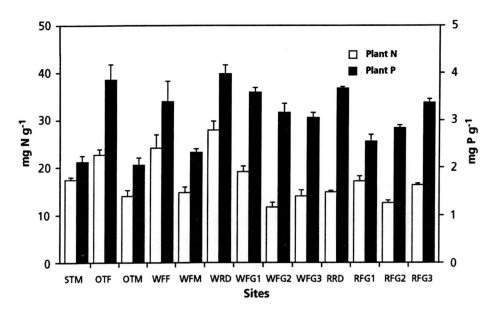

Fig. 5. Plant nitrogen and phosphorus concentrations. Site codes as in Table 1. Error bars indicate SE.

Nitrogen mineralization as well as phosphorus release correlated significantly with Factor 2 (soil P richness), and to a smaller degree also with Factor 1 (soil organic matter and N richness) (Table 3). Denitrification was significantly related to Factor 2, which explained only 14% of the variance. Plant N correlated significantly with Factor 3 (soil pH and nitrate content, 9% explained variance), whereas plant P content correlated with Factors 3 and 2 (25% explained variance).

Table 3. Multiple regression of process rates and plant N and P concentrations against the principal components (see Table 2). F1, Factor 1; F2, Factor 2; F3, Factor 3.

Dependent variable	Model	R^2	P
N mineralization	Nmin = 0.52 F2 + 0.27 F1	0.34	<0.0001
P release	Prel = 0.70 F2 + 0.20 F1	0.67	<0.0001
denitrification	denitr = 0.38 F2	0.14	0.0018
plant N concentration	Nplant = 0.29 F3	0.09	0.0158
plant P concentration	Pplant = 0.44 F3 + 0.23 F2	0.25	0.0002

5. Discussion

This study carried out in a limited number of floodplain and freshwater tidal wetlands in The Netherlands and Belgium allows some preliminary conclusions to be drawn on the characteristics of their nutrient dynamics. The floodplains in the Rhine and Scheldt delta have been enriched with phosphorus, and this has led to higher rates of phosphate release and nitrogen mineralization. The enrichment with phosphorus can be deduced from the extremely high values for total and/or extractable phosphorus in the soils of the freshwater tidal wetlands which have been in much more frequent contact with the river water than all the other sites studied. Another indication of enrichment of the Dutch floodplains with P is the much lower C/P ratio in the Dutch floodplain grasslands (50-80) than Van Oorschot (1996) found in grasslands along the Torridge River in Devon, UK (120-430) or the Shannon River, Ireland (100-420), whereas C/N ratios of the soils in all three areas were similar and in the range 11-20. The occasional flooding with polluted Rhine water, which used to be very high in particulate phosphates in the period between 1960 and 1990 (Van Dijk *et al.* 1995), is the most probable cause.

The correlation of the process rates with the Principle Components of soil variables showed that P release, N mineralization as well as denitrification were significantly correlated with soil P richness (Factor 2). This indicates that P release and N mineralization have both increased as a result of the enrichment of the floodplains with P. For denitrification, the percentage variance explained is so small that it will probably not have been affected much. This process is very dependent on the availability of nitrate, which is determined by the nitrification process (Patrick & Tusneem 1972; Reddy & Patrick 1984). Fluctuating water tables lead to high nitrification and denitrification rates (De Klein & Van Logtestijn 1994); the values we found in STM and WFF are higher than generally found in wetlands (Verhoeven *et*

al. 1996a), which is probably due to the combination of nutrient richness and fluctuating water tables at these sites.

The high availability of N and P to the vegetation, which is a natural phenomenon
in floodplains, has been amplified by contact with the polluted river water. We cannot say if this increased nutrient availability has led to higher primary productivity
and plant biomass because no historic records of primary production are available.
The N and P concentrations in the herbaceous plant material can be used as an indication of the degree of limitation of plant growth by these nutrients (Verhoeven et al.
1996b). The 'critical' values for N and P are 14 mgN g^{-1} and 0.7 mgP g^{-1}, respectively. The high P concentrations definitely indicate a surplus of P in all stations studied.
The N concentrations indicate N-limited growth in the tidal marsh, the claypit marsh,
and two of the grassland sites.

Plant biomass in July was greater than 1100 g m^{-2} in both *Phragmites* marshes,
which is too high to permit the coexistence of a large number of species in a small
area in wetlands (Wheeler & Giller 1983; Wisheu & Keddy 1989). Establishment of
plant communities with a high species density, such as the typical floodplain grasslands in the 'callows' along the Shannon (Ireland), or in parts of the Rhine floodplain
which are totally cut off from the river (Rijnstrangen), would require biomass values
below 700 g m^{-2}. The biomass values in the grasslands in the Millingerwaard and the
Blauwe Kamer are close to this maximal value.

Will the restoration of the connection with the river by removing the summer
dykes lead to further enrichment of the Rhine floodplain grasslands, or will nutrients be flushed out of the soils? The current Rhine water quality has improved drastically compared to that during the 1960-1980's (Van Dijk & Marteijn 1993; Van
Dijk et al. 1994); this is primarily the case for phosphorus, however, nitrogen loads
have decreased little. A more frequent flooding with Rhine water, therefore, may
lead to further eutrophication of the grasslands, as the phosphorus in the soils is not
likely to be removed to the extent that it becomes limiting to the vegetation, whereas the nitrogen load of the water is likely to be partly captured by the floodplain ecosystem, which will impact the N-limited vegetation.

In view of the fact that the Blauwe Kamer grasslands have been in closer contact with the river than those in the Millingerwaard because of the removal of the
summer dyke in the former area in 1993, it is interesting to look for differences
between the two areas in the nutrient-related variables we measured. Three out of
four stations are higher in the Millingerwaard for N mineralization as well as for P
release (Fig. 3). There are no clearcut differences in the soil factors (Table 1), except
for a significant difference in soil pH: the Blauwe Kamer soils are 1-2 pH units
lower than the Millingerwaard soils. This is probably directly related to a higher
flooding frequency in the former area, as alkalinity was shown to be inversely related with flooding frequency in floodplain lakes by Van den Brink et al. (1993). It
must be concluded that the more frequent flooding of the Blauwe Kamer sites is not
(yet) reflected in higher nutrient richness or availability, as would be predicted by
the 'flood pulse concept' (Junk et al. 1989). The short period (2 years) passed after
the removal of the summer dykes, and the occurrence of extremely high river discharge leading to water levels as high as 3 m above the floodplain in both areas in
two successive winters (1994-1995) may have been important here.

If the higher frequency and longer duration of flooding would indeed lead to a higher nitrogen availability to the vegetation on the longer term, an even higher biomass production is to be expected and species density certainly will not increase. The actual biomass production in these systems is in a range where a relatively small decrease would permit a larger number of species to coexist in the plant community. Restoration of the traditional form of floodplain land use, i.e., harvesting for hay, is expected to have a positive influence on botanical diversity (Bakker 1989; Koerselman *et al.* 1990). The restoration of the connection with the river together with a grazing regime, however, will probably result in an increase of plant productivity and a further reduction in botanical grassland diversity.

Acknowledgements

The investigations in the claypits and tidal wetlands were part of an international collaboration supported by NATO. Dr. D.F. Whigham (SERC, Md, USA) contributed to various activities related to this study and critically read the manuscript. Dr H. Coops (RIZA, Lelystad) kindly introduced us to the tidal habitats. Dr B. Bedford (Cornell University, NY, USA) and two anonymous reviewers provided helpful comments to an earlier version of the manuscript.

References

Admiraal, W., Van der Velde, G., Smit, H. & Cazemier, W.G. 1993. The rivers Rhine and Meuse in The Netherlands: present state and signs of ecological recovery. Hydrobiologia 265: 97-128.
Bakker, J.P. 1989. Nature management by grazing and cutting. Kluwer Academic Publishers, Dordrecht. 400 pp.
De Klein, C.A.M. & Van Logtestijn, R.S.P. 1994. Denitrification in the top soil of managed grasslands in The Netherlands in relation to soil type and fertilizer level. Plant and Soil 163: 33-44.
Forsberg, B.R., Devol, A.H., Richey, J.E., Martinelli, L.A. & Dos Santos, H. 1988. Factors controlling nutrient concentrations in Amazon floodplain lakes. Limnol. Oceanogr. 33: 41-56.
Junk, W.J., Bayley, P.B. & Sparks, R.E. 1989. The flood pulse concept in River-Floodplain systems. Can. Spec. Publ. Fish. Aquat. Sci. 106: 110-127.
Koerselman, W., Bakker, S.A. & Blom, M. 1990. Nitrogen, phosphorus and potassium mass balances for two small fens surrounded by pastures. J. Ecol. 78: 428-442.
Maltby, E., Hogan, D.V., Immirzi, C.P., Tellam, J.H. & Van der Peijl, M. 1994. Building a new approach to the investigation and assessment of wetland ecosystem functioning. In: Mitsch, W.J. (ed.) Global Wetlands: Old World and New, Elsevier, Amsterdam.
Maltby, E., Hogan, D.V. & McInnes, R.J. 1996. EUR 16132. Functional analysis of European wetland ecosystems – Phase 1 (FAEWE). European Commission, Office for Official Publications of the European Communities, Luxemburg. 448 pp.
Page, A.C., Miller, R.H. & Keeney, D.R. 1982. Methods of soil analyses, Part 2, Chemical and microbiological properties. American Society of Agronomy, Madison, Wisconsin, USA. pp.
Patrick, W.H. & Tusneem, M.E. 1972. Nitrogen loss from flooded soil. Ecology 53: 735-737.
Reddy, K.R. & Patrick, W.H. 1984. Nitrogen transformations and loss in flooded soils and sediments. CRC Critical Reviews in Environmental Control 13: 273-309.
SAS. 1985. SAS/STAT guide for personal computers. SAS Institute, Cary NC, USA. 378 pp.
Sokal, R.R. & Rohlf, F.J. 1981. Biometry. Freeman, San Francisco. 859 pp.
Sparks, R.E. 1992. Risk of altering the hydrologic regime of large rivers. In: Cairns, J., Niederlehner, B.R. & Orvos, D.R. (eds.) Predicting Ecosystem Risk, pp. 119-152, Princeton Scientific Publishing Company, Princeton, N.J.

Sparks, R.E. 1995. Need for ecosystem management of large rivers and their floodplains. BioScience 45: 168-182.

Sparks, R.E., Bayley, P.B., Kohler, S.L. & Osborne, L.L. 1990. Disturbance and recovery of large floodplain rivers. Environm. Manage. 14: 699-709.

Van den Brink, F.W.B., De Leeuw, J.P.H.M., Van der Velde, G. & Verheggen, G. 1993. Impact of hydrology on the chemistry and phytoplankton development in floodplain lakes along the lower Rhine and Meuse. Biogeochemistry 19: 103-128.

Van Dijk, G. & Marteijn, E.C.L. 1993. Ecological Rehabilitation of the Rhine 1988-1992. RIZA, Lelystad. 63 pp.

Van Dijk, G., Van Liere, L., Admiraal, W., Bannink, B.A. & Cappon, J.J. 1994. Present state of the water quality of European rivers and implications for management. The Science of the Total Environment 1994: 1-9.

Van Dijk, G.M., Marteijn, E.C.L. & Schulte-Wülwer-Leidig, A. 1995. Ecological rehabilitation of the river Rhine: plans, progress and perspectives. Regulated Rivers: Research & Management 11: 377-388.

Vannote, R.L. 1981. The river continuum: a theoretical construct for analysis of river ecosystems. Proc. Nat. Symp. on Freshwater Inflow to Estuaries II: 289-304.

Van Oorschot, M.M.P. 1996. Effects of the vegetation on carbon, nitrogen and phosphorus dynamics in English and French riverine grasslands. Ph.D. Dissertation, Utrecht University, 149 pp.

Verhoeven, J.T.A., Maltby, E. & Schmitz, M.B. 1990. Nitrogen and phosphorus mineralization in fens and bogs. J. Ecol. 78: 713-726.

Verhoeven, J.T.A., Whigham, D.F., Van Kerkhoven, M., O'Neill, J. & Maltby, E. 1994. A comparative study of nutrient-related processes in geographically separated wetlands: towards a science base for functional assessment procedures. In: Mitsch, W.J. (ed.) Global Wetlands; old world and new, pp. 91-106, Elsevier, Amsterdam.

Verhoeven, J.T.A., Keuter, A., Van Logtestijn, R., Van Kerkhoven, M.B. & Wassen, M. 1996a. Control of local nutrient dynamics in mires by regional and climatic factors: a comparison of Dutch and Polish sites. J. Ecol. 84: 647-656.

Verhoeven, J.T.A., Koerselman, W. & Meuleman, A.F.M. 1996b. Nitrogen- or phosphorus-limited growth in herbaceous mire vegetation: relations with atmospheric inputs and management regimes. TREE 11: 494-497.

Westhoff, V. & Den Held, A.J. 1969. Plantengemeenschappen in Nederland. Thieme, Zutphen. 324 pp. (in Dutch).

Wheeler, B.D. & Giller, K.E. 1983. Species richness of herbaceous vegetation in Broadland, Norfolk, in relation to the quantity of above-ground plant material. J. Ecol. 70: 179-200.

Wisheu, I.C. & Keddy, P.A. 1989. Species richness – standing crop relationships along four lakeshore gradients: constraints on the general model. Can. J. Bot. 67: 1609-1617.

WWF. 1993. Living Rivers. WorldWide Fund for Nature, Zeist, The Netherlands. 28 pp.

ASSESSING CUMULATIVE IMPACTS OF MULTIPLE STRESSORS ON RIVER SYSTEMS

R.S.E.W. Leuven[1], J.L.M. Haans[1], A.J. Hendriks[2], R.A.C. Lock[3] &
S.E. Wendelaar Bonga[3]
*[1]Department of Environmental Studies, Faculty of Science, University of Nijmegen,
P.O. Box 9010, 6500 GL Nijmegen, The Netherlands; [2]Institute for Inland Water
Management and Waste Water Treatment (RIZA), P.O. Box 17, 8200 AA Lelystad,
The Netherlands; [3]Department of Animal Physiology, Faculty of Science,
University of Nijmegen, P.O. Box 9010, 6500 GL Nijmegen, The Netherlands*

Abstract

The cumulative impacts of multiple stressors on water systems are of rapidly growing concern within the field of environmental sciences and management. Most studies have focused on mixture toxicity and have dealt with responses of biota at either organismal or population level. Few studies have addressed responses of organisms exposed to combinations of chemical and physical stressors. Although antagonistic, additive and synergistic effects have been described for exposure of biota to combinations of chemical stressors, it seems to be agreed that concentration addition proves to be a reasonable worst case estimation. Therefore, aggregation of physico-chemical parameters in water quality indices and supplementary specifications of environmental quality objectives to account for mixture toxicity are generally based on concentration addition.

In spite of a growing interest in multiple stressors, basic data are often lacking or inadequate to allow precise predictions of the cumulative impacts of multiple stressors at the ecosystem level. Even in the long term, investigation of all probable ecotoxicological responses to exposure to all possible combinations of stressors does not seem practically or economically feasible. Monitoring of a sophisticated combination of physico-chemical and biological parameters improves detection and ecotoxicological risk assessment of multiple stressors. Application of quantitative structure-activity relationships, algorithms for mixture toxicity of known substances, (bio)chemical group parameters and response-oriented sum parameters may reduce uncertainties of cumulative impact assessment and can improve water quality management.

1. Introduction

River systems are affected by a wide variety of environmental stressors, including those associated with human activities (e.g. complex mixtures of pollutants and disturbance of temperature or light regimes) as well as those that occur naturally (e.g. competition between species, diseases, fluctuations of physico-chemical properties and disasters such as extremely low or high river discharge). The possibility of riverine ecosystems being exposed simultaneously or sequentially to multiple stressors requires consideration of the interactions between the stressors themselves and between their effects on organisms. According to the 'balance of nature' paradigm, an ecosystem will appear to be resistant or resilient to stress until a certain threshold value is exceeded (Pimm 1991). When an ecosystem is forced into an unstable

New concepts for sustainable management of river basins, pp. 241–259
edited by P.H. Nienhuis, R.S.E.W. Leuven and A.M.J. Ragas
© 1998 Backhuys Publishers, Leiden, The Netherlands

situation by environmental stressors, it can form a new dynamic equilibrium with a simpler structure (Aber & Melillo 1991, Scheffer *et al.* 1993). The concept of sustainable management is theoretically applicable to all dynamic equilibria of an ecosystem, notwithstanding the fact that they may differ markedly in structural and functional complexity (cf. Nienhuis & Leuven 1997). Establishing the thresholds beyond which a river ecosystem in equilibrium shifts to another state of equilibrium, and defining when they will be exceeded (i.e. ecological risk assessment) is essential for the sustainable management of river basins.

Due to existing controversies and general lack of precise data, many environmental scientists have not yet paid attention to cumulative impact assessment (cf. Burris & Canter 1997). As the emerging field of ecological risk assessment grows beyond assessing the impact of single chemical contaminants on single species to assessing the combined effects of multiple stressors on ecosystems, others are struggling to establish the methodologies, tools, procedures and environmental quality objectives needed for environmental management (Abbruzzese & Leibowitz 1997, EC 1996, CEHR 1996, Renner 1996).

The goal of the present paper is to present concepts for cumulative impact assessment (CIA) of multiple stressors on river systems. Section 2 indicates trends in CIA research and describes the subject matter of papers in renowned environmental journals (e.g. stressors investigated, structural parameters and ecotoxicological endpoints of test systems). Section 3 deals with the different types of physiological responses of (river) organisms to multiple stressors. Section 4 reviews CIA methodologies in Dutch river management, while section 5 discusses available methodologies, draws conclusions and gives recommendations for further research. The various sections are based on the updated introductory talks and discussions during a workshop at the symposium *New concepts for sustainable management of river basins*, held on November 29, 1996 at the University of Nijmegen (The Netherlands). The present paper mainly focuses on mixture toxicity, because nearly all available studies of CIA of multiple stressors deal with the combined effects of chemical substances.

2. Research trends

Until very recently, most ecological risk assessments have dealt with the effects of a single stressor on cohorts or populations of a single species under laboratory conditions. Over the last decade, multi-species tests have attracted growing interest (Brock & Budde 1994, Van Leeuwen 1995). An extensive review of structural parameters and endpoints indicating responses to pesticides in 127 freshwater field tests illustrates that few multi-species studies have focused on combinations of contaminants, including their degradation products (Brock & Budde 1994). In the early years, most of the studies on combined effects of chemical substances on freshwater fish and other aquatic life were often carried out with binary mixtures (EIFAC 1987, Könemann & Pieters 1996).

The subject matter of 622 publications in recent editions of three renowned environmental journals still shows a relatively high percentage of articles dealing with responses to a single stress factor (mostly a toxic chemical such as a metal or an organic compound). Surprisingly, over the years 1995-1996, multiple stressors (mainly mixtures of chemicals) also received much attention (Table 1). In spite of considerable interest in mixture toxicity, combinations of chemical and physical stressors seem to have attracted little attention. Few articles deal with responses of organisms exposed to a combination of temperature shocks and various (mixtures of) chemicals, in order to assess cumulative impacts of discharges of cooling water or winter stress in polluted rivers.

In the publications reviewed, a total of 170 combinations of stress factors can be distinguished. The effects of mixtures of polychlorinated hydrocarbons have been most frequently studied (24%), followed by mixtures of (heavy) metals (22%), mono-aromatic hydrocarbons (7%), pesticides (5%), chlorinated hydrocarbons (4%), poly-cyclic aromatic hydrocarbons (4%), tributyltins (3%) and several other mixtures of chemicals (11%). Most mixtures investigated consisted of well-known priority substances of European water pollution control. The share of studies on the effects of unknown substances, i.e., in whole effluent and in river water and sediment samples, is relatively low (16%). As already mentioned above, combinations of chemicals and other stressors (physical factors) have been rare (4%). In the papers reviewed, combinations with biological stressors have not received any attention.

In total, 94.8% of the multiple stressor studies reviewed deal with single species tests (i.e. cohorts of populations), whereas only 5.2% focus on multi-species (micro- and mesocosms) or field tests. A total of 229 species/taxa were used in the tests. Ranked by relative frequencies, important taxonomical groups include fish (24.7%), macroinvertebrates (22.2%), mammals (15.1%), algae (11.7%) and birds (10.9%). Amphibians (4.2%), macrophytes (2.5%) and other taxa (8.7%) have received relatively little attention. Among the test species/taxa are several representatives of large rivers and estuaries in Western Europe (e.g. fish species such as common carp, eel and trout).

Table 1. Subject matter of papers in three environmental journals over the years 1995-1996.

Journal	Number (n) of papers reviewed per journal (n_{total} = 622)	Subjects			
		Single stressor (in %)	Multiple stressors		Other subjects* (in %)
			Mixture(s) of chemicals (in %)	Combination(s) of chemical and physical stressors (in %)	
Aquatic Toxicology	96	55	34	3	7
Archives of Environmental Contamination and Toxicology	246	42	36	1	21
Environmental Pollution	280	12	11	1	76

*: e.g. methodological studies and monitoring data.

Relative frequencies of the response parameters investigated indicate that bioaccumulation in (fat) tissue or organs (32.0%), changes in cell and tissue physiology (25.7%) and mortality (15.4%) have been most frequently used to measure effects of multiple stressors. Other response parameters investigated have included growth (9.6%), vitality/behaviour (5.9%), reproduction (5.5%), histopathological effects (4.0%) and osmoregulation (1.8%).

In spite of growing interest in effects of mixtures on individual and population performances of single species and in multi-species tests, none of the papers explicitly deals with the cumulative impacts of multiple stressors on whole river ecosystems. According to Ramade (1995), the overall impact of stressors on the whole ecosystem must include the behavioural and biochemical responses impinging upon individual performances (development, growth and reproduction) as well as the impact of alterations in these individual performances on populations (abundance, distribution and age structure), community structure and dynamics (e.g. population extinction, dominance, diversity and biomass), sytem functioning (e.g. productivity, nutrient cycling and water cycle) and system properties (e.g. homeostasy and resilience). Moreover, the cumulative impacts on river ecosystems dependend on scale, time and space (Constanza 1995, Dyer *et al.* 1997).

Measures of whole ecosystem performance are inherently more difficult and more comprehensive, requiring more modeling and synthesis and involving less precision, but they are more relevant than endpoints and indicators from which they are built (Constanza 1995). Until now, however, there is no simple solution to a quick and quantitative assessment of cumulative impact on river ecosystems at various scales. Assessing cumulative impacts of multiple stressors from both structural and functional standpoints needs further basic studies (cf. Ramade 1995).

3. Combined actions of multiple stressors

The effects of multiple stressors on aquatic organisms can be divided into direct effects and the stress responses of organisms to these effects. Many direct effects at biochemical level are detrimental, at least in the longer term, comprising cell and tissue damage, reduced growth and reproduction, and increased susceptibility to diseases (section 2). By way of example, Box 1 describes in detail the stress responses in teleost fish.

Theoretically, four concepts are available for the cumulative impact assessment of multiple stressors on organisms (Table 2). Stressors may evoke a combined action that is similar or dissimilar depending on whether the sites of primary action of the stressors are the same or different. Moreover, interactive and non-interactive actions are possible, depending on whether one stress factor does or does not influence another. Problems can arise when the classification is applied to more than two stress factors, e.g. complex mixtures of chemicals. The pairings may fall into different classes of combined actions and different modes of action may be possible between various pairs (Van Leeuwen 1995). Moreover, adequate information about the underlying mechanisms of combined action is often lacking (Könemann & Pieters 1996). Therefore, several authors have used approaches dealing more exclusively with the quantitative results of mixture toxicity studies.

Box 1. Stress responses in teleost fish (Wendelaar Bonga 1997).

Stress responses in teleost fish are primarily related to the aquatic environment of fish. Fish are exposed to toxic stressors (aquatic pollutants) through the extensive and delicate respiratory surface of the gills and, in salt or brackish water, also through drinking. The high bioavailability of many chemicals in water is an additional factor. Together with the variety of highly sensitive perceptive mechanisms in the integument, this may explain why so many pollutants evoke an integrated stress response in fish in addition to their toxic effects at cellular and tissue levels. A stress response will be aroused if the intensity (or concentration) of the stressor surpasses a threshold value. This response may be a non-specific alarm and mobilization response of the central nervous system, directed at the adaptive mechanism of the organism to the stressor. However, excessively intensive or chronic stress response causes a decrease in growth, reproduction and resistance to diseases, often combined with accelerated ageing and increased mortality.

Chemical stressors increase the permeability of the surface epithelia, including the gills, to water and ions, and thus induce systemic hydromineral disturbances. High circulating catecholamine levels as well as structural damage to the gills and perhaps the skin are prime causal factors. This is associated with increased cellular turnover in these organs. Cortisol combines glucocorticoid and mineralocorticoid actions, the latter being essential for the restoration of hydromineral homeostasis, in concert with hormones such as prolactin (in fresh water) and growth hormone (in seawater). Exposure to chemical stressors may also directly compromise the stress response by interfering with specific neuroendocrine control mechanisms. This concerns the principal messengers of the brain-sympathetic-chromaffin cell axis and the brain-pituitary-interrenal axis, as well as their functions, involving stimulation of oxygen uptake and transfer, mobilization of energy substrates and reallocation of energy away from growth and reproduction. There is also growing evidence for intensified interaction between the neuroendocrine system and the immune system (mainly suppressive effects).

Since hydromineral disturbance is inherent to stress in fish, external factors affecting homeostasis such as water temperature, acidity (pH), mineral composition and ionic calcium levels also have a significant impact on stressor intensity.

Table 2. Four types of combined action of multiple stressors (according to Plackett & Hewlett 1952).

	Similar action	**Dissimilar action**
Interaction absent	simple similar action (concentration addition)	independent action (response multiplication)
Interaction present	complex similar action	dependent action

Combined effects of chemical stressors (e.g. chlorophenols, anilines, metals and reactive organic chemicals) on fish and daphnids often appear to be additive (Boedeker *et al.* 1993, EIFAC 1987, Enserink *et al.* 1991, Hermens *et al.* 1984b,c and 1985, Könemann 1981, Van Loon & Hermens 1995). In this kind of studies, equitoxic mixtures of up to 50 chemicals have been used. Concentration addition also seems to be valid for very low concentrations of narcotic chemicals in complex mixtures (Deneer *et al.* 1988). The effects of Rhine water exposure in combination with temperature elevation (5-7°C for one to three hours, mimicking thermal cooling water plumes of an electric power plant) on Rainbow trout and Sea trout have been studied at the KEMA Rhine Laboratory facilities near Arnhem (Nolan et al. 1998). In spite of an overall improvement in water quality due to the Rhine Action Programme, exposure to Rhine water alone still induces clear stress responses in the fish, as indicated by endocrine and histological parameters. Typical phenomena for stressed fish, such as damage to and increased ageing of the epithelia of skin and gills, as well as invasion of these epithelia by leucocytes, are apparent. These effects can be ascribed to the mixture of toxic substances in the Rhine water. A temperature shock produces a similar response. When Rhine water adapted fish are exposed to a temperature shock, the stress parameters measured clearly indicate additive effects of both treatments, which remain noticeable for three weeks after the high-temperature episode. Additive effects on fish may be mediated through elevated cortisol levels (Pelgrom 1995).

Stressors can also exert complicated interactions (i.e. complex similar and dependent actions) between their specific effects, as is known from the toxicological literature, and these may interfere with the non-specific effects. Antagonistic effects and synergystic effects have also been described for exposure to a combination of stressors (EIFAC 1987, Hermens & Leeuwangh 1982, Hermens et al. 1984a, Pelgrom 1995, Van Leeuwen 1995). An adaptive mechanism is the formation of stress proteins in response to both toxic and non-toxic stressors, which may confer resistance to other stressors. Induction of metallothioneines by a toxic metal may provide protection against other metals, as is indicated for instance by the antagonistic effects of copper and zinc on fish (Pelgrom 1995).

The results of mixture toxicity studies can be summarized as follows (Könemann & Pieters 1996):

– mixtures were never less toxic than the most toxic component, so an overall antagonism was never observed;
– all compounds together were never more toxic than could be predicted by assuming concentration addition;
– in some mixtures partial concentration addition was observed, leading to a combined effect that was always significantly greater than the effect of response addition alone;
– potentiation of toxicity (synergystic effect) was never observed.

Nowadays, experts seem to agree that mixture toxicity is reasonably well predicted by models based on the concepts of simple similar action and independent action, i.e., concentration addition response multiplication (Greco et al. 1993). The phenomenon of concentration addition appears to be an excellent approximation for chemicals that have comparable modes of action (Könemann & Pieters 1996). Concentration addition has also proved to be a reasonable worst case estimation for substances with independent action and has therefore been recommended as a leading principle in calculating mixture toxicity for regulatory purposes (Boedeker et al. 1993).

4. River management tools

At present, European water quality management mainly focuses on a few (<200) chemicals, called priority substances (e.g. IRC 1987). Studies have been carried out to locate sources, to determine exposure concentrations, to track distribution, to derive 'safe levels' and to reduce emissions. This has certainly improved the overall water quality of several European rivers, for example of the Rhine (V&W 1996). In Dutch rivers, the number of chemical substances violating environmental quality objectives (EQOs) has been reduced over the period 1985-1995 (V&W 1996). However, the European Inventory of New and Existing Commercial Chemical Substances (EINECS) lists about 100,000 compounds (Van Leeuwen & Hermens 1995), including 2000 high production volume chemicals (HPVC). Many of these are discharged or deposited in river basins. During the last decades, the number of chemicals involved in monitoring programmes and the number of EQOs has been continuously increased, while ecotoxicological support is constantly improving. However, the number of chemicals monitored is still rather low in comparison with the number of chemicals on the EINECS or HPVC list. Fig. 1 illustrates the trends in the numbers of (commercial) chemicals in river water and included in monitoring programmes as well as trends in EQOs and EQO violations. Moreover, basic data are very often lacking or do not allow precise predictions of the effects of multiple stressors (Van Leeuwen & Hermens 1995). The lack of data applies to ecotoxicological data, as well as to data regarding emissions and exposure concentrations of organisms in river ecosystems. According to Van der Zandt & Van Leeuwen (1992) the lack of data applies to most commercial chemical substances, and even to 2000 high production volume chemicals. Nowadays, it is also recognized that current chemical monitoring is unable to provide full assessment of river water quality. At present, only 5-25 percent of organic compounds can be determined (cf. Van Loon & Hermens 1995). It is concluded that the number of chemicals lacking

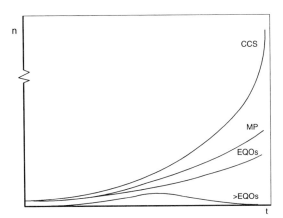

Fig. 1. Tentative numbers (n) of chemical substances (CCS: commercial chemical substances in river water; MP: European monitoring programmes; EQOs: environmental quality objectives; >EQOs: violation of environmental quality objectives; t: time).

water quality and emission reduction targets is very high, whereas the major part of the organic compounds in river water and sediments is still unknown.

Even in the long term, adequate monitoring and detection of all individual chemicals in river systems and examination of all probable responses of organisms and ecosystems to exposure to all possible combinations of physico-chemical stressors does not seem practically and economically feasible. Therefore, the following paragraphs present methods and management tools for dealing with mixture toxicity of known substances (4.1) and monitoring strategies for complex mixtures and unknown substances (4.2).

4.1. Dealing with mixture toxicity of known substances

Mixture toxicity of compounds with a simple similar action (concentration addition) can be calculated by adding up the ratios between their concentrations ([Ci]) and their lethal concentrations to for 50% of the individuals tested or their no observed effect concentrations (LC_{50} and NOEC, respectively). The ratios C/LC_{50} and $C/NOEC$ are termed acute toxic unit (TU_a) and chronic toxic unit (TU_c), respectively. Concentration addition means that the LC_{50} or NOEC of a mixture, taking the sum of the concentrations of *n* individual compounds, expressed as fractions of their LC_{50} or NOEC, respectively, is 1.0. In mathematical terms this is expressed as:

$$\sum_{i=1}^{n} [C_i]/LC50_i = 1$$

or

$$\sum_{i=1}^{n} [C_i]/NOEC_i = 1$$

In the case of lacking or insufficient toxicity data, quantitative structure-activity relationships (QSARs) can be used for the classification of pollutants into groups with a similar mode of action, for which concentration addition applies (Van Leeuwen & Hermens 1995, Könemann & Pieters 1996). Several toxicity tests with aquatic organisms have shown that the combined action of mixtures of chemicals that can be described by a particular QSAR indeed corresponds very well with concentration addition (Van Loon & Hermens 1995).

Until now, few EQOs for river systems have taken mixture toxicity into account. EQOs are generally derived from lethal or no observed effect concentrations in single species tests with a single toxic compound. Although these tests cannot be used to predict mixture toxicity (see section 3), derived EQOs may be protective when applied with an appropriate safety factor (La Point *et al.* 1989). The US-EPA (1985) has already proposed to apply safety factors (SF) ranging from 1 to 10 for synergistic effects of other chemicals. An advantage of the introduction of such an assessment factor is its simplicity, but there is the disadvantage of the lack of ecotoxicological data supporting it. This means that the derived EQOs may be too flexible or too rigid. Dutch general EQOs for surface waters are based on scientifically derived risk limits, but are also determined by actual concentrations, economics, social interest, and technical options (Kalf *et al.* 1997). A distinction is made between limit and target values, which are currently derived from maximum permissible concentrations (MPCs) and negligible concentrations (NCs), respectively. MPC is the concentration above which the risk of adverse effects is considered to be unacceptable. NC is defined as MPC/100 and takes into account possible effects of combination toxicity due to the presence of other substances. The methods used for the derivation of MPCs are the statistical extrapolation method of Aldenberg & Slob (1993) and the preliminary effect assessment method used by the US-EPA (OECD 1992). In general, target values may ensure protection of river ecosystems to mixture toxicity. However, target values do not account for negligible risks in all cases where organisms are exposed to mixtures of many pollutants with simple similar combined action or synergistic effects and other severe environmental stressors. Moreover, in Dutch water pollution control, target values have a more or less 'symbolic' value for long term measures. They may be the precursors of an additional range of quality requirements and only require authorities to make an compulsory effort. Implementation of Dutch emission and water quality approach is currently based on limit values (V&W 1989).

In addition to using EQOs for individual substances and then assuming a simple similar action (concentration addition), a supplementary specification (EQO_m) accounting for mixture toxicity of *n* substances may also be used for mixtures of chemicals (*m*) (Calamari & Vighi 1992):

$$EQO_m = \sum_{i=1}^{n} [C_i]/EQO_i \leq 1$$

In the Netherlands, the equation ($EQO_m \leq 1$) is used for some groups of pesticides (e.g. the limit values for Dutch water quality standards for organophosphorus and pyrethroïd pesticides), whereas sum parameters are applied to some other groups of pollutants (e.g. 6 PAHs of Borneff). Sum parameters have been defined as the total concentrations of a selection of target compounds (Van Loon & Hermens 1995).

Over the last decades, various water quality indexing systems for rivers and streams have been developed (e.g. Smith 1990, NRA 1994, Latour *et al.* 1996). BKH/RIZA (1994) describes parameters (including sub-indices), aggregation methods and mathematical equations of 28 water quality indices. Most aggregation formulas are based on the weighted or unweighted (geometric) mean of physico-chemical parameters or subindices such as distances to targets (Couillard 1985). The allotment of the weight factors generally takes place on the basis of expert judgement, while in a few cases it is based on specific physico-chemical requirements related to functions of water systems. Different types of combined action of multiple stressors are not (yet) explicitly taken into account.

4.2. Monitoring strategies for complex mixtures and unknown substances

Besides well-known priority substances, thousands of other, largely unknown, substances are present in our major rivers, lakes and estuaries. As was mentioned in section 3, the response induced by one stressor may depend on other stress factors, including those of unknown compounds. How can we identify unknown environmental stressors and quantify their cumulative impact? Theoretically, this calls for the incorporation of chemical group parameters and response-oriented sum parameters in monitoring programmes for river water, sediments and effluents.

Chemical group parameters are based on chemical analysis techniques and determine specific elements or chemically defined groups of (toxic) compounds (e.g. extractable organohalogen compounds). Chemical group parameters usually determine the effects of roughly defined groups of compounds (e.g. organophosphate esters) on enzymes (e.g. cholinesterase inhibition). Many procedures for extraction, concentration and fractionation of organic compounds from water samples have been developed (Van Loon & Hermens 1995).

Response-oriented sum parameters are measured in biochemical and biological assays. They have been developed in order to indicate total toxicity, mutagenicity and bioaccumulation (Hendriks 1995). Both types of assay may be carried out with individual water samples (static assays) or with water flowing continuously through a basin (continuous assays). Biochemical assays, better known as biomarkers (static assays) or biosensors (continuous assays) are being applied in specific projects.

As an example, the methods and results of a study that aimed to quantify the contribution of organic microcontaminants to the overall response of biota in the Rhine and Meuse (Hendriks *et al.* 1994) will be briefly recapitulated. The methods used are illustrated in Fig. 2.

As a first step, Rhine water was concentrated and tested for toxicity and mutagenicity in standard assays with water fleas (*Daphnia magna*) and bacteria (*Salmonella typhimurium*), respectively. After 5-fold concentration, reproduction of *Daphnia magna* was inhibited, suggesting that more sensitive species still cannot survive in Rhine water. The substances of the sample were distributed over different fractions using different solvents. Toxicity tests showed that the fraction with the hydrophobic compounds was most toxic. In this fraction, as many compounds as possible were analysed. Next, the toxicity of the compounds identified was obtained from databases and added up using a common model for mixture toxicity. The combination of substances was considered to follow concentration addition, a reasonable assumption for organic microcontaminants (e.g. Hermens *et al.* 1984b,c, Van Loon & Hermens 1995; see also section 3). A maximum of 15% of the toxicity observed in the assays with Rhine water could be explained by the compounds detected chemically. This discrepancy was possibly caused by unknown compounds, i.e., substances that were either not detected in the chemical analysis or that were detected but for which no toxicity information was available (Hendriks *et al.* 1994). A similar study was carried out with water of the river Meuse (Maas *et al.* 1994). It was found that toxicity in samples from some locations could fully be explained on the basis of one single compound (i.e. diazinon), while at other locations most of the toxicity could not be explained by the substances detected. The same was concluded in a survey of effluents (De Graaf *et al.* 1997). These results

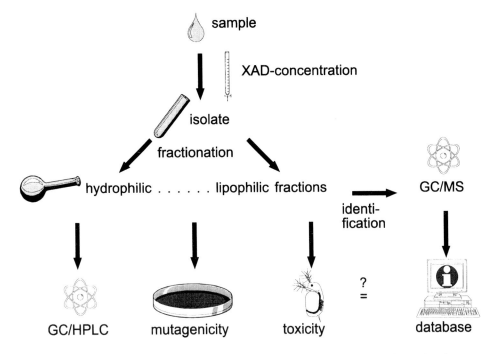

Fig. 2. Scheme of the experimental methods used to quantify the contribution of organic microcontaminants to the overall response of aquatic biota (from Hendriks *et al.* 1994; GC: gas chromatography; HPLC: high performance liquid chromatography; MS: mass spectrography; XAD: polymeric extraction).

should not be too much of a surprise. Emissions of priority substances from point sources have been reduced substantially over the last decades, and the relative importance of other compounds is likely to have increased (V&W 1996).

A promising method for the assessment of accumulation seems to be the development of artificial biological matter (e.g. Verhaar *et al.* 1995). Sorption to this material can be quantified in a way that mimics bioaccumulation in aquatic species. The total of organic compounds sorbed can be compared with body burdens that are lethal to organisms. The approach is a combination of worst-case and best-case assessment. On the one hand, biotransformation of compounds is not taken into account, while on the other hand, all compounds are assumed to act through a general mode of action, viz. narcosis. All compounds cause death by this mode of action at about 1 mmol per kg of organism, although some compounds are lethal at lower concentration via other modes of action. Neglecting biotransformation to less toxic compounds (deactivation) may be considered a worst-case approach, whereas excluding compounds with a different mode of action leads to best-case scenarios. In a preliminary study using Rhine water samples, the total body burden in artificial biological matter was about 0.05-0.15 mmol per kg of organism (Van Loon & Hermens 1994), whereas the total of compounds detected in an extensive chemical analysis of mussels and fish was 0.01 mmol per kg of organism or less (Hendriks *et al.* 1998).

River water is monitored by static assays with bacteria (*Photobacterium phosphoreum*). In the nearby future, the number of species used will be extended. Biological Early Warning Systems (BEWS), i.e. continuous assays with luminescent bacteria, algae, daphnids, molluscs and fish, are used to detect peak loads or adverse effects at several locations along the Rhine and Meuse (Hendriks & Stouten 1993, Tonkes *et al.* 1995). BEWS produces an alarm signal when triggered by the violation of a certain set point. It does not provide insight into the causes of the responses observed, but can be used to take precautionary measures (e.g. additional monitoring and warning drinking water companies).

Developments regarding monitoring and (ecological) risk assessment of polluted sediments seem to be in progress in many European countries (Den Besten *et al.* 1995, Tonkes *et al.* 1995, Van de Guchte 1995). The Dutch TRIAD approach bases assessment on three kinds of variables: physico-chemical analyses, laboratory bioassays and biological field surveys. This approach takes into account the mixture toxicity of polluted sediments under laboratory as well as field conditons.

Tonkes & Botterweg (1994) drafted a proposal for assessment of Whole Effluent Environmental Risk (WEER). The method proposed is summarized in Fig. 3. WEER is meant to assess risks of mixtures of known and unknown components in effluents. It uses more or less the same parameters as those described above for water quality monitoring (acute and chronic toxicity, bioaccumulation, persistence, oxygen demand and mutagenicity). The WEER assessment should make it possible

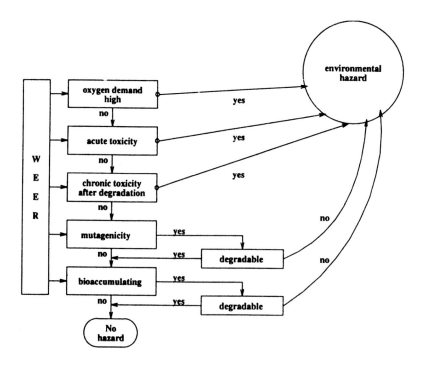

Fig. 3. Whole Effluent Environmental Risk (WEER), from Tonkes & Botterweg (1994).

to demand an (additional) improvement effort in those cases where current chemical approaches for known substances are incomplete or unreliable. WEER is not meant to predict effects on the receiving surface water. The method should be distinguished from Whole Effluent Toxicity (WET), which has already been applied as an emission requirement in environmental permitting. WET only focuses on total toxicity. Toxicity requirements can be applied to waste water discharges which strongly and unpredictively differ in quality or with discharges containing (known) chemicals which are difficult to analyse (Tonkes & Botterweg 1994).

Before monitoring programmes are extended with new (expensive) chemical group parameters and response-oriented sum parameters, the contribution of unknown substances to the overall response should be investigated in real-world environmental samples. However, section 2 illustrates that relatively few studies have attempted to estimate the relative importance of mixtures of unknown substances. So far, biochemical assays have not been implemented in Dutch monitoring programmes. Biochemical parameters may be especially useful if they are cheaper than monitoring chemical and biological parameters and if they cover substances and responses not covered by other parameters. While accumulation and biochemical parameters are in the developmental phase, biological parameters have already been implemented in water quality monitoring programmes for Dutch rivers. The assays used in monitoring programmes and the sampling locations are shown in Fig. 4 and Table 3, respectively.

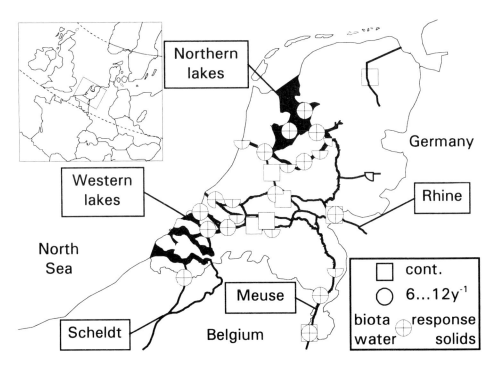

Fig. 4. Monitoring locations for concentrations of chemicals in surface water, sediment and organisms and for response to surface water and sediment in the Dutch Rhine-Meuse delta (from Hendriks & Van de Guchte 1997).

Table 3. Chemical, biological and toxicological monitoring in major rivers and lakes in the Dutch Rhine-Meuse delta (from Hendriks & Van de Guchte 1997).

Compartments/ Taxa	Compounds	Sampling frequency Y^{-1}	Locations n	Costs K$
Concentrations				
Surface water	metals, PAHs, Cl-R	6-12	25	1[a]
	N-R, P-R, metals	4	25	2[a]
	several substances	365[b]	2	-
Sediments	metals, PAHs, Cl-R	1[c]	12	1-2[a]
Molluscs	metals, PAHs, Cl-R	1/4	12	2[a]
Fish	Cl-R, Hg[e]	1	10[e]	1[a]
Response in bioassays				
Surface water	bacteria, algae, rotifers and crustaceans[e]	1/4	10-20	1[a]
	algae, daphnids and fish	∞	1-8	35[d]
Effluents	daphnids or fish	6-12	≈15	1-2[a]
Sediments	chironomids and daphnids	1/4[c]	12-20	2+5[a]

Approximate staff and equipment costs [a]per sample, [b]screening, [c]in addition chemical and toxicological analysis during 1986-1992 at circa 100 and 500 sites of specific interest and [d]early warning system per year; [e]data collected by or in cooperation with RIVM, RIVO, RIWA or RWS directorates; R: aromatic hydrocarbons (Cl-: biphenyls, N-: benzenes and P-: organophosphorus pesticides); PAHs: polycyclic aromatic hydrocarbons.

5. Discussion

What are the implications of the foregoing for river management in the nearby future? Due to specific as well as non-specific effects of stressors, simultaneous as well as serial exposure to multiple stressors causes cumulative impacts on river systems. This is the rule rather than the exception in many rivers and estuaries, as well as in other water systems, where combinations of disturbance (e.g. caused by nuisance of shipping traffic), increased turbidity (due to either erosion, eutrophication or shipping traffic), rapid changes in temperature (cooling water plumes) and a broad variety of contaminants are foreseeable phenomena resulting from multifunctional water use. Present knowledge regarding the cumulative impacts on entire river ecosystems is still limited. In practice, ecotoxicological risk assessments are mostly based on simple dose-response relations in single species tests under experimental conditions. Results of experiments with a single stressor in single species tests do not allow prediction of the cumulative impacts of multiple stressors on a population, let alone on entire ecosystems (cf. Constanza 1995, Hendriks 1995, Van Leeuwen 1995). Therefore, ecotoxicological risk assessments and EQOs based on single contaminant exposure in single species tests cannot be used without stint for the evaluation of situations with multiple stressors.

The past approach of measuring concentrations of chemicals and comparing them with EQOs and emission reduction targets has proved to be successful in reducing emissions of the well-known priority substances in Western European rivers (cf. V&W 1996). For priority substances that still do not meet their EQOs or emission reduction targets, European water pollution control should continue in this direction.

An additional approach for less well-known substances, complex mixtures and other environmental stressors is needed. Several methodologies for assessing cumulative impacts of known and unknown mixtures of chemicals on species or populations are already available and may be useful for underpinning sustainable management of river basins. However, application of these methodologies requires monitoring of a sophisticated combination of physico-chemical and ecotoxicological parameters in river water, sediment and effluent samples. Here, (bio)chemical group and response-oriented sum parameters will have to do the job. If (bio)chemical group and sum parameters for accumulation or toxicity indicate that pollution is severe, one may try to identify or characterize the substances that are responsible for the effect. However, one may also decide to increase the number of locations (for instance, in or close to effluents) and periods tested, thus tightening the net around the trouble spot. A strategic approach as proposed in section 4 provides coherent management tools.

The scientific validation of algorithms for combined effects of multiple stressors is still insufficient. Lack of basic ecotoxicological data, various modes of action of complex mixtures of toxic substances and their metabolites, uncertainties regarding carcinogenic, mutagenic and delayed effects of chemicals, including those causing endocrine disruption, and natural dynamics of populations and ecosystems complicate cumulative impact assessment. Moreover, decrees of test protocols and EQOs properly taking into account exposure to multiple stress factors are lacking, so further development of CIA methodologies and river management tools is recommended. Special attention must be focused on the scientific support for causality at population as well as ecosystem levels. Examination of all probable responses and all possible combinations of physical and chemical stressors does not seem practically and economically feasible. Therefore, attention should be paid to combined effects of priority substances of water pollution control which still violate EQOs, and to effects of unknown mixtures in whole effluent, river water and sediment samples. Combined effects of chemicals and other stressors (i.e. physical as well as biological factors) also need more attention.

Recently, the US-EPA has developed a synoptic approach to assessing cumulative impacts on wetlands (Abbruzzese & Leibowitz 1997). It is a framework for making comparisons between landscape subunits, such as watersheds and ecoregions, allowing cumulative impacts to be considered in management decisions. These comparisons are made by evaluating indices for each subunit, based on principles from landscape and stress ecology. Because there is still a lack of management tools that can be used within regulatory constraints, the synoptic approach has been designed as a method that can make use of available information and best professional judgement. It is a compromise between the need for rigorous results and the need for timely information. Although the US-EPA approach does not explicitly focus on risks of chemicals and some other important physical stressors of river systems (including wetlands), it may be customized to account for the specific needs of river management.

In spite of a lack of scientific proofs of causality regarding effects of multiple stressors on river ecosystems, the Dutch National Policy Document on Water

Management uses a multi-track approach as its strategy and advocates a combination of measures such as accelerated reduction of pollution, improvement of hydraulic design, restauration and rehabilitation of ecosystems, and guided use of water systems (V&W 1989). The implementation of MPCs for response-oriented sum parameters in water and sediment monitoring has recently been announced (V&W 1997).

Acknowledgements

The authors would like to thank Prof. Dr. P.H. Nienhuis and Mr. A.M.J. Ragas for critical remarks, Mrs. M.S. Mudde for her help with literature search and Mr. J. Klerkx and Dr. V.R. Edmonds-Brown for reviewing the manuscript.

References

Aber, J.D. & Melillo, J.M. 1991. Terrestrial ecosystems. Saunders, Philadelphia.

Abbruzzese, B. & Leibowitz, S.G. 1997. Environmental auditing: a synoptic approach for assessing cumulative impacts to wetlands. Environmental Management 21/3: 457-475.

Aldenberg, T. & Slob, W. 1993. Confidence limits for hazardous concentrations based on logistically distributed NOEC toxicity data. Ecotoxicology and Environmental Safety 25: 48-63.

BKH/RWS-RIZA 1994. Chemische waterkwaliteitsindices: Internationale inventarisatie van technieken en methodieken voor de aggregatie en presentatie van chemische waterkwaliteitsgegevens. BKH Adviesbureau: Raadgevende Ingenieurs Milieu Bouw Infrastructuur (BKH) and Rijkswaterstaat-RIZA, Delft (in Dutch).

Boedeker, W., Drescher, K., Altenburger, Faust, M., Grimme, L.H. 1993. Combined effects of toxicants: the need and soundness of assessment approaches in ecotoxicology. The Science of the Total Environment, Supplement: 931-939.

Brock, T.C.M. & Budde, B.J. 1994. On the choice of structural parameters and endpoints to indicate responses of freshwater ecosystems to pesticide stress. In: Hill, I.R., Heimbach, F., Leeuwangh, P. & Matthiessen, P., Freshwater field tests for hazard assessment of chemicals. Lewis Publishers, London.

Burris, R.K. & Canter, L.W. 1997. Cumulative impacts are not properly addressed in environmental assessments. Environ. Impact Assess Rev. 17: 5-18.

Calamari, D. & Vighi, M. 1992. A proposal to define quality objectives for aquatic life for mixtures of chemical substances. Chemosphere 4: 531-542.

CEHR 1996. From cumulative impacts toward sustainable solutions: critical methodologies for the study of ecosystem health. Center for Ecological Health Research (CEHR), University of California.

Constanza, R. 1995. Ecological and economic system health and social decision making. In: Rapport, D.J., Gaudet, C.L. & Calow, P. (eds.). Evaluating and monitoring the health of large-scale ecosystems. NATO Advanced Science Institutes Series 1: Global environmental change 28. Springer-Verlag, Berlin.

Couillard, D. & Lefebre, Y. 1995. Analysis of water quality indices. Journal of Environmental Management 21: 161-179.

De Graaf, P.J.F., Graansma, J., Tonkes, M., Ten Kate, E.V., Beckers, C.M.H. 1997. De acute toxiciteit van 17 industriële effluenten uit het beheersgebied van de regionale directies Noord-Nederland en Zuid-Holland. Institute for Inland Water Management and Waste Water Treatment (RIZA), Lelystad, The Netherlands (in Dutch).

Den Besten, P.J., Schmidt, C.A., Ohm, M., Ruys, M.M., Van Berghem, J.W. & Van der Guchte, C. 1995. Sediment quality assessment in the delta of rivers Rhine and Meuse based on field observations, bioassays and food chain implications. Journal of Aquatic Ecosystem Health 4: 257-270.

Deneer, J.W., Sinnige, T.L. Seinen, W. & Hermens, J.L.M. 1988. The joint acute toxicity to Daphnia magna of industrial organic chemicals at low concentrations. Aquatic Toxicology 12: 33-38.

Dyer, S.D., White-Hull, C.E., Johnson, T.D., Carr, G.J. & Wang, X., 1997. The importance of space in understanding the risk of multiple stressors on the biological integrity of receiving waters. In: Ale, B.J.M., Janssen, M.P.M. & Pruppers, M.J.M. (eds.), Book of Papers Risk 97: International Conference Mapping Environmental Risks and Risk Comparison, National Institute of Public Health and the Environment, Bilthoven, The Netherlands.

EC 1996. Study on the assessment of indirect and cumulative impacts, as well as impact interactions within the Environmental Impact Assessment process. Tender B2/ETU/960049, European Commission (EU), Directorate-General Environment, Nuclear Safety and Civil Protection, Brussels, Belgium.

EIFAC 1987. Revised report on combined effects on freshwater fish and other aquatic life. Technical Paper 37 Rev. 1, European Inland Fisheries Advisory Commission (EIFAC)/FAO, Rome.

Enserink, E.L., Maas-Diepeveen, J.L. & Van Leeuwen, C.J. 1991. Combined effects of metals; an ecotoxicological evaluation. Water Research 25/6: 679-687.

Greco, W. Unkelbach, H.D., Pöch, G., Sühnel, J., Kundi, M. & Boedeker, W. 1992. Concensus on concepts and terminology for combined-action assessment: tthe Saariselkä agreement. Archive Complex Environmental Studies 4/3: 65-69.

Hendriks, A.J. 1995. Concentrations of microcontaminants and response by organisms in laboratory experiments and Rhine-delta field surveys: Monitoring and modelling instruments in applied research and management. Thesis, Research Institute for Toxicology (RITOX), Utrecht University, The Netherlands.

Hendriks, A.J. & Van de Guchte, C. 1997. Optimal modelling and monitoring in ecotoxicological assessments: Choosing instruments for management and applied research with examples from the Rhine-Meuse delta. Environmental Toxicology and Water Quality 12: 321-333.

Hendriks, A.J. & Stouten, D.A. 1993. Monitoring the response of microcontaminants by dynamic *Daphnia magna* and *Leuciscus idus* assays in the Rhine delta: Biological early warning as a useful supplement. Ecotoxicology and Environmental Safety 26: 265-279.

Hendriks, A.J., Maas-Diepeveen, J.L., Noordsij, A. & Van der Gaag, M.A. 1994. Monitoring response to XAD-concentrated water in the Rhine delta: a major part of the toxic compounds remains unidentified. Water Research 28: 581-598.

Hendriks A.J., Pieters, H. & De Boer, J. 1998. Concentrations of metals, polycyclic aromatic hydrocabons, chlorobenzenes, chlorophenols, chloronitrobenzenes, chloro- and bromobiphenyls, bromodiphenylethers, chlorobiocides, nitrobiocides, phosphorbiocides and phtalates. Environmental Toxicology and Chemistry (submitted).

Hermens, J.L.M. & Leeuwangh, P. 1982. Joint toxicity of mixtures of 8 and 24 chemicals to the guppy (*Poecilia reticulata*). Ecotoxicological and Environmental Safety 8: 388-394.

Hermens, J.L.M., Leeuwangh, P. & Musch, A. 1984a. Quantitative structure-activity relationships and mixture toxicity studies of chloro- and alkylanilines at an acute toxicity level to the guppy (*Poecilia reticulata*). Ecotoxicological and Environmental Safety 8: 388-394.

Hermens, J.L.M., Canton, H., Janssen, P. & De Jong, R. 1984b. Quantitative structure-activity relationships and toxicity studies of mixtures of chemicals with anaesthetic potency: acute lethal and sublethal toxicity to *Daphnia magna*. Aquatic Toxicology 5: 143-154.

Hermens, J., Canton, H., Steyger, N. & Wegman, R. 1984c. Joint effects of a mixture of 14 chemicals on mortality and inhibition of reproduction of *Daphnia magna*. Aquatic Toxicology 5: 315-322.

IRC. 1987. Rhein Aktionsprogram. International Rhine Committee, Strasburg, France (in German).

Kalf, D.F., Crommentuijn, T. & Van de Plassche, E.J. 1997. Environmental quality objectives for 10 Polycyclic Aromatic Hydrocarbons (PAHs). Ecotoxicology and Environmental Safety 36: 89-97.

Könemann, W.H. 1981. Fish toxicity tests with mixtures of more than two chemicals. A proposal for a quantitative approach and experimental results. Toxicology 19: 229-238.

Könemann, W.H. & Pieters, M.N. 1996. Confusion of concepts in mixture toxicity. Food and Chemical Toxicology 34: 1025-1031.

Latour, P.J.M., Stutterheim, E. & Schäfer, A.J. 1996. From datum to information: the WATER DIALOGUE. H_2O 29/23: 693-696.

La Point, T.W. & Perry, J.A. 1989. The use of experimental ecosystems in regulatory decision making. Environmental Management 13: 539-544.

Maas, J.L., De la Haye, M.A.A. & Beek, M.A. 1994. Ecotoxicologisch onderzoek aan Maaswater en sediment (1991, 1992), Report 23, Project Ecological Rehabilitation of the River Meuse, Institute of Inland Water Management and Waste Water Treatment RIZA, Lelystad, The Netherlands (in Dutch).

Nienhuis, P.H. & Leuven, R.S.E.W. 1997. The role of the science of ecology in the sustainable development debate in Europe. Verhandlungen der Gesellschaft für Ökologie 27: 1-9.

Nolan, D.T., Hadderingh, R.H., Jenner, H.A. & Wendelaar Bonga, S.E. 1998. The effects of exposure to Rhine water on the Sea trout smolt (*Salmo trutta* L.): an ultrastructural and physiological study. In: Nienhuis, P.H., Leuven, R.S.E.W. & Ragas, A.M.J. (eds.), New concepts for sustainable management of river basins. pp. 261-271. Backhuys Publishers, Leiden.

NRA 1994. Water quality objectives: procedures used by the National Rivers Authority for the purpose of the surface waters (river ecosystem classification) regulations. National Rivers Authority (NRA), Bristol.

OECD 1992. Report of the OECD workshop on the extrapolation of laboratory aquatic toxicity data to real environment. OECD Environmental Monographs 59: 43.

Pelgrom, S.M.G.J. 1995. Interaction between copper and cadmium in fish: metal accumulation, physiology and endocrine regulation. Thesis University of Nijmegen.

Pimm, S.L. 1991. The balance of nature? Ecological issues in the conservation of species and communities. The University of Chicago Press, Chicago.

Plackett, R.L. & Hewlett, P.S. 1952. Quantal responses to mixtures of poisons. J. Roy. Stat. Soc. B. 14: 141-163.

Ramade, F. 1995. Qualitative and quantitative criteria defining a "healthy" ecosystem. In: Rapport, D.J., Gaudet, C.L. & Calow, P. (eds.). Evaluating and monitoring the health of large-scale ecosystems. NATO Advanced Science Institutes Series 1: Global environmental change 28. Springer-Verlag, Berlin.

Renner, R. 1996. Ecological risk assessment struggles to define itself. Environmental Science & Technology 30/4: 172- 174.

Scheffer, M., Hosper, S.H., Meijer, M.L., Moss, B. & Jeppesen, E. 1993. Alternative equilibria in shallow lakes. Trends in Ecology and Evolution 8: 275-279.

Smith, D.G. 1990. A better water quality indexing system for rivers and streams. Water Research 24/10: 1237-1244.

Tonkes, M. & Botterweg, J. 1994. Totaal effluent milieubezwaarlijkheid. Beoordelingsmethodiek milieubezwaarlijkheid van afvalwater: literatuur- en gegevensevaluatie. Report 94.020, Institute of Inland Water Management and Waste Water Treatment (RIZA), Lelystad, The Netherlands. Hageman Verpakkers, Zoetermeer (in Dutch).

Tonkes, M., Van de Guchte, C., Botterweg, J., De Zwart, D. & Hof, M. 1995. Monitoring water quality in the future. Volume 4: monitoring strategies for complex mixtures. Distribution Office, Ministry of Housing, Spatial Planning and the Environment, Zoetermeer.

US-EPA 1985. Federal register 50, 46830 and 46936-47025. United States of America Environmental Protection Agency (US-EPA).

Van de Guchte, C. 1995. Ecological risk assessment of polluted sediments. European Water Pollution Control 5/5: 16-24.

Van der Zandt, P.T.J. & Van Leeuwen, C.J. 1992. A proposal for priority setting of existing chemical substances. Directorate-General for Environmental Protection, The Hague, The Netherlands.

Van Leeuwen, C.J. 1995. Ecotoxicological effects. In: Van Leeuwen, C.J. & Hermens, J.L.M. (eds.), Risk assessment of chemicals: an introduction. Kluwer Academic Publishers, Dordrecht

Van Leeuwen, C.J. & Hermens, J.L.M. (eds.) 1995. Risk assessment of chemicals: an introduction. Kluwer Academic Publishers, Dordrecht.

Van Loon, W.M.G.M. & Hermens, J.L.M. 1994. Sum parameter to estimate bioconcentration and baseline-toxicity of hydrophobic compounds in river water. Research Institute for Toxicology RITOX, Utrecht University, The Netherlands.

Van Loon, W.M.G.M. & Hermens, J.L.M. 1995. Monitoring water quality in the future. Volume 2: mixture toxicity parameters. Research Institute for Toxicology RITOX, Utrecht University, Distribution Office, Ministry of Housing, Spatial Planning and the Environment, Zoetermeer, The Netherlands.

Verhaar, H.J.M., Busser, F.J.M. & Hermens, J.L.M. 1995. Surrogate parameter for the baseline toxicity content of contaminated water: simulating the bioconcentration of mixtures of pollutants and counting molecules. Environmental Science and Technology, 29: 725-734.

V&W 1989. Water in the Netherlands: a time for action. National policy document on water management. Ministry of Transport and Public Works (V&W), The Hague, The Netherlands.

V&W 1996. Achtergrondnota Toekomst voor Water. Watersysteemverkenningen. Ministerie van Verkeer en Waterstaat (V&W), Directoraat-Generaal Rijkswaterstaat, Den Haag (in Dutch).

V&W 1997. Water kader: Vierde Nota Waterhuishouding – Regeringsvoornemen. Ministerie van Verkeer en Waterstaat (V&W), Den Haag (in Dutch).

Wendelaar Bonga, S.E. 1997. The stress response in fish. Physiological Reviews 77: 591-625.

THE EFFECTS OF EXPOSURE TO RHINE WATER ON THE SEA TROUT SMOLT (*SALMO TRUTTA TRUTTA L.*): AN ULTRASTRUCTURAL AND PHYSIOLOGICAL STUDY

D.T. Nolan[1], R.H. Hadderingh[2], H.A. Jenner[2] & S.E. Wendelaar Bonga[1]
[1]*Department of Animal Physiology, University of Nijmegen, The Netherlands;*
[2]*KEMA Environmental Services, Arnhem, The Netherlands*

Abstract

Sea trout smolts (*Salmo trutta trutta*) were continuously exposed to water from the river Rhine for 29 days during the natural seaward migration period of this species. Control and Rhine water-exposed groups were sampled after 3 and 24 hours, 8, 18 and 29 days in Rhine water and skin ultrastructure as well as a variety of blood parameters were examined to assess the effects. In the skin, exposure to Rhine water resulted in an increased incidence of apoptosis (physiological programmed cell death) and necrosis (toxin-induced cell death) in the filament cell populations. The intracellular vesicles of the upper filament cell populations were depleted and the microfilament bundles of the upper and basal filament cells were disrupted and aggregated after 3 hours in Rhine water. Microridge structures on the pavement cells, which anchor mucus to the body surface, disappeared on exposure to Rhine water, while numbers of mucous cells in the epidermis were unaffected. Qualitative examination revealed that in Rhine water, immature mucous cells occurred in the upper epidermis and were observed discharging at the surface. This did not occur in control fish and indicates an increased rate of mucus discharge. These cellular changes in the epidermis of Rhine water fish caused the formation of intercellular spaces, disrupting the structural integrity of the epithelium. Throughout these spaces, leucocytes were frequently seen, indicating effects on the immune system. These results are discussed in relation to the water quality of the lower Rhine and the effects on populations of migrating fish.

1. Introduction

The water quality of the river Rhine has been the focus of much international attention as the river system is influenced by many anthropogenic factors which have seriously affected the migratory species, in particular the salmonids (for general anthropogenic effects see: Crisp 1989, Ward & Stanford 1989; for the Rhine system specifically: Friedrich & Muller 1984, Van Dijk & Marteijn 1993, Tittizer *et al.* 1994). Although the quality of the water has been improved through international efforts, the river is still a complex mixture of contaminants (Friedrich & Muller 1984, Van Dijk & Marteijn 1993, Hendriks 1994, Streit 1994), whose specific and combined effects on fish are largely unknown.

As salmonid species have high water quality requirements, their presence is widely accepted as indicative of a healthy river system. Much attention has focused on the decline of Atlantic salmon (*Salmo salar*) in the river Rhine and the re-establishment of a self-sustaining population of migrating salmon (Van Dijk & Marteijn

New concepts for sustainable management of river basins, pp. 261–271
edited by P.H. Nienhuis, R.S.E.W. Leuven and A.M.J. Ragas
© *1998 Backhuys Publishers, Leiden, The Netherlands*

1993, Cazemier 1994, Roche 1994, Schulte-Wulwer-Leidig 1994). It has been shown that exposure to Rhine water induces stress effects in the skin of the rainbow trout, *Oncorhynchus mykiss* (Iger *et al.* 1994a) and furthermore, that many of these effects are mediated by cortisol (Iger *et al.* 1995), which is the primary stress hormone in fish (Wendelaar Bonga 1993, 1997). However, the rainbow trout is not an indigenous species to the Rhine system. Therefore we studied a salmonid species previously abundant in the Rhine, the sea trout, *Salmo trutta trutta*.

The purpose of the present study was to investigate the effects of exposure to Rhine water on the sea trout smolt, the juvenile stage which migrates to seawater. The salmonid smoltification process is extremely complex and combines physiological, morphological and behaviourial changes which enable the freshwater smolt to pre-adapt to and migrate into seawater and to survive there (Boeuf 1993, McCormick 1994). Rhine water combines both thermal pollution and complex chemical contaminants together in a manner likely to be deleterious to smolt welfare. However, there have always been sea trout in the Rhine and spawning and migration have been studied in this species as part of the rehabilitation plan (Van Dijk & Marteijn 1993). To date, nothing is known about the effects of exposure to increasingly polluted water on the seaward migrating smolt.

Stress effects in the skin epithelium were examined, as the skin and gill epithelia come into contact with changing environmental conditions and form the first barrier between the fish and the external environment. In addition, several blood parameters (osmotic, ionic, hormonal and metabolic) were examined to provide further data on any effects at the whole animal level.

2. Materials and Methods

Groups of 35 pre-smolt sea trout (39.37±6.16 grams, fork length 15.55±1.02 cm) were held in 400-l black plastic tanks for 6 weeks acclimatization in non-chlorinated tapwater as described previously (Iger *et al.* 1994a) at a flow through rate of 600 l·hour⁻¹. The fish were fed a commercial trout diet at 1% of body weight daily. Photoperiod was controlled by timeswitch, and adjusted periodically to match increasing natural daylength during March and April.

After acclimation, the water supply to two tanks was changed from tapwater to Rhine water, as described previously (Iger *et al.* 1994a). This water was pumped from the river Rhine at the KEMA property near Arnhem, the Netherlands and filtered by a lamellar filter system in a sediment chamber to remove particles larger than 2 mm before reaching the fish. Two groups of trout remained in running tapwater as controls. The temperature profile for both the Rhine water and the tap water was measured daily and Rhine water temperature increased faster than the tapwater during the period (Fig. 1). Dissolved oxygen content of the water ranged from 8.7-11.5 mg/l in tap water and 8.7-10.7 mg/l in Rhine water. Fish were sampled at 3 and 24 hours, 8, 18, and 29 days after transfer to Rhine water. Four fish from each treatment were sampled each time and alternate replicate tanks were used to avoid repetitively sampling the same tank.

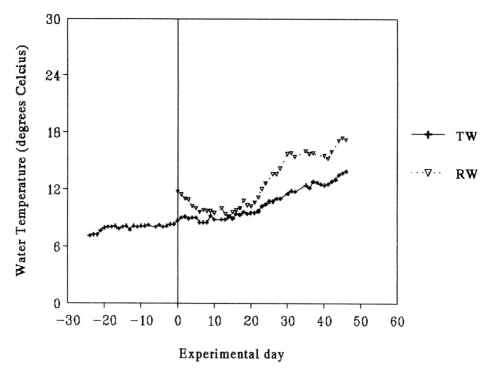

Fig. 1. Water temperature of the tapwater and Rhine water during the experimental period.

For light microscopy, skin biopsies were taken by scalpel blade from the dorsal part of the head, fixed in Bouin's fixative for 24 hours and processed by conventional methods. Sections (5 µm thick) were cut, mounted and stained by the PAS+ method to stain total mucous cells or Alcian Blue (pH 2.5) to stain acidophilic mucous cells (Blackstock & Pickering 1982a, b). Numbers of mucous cells per mm of epidermis were quantified by counting 6 independent views per fish with a microscope calibrated with a micrometer eyepiece.

For electron microscopy, skin biopsies (about 3 x 4 mm) were fixed and processed as described previously (Wendelaar Bonga *et al.* 1990) and viewed in a Jeol 100 CXII transmission electron microscope at 40kV.

Blood samples were withdrawn by needle from the caudal blood vessel into Na^+-heparinised syringes, the plasma was separated by centrifugation and immediately frozen in liquid nitrogen for analysis. Plasma cortisol was measured by radioimmunoassay (Lamers *et al.* 1992), plasma osmolality with a Roebling cryoscopic micro-osmometer, plasma sodium and chloride were determined by flame photometry (model IV auto-analyzer, Technikon) and plasma glucose using the Boehringer UV test kit (Boehringer, Mannheim, Germany).

Data were analyzed by non-parametric ANOVA with appropriate post tests. Statistical significance was accepted at $P<0.05$.

3. Results

3.1. Control fish

The ultrastructure of Salmo trutta epidermis is as described for teleost fish generally (Hendrickson & Matoltsy 1968, Whitear 1986), the rainbow trout (Iger et al.
1994a, b) and the brown trout specifically (Harris & Hunt, 1975). The epidermis is
composed primarily of filament cells and mucous cells. The outermost layer of filament cells is differentiated into the pavement cell layer the cells of which have a
microridge structure apically (Fig. 2a). This microridge structure is understood to
anchor the mucus to the body surface, enhancing the functional life of discharged
mucus. The population of filament cells proximal to the pavement cell layer are
spheroid cells which are highly active, synthesising vesicles. This population of cells
is interconnected by many desmosomes, with little intercellular spacing (Fig. 2a).
   Mucous cells occur throughout the upper epidermal cell layers, and mature and
increase in size as they migrate to the pavement cell layer to discharge at the surface. Mucosomes in these mucous cells are electron lucent, and have a stacked
appearance (Fig. 2a). The basal layer of filament cells is composed of elongated
cells, which are endocytotically active at the basal pole and contain bundles of
microfilaments (Fig. 2b). Spheroid cells close to the pavement cell layers also have
microfilament bundles. The structure of the epidermis of control fish was
unchanged throughout the experimental period. Occasional sloughing of the super-
ficial pavement cells was observed which is part of the normal renewal, but necrotic and apoptotic cells were seldom seen.
   Plasma osmolality did not vary throughout the experimental period and plasma
sodium and chloride concentrations were constant (Table 1). The levels of circulating
cortisol in the control groups of fish sampled ranged from 1 to 256 ng/ml plasma during experimental period (Table 1). Plasma glucose level were constant throughout the
period and did not vary significantly between sample points (Table 1).

3.2. Fish in Rhine water

Exposure to Rhine water resulted in an increased incidence of apoptosis and necrosis among the filament cell populations. The pavement cell layer frequently included apoptotic cells, seldom seen in the inner cell layers of controls, and the pavement
cell ridges were absent (Fig. 2c). In the inner cell layers, apoptosis was frequently
seen. After 3 hours in Rhine water, populations of vesicles became depleted in the
inner filament cell layers and there was a reduction in cell synthetic activity (Fig.
2c). Severe disruption to the structural organisation of the epidermis was apparent.
The filament bundles in the upper layers of filament cells in control fish were disrupted and wavy at three hours and intercellular spaces were apparent and quite
extensive. In the basal layer of filament cells, bundles of collapsed microfilaments
could be seen and the cellular organisation was disrupted (Fig. 2d). Lymphocytes
and other leucocyte types were commonly found throughout the epidermis from
three hours onwards (Figs. 2d and 2f).
   By day 29, the overall structure of the epidermis in these fish did not show
recovery (Fig. 2e). Sloughing of necrotic pavement cells was frequently observed

Table 1. Blood parameters measured in sea trout smolts (*Salmo trutta trutta*) in tap water and during exposure to Rhine water. Data from Rhine water fish were not significantly different at any sample point and values from all sample points are pooled and expressed as mean ± S.D. for n=20.

	Control	**Rhine water**
Cortisol (ng/ml)	59.3 ± 55	47.4 ± 52
Glucose (mg/dl)	54.9 ± 12	50.5 ± 14
Osmolality (mOsm/kg)	319 ± 11	320 ± 5
Sodium (mMol/l)	144 ± 13	150 ± 9
Chloride (mMol/l)	128 ± 13	130 ± 9

and necrosis and apoptosis were common throughout the upper epidermal cell layers. Intercellular spaces remained and immature mucous cells were still common close to the surface of the skin. Macrophages and lymphocytes were seen less frequently than in the earlier stages, but were still more prevalent than in control fish.

Neither the width of the epidermis nor the epidermal mucous cell counts were significantly different from controls at any sample point during the experiment.

Plasma osmolality of Rhine water fish did not vary over time and was not different from that of control fish, indicating that osmotic homeostasis of the blood compartment was maintained. This was also reflected by the concentrations of plasma electrolytes which remained stable over time, and comparable to controls. The mean plasma cortisol values measured in this group of fish varied considerably, but were not significantly different from controls (Table 1). Plasma glucose levels did not change between sample points and were not significantly different from those of control tap water fish (Table 1).

4. Discussion

The integrity of the skin epithelium was compromised by exposure to Rhine water. Acute effects included the opening of intercellular spaces within the tissue and a disruption of epithelial integrity. As there was no overall change in epidermal thickness, these spaces probably result from an interplay of three factors. First, because of removal of cells from the epithelium through apoptosis and necrosis, which was evident throughout the upper layers of the epidermis. Second, through increased mucous cell discharge to maintain the protective mucus coat on the body surface. Although overall mucous cell numbers were not reduced in Rhine water fish, the presence of smaller immature mucous cells in the upper layers and reduction in the proportion of large mature mucous cells present in the upper and middle epidermal layers can also explain the intercellular spaces. Third, swelling in freshwater is caused by osmotic effects and water coming into the tissue by osmotic drag across disrupted epithelia. However, this was not reflected in the osmolality of the blood, and therefore any additional water influx was probably compensated by increased elimination by the kidney.

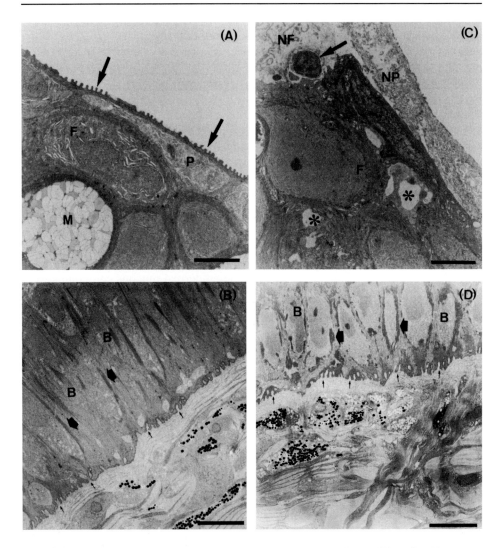

Fig. 2a. Upper epidermal layer of TW control trout skin. The upper cells are differentiated into pavement cells (P) which have distinctive microridge structures (arrows) at the water side. Below these is a layer of filament cells (F) and mucous cells (M). Cell-cell contacts are made by desmosomes and tight junctions which prevent intercellular spaces opening and thus preserve the integrity of the tissue.

Fig. 2b. Basal epidermal layer of TW control trout skin. The lower filament cells are differentiated into basal cells (B) with a distinct columnar appearance. These cells contain bundles of microfilaments (arrowheads) and are endocytotically active at the basal pole (small arrows), which is the contact point with the dermis.

Fig. 2c. Upper epidermal layer of Rhine water-exposed trout after three hours. The pavement cells are necrotic (NP) and some of the filament cells below also (NF). The microridge structures at the water face are gone. Intercellular spaces are opening up in the tissue (∗) and the overall structure is disrupted. A lymphocyte (arrow) is present beside the necrotic filament cell.

Fig. 2d. Basal epidermal layer of Rhine water-exposed trout after three hours. The basal cells (B) are disrupted and there are many aggregated microfilament bundles associated with this disruption (arrowheads). As a result, the contact with the dermis is wavy at the endocytotic pole (small arrows). Scale bar = 10 μm.

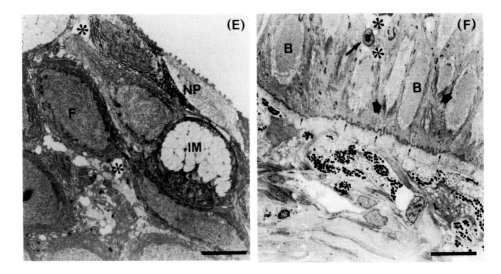

Fig. 2e. Upper epidermal layer of Rhine water-exposed trout at 29 days. Necrotic pavement cells are still evident (NP) and immature mucous cells are located in the upper cell layers, close to the surface (IM). Intercellular spaces (∗) are still present, probably related to the poor cell-cell contacts of the filament cells (F).

Fig. 2f. Basal epidermal layer of Rhine water-exposed trout at 29 days. The basal cells (B) still contain aggregated microfilament bundles (arrowheads), and the endocytotic basal pole is less wavy than earlier (small arrows). Intercellular spaces occur just above the basal cells (∗) and a lymphocyte infiltrates this space (large arrow).
Scale bar = 10 μm.

Increased cell turnover was indicated by increased levels of apoptosis and necrosis in both the epidermal cell layers. Necrosis was confined to the uppermost cells close to the interface with the Rhine water, and may be considered a direct toxic effect. By comparison, apoptosis occurred throughout the epidermal layers and indicates increased ageing of the cell populations. This may be considered an indirect effect of exposure to Rhine water, and is probably mediated by an internal hormonal factor. It has been shown in vitro that cortisol can induce apoptosis in the gill cells of the tilapia *Oreochromis mossambicus* (Bury *et al.* 1997).

As the microridges were absent on the pavement cells of Rhine water fish, a higher mucus secretion rate is necessary to replace unanchored mucus washed or sloughed off. Immature mucous cells located close to the upper cell layers indicate accelerated turnover of mucous cells caused by increased mucus discharge onto the body surface. However, this was not reflected in the total numbers of mucous cells which were present in the epithelia, so any increased discharge rate could be sustained by the mucous cell population of the epidermis.

Increased numbers of macrophages and lymphocytes penetrating through the epidermal cell layers may result from direct chemotaxis induced in response to an influx of foreign antigens from the Rhine water. The production of macrophage activating factor in rainbow trout is temperature-dependent, and inhibited at low temperature, but stimulated by exposure to higher temperatures (Hardy *et al.* 1994).

In the present experiment, transfer to Rhine water brought an immediate increase in water temperature of ±5°C. Macrophages may also be attracted into the epithelia to scavenge the cellular debris from apoptotic and necrotic cells.

The growth of the fish was not studied for several reasons. Firstly, different thermal regimes of the Rhine water and the tap water during the period (Fig.1) would result in differing metabolic rates, and therefore different food conversion rates between groups. Secondly, where the species is a smoltifying one, metabolic resource partitioning during the pre-smolt period might be expected to lead to investment into the production of a morphologically and physiologically differentiated smolt, and not necessarily somatic growth. Therefore examining physiological parameters appears more promising.

Condition factors (CF), were calculated for the fish. This parameter is often used to quantitatively evaluate the condition of sexually immature salmonids, and does so by expressing the individual body weight as a function of fork length, thus eliminating any effect of differing size between individuals. The calculation used is;

$$CF = (100*W)/L^3$$

where W=body weight in grams and L=fork length in centimetres. The CF of control fish dropped to about 1 as the smoltification progressed and as is known in smoltification process (Boeuf 1993). In the Rhine water fish, the CF fell steadily with time, and trend analysis indicated that this was statistically significant (slope - 0.026; r^2=0.347; F=12.226; p=0.002). This suggests that these fish were losing condition (i.e. not maintaining or gaining body weight) through the holding period.

Analysis of circulating cortisol levels in the blood are used in many fish studies to assess the level of stress (Fevolden & Roed 1993, Pottinger & Moran 1993, Waring *et al.* 1996). However, basal cortisol levels as well as the cortisol stress response are known to be different in smoltifying salmonids (Barton *et al.* 1985, Virtanen & Soivio 1985, Young *et al.* 1989, Avella *et al.* 1990, Franklin *et al.* 1992, Olsen *et al.* 1993) and this is a complicating factor. The sampling protocol in the present study necessitated handling the fish and inducing a stress response. While other studies have demonstrated an impaired cortisol stress response to handling stress in fish from polluted environments (Hontela *et al.* 1992, 1993, 1995), the circulating plasma cortisol levels in control and Rhine water fish were the same in this study.

Plasma osmolality and ions indicated that the fish were able to hyperosmoregulate normally, and maintain homeostasis in the blood. The values obtained for plasma osmolality, sodium, and chloride agree with those reported in the literature for salmonids (Williams *et al.* 1994). However, although ionic homeostasis was maintained overall, we have no data about changes in fluxes or turnover of ions in these fish. The reduction in condition factor in the Rhine water fish may be caused by increased energetic expenditure on active ion uptake over the 29 day period to compensate for enhanced diffusional losses of ions across damaged epithelia.

Changes in epidermal width, noted in Rhine water-exposed rainbow trout (Iger *et al.* 1994a), were not found in sea trout. Overall, the level of epidermal damage caused by exposure to Rhine water in sea trout appears to be greater than that reported previously in the study on rainbow trout (Iger *et al.* 1994a), indicating that the smolt may be more sensitive to Rhine water. In addition, the epidermal ultrastructural changes reported here are similar to those reported recently in a study of the effects of waste water effluents on brown trout (Burkhardt-Holm *et al.* 1997).

Identifying the specific factor(s) which might be responsible for the changes reported is problematic as the pollutant loading of the river is a low-level mixture of many toxic and potentially toxic elements and compounds. The stress effects induced by one factor alone may be negligible while the presence of a second factor may potentiate the toxicity of the first to the fish. This has been shown in goldfish (*Carassius auratus*) for catabolic ammonia and cadmium toxicity (Gargiulo *et al.* 1996). In addition the increase of ±5°C in water temperature experienced by the sea trout smolts on transfer to Rhine water may have brought about temperature shock-induced effects in the epithelia. It has been shown that a 3 hour temperature shock of +7°C can induce a number of cellular alterations in the epidermis of the rainbow trout (Iger *et al.* 1994b). Elevated water temperature can also interact with pollutants and increase the toxicity to fish (Reid *et al.* 1997).

The other naturally occurring salmonid species in the Rhine system is the Atlantic salmon (*Salmo salar*). The response of Atlantic salmon smolts to Rhine water is unknown at this time. As the smaller salmon smolt has a much larger surface area-volume ratio than the larger sea trout smolt, greater stress effects are likely.

5. Conclusions

This study shows that exposure to Rhine water has profound effects on the epidermis of the sea trout smolt. The most important of these are increased cell apoptosis and necrosis, and disruption of the structural integrity and intercellular swelling, at least for 29 days. Increased amounts of leucocytes in the epidermis indicate effects on the immune system.

The influence of this experience on the longterm survival of the sea trout smolt, and its subsequent performance in the marine environment remains to be shown. The water quality of the river may have improved dramatically in recent years, yet our data indicate that in a species which naturally occurs in the Rhine river system, exposure to water of the lower Rhine induces histo-pathological changes in the surface epithelia which could affect their ability to adapt to seawater. The longterm result of a stressed population of smolts at seawater entry is lower marine survival and low returns of sexually mature adults to breed.

As the composition of the river is a complex mixture of low level pollutants, identifying the effects of individual factors which are responsible for the histo-pathology observed is impossible. It is likely that the collective fish response to the combined pollutants may be greater than the response to individual compounds.

References

Avella, M., Young, G., Prunet, P. & Schreck, C.B. 1990. Plasma prolactin and cortisol concentrations during salinity challenges of coho salmon (*Oncorhynchus kisutch*) at smolt and post-smolt stages. Aquaculture 91: 359-372.

Barton, B.A., Schreck, C.B., Ewing, R.D., Hemmingsen, A.R. & Patiño, R. 1985. Changes in plasma cortisol during stress and smoltification in coho salmon, *Oncorhynchus kisutch*. Gen. Comp. Endocrinol. 59: 468-471.

Blackstock, N. & Pickering, A.D. 1982a. Acidophilic granular cells in the epidermis of the brown trout, *Salmo trutta L.* Cell Tissue Res. 210: 259-269.

Blackstock, N. & Pickering, A.D. 1982b. Changes in the concentration and histochemistry of epidermal mucous cells during the alevin and fry stages of the brown trout *Salmo trutta.* J. Zool., Lond. 197: 463-471.

Boeuf, G. 1993. Salmonid smolting: a pre-adaptation to the oceanic environment. In: Rankin, J. C. & Jensen, F. B. (eds), Fish Ecophysiology. pp 105-135. Chapman & Hall, London.

Burkhardt-Holm, P., Escher, M. & Meier, W. 1997. Waste-water management plant effluents cause cellular alterations in the skin of brown trout. J. Fish Biol. 50:744-758.

Bury, N.R., Li, J., Lock, R.A.C. & Wendelaar Bonga, S.E. 1998. Cortisol protects against copper induced necrosis and promotes apoptosis in fish gill chloride cells in vitro. Aquat. Toxicol. 40: 193-202.

Cazemier, W.G. 1994. Present status of the salmonids Atlantic salmon and sea-trout in the Dutch part of the river Rhine. Water Sci. Technol. 29: 37-41.

Crisp, D.T. 1989. Some impacts of human activities on trout, *Salmo trutta*, populations. Freshwater Biol. 21: 21-33.

Fevolden, S.E. & Roed, K.H. 1993. Cortisol and immune characteristics in rainbow trout (*Oncorhynchus mykiss*) selected from high or low tolerance to stress. J. Fish Biol. 43: 919-930.

Franklin, C.E., Davison, W. & Forster, M.E. 1992. Seawater adaptability of New Zealand's sockeye (*Oncorhynchus nerka*) and chinook salmon (*O. tshawytscha*): physiological correlates of smoltification and seawater survival. Aquaculture 102: 127-142.

Friedrich, G. & Muller, D. 1984. Rhine. In: Whitton, B. A. (ed), Ecology of European rivers. pp 265-315. Blackwell Scientific Publications, Oxford.

Gargiulo, G., de Girolamo, P., Ferrara, L., Soppelsa, O., Andreozzi, G., Antonucci, R. & Battaglini, P. 1996. Action of cadmium on the gills of *Carassius auratus L.* in the presence of catabolic NH_3. Arch. Environ. Contam. Toxicol. 30: 235-240.

Hardy, L.J., Fletcher, T.C. & Secombes, C.J. 1994. Effect of temperature on macrophage activation and the production of macrophage activating factor by rainbow trout (*Oncorhynchus mykiss*) leucocytes. Dev. Comp. Immunol. 18: 57-66.

Harris, J.E. & Hunt, S. 1975. The fine structure of the epidermis of two species of salmonid fish, the Atlantic salmon (*Salmo salar L.*) and the brown trout (*Salmo trutta L.*). I. General Organisation and Filament-containing cells. Cell Tissue Res. 157: 553-565.

Hendrickson, R.C. & Matoltsy, A.G. 1968. The fine structure of teleost epidermis. I. Introduction and filament-containing cells. J. Ultrastruct. Res. 21: 194-212.

Hendriks, A.J. 1994. Monitoring and estimating concentrations and effects of microcontaminants in the Rhine-delta: chemical analysis, biological laboratory assays and field observations. Water Sci. Technol. 29: 223-232.

Hontela, A., Rasmussen, J.B., Audet, C. & Chevalier, G. 1992. Impaired cortisol stress response in fish from environments polluted by PAHs, PCBs, and mercury. Arch. Environ. Contam. Toxicol. 22: 278-283.

Hontela, A., Rasmussen, J.B. & Chevalier, G. 1993. Endocrine responses as indicators of sublethal toxic stress in fish from polluted environments. Water Poll. Res. J. Can. 28:767-780.

Hontela, A., Dumont, P., Duclos, D. & Fortin, R. 1995. Endocrine and metabolic dysfunction in yellow perch, *Perca flavescens*, exposed to organic contaminants and heavy metals in the St. Lawrence river. Environ. Toxicol. Chem. 14: 725-731.

Iger, Y., Jenner, H.A. & Wendelaar Bonga, S.E. 1994a. Cellular responses in the skin of the rainbow trout (*Oncorhynchus mykiss*) exposed to Rhine water. J. Fish Biol. 45: 1119-1132.

Iger, Y., Jenner, H.A. & Wendelaar Bonga, S.E. 1994b. Cellular responses in the skin of the trout (*Oncorhynchus mykiss*) exposed to temperature elevation. J. Fish Biol. 44: 921-935.

Iger, Y., Balm, P.H.M., Jenner, H.A. & Wendelaar Bonga, S.E. 1995. Cortisol induces stress-related changes in the skin of rainbow trout (*Oncorhynchus mykiss*). Gen. Comp. Endocrinol. 97: 188-198.

Lamers, A.E., Flik, G., Atsma, W. & Wendelaar Bonga, S.E. 1992. A role for di-acetyl alpha-melanocyte-stimulating hormone in the control of cortisol release in the teleost *Oreochromis mossambicus*. J. Endocrinol. 135: 285-292.

McCormick, S.D. 1994. Ontogeny and evolution of salinity tolerance in adromous salmonids: hormones and heterochrony. Estuaries 17: 26-33.

Olsen, Y.A., Reitan, L.J. & Roed, K.H. 1993. Gill Na,K-ATPase activity, plasma cortisol level, and non-specific immune response in Atlantic salmon (*Salmo salar*) during parr-smolt transformation. J. Fish Biol. 43: 559-573.

Pottinger, T.G. & Moran, T.A. 1993. Differences in plasma cortisol and cortisone dynamics during stress in two strains of rainbow trout (*Oncorhynchus mykiss*). J. Fish Biol. 43: 121-130.

Reid, S.D., McDonald, D.G. & Wood, C.M. 1997. Interactive effects of temperature and pollutant stress. In: Wood, C.M. & McDonald, D.G. (eds), Global warming: Implications for freshwater and marine fish. pp 325-349. Society of Experimental Biology Seminar Series 61, University Press, Cambridge.

Roche, P. 1994. Habitat availability and carrying in the French part of the Rhine for Atlantic salmon (*Salmo salar L.*). Water Sci. Technol. 29: 257-265.

Schulte-Wulwer-Leidig, A. 1994. Outline of the ecological master plan for the Rhine. Water Sci. Technol. 29: 273-280.

Streit, B. 1994. Bioaccumulation processes of organic pollutants by animals of the river Rhine. Water Sci. Technol. 29: 145-147.

Tittizer, T., Scholl, F. & Dommermuth, M. 1994. The development of the macrozoobenthos in the river Rhine in Germany during the 20th century. Water Sci. Technol. 29: 21-28.

Van Dijk, G.M. & Marteijn, E.C.L. 1993. Ecological rehabilitation of the River Rhine, the Netherlands research summary report (1988-1992). Report of the project "Ecological Rehabilitation of the rivers Rhine and Meuse", report no. 50. RIZA/RIVM/RIVO-DLO/IBN-DLO/SC-DLO, the Netherlands.

Virtanen, E. & Soivio, A. 1985. The patterns of T3, T4, cortisol and Na^+-K^+-ATPase during smoltification of hatchery-reared *Salmo salar* and comparison with wild smolts. Aquaculture 45: 97-109.

Ward, J.V. & Stanford, J.A. 1989. Riverine ecosystems: the influence of man on catchment dynamics and fish ecology. In: Dodge, D.P. (ed), Proceedings of the International Large River Symposium. pp 56-64. Canadian Special Publications on Fisheries and Aquatic Science.

Waring, C.P., Stagg, R.M. & Poxton, M.G. 1996. Physiological responses to handling in the turbot. J. Fish Biol. 48: 161-173.

Wendelaar Bonga, S.E. 1993. Endocrinology. In: Evans D.H. (ed), The Physiology of Fishes. pp 469-502. CRC Press, Florida.

Wendelaar Bonga, S.E. 1997. The stress response in fish. Physiol. Rev. 77: 591-625.

Wendelaar Bonga, S.E., Flik, G., Balm, P.H.M. & van der Meij, J.C.A. 1990. The ultrastructure of chloride cells in the gills of the teleost *Oreochromis mossambicus* during exposure to acidified water. Cell Tissue Res. 259: 575-585.

Whitear, M. 1986. The skin of fishes including cyclostomes – Epidermis. In: Bereiter-Hahn J., Matoltsy, A.G. & Richards, R.J. (eds), Biology of the integument, vol 2. pp 8-38. Springer-Verlag, Berlin.

Williams, J., Gibney, E. & Timpson, P. 1994. Biochemical reference ranges for trout and salmon. J. Biomed. Sci. 4: 92-97.

Young, G., Björnsson, B.T., Prunet, P., Lin, R.J. & Bern, H.A. 1989. Smoltification and seawater adaptation in coho salmon (*Oncorhynchus kisutch*): plasma prolactin, growth hormone, thyroid hormones, and cortisol. Gen. Comp. Endocrinol. 74: 335-345.

EMISSION OF METALS FROM MINE STONE IN HYDRAULIC ENGINEERING STRUCTURES IN DUTCH RIVER BASINS

R.S.E.W. Leuven[1], W.A. Zwart[1], J.M.A. Kesseleer[2] & P.H. Nienhuis[1]
[1]Department of Environmental Studies, Faculty of Science, University of Nijmegen, P.O. Box 9010, 6500 GL Nijmegen, The Netherlands; [2]Dutch Standardization Institute, P.O. Box 5059, 2600 GB Delft, The Netherlands

Abstract

The present paper estimates the cumulative emissions of eight (heavy) metals (arsenic, cadmium, chromium, copper, lead, mercury, nickel and zinc) from mine stone applications in hydraulic engineering structures in drainage basins of Dutch rivers. Two leaching models (a diffusion and a percolation model) and three application scenarios for the period 1996-2010 (the stop, current perception and increase scenario) have been used. It is concluded that under the current scenarios the contributions of most metals (except arsenic and nickel) to actual loads are rather low (i.e. < 1%). Continued and widespread large-scale applications of contaminated secondary building materials can mean an extra obstacle on the way to meeting national and international emission reduction targets.

1. Introduction

Dutch environmental policy intends to scale down the utilization of primary building materials (e.g. sand and gravel) and to promote the substitution of these resources by secondary raw materials (VROM 1993). The desire to use alternative materials, such as mine stone, in hydraulic engineering structures has been motivated by the environmental hazards connected with the mining of primary resources, the over-exploitation of surface minerals and the growing problems of waste disposal.

Mine stone is a by-product of coal mining (synonyms of mine stone are coal mining waste, colliery spoil, colliery discard, grained carbon waste and quarry waste) and consists of fragments of the rock accompanying coal beds or brought to the surface during the construction of mine shafts. It can be used in a variety of ways, e.g. in constructing dams, dikes, breakwaters, quays and in protective layers which prevent damage to river beds, embankments and shores exposed to erosion. The (potential) utilization of mine stone as a building material has important and undeniable national implications with respect to economic and environmental impact (Skarzynska 1993, 1995a,b). On the one hand, mine stone is an abundant and inexpensive secondary building material, whereas the possibilities for transport along water routes are relatively good. On the other hand, this building material contains various harmful substances, which leach into the groundwater and surface water when it is used in hydraulic engineering structures and fills.

In order to prevent environmental damage, the utilization of mine stone in Dutch surface waters is regulated by the Pollution of Surface Waters Act (PSWA) and the

New concepts for sustainable management of river basins, pp. 273–282
edited by P.H. Nienhuis, R.S.E.W. Leuven and A.M.J. Ragas
© 1998 Backhuys Publishers, Leiden, The Netherlands

Building Materials Decree (BMD). Until now, the competent authorities for notification procedures and environmental permitting have only considered the leaching
of toxic substances for each single project. The impact of a single project on water
quality is generally negligible, due to low leaching rates and high rates of water flow
in rivers and estuaries. The consequences of cumulative emissions for a river basin
or on a national scale are unknown. According to the jurisprudence of the Dutch
Council of State they must be taken into account in the case of continued application of mine stone (Raad van State 1994).

The aim of this paper is to estimate the utilization of mine stone and the cumulative emissions of eight metals from mine stone used in hydraulic engineering
structures in the Dutch parts of the drainage basins of the rivers Rhine and Meuse
(including their estuaries). The consequences of various utilization scenarios for the
feasibility of national and international emission reduction targets will be discussed.

2. Materials and methods

Data

Historical data on the utilization of mine stone in hydraulic engineering structures
were collected from the environmental permitting files of the Dutch Ministry of
Transport, Public Works and Water Management (Directorate-General for Public
Works and Water Management), from the archives of the Dutch Society for
Environmental Conservation, from the notifications in the Dutch Gazette, from the
import files of the sand and gravel trading *De Beijer b.v.* and from literature
(Kesseleer 1993, Saft 1992, VROM 1984). Data concerning the contents of arsenic
(As), cadmium (Cd), chromium (Cr), copper (Cu), lead (Pb), mercury (Hg), nickel
(Ni) and zinc (Zn) in mine stone were obtained from an inventory prepared by the
Dutch Institute for Inland Water Management and Waste Water Treatment and the
National Institute for Public Health and Environmental Protection (Aalbers *et al.*
1993). The average metal contents of sorted and unsorted mine stone (sizes 10-125
mm and 0-70 mm, respectively) showed remarkable variability (Table 1).

Table 1. Average chemical composition of sorted and unsorted mine stone (Aalbers *et al.* 1993).

Metal	Unsorted			Sorted		
	N	[X]	SD	N	[X]	SD
As	30	13.84	11.19	11	4.19	1.60
Cd	30	0.83	0.40	10	0.63	0.48
Cr	30	32.98	21.47	10	40.07	20.06
Cu	30	35.55	13.61	9	27.03	10.27
Hg	7	0.17	0.17	10	0.11	0.14
Ni	29	38.96	14.24	12	29.27	14.08
Pb	30	26.71	22.38	11	15.00	3.60
Zn	30	138.66	119.98	11	67.00	27.90

N: number of samples; [X]: average content in mg/kg; SD: standard deviation.

Maximum leaching percentages of (heavy) metals were determined by TAUW (1986, 1987, 1988), whereas data with respect to leaching in batch and column tests were extracted from Gemeentewerken Rotterdam (1991) and Aalbers *et al.* (1993), respectively. The batch and diffusion test were performed according to the final drafts for the Dutch standards NEN 7345 and 7343 (NNI 1995 a,b), in order to simulate diffusion and percolation, respectively. Available data were summarized by Zwart (1996).

Scenarios

Three scenarios for the expected annual utilization of mine stone in the period 1996-2010 were designed; the stop, current perception and increase scenarios. Different figures were used for the assumed utilization in works predominantly exposed to river water and ground water (see Fig. 2 and Table 2). The stop scenario assumes the utilization of mine stone to have ceased in 1996. In the current perception scenario, the estimated utilization of mine stone in 1996 is based on the application procedures for environmental permits, while using the average of the annual utilization of mine stone in structures predominantly exposed to river water over the period 1980-1995 (real data) to extrapolate over the period 1997-2010. In the increase scenario, the utilization of mine stone in structures predominantly exposed to river water in 1996 equals that of the current perception scenario, and gradually increases to twice that of the current perception scenario in the period 1997-2010. It assumes that over the period 1997-2005 $2,600 \cdot 10^6$ kg·year^{-1} will be applied in fills predominantly exposed to groundwater.

Modelling and data processing

Because there is considerable similarity between the physico-chemical properties of mine stone from different sources and countries (Skarzynska 1995a), average values were used for the metal content of the most frequently applied sorted and unsorted mine stone. Average data of metal leaching in batch and column tests were transformed to field conditions by test-specific modelling (diffusion and percolation model) in order to estimate the cumulative leaching of metals from mine stone into surface water (Zwart 1996). Both models distinguished between the application of sorted and unsorted raw materials, as well as between hydraulic engineering structures predominantly exposed to surface water (e.g. constructing dams, breakwaters, quays and protective layers which prevent damage to river beds) and predominantly exposed to groundwater (i.e. fills), because of differences in chemical composition and leaching rates of metals under various field conditions. Leaching in fresh water was only considered, because available quantitative data on utilization of mine stone mainly concerned hydraulic structures in rivers and groudwater with a low salt content. For fills, it was assumed that only 10 percent of the leached metals contributes to pollution of river water and 90 percent remains in groundwater. Liquid/solid (L/S) rates used in the percolation model are determined as a function of percolation and height of the hydraulic engineering structure. Lowest, average and highest L/S rates were simulated using the Monte Carlo technique (5000 iterations), using available minimum, likeliest and maximum values for the height of the hydraulic engineering structures as well as for the percolation of water through mine stone and assuming triangular distributions. Based on historical data and the three scenarios for the application of mine stone in the period 1996-2010, the annual leaching of metals was calculated as a percentage of total Dutch emissions to surface waters in 1995 (the target year of the Dutch *National Policy Document on Water Management, Rhine Action Programme* and *North Sea Action Plan*). All model formulations can be found in Zwart (1996). The model formulations were programmed in the spreadsheet program Microsoft Excel 5.0® (Microsoft 1994). Monte Carlo simulations of percolation were performed with Crystall Ball®(Decisioneering Inc. 1993). The STIPT®version 4.6 program (Frigge 1994) was used for geographical mapping of known locations of mine stone applications (Fig. 1).

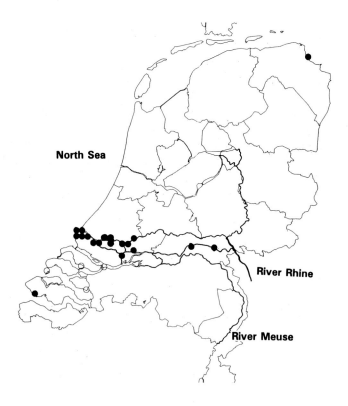

Fig. 1. Known locations of mine stone applications in hydraulic engineering structures and fills in drainage basins of Dutch rivers (•: quantitative data available; ° : no quantitative data available).

3. Results

Fig. 1 shows the known locations of hydraulic engineering structures in which mine stone has been used as a building material. Most locations are situated in the south-western part of the country (i.e. in the lower reaches of rivers Rhine and Meuse).

Fig. 2 illustrates the annual utilization of sorted and unsorted mine stone in drainage basins of Dutch rivers, according to available historical data (period 1980-1995) and the three scenarios (period 1996-2010). Although it is known that in the Netherlands mine stone was already used for hydraulic engineering before the 1980's (e.g. the Delta Works), quantitative data or estimates are lacking. Over the period 1980-1990, mine stone was used in fairly large quantities. However, these figures are mainly based on estimates (Saft 1992, VROM 1984, Zwart 1996), whereas real data are only available for the years 1982 and 1983. Until 1990, the competent authorities tolerated the utilization of mine stone in surface waters without PSWA-permit procedures, and the registration of secondary building materials applied was very limited. Over the period 1990 -1995, the utilization of mine stone was reduced compared with the period 1980-1990, due to the enforcement of PSWA (ban on dumping waste materials in surface waters without a proper permit) and due to objections and appeals against PSWA-permits for the application of secondary building materials in surface waters.

Until 1996, mine stone was occasionally used in fills along Dutch rivers. Table 2 summarizes available data (Zwart 1996). According to an environmental impact assessment that is required for an apply for environmental permits, large amounts of mine stone will be used over the period 1996-2005 as filling material for reconstruction of harbours in the city of Rotterdam (Gemeentewerken Rotterdam 1991).

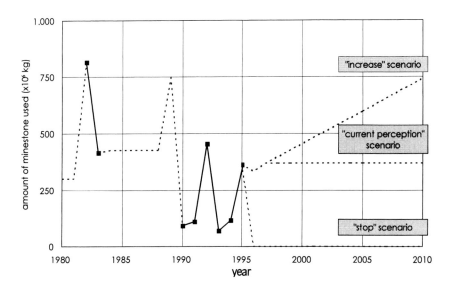

Fig. 2. Annual utilization of sorted and unsorted mine stone in hydraulic engineering structures, predominantly exposed to river water (•—•: real data; -----: estimates for the periods 1980 -1982 and 1984 – 1990 and scenarios for the period 1996 – 2010).

Table 2. Annual utilization of sorted and unsorted mine stone in hydraulic engineering structures, predominantly exposed to groundwater (in 10^6 kg.year^{-1}).

Scenario	Period/year	10^6 kg.year^{-1}
Historical data	1990-1992	50
	1993	5
	1994-1995	0
Expected utilization	1996	3050
Stop and current perception scenario	1997-2010	0
Increase scenario	1997-2005	2600
	2005-2010	0

Fig. 3 shows results of calculations using the leaching models developed. As is indicated for the case of arsenic, the leaching of metals from mine stone in hydraulic engineering structures and fills will lag for a long time even in case of the stop scenario. Based on the diffusion model, the annual leaching of arsenic ranges from 0.5 to 2.0 per cent of the total emission of this metal in Dutch surface waters in the year 1995. The percolation model yields much lower leaching values (range 0.01-0.12 percent) than the diffusion model.

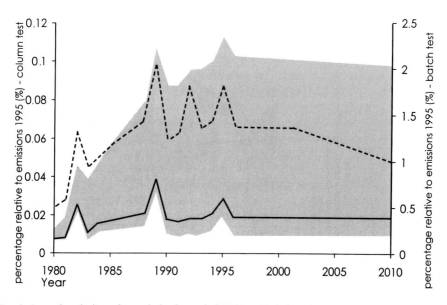

Fig. 3. Annual emission of arsenic in the period 1980 – 2010, based on the stop scenario and percolation model (– : using leaching data from column tests and average L/S-ratio; shading indicates range of lowest and highest L/S-ratio) and diffusion model (-----: using leaching data from batch tests).

Table 3 presents the leaching of metals in the year 2010, based on the current perception and increase scenarios. Expressed as a percentage of the total emission to Dutch surface waters in 1995 arsenic shows the highest level of annual leaching. In the diffusion model, this level may be as much as 2.67 or 3.70 per cent, based on the current perception and increase scenarios, respectively. Using the percolation model, annual leaching may vary from 0.025 to 0.199 and from 0.035 to 0.260 per cent, based on the current perception and increase scenarios, respectively. All other (heavy) metals studied show much lower values.

Based on the increase scenario, utilization of mine stone in 2010 will result in a total annual import of metals that varies between 10.8-45.0 per cent of the lowest known estimates of natural background loads (Table 4). Leaching of metals may range between 0.1-2.3 per cent of the natural background loads.

Table 3. Annual leaching of metals from mine stone in the year 2010, expressed as a percentage of total emission to Dutch surface waters in 1995.

Metal	Current perception scenario			Increase scenario		
	Column test		Batch test	Column test		Batch test
	Minimum	Maximum		Minimum	Maximum	
As	0.025	0.199	2.67	0.035	0.260	3.70
Cd	0.004	0.016	0.10	0.005	0.022	0.19
Cr	0.002	0.014	0.30	0.003	0.018	0.60
Cu	0.001	0.004	0.27	0.001	0.006	0.44
Hg	0.004	0.031	0.26	0.006	0.039	0.51
Ni	0.001	0.007	0.74	0.002	0.010	1.31
Pb	0.001	0.003	0.51	0.001	0.004	0.34
Zn	0.000	0.003	0.51	0.001	0.004	0.70

Table 4. Import and cumulative leaching of metals from mine stone in hydraulic engineering structures in comparison with natural background loads of Dutch rivers (in ton.year[-1]).

Metal	Natural background loads[1]	Year 2010/increase scenario	
		Import	Cumulative leaching[2]
As	n.a.	n.a.	0.80
Cd	1.2	0.54	0.01
Cr	248.0	26.87	0.27
Cu	106.0	23.34	0.98
Hg	0.7	0.10	0.01
Ni	n.a.	25.46	0.69
Pb	73.0	15.69	0.77
Zn	356.0	77.67	8.31

1: lowest known estimates of natural background loads (J. Dogterom, personal communication); 2: based on batch tests/diffusion model; n.a.: not available

4. Discussion

Some difficulties were encountered during the collection of historical data. Before 1990, the competent authorities usually tolerated the application of secondary building materials without environmental permitting or formal notification procedures. In several cases (e.g. the Delta Works) the amounts, sources and properties of the mine stone used were not or incompletely documented. Due to this lack of data, the present study probably underestimates the utilization of mine stone in hydraulic engineering structures over the above period.

Over the period 1996-2010, mine stone will be used mainly as filling material for recultivation of harbours in the city of Rotterdam. However, new legislation (BMD) and liberalization of quality standards for secondary building materials may lead to a large increase in the utilization of mine stone. When the BMD fully comes into force law in 1998, it will be allowed to use mine stone and several other building materials after a simple notification procedure, as long as product quality standards are met. It is to be expected that this will cause an increase in the application of minestone. Therefore, the real utilization over the period 1996-2010 is expected to be higher than that predicted by the current perception scenario, and may be nearer or even higher than that in the increase scenario.

Most of the mine stone used in Dutch river basins is originating from Germany and Belgium. The total annual import of metals related to the utilization of mine stone in hydraulic engineering structures is rather high in comparison with natural background loads (Table 4). Mine stone used in the past will remain an emission source of (heavy) metals for a long time, and continued utilization of this building material will add new diffuse sources of river water pollution. On the basis of the increase scenario and the diffusion model, mine stone will have a maximum share in annual Dutch emissions of (heavy) metals to surface water between 0.34-3.70 percent in 2010 (relative to the total emission in 1995). Percolation model yields a much lower share (0.00-0.26 percent). According to the Dutch *National Policy Document on Water Management*, *Rhine Action Programme* and *North Sea Action Plan*, emissions of (heavy) metals from diffuse and point sources must be further reduced in the period 1995-2010. Consequently, the relative contribution of mine stone to the total emission will probably increase with a factor 1.7-5.0 over the coming years. However, even in comparison with the lowest known estimates of the natural background loads the cumulative emissions of metals from mine stone are rather low (Table 4), due to low leaching rates of metals from mine stone.

In the Netherlands, the emission reduction targets for the period 1985-1995 have not been met for several pollutants (e.g. mercury, copper, nickel, zinc and lead), whereas meeting the reduction targets and water quality objectives for the years 2000 and 2015 will be very difficult (V&W 1996). The results of the present scenario study imply that the emission of metals from secondary building materials, e.g. arsenic and nickel from mine stone in hydraulic engineering structures, may be a factor contributing to these problems. Moreover, an overall increase in the utilization of mine stone and several other contaminated secondary building materials (e.g. metal and phosphorous slags) may be expected under BMD. This means that extra efforts will have to be made to reduce other sources of water pollution if we are to meet the national and international emission reduction targets. Therefore, it is recommended that policy makers should weigh up all pros (e.g. less use of primary materials and cost reduction), cons (e.g. additional effort to meet emission reduction targets) and their quantitative uncertainties on a national level, especially if future developments force emission reduction targets to be set even lower than in present plans.

The predicted level of leaching always varies greatly, depending on the models used and the metals considered. Under field conditions, leaching will depend on a combination of diffusion and percolation. The process intensity and ultimate amount of contaminants washed-out are also dependent on how minestone is incorperated in hydraulic structures, the degree of compaction and the salt content of ground- and river water. The real contribution of all involved processes varies for each application, and is actually unknown as model assumptions and uncertainties of input parameters are intrinsic to scenario studies. In the present study the range of leaching has been modelled using several models and percolation rates. Further research on leaching of metals and other contaminants (i.e. polycyclichydrocarbons) from secondary building materials under various field conditions can validate model assumptions and will reduce uncertainties in pros and cons.

Acknowledgements

The authors sincerely thank Mr. J.H.H.M. Klerkx, Mr. A.M.J. Ragas and two anonymous referees for reviewing the manuscript and the Ministry of Transport, Public Works and Water Management (Directorate General for Public Works and Water Management) and the Society for Environmental Conservation for permission to consult their archives.

References

Aalbers, Th.G., De Wilde P.G.M., Rood G.A., Vermij P.H.M., Saft R.J., Van de Beek A.I.M., Broekman M.H., Masereeuw P., Kamphuis Ch., Dekker P.M. & Valentijn, E.A. 1993. Milieuhygiënische kwaliteit van primaire en secundaire bouwmaterialen in relatie tot hergebruik en bodem- en oppervlaktewaterenbescherming. RIVM-rapport 771402006. Rijksinstituut voor Volksgezondheid en Milieuhygiëne, Bilthoven (in Dutch).

CUR 1992. Toepassing van alternatieve materialen in de waterbouw. Rapport 92-10, Civieltechnisch Centrum Uitvoering Research en Regelgeving, Gouda (in Dutch).

Decisioneering Inc 1993. Cristall Ball Version 3.0. Forecasting and risk analysis for spreadsheet users. Decisioneering Inc, Denver.

Frigge, P.J. 1994. Gebruikershandleiding STIPT versie 4.6 en IN versie 1.0. Informatie en Kennis Centrum Natuurbeheer, Wageningen (in Dutch).

Gemeentewerken Rotterdam 1991. MER-mijnsteen (Hoofdrapport en Achtergronddokument 1 t/m 5). Ingenieursbureau Havenwerken, Rotterdam (in Dutch).

Kesseleer, J.M.A. 1993. Mijnsteen, een nuttige toepassing of een milieuprobleem? Verslagen Milieukunde 64, Katholieke Universiteit Nijmegen (in Dutch).

Microsoft 1994. Microsoft Excel Version 5.0. Mircosoft Corporation.

NNI 1995a. Nederlandse Norm NEN 7343: uitloogkarakteristieken van vaste grond- en steenachtige bouwmaterialen en afvalstoffen. Uitloogproeven. Bepaling van de uitloging van anorganische componenten uit poeder- en korrelvormige materialen met de kolomproef. Nederlandse Normalisatie-instituut, Delft. UDC 628.516.66.061.34:543.21 (in Dutch).

NNI 1995b. Nederlandse Norm NEN 7345: uitloogkarakteristieken van vaste grond- en steenachtige bouwmaterialen en afvalstoffen. Uitloogproeven. Bepaling van de uitloging van anorganische componenten uit vormgegeven en monolitische materialen met de diffusieproef. Nederlandse Normalisatie-instituut, Delft. UDC 628.403-405:691.4:543.21 (in Dutch).

Raad van State 1994. Uitspraak in het geschil tussen de Stichting Natuur en Milieu te Utrecht en de Minister van Verkeer en Waterstaat. No. G05.91.1407, Raad van State, Afdeling Bestuursrechtspraak, Den Haag (in Dutch).

RWS/TAUW 1986. Uitloging van mijnsteen. Rijkswaterstaat, Dienst Binnenwateren/riza, Lelystad & TAUW Infraconsult B.V., Deventer (in Dutch).

Saft, R.J. 1992. Inventarisatie van het gebruik van secundaire materialen in de waterbouw. Rijkswaterstaat RIZA, Lelystad (in Dutch).

Skarzynska, K.M. (Ed.) 1993. Proceedings of the fourth International Sympoisum on the reclamation, treatment and utilization of coal mining wastes. Volumes 1 and 2. University of Agriculture, Kraków.

Skarzynska, K.M. 1995a. Reuse of coal mining wastes in civil engineering – Part 1: properties of minestone. Waste Management 15/1: 3-42.

Skarzynska, K.M. 1995b. Reuse of coal mining wastes in civil engineering – Part 2: utilization of minestone. Waste Management 15/2: 83-126.

TAUW 1986. Uitloging van mijnsteen. TAUW Infraconsult B.V./RIZA Rijkswaterstaat, Deventer/Lelystad (in Dutch).

TAUW 1987. Milieuhygiënische kwaliteit mijnsteen Auguste Victoria 0-150 mm. TAUW Infraconsult B.V., Deventer (in Dutch).

TAUW 1988. Milieuhygiënische kwaliteit mijnsteen Auguste Victoria. TAUW Infraconsult B.V., Deventer (in Dutch).

VROM 1984. Kwantitatieve inventarisatie gebruik van secundaire grondstoffen. Ministerie van Volkshuisvesting, Ruimtelijke Ordening en Milieubeheer (VROM). DHV/Broers & Partners, Den Haag (in Dutch).

VROM 1993. Nationaal Milieubeleidsplan 2. Milieu als maatstaf. Tweede Kamer, vergaderjaar 1993-1994, 23 560, nrs. 1-2, Ministerie van Volkshuisvesting, Ruimtelijke Ordening en Milieubeheer (VROM), Den Haag (in Dutch).

V&W 1996. Nota watersysteemverkenningen: Toekomst voor water. Ministerie van Verkeer en Waterstaat, Directoraat-Generaal Rijkswaterstaat, Den Haag.

Zwart, W.A. 1996. Milieubelasting van mijnsteen als grondstof in de waterbouw. Verslagen Milieukunde 124, Katholieke Universiteit Nijmegen (in Dutch).s

UNCERTAINTIES IN EVALUATING THE COHERENCE OF INDEPENDENTLY DERIVED ENVIRONMENTAL QUALITY OBJECTIVES FOR AIR, WATER AND SOIL

R.S. Etienne[1], F.H. Willemsen[1], A.M.J. Ragas[1] & D. Van de Meent[2]

[1]Department of Environmental Studies, Faculty of Science, University of Nijmegen, P.O. Box 9010, 6500 GL Nijmegen, The Netherlands; [2]National Institute of Public Health and the Environment (RIVM), P.O. Box 1, 3720 BA Bilthoven, The Netherlands

Abstract

The multimedia fate model SimpleBox (Van de Meent 1993) can be used to test the coherence of independently derived Environmental Quality Objectives (EQOs). A set of EQOs is called coherent if maintenance of an EQO in one compartment does not result in an EQO violation in another compartment due to intercompartmental exchange. Whether an incoherent set of EQOs should be adjusted, depends, among other things, on the uncertainties involved in coherence testing. In the present paper, these uncertainties are described, categorised and – where possible – quantified. A distinction is made between fundamental uncertainties (e.g. model assumptions) and operational uncertainties (uncertainties which can be quantified in terms of input parameters). The results show that the uncertainties involved in coherence testing are highly substance- and scenario-specific. Further research is recommended to develop methods for dealing with fundamental uncertainties. The results of the operational uncertainty analysis show that politicians need to determine an appropriate scenario and (in)coherence percentages for the purpose of coherence testing of EQOs.

1. Introduction

One of the goals of environmental management is to improve environmental quality by controlling the emission of pollutants. EQOs play a key role in achieving this goal. EQOs indicate the level of environmental quality at which no unacceptable adverse impacts on human health and ecosystems are expected. They can be used in environmental management to assess environmental quality and to determine corresponding emission limits (Ragas *et al.* 1998).

Since each system has its own characteristic quality features, it seems logical to determine specific EQOs for each system, e.g. for river basins. However, deriving system-specific EQOs is often considered unfeasible because of the huge numbers of different pollutants and a general lack of scientific knowledge. Most countries content themselves to general EQOs which are derived and applied on a national scale. Since general EQOs are thus often applied in the management of river basins, the present paper concentrates on deriving general EQOs.

In the Netherlands, EQOs are derived independently for soil, water and air. This implies that intercompartmental exchange of substances is not accounted for, which may result in incoherent EQOs. A set of EQOs is called incoherent if maintenance of an EQO in one compartment results in an EQO violation in another compartment.

The Dutch National Institute of Public Health and the Environment (RIVM) has developed a computer model, SimpleBox, to check the coherence of EQOs (Van de Meent 1993; Fig. 1). SimpleBox is a multimedia fate model of the "Mackay type" (Mackay 1991), in which the Netherlands is represented by eight homogeneous boxes: air, water, suspended particles, aquatic organisms, sediment and three soil compartments. SimpleBox can perform non-equilibrium, steady-state computations (level 3) and quasi-dynamic non-equilibrium, non-steady-state computations (level 4). To check the coherence of EQOs, the model is used in its level 3 mode: import and export of pollutants can take place, but the concentration levels within the compartments remain constant.

The Health Council of the Netherlands (Gezondheidsraad 1995) recently recommended that SimpleBox should not be used for coherence testing, because the model has not yet been validated in laboratory or field experiments and because a detailed sensitivity and uncertainty analysis is lacking. The aim of the present paper is to present the results of a study conducted in order to reveal the uncertainties involved in the application of SimpleBox for testing the coherence of EQOs in the Dutch situation. One way to assess these uncertainties is validation, which is however impeded by the lack of validation criteria, the complexity of the real world and the costs involved. Therefore, a different strategy was followed, in which it was attempted to identify the different sources of uncertainty and to assess the acceptability of these uncertainties within the context of coherence testing of EQOs.

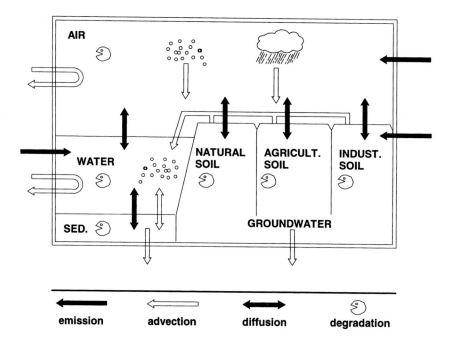

Fig. 1. Schematic representation of SimpleBox, version 1.1 (Van de Meent 1993).

2. Materials and Methods

Two types of uncertainties were distinguished:
- fundamental uncertainties, which cannot be quantified in terms of input parameters, e.g. model assumptions;
- operational uncertainties, which can be quantified in terms of input parameters, e.g. uncertainty about the vapour pressure of a substance.

Since fundamental uncertainties cannot be quantified, they were identified and assessed qualitatively. Identification of fundamental uncertainties was based on the classification of uncertainties presented by Morgan & Henrion (1990), in combination with a detailed analysis of SimpleBox parameters and model assumptions. To assess the acceptability of the fundamental uncertainties, seven scientists and policy makers active in relevant fields were interviewed. They were asked for their opinion on coherence testing of EQOs, the application of SimpleBox and application criteria for environmental models in general.

Operational uncertainties were identified and assessed quantitatively by means of an uncertainty analysis of SimpleBox model output. This output consists of concentration ratios between compartments (SimpleBox concentration ratios or SBCRs). In the present study, uncertainty analysis was performed for air-water SBCRs of 11 volatile substances (Table 1).

Input parameters were divided into three classes, depending on the origin of the dominant type of uncertainty. Table 2 lists these classes, together with examples and the approach chosen to deal with these uncertainties. Operational uncertainty was not quantified for those parameters which are defined by model assumptions, e.g. spatial variability (since the spatial dimensions are determined by the domain scenario chosen). Monte Carlo simulation was used for parameters whose uncertainty can be described by a probability distribution. This simulation technique assigns a probability density function to each input parameter, then randomly selects values

Table 1. Names and CAS numbers of the 11 volatile compounds considered in the operational uncertainty analysis.

Chemical name	CAS Registry number
dichloromethane	75-09-2
ethylene oxide	75-21-8
1,1-dichloroethane	75-34-3
1,2-dichloropropane	78-87-5
trichloroethene	79-01-6
styrene	100-42-5
acrylonitrile	107-13-1
toluene	108-88-3
2-chloro-1,3-butadiene	126-99-8
tetrachloroethene	127-18-4
1,2,3,4-tetrachlorobenzene	634-66-2

from each of the distributions and inserts them into the model equations. Repeated calculations (iterations) produce a distribution of output values, reflecting the combined impact of operational uncertainty in each input parameter. The input uncertainty distributions were defined by collecting data mainly from handbooks and databases. The software package Crystal Ball 3.0© was used to perform the Monte Carlo simulations (Decisioneering Inc. 1993). Each model run consisted of 10,000 iterations, which is generally considered sufficient to obtain a representative picture of the output uncertainty distribution (Morgan & Henrion 1990).

Scenarios were formulated for some of the parameters whose value is influenced by policy decisions, e.g. import concentrations. The scenario parameters were chosen in such a way as to represent the Dutch situation in one of the following scenarios:
- Scenario 1: import concentration to air and water at EQO level;
- Scenario 2: import concentration to air at EQO level, to water negligible;
- Scenario 3: import concentration to water at EQO level, to air negligible.

In order to test the coherence of EQOs, one compartment needs to be chosen in which the EQO is maintained; this is called the primary compartment. The concentration in the other compartment is then predicted by SimpleBox. In scenario 1 the primary compartment can be either water or air. In scenarios 2 and 3 the primary compartment is determined by the scenario assumptions, resulting in air as primary compartment in scenario 2 and water as primary compartment in scenario 3.

To obtain a coherence indicator, the SimpleBox output distribution of SBCRs (resulting from the operational uncertainty analysis) is divided by the air-water EQO concentration ratio (EQOCR). The interpretation of this indicator depends on which compartment is the primary one. If water is the primary compartment, an indicator value of more than 1 implies that the EQO in air is being exceeded. If air is the primary compartment, an indicator value of less than 1 implies that the EQO in water is being exceeded. This coherence indicator does not account for the fundamental uncertainty in model predictions.

Table 2. Input uncertainty.

Uncertainty class	Uncertainty subclass	Example	Method
Scenario uncertainty	Domain scenario uncertainty Decision scenario uncertainty	system area emission ratio to air/water; emission rate to soil	scenario scenario; Monte Carlo
Variability (Stochasticity)	Temporal variability Spatial variability	wind speed water depth	Monte Carlo none
Inaccuracy	Empirical Inaccuracy (Error) Lack of data (Ignorance)	vapour pressure water depth	Monte Carlo Monte Carlo

3. Results

3.1. Fundamental uncertainties

Fundamental uncertainties in SimpleBox are present at different levels of the model (Willemsen 1996), and arise from two main sources. Firstly, SimpleBox makes various assumptions with respect to the environmental compartments (e.g. the size of the compartments, how many different compartments must be modelled), and the behaviour of substances in these compartments (e.g. homogeneity within the compartments). These assumptions, which define the larger part of the model, are to some extent made by the modelmaker, but must also correspond with assumptions made earlier in setting the policy on EQOs. Because these assumptions define the model, their uncertainty cannot be assessed within the model itself and these uncertainties are therefore fundamental.

A second category of fundamental uncertainties arises from the use of formulas for estimating empirical quantities that cannot be entered directly, usually because of a lack of data on that particular quantity. Derivation of the bioconcentration factor from the more readily available K_{ow} (optional in SimpleBox) is an example of such a formula. The optional character of some model formulations implies that fundamental uncertainty may differ for different model applications.

The results of the interviews indicated that there was no consensus as to what were the most important (fundamental) uncertainties (Willemsen 1996). Opinions also differed on the importance and feasibility of (partial) validation. A direct relationship between the fundamental uncertainties distinguished and the acceptance of the model could therefore not be established.

3.2. Operational uncertainties

The uncertainties in the air-water SBCRs of the 11 selected volatile substances were found to be highly dependent on the nature of the substance and on the scenario (Etienne 1996). The ratio of the upper and lower bounds of the 95% confidence intervals ranged from 6.49 (for acrylonitrile in scenario 1) to 7,433 (for 2-chloro-1,3-butadiene in scenario 2) with a median of 11.84 (for 1,2,3,4-tetrachlorobenzene in scenario 3).

To illustrate the results of coherence testing, Fig. 2 shows a simplified output uncertainty distribution for acrylonitrile in scenario 1. It indicates that the EQO in air will be exceeded with a probability of 94.5% if water is the primary compartment. If air is the primary compartment, there is a probability of 5.5% that the EQO in water will be exceeded. An overview of the coherence indicator distributions for the other substances and scenarios is presented in Fig. 3.

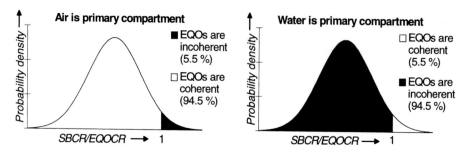

Fig. 2. The output distribution of the coherence indicator for acrylonitrile in scenario 1.

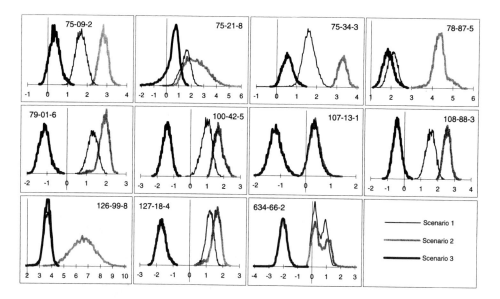

Fig. 3. Output uncertainty distributions of the logarithm of $(SBCR/EQOCR)_{air-water}$ for each scenario and each substance (see Table 1 for their names).

4. Discussion and conclusions

Acceptance of SimpleBox for coherence testing of EQOs would imply that the uncertainties of the model predictions are of acceptable magnitude. The results indicate, however, that general acceptance of SimpleBox for coherence testing is debatable since the magnitudes of these uncertainties are substance- and scenario-specific. General acceptance of this model would be a strategy which in some cases may still result in an unacceptable level of uncertainty. Fundamental uncertainties vary due to optional model formulations in SimpleBox, while operational uncertainties strongly depend on the available input data. This implies that the acceptability of SimpleBox model results for coherence testing would have to be assessed for each model application separately. This may result in acceptance of the model predictions for some situations and in rejection for others.

Fundamental uncertainties in SimpleBox can be identified and described, but a suitable method for dealing with these uncertainties in terms of model acceptance is lacking. Subjective quantification by experts and other persons involved turned out to be unsuccessful, mainly because most of the interviewed persons could not discriminate between fundamental uncertainties and other (political) factors influencing model acceptance. Further research is recommended to develop methods for dealing with fundamental uncertainties in model acceptance.

Operational uncertainty can be quantified by modelling different scenarios and by applying of the Monte Carlo simulation technique. The results indicate that the coherence of a set of EQOs depends on three variables: (1) the scenario chosen, (2) the primary compartment chosen and (3) the acceptable probability percentage of (in)coherence. A decision tree can be set up illustrating which substances in which cases have an incoherent set of EQOs (Fig. 4).

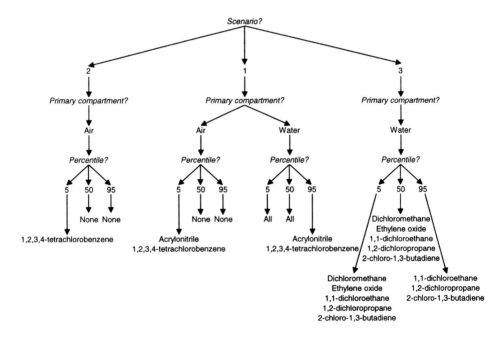

Fig. 4. Coherence decision tree. "Percentile?" asks for the permissible *in*coherence percentage of the output distribution (black in Figure 2). The substances listed have an *in*coherent set of EQOs.

The question is whether the results presented in this paper justify the adjustment of existing EQOs. An example: "Should the EQO of acrylonitrile in water be adjusted, because SimpleBox predicts that in scenario 1 the EQO in air will be violated with a probability of 94.5% if water quality equals its EQO? And what if this probability were 80% or 50%?" First, it should be stated that adjustment of EQOs is a political issue. So, politicians should determine an appropriate scenario and primary compartment, as well as the acceptability of fundamental and operational uncertainties in model predictions. An appropriate scenario and primary compartment should be based on a valuation of existing or future environmental conditions. The acceptability of fundamental and operational uncertainties should be determined within the framework of setting EQOs, which comprises the weighing of adverse impacts of pollutants and the probability of these adverse impacts occurring against the costs involved in realising EQOs. Further research is necessary to gain more insight in this decision making process and for the development of decision support instruments.

As long as the existing EQOs are not yet adjusted, actors in the field of environmental management should be aware that maintenance of an EQO in one compartment may result in an EQO violation in another. More specific, the results presented in this paper indicate for several volatile substances, that the EQO in air will be violated with a considerable likelihood if the EQO in water is maintained. Water managers in the Netherlands are therefore advised to aim for a water quality which lies well below the existing EQO. Since the substances involved are no major water pollutants, realising this better water quality will not be very problematic for water managers.

References

Decisioneering Inc. 1993. Crystal Ball Version 3.0 User Manual. Decisioneering Inc., Denver, USA.

Etienne, R.S. 1996. Operational uncertainties in SimpleBox; operational uncertainty analysis of the air-water concentration ratio computed by SimpleBox for 11 volatile compounds. Department of Environmental Studies, Reports Environmental Studies No. 136, University of Nijmegen, The Netherlands.

Gezondheidsraad. 1995. Het project Integrale Normstelling Stoffen: advies van een commissie van de Gezondheidsraad. Rapport No. 1995/07, Den Haag. The Netherlands (in Dutch).

Mackay, D. 1991. Multimedia environmental models. The fugacity approach. Lewis Publishers, Chelsea, USA.

Morgan, M.G. & Henrion, M. 1990. Uncertainty. A guide to dealing with uncertainty in qualitative risk and policy analysis. Cambridge University Press, New York, USA.

Ragas, A.M.J., Laar, B.J. van de, Schijndel, A.M.J. van, Stortelder, P.B.M. & Klapwijk, S.P. 1998. Application of the water-quality based approach and models in water pollution control: possibilities and restrictions. In: Nienhuis, P.H., Leuven, R.S.E.W. & Ragas, A.M.J. (eds), New concepts for sustainable management of river basins. pp. 191-209. Backhuys Publishers, Leiden, The Netherlands.

Van de Meent, D. 1993. SIMPLEBOX: a generic multimedia fate evaluation model. National Institute of Public Health and the Environment, Report No. 672720001. Bilthoven, The Netherlands.

Willemsen, F.H. 1996. Fundamentele onzekerheden in SimpleBox; een onderzoek naar de invloed van fundamentele onzekerheden in SimpleBox op de acceptatie van het model. Vakgroep Milieukunde, Verslagen Milieukunde no. 131, Katholieke Universiteit Nijmegen. The Netherlands (in Dutch).

ON THE WAY TO TOTAL WATER MANAGEMENT FOR LARGE RIVERS IN THE NETHERLANDS

S.P.G. Van de Kamer, R. Postma, E.C.L. Marteijn & C. Bakker
Department of Public Works and Water Management, Institute for Inland Water Management and Waste Water Treatment RIZA, P.O. Box 9072, 6800 ED Arnhem, The Netherlands

Abstract

The type of water management that takes account of directive developments in terms of economy as well as ecology and sociology is indicated by the phrase "total water management". However, the development from integrated into total water management would appear to be a conceptual one rather than a chronological one: total water management has always existed.

In the last few decades, however, the claims of sectoral interests have grown to the extent that they can no longer all be honoured. A choice must be made, necessitating the integrated weighing of such interests. On the one hand, this will require sufficient knowledge to be able to define the various options and, on the other, sufficient public support.

In making use of knowledge for the benefit of policy analyses, it has become evident that the use of ecotopes considerably improves the communication between the disciplines. In order to obtain public support, the integrated surveys detailed in the "Landscape Planning of the River Rhine in the Netherlands" are suitable for encouraging a wide public to contribute ideas about problems and solutions. In the execution of restoration plans, such as the nature development project at the floodplains of the river Waal, the support from all authorities involved as well as other interested parties is an absolute precondition for success.

After the high waters of 1994 and 1995, a decision on an international level was made remarkably quickly with regard to the improvement of protection against high waters in the Rhine basin. This was because the hydrologists, who had been working together for many years, now had the necessary knowledge at hand. Moreover, public support for the changes was very wide, because all parties involved had suffered their damage only very recently.

1. Introduction

The "Space for Water" working paper (Project team NW4 1995), which is meant to instigate discussions and to prepare the way for the Fourth National Policy Document on Water Management, characterizes the present conceptual development of water management as follows: "Water management is taking more and more account of directive developments in terms of economy as well as ecology and sociology" (Fig. 1). In other words: the interaction between water management and its surroundings is becoming stronger.

Van Rooy & De Jong (1995) call the type of water management based on this description "total water management". In their opinion, total water management is the (tentative) end of a historical development, which started with the presence of modern human life on this planet. We have successively had "no management" in

New concepts for sustainable management of river basins, pp. 291–307
edited by P.H. Nienhuis, R.S.E.W. Leuven and A.M.J. Ragas
© *1998 Backhuys Publishers, Leiden, The Netherlands*

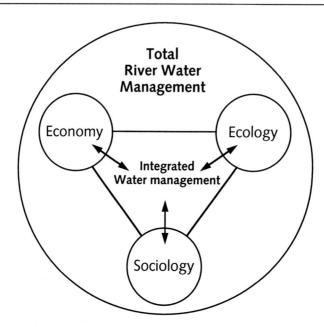

Fig. 1. Water management is taking more and more account of directive developments in terms of economy, ecology and sociology.

prehistory, "basal management" from Roman days, "sectoral management" as from the industrial revolution and "integrated management" since 1985, which will subsequently evolve into "total management". Integrated water management is still inwards-oriented, towards the multifunctional and durable use of the coherent whole of water, bed, bank, technical infrastructure and the biological component. Total water management makes water management part of society, where economy, ecology and sociology become directive. Economy is directive with its awareness of scarcity of resources, ecology with its awareness of the vulnerability of natural resources and relationships, and sociology with its human standards and values. The overall support of water management will be determined by yield, durability and feelings.

In systems analysis, however, the idea of an interrelationship of (water) systems and their surroundings is quite familiar (e.g. Quade & Miser 1981), so that the development into total water management is a conceptual one rather than a chronological one: Hasn't there always been total water management?

The aim of this paper is to describe the policy process towards total water management for large rivers. In the second paragraph the conceptual development of water management will be discussed, followed by an exemplification of the key-concept "ecotope" and the use of a Decision Support System for making the proper policy integrations. The fourth paragraph deals with a case study, in order to demonstrate trial and and error in persuing policies. The paper ends with a discussion on the most recent policy item of the International Rhine Commission, the protection against exceptional river floods.

2. Conceptual development

The restoration of the upper area of the river Rhine in the first part of this century enjoyed great public support because it was permanently adapted to meet the sectorial needs. In the preceding centuries, this gearing caused many conflicts, induced by different interests. In short, management used to be primarily focused on regional flood protection and land reclamation for agricultural purposes. Only later, these interests were advanced from a more national point of view. In this context, the defence interests played a stimulating part. Finally, the needs of the shipping trade were met (Ploeger 1992).

Even before the first dikes were built in the late middle ages, floodplain forests had been cut down on a large scale. The floodbanks were excellent settlement sites in the boggy Netherlands. Wood was still the primary source of fuel. In the following centuries, rivers continued to be characterized by a dynamic main channel, shallow, sandy secondary channels, steep and gradually sloping banks, sand and silt banks, in spite of all the land reclamations. There still was an abundance of marshes and open pastures in addition to what was left of the floodplain forests. But, particularly in the previous century and in this one, these ecotopes disappeared because of the rivers being regulated. Summer dikes were built to serve agriculture. The river became a single deep channel with wide strips of pastures along its sides, enclosed by strong dikes. Water management was multifunctional and was widely supported.

The relationship between water management and society has always been a close one. But until the latter half of this century there had been, literally and figuratively, enough space for sectoral solutions. Around 1900, some 10% of the river area consisted of so-called "non-land", which could be reclaimed if necessary with a little extra effort. The emphasis was on economic development and there was ample space for this. By the middle of this century, space became more cramped: the population of the Netherlands grew from 5 million in 1900 to about 15 million now. The buffer space, the amount of "non-land", diminished to about 1% of the river area. Prosperity increased as well as the emancipation of people and social and ecological awareness. The little bit of "non-land" left, suddenly became very valuable and a fight was put up for its preservation, protection and expansion. But all interests and sectoral decisions can no longer be fully honoured: a choice must be made. Economy, sociology and ecology have found a new balance.

A milestone in the development into this new balance was the advice to the government of the Becht Committee in 1977. This committee had been set up after certain dikes had been strengthened too rigorously, such as the one at Brakel. Becht was clearly fully aware of the various functions of the river area; in addition, the committee insisted on a wider form of decision-making. But the method of strengthening dikes was not really changed until the Boertien Committee was set up in 1992. Potman (1995) indicates several causes, such as the lower priority that was given to the strengthening of river dikes by the Dutch government due to the economic recession, the monoculture of civil engineers at the various government departments involved, and the individual character of the separate plans for each dike section. In 1992, the Boertien Committee acknowledged Becht's range of ideas and introduced the Environmental Impact Assessment (EIA) as a tool. Boertien made the last move to cut across the monoculture of civil engineers and opened up the forming of plans. After the 1995 high waters, the Delta Act on Large Rivers gave top priority to the strengthening of 150 km of dikes: to be realized before 1997. In spite of the fact that the EIAs, which had only just been introduced, were ignored, the various parties involved, seem to be reasonably satisfied with the results. Work is being carried out along Boertien's lines, there has been no relapse into the sectorial approach. Use has been made of the technical options linked up with the requirements of society. For this reason, Potman (1995) believes we can have confidence in the dikes strengthened after 1996 within the framework of the Flood Protection Act.

The increasing ecological and social awareness also had consequences for the riverbed between the main dikes. In the working paper "Dealing with Water" (Ministry of Transport, Public Works and Water Management 1985) the concept of integrated water management was first introduced. The Rhine Action Programme (IRC 1987) and the Third National Policy Document on Water Management (Ministry of Transport, Public Works and Water Management 1989) defined the aim of creating a more natural river area and the return of characteristic species in international and national policies. Visionary plans, such as the Black Stork Plan (De Bruijn et al. 1987) and Living Rivers (WWF 1992), described in an appealing way how river nature might look and how this could be realized in combination with other functions of the river area. The pilot projects carried out, such as the one at the Duursche Waarden at the river IJssel (Cals 1994), resulted in even greater public support for nature development.

As a consequence of the Second Structure Plan for Traffic and Transport (Ministry of Transport, Public Works and Water Management 1990) more space was claimed for the shipping trade. After the high waters of 1995, the river itself claimed more space for its discharge of water, sediment and ice (Ministry of Transport, Public Works and Water Management & Ministry of Housing, Physical Planning and the Environment 1996, IRC 1995). This space is not likely to be found a priori in another round of strengthening of the dikes. After 2000, measures to lower the water level will be preferred, where possible, such as lowering of the floodplain level.

Total water management appears more successful than earlier water management concepts as it is less restrained by gaps in scientific knowledge and as the decisions made fit in better with the existing balance between economy, ecology and sociology (Van Rooy 1995a). In other words, at stake are knowledge of the aquatic environment (hydrology, ecology, morphology), and public support. At the end of the day, both issues are taken into account and used to the optimum. This may explain the success of the Boertien Committee.

But not all the available knowledge of the aquatic environment and estimates of public support are always used:
– At weirs, even in brooks, fish ladders are still commonly used to allow for fish migration. From the points of view of dehydration and high-water control, a more integrated solution, such as re-meandering, would be more obvious. However, this is seldom taken into consideration.
– The dikes along the river Meuse in Limburg were only built because there was no public support in the region for a better integrated solution for the protection against high waters: the creation of more space for the river. Internationally, on the other hand, there is support for this alternative. Dikes take away space from

the river both directly and indirectly: diking part of the riverbed implies that the water must be discharged through a smaller channel. Moreover, pressure to build on the area behind the quays will increase, in spite of the fact that there is no guarantee of protection against floods. This will increase the risk of casualties in the event of extremely high waters.

3. Steps in policymaking

The factors determining the success of water management are scientific knowledge and public support. Progress has recently been made in both areas. The use of ecotopes has facilitated the communication between engineers and ecologists. With ecotopes it is possible to find a technical-scientific connection between nature, shipping and flood protection. This is especially important for integrated considerations in policymaking. The introduction of integrated surveys is the first step of a joint planning process. A joint planning process is seen as one of the best opportunities to develop sufficient public support for water management (Van Rooy 1995b). A healthy first step is joint problem analysis, so that the parties involved (organizations and inhabitants) have a problem in common as well as some insight into the possible solutions. It is important that all the relevant interests are included. Talking about solutions without a common problem is useless. This was demonstrated once again by the "depoldering" discussions in the province of Zeeland.

3.1. Ecotopes

Policymaking is generally based on a comparison of various variants. Apart from the financial aspect, the effect on the various interests will determine the decision. Where the restoration of river areas is concerned, physical space is an important aspect. Flood protection, nature and shipping all claim a part of the limited space. Consequently, it is convenient to use a spatial unit which is related to hydraulic, ecological and morphological characteristics, so that direct connections can be found between flood protection, nature and shipping. Ecotopes offer this possibility for the Dutch river area. Ecotopes are defined here as (Wolfert 1996): "ecological units, the space of which can be limited and the composition and development of which are determined by local abiotic, biotic and anthropogenic conditions".

Rademakers & Wolfert (1994) have set up a classification of ecotopes for the Dutch river area, consisting of 65 ecotopes (Table 1), which allows us to make a surface-covering chart of the river including the floodplains on a scale of about 1:25,000 to 1:100,000. The ecotopes are distinguished on the basis of 3 characteristics: hydrodynamics, morphodynamics and vegetation structure (Amoros *et al.* 1987, Rademakers & Wolfert 1994). The hydrodynamic and morphodynamic characteristics together form the abiotic part of the ecotope: the physiotope. Both characteristics include a wide range of physical properties, but are calculated in practice by a limited number of parameters, such as flooding frequency and flow rate (Pedroli & Rademakers 1995) or bed properties (Harms & Roos-Klein Lankhorst 1994, Reijnen *et al.* 1995). The vegetation structure, which is determined e.g. by pasture management, can be deduced for the greater part from aerial photographs.

Table 1. In the Dutch river area, 65 ecotopes can be distinguished, divided into 18 clusters. The table shows the "wooded levee" cluster.

Ecotopes of forested natural levee	
forested natural levee	natural levee hardwood forest
	natural levee hardwood shrubs
	natural levee softwood forest
	natural levee softwood shrubs
	natural levee production forest

With the aid of a geographical information system, the surface-covering ecotope chart can be combined very easily with the geometric representation of the river used in hydraulic models. Moreover, the type of vegetation of each ecotope can be related unambiguously to hydraulic roughness: this is the flow resistance caused by riverbed and vegetation (Schutte & Van der Veen 1996). Through intervention, the geometry, ecotope chart and hydraulic roughness can be changed. It is possible to make a coherent analysis of the consequences for nature and high-water protection, because, on the one hand, the potential supporting power for characteristic species can be deduced from surface areas and ecotope patterns (Duel *et al.* 1995), and, on the other hand, water levels can be calculated by entering the hydraulic roughness value into a hydraulic model. In order to simulate the morphological development as well, factors such as sediment grain size will be needed in addition to the ones mentioned.

By now, river ecotopes have been used in several studies:

– "Target models for the rivers Rhine and Meuse for the benefit of Aquatic Outlooks" (Postma *et al.* 1995). This study deals with the ecotopes which can still develop in the present conditions within the river's winter bed (Rademakers *et al.* 1995). Moreover, based on surfaces and ecotope patterns, an estimate is made of the potential supporting power for characteristic species (Duel *et al.* 1995).

– "Rhine-Econet" describes the development of a method to assess the durability of populations under a certain landscaping variant (Reijnen *et al.* 1995). The method has been developed for a section of the German-Dutch Rhine. Based on the current physiotopes in the winter bed, three landscaping alternatives have been set up with various three-dimensional ecotope patterns. With the aid of e.g. population dynamic models, the durability for the populations of six species has been determined.

– "Method for the evaluation of effects of landscaping variants on potential natural values at the Zandmaas EIA" (Postma *et al.* 1996). This method makes it possible to indicate the future options for nature development under the various landscaping alternatives. To this effect, the development options for ecotopes are compared with the natural target models.

– "Monitoring strategy for nature development projects in inland waters" (Buijse *et al.* 1996). The decisive criteria for the monitoring of nature development projects are related to, amongst other things, expected ecotope development.

– "Hydraulic Models" (Schutte & Van der Veen 1996). By linking the vegetation structure of each ecotope, deduced from aerial photos, to a hydraulic roughness value, the calculation of water levels is improved with the aid of hydraulic models.

– "River Waal Dredging Strategy". Using simulations with morphological models, an optimum strategy will be determined for maintaining the channel depth by means of dredging or by stabilising the distribution of discharge between summer and winter beds through afforestation or natural levee development. Ecotopes might be useful in a study like this.
– "Landscape Planning of the River Rhine in the Netherlands" (LPR) (Silva & Kok 1996). LPR is a decision supporting system for surveying the integrated effects of landscaping alternatives on the Rhine branches. Landscaping alternatives are expressed in terms of ecotopes, from which the effects on nature and water levels can be deduced.

In all these studies, the 65 ecotopes are clustered, one way or another, into 10 to 15 ecotopes. Clustering is often necessary to ensure that the degree of detail is in proportion to the purpose and the information available. In the target models, for example, no distinction is made between the hardwood thicket and hardwood floodplain forest ecotopes, because this is difficult to predict on the 1:50,000 scale used.

3.2. Integrated surveys

The first step in a joint planning process is problem analysis. An appropriate form for this is the integrated survey. This is illustrated by the report titled "Landscape Planning for the River Rhine in the Netherlands: towards a balance in river management" (Silva & Kok 1996). This report finds connections between the various developments started up in the Rhine branches: the entire floodplain area, for example, is part of the Ecological Primary Structure and it is the intention to take away 7,000 ha of agricultural land out of production in the next few decades for the benefit of nature development (Ministry of Agriculture, Nature Management and Fisheries 1989 and 1992). In order to meet the growing demands of the shipping trade, the navigational channel of the river Waal main artery is being improved. In addition, since the high waters of 1993 and 1995, the execution of any old plans to strengthen the dikes has been accelerated. Finally, extra measures will be needed at short notice in order to maintain flood protection levels. In the year 2001, the so-called design discharge, in other words: the discharge linked to the protection level, will be reassessed. It is already clear that the new design discharge should be higher than the present one. Due to climatic changes, these discharge criteria may rise even more in the longer term. In order to be able to safely discharge these higher volumes of river water in the near future, serious thought is being given to measures creating more space for rivers rather than building higher dikes.

The various developments must be taken into consideration as a whole, because measures for the benefit of the one sector may have negative effects on the other sector (Table 2). But win-win situations may also occur. With the aid of a Decision Supporting System (LPR-DSS), the effects of integrated landscaping variants on the entire Rhine branch area have been charted. The relevant landscaping variants consist of combinations of measures pertaining to nature, the shipping trade and high-water protection (Fig. 2).

Intervention in the river

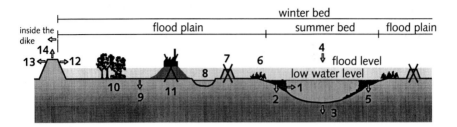

1 = narrowing
2 = lowering of groynes
3 = dredging
4 = redumping of sediment
5 = permanent layer
6 = natural bank
7 = removing summer embankment

8 = secondary channel
9 = lowering of flood plain (excavation of clay/sand)
10 = nature development
11 = removing of high-water free areas
12 = dike reinforcement
13 = dike repositioning
14 = dike raising

Fig. 2. Typical cross section of the Rhine branches with the various measures that may be taken for the benefit of a variety of interests.

The LPR-DSS is based on a one-dimensional model for the simulation of water movements and morphology, which tests the effects of certain measures on the river. In addition, the distribution of ecotopes in the floodplains of the river Rhine forms an important part of the LPR-DSS system. In many cases of intervention, it is possible to roughly estimate the effects on the characteristics of hydrodynamics, morphodynamics and vegetation structure. By means of rules of thumb, the new ecotope distribution created after a number of measures is carried out is deduced from the ecotope chart of the present situation (Buijsrogge & Nieuwkamer 1995). The distribution of ecotopes as a result of a landscaping variant produces a quick summary of the new scenery. Subsequently, the ecotopes are translated into effects on e.g. nature and water levels.

After the summer dike has been removed alongside the floodplain, the winter bed will be more likely to be flooded, while flow rates will increase locally. Expansion of pastures will allow for the development of higher successive stages of

Table 2. Effect of 3 measures on the shipping trade, high-water protection and morphology.

Effect measure	Navigable depth + = deeper − = shallower	High-water level + = higher − = lower	Riverbed inclination + = larger − = smaller
secondary channel	−	−	+
floodplain forest	+	+	−
dredging	+	−	−

vegetation types. This is how, after removal of the summer dike and expansion of the pastures, the floodplain pasture ecotope will partly change in due time into the ecotopes of floodplain brushwood, floodplain forest dominated by willows, etc., and softwood thicket (Buijsrogge & Nieuwkamer 1995).

The landscaping variants are checked against a series of criteria which serve as a model for the various sectors. The checking criteria include the water levels occurring at the specified discharge criterion, the similarity of the distribution of ecotopes to the target model, the dredging work required for maintenance of the channel and the costs of landscape planning. The result is displayed in a table of effects.

As it is not yet certain what the design discharge will be in the near future and thereafter, three scenarios have been studied with different design discharge values: the present value of 15,000 m³s⁻¹ and two future scenarios of 16,000 m³s⁻¹ and 18,000 m³s⁻¹ (Silva & Kok 1996).

These studies show that if the current landscaping plans are carried out at the present design discharge, high-water levels will rise throughout half the area. As a consequence, it will be impossible to obtain permits under the dutch River Act. The plans do not contain enough measures to lower water levels, such as declaying to compensate for vegetation obstructing the flow. Besides, it has been noted that nature reserves are disintegrating on a large scale. These results emphasize the importance of integrated considerations.

One may think of many variants which will meet the requirements of both the shipping trade and high-water protection. At a design discharge of 16,000 m³s⁻¹, they are as follows:
- a variant under which the present agricultural use of land is maintained and the floodplains are excavated to 0.5 m above the median water level;
- a variant under which the target model is virtually realized, the summer dikes are removed, secondary channels are constructed and the floodplains are lowered to 0.5 m above the median water level;
- a variant under which 50% of the scenery is left intact because of actual cultural and natural values, the other floodplains are lowered to 0.5 m above the median water level and higher dikes are built.

In these variants, problems with morphological stability may arise in various degrees. Large-scale excavations will disrupt the clay and sand market. Moreover, it has become evident that if the design discharge rises any further, extra measures, such as floodplain expansion, will be necessary.

The surveys with LPR-DSS give an insight into problems and possible solutions. It has become clear that the surveys provide an excellent policymaking basis within the framework of the coming Fourth National Policy Document on Water Management. Because of the insight provided, a wide group of interested parties is able to participate in the process, which will increase public support in the planning process on a regional level.

4. Trial and error in pursuing policies

Knowledge of the aquatic environment and public support play an equally important part in the persuasion of policy makers. In the draft for a secondary channel at "De Stiftse Uiterwaarden" (floodplain of the river Waal) nature development project, optimum use has been made of any ecological and physical knowledge available. Both during the construction and afterwards, the morphological, hydrological and ecological developments will be measured in order to fill any gaps in our knowledge. The project organization also aims at acquiring public support in the surrounding area.

When the high-water problems were discussed on an international level, the International Rhine Commission proved to be able to translate the general policy statements into 10 principles forming the basis for a Flood Protection Action Programme at very short notice. Part of this campaign has already been put into practice.

4.1. De Stiftse Uiterwaarden

The "Stiftse Uiterwaarden" project is part of a much larger nature development plan around Fort St Andries, covering ± 1,000 ha. A policy statement has been defined for this large area by the Fort St Andries advisory committee (previously the steering committee). It includes a secondary channel for the Stiftse Waard area. A basic design has been made for this secondary channel on the basis of ecological requirements and river-technological preconditions (Schropp 1995; Schropp & Bakker 1996). At the same time, the owner and manager of a large part of the Stiftse Waard has translated the policy statement into a rough landscaping plan. Since then, all parties have joined in drawing up an overall plan. As a result of the Delta Act on Large Rivers, the execution of the plan has been accelerated, the first phase has already been carried out by special legislation.

The Stiftse Waard area is situated along the free-flowing Waal, a river branch with a high potential for the development of "dynamic countryside", where nature is strongly influenced by river processes such as sedimentation and erosion (Postma *et al.* 1995). From an ecological point of view, it is desirable to create space for these processes, so that the river itself is able to produce the characteristic ecotopes. For this reason, the ecological target model drawn up for the planning area consists of a rough outline of the final situation in the shape of a distribution of ecotopes. The targeted ecotopes, such as shallow areas, flowing water, floodplain forest and floodplain marshes, are hardly present at the moment, if at all.

The construction of a secondary channel and the spontaneous development of forest, however, will affect the high-water design discharge. New forests will hinder the rapid discharge of water and will therefore cause higher water levels. The construction of a secondary channel is counterproductive and may result in lower water levels. Besides, erosion in the outside bend of the secondary channel may put the main dikes at risk. Moreover, serious problems were expected for the shipping trade on the heavily used Waal river. The construction of a secondary channel will reduce the amount of water in the primary channel, causing the flow rate to drop. The lower flow rates will cause sand sediments and unacceptable bars in the shipping channel. Theoretical models and the study of literature have provided technical solutions which, however, will limit the free space for the creation of natural ecotopes (Table 3).

Table 3. Summary of problems and solutions in the planned process for the "De Stiftse Uiterwaarden" nature development project.

Problem	(Alleged)cause	Solution
rising water levels	upward pressure from new forests	concentrate flood plain forest in shade of flow, compensate by excavating
accretion in primary channel	discharge is distributed through primary and secondary channel	regulate discharge, slow down flow rate
dikes & levees erode/collapse	more and faster flow through flood plains	locate flow line 100m from dike, slow down flow rate
seepage inside dikes	more water in floodplains	maintain clay layer at foot of dike
loss of riverbank pastures, bird sanctuary	more frequent flooding, loss of acreage due to slopes and increasing water surface	put up steeper banks locally or (ecologically interesting) steep-sided edges to preserve pastures
less produce from hayfields	rougher types of pasture, natural pastures	adjust pasture management locally
higher management costs	reduced accessibility, uncertainties about water management costs (dredging)	open up, share management costs
uncertainty future nature	desire to know exactly what will grow/establish itself where	specify ecological target model, include "what-if" constructions in management plan (monitor properly and adjust undesirable developments)
mosquito plagues	marshes	inform the public and/or reduce marshlands near residential areas
increased soil pollution floodplain beds	clogging of sand/silt traps withpolluted river sediment	concentrate silting-up, deposit outcoming silt on flood plains
high cost of earthmoving locally	local category-4 beds	adjust flow line of secondary channel
rising land prices	effect of the market	negotiate
vandalism, motorcross	much fallow land due to earthmoving, obscure object of nature reserve	inform the public, put up information boards, limit access for cars/motorbikes

The design still contains a number of uncertainties. On the basis of current knowledge, however, these cannot be specified, only research into the behaviour of secondary channels in the Dutch situation would provide some insight. The Stiftse Waard project will only be completed in about 10 years' time, because of the time required by the process of land acquisition and clay extraction. For this reason a small secondary channel will be constructed in the part of the floodplain outside the dikes, where experience can be gained with the behaviour of secondary channels and the effects on the primary channel. On the basis of the results of this small channel, the design of the larger secondary channel can be improved.

The secondary channel was not only designed in consultation with ecology and river technology. The working group set up to prepare the plans included, apart from the Department of Public Works and Water Management, the largest owner, the Polder Board and the excavation firm involved. At the start of the consultations, unsurmountable problems seemed to arise concerning the management of sediment interception and the degree of pollution of the soil to be excavated, aspects which had not been discussed when the basic design was drawn up. Before the plan can be finally realized, several plots of land will have to be acquired. In this context, it is important that the area in the region is embraced as a nature development project. It is also important in order to reduce the chances that the area will still be used as a motorcross track after the bulldozers have left.

A working group has been set up to draw up the landscaping plan as well as a project group in which the regional administrators (Polder Board, Municipality, Province) will check the plans. These groups are supervised by the Fort St Andries advisory committee with representatives from the government, province and local authorities. In practice, the communication between the project group and the advisory committee only started in a late phase. The project group drew up the landscaping plan in a short period of time, because it was possible to start the excavation work quickly thanks to the Delta Act on Large Rivers. The formal procedure for the landscaping plan will include the approval of the zoning plan and the granting of permits as well as the possibility of inspection and objection. Apart from that, more informal meetings were held in the region, whereby reactions from the public led to more detailed investigations and modifications of the plan. The inhabitants are also notified in writing by means of brochures, information boards on the spot and notices in the local press.

Because of the experience gained with the project organization of the Stiftse Waard, one of the first nature development projects of this magnitude, a project organization has been set up for new projects in which the responsibilities are made clear from the very beginning and the details of communication with the region are specified.

4.2. Flood Protection Action Programme

After the high waters of 1995, wide-spread public support was soon found to tackle high-water problems on an international level. The Declaration of Arles by the European Environment Ministers was an important impulse (Anonymus 1995). It was decided to set up a campaign to tackle high-water problems, in which the water basin approach became the most important criterion and measures in the scope of physical planning were also covered. Any available hydrological knowledge was used immediately. The International Rhine Commission (IRC) accepted the challenge by setting up a high-water working group and simultaneously gave new meaning to the resolution of the Congress of Ministers of the riparian Rhine Countries held in 1994, by adding water quantity to the area for special attention (IRC 1994). Up till then, the IRC had been primarily engaged in the water quality and ecology of the river Rhine (IRC 1992).

For hydrologists it is quite normal and even necessary to look at the water basin as a whole. As a matter of fact, the water flowing through the river has come from precipitation elsewhere in the basin. The hydrological processes of precipitation, meltage, evaporation, storage on and in the soil, flow and outflow, cause the water to flow into brooks. After that the water carries on flowing through the tributaries and, finally, through the river Rhine to the North Sea (Fig. 3).

The widening of the scope of the IRC has given a new impulse to the original area for special attention, i.e. water quality. After all, the persistent pollution as a result of diffuse sources follows the same route as the precipitation. Likewise, the cooperation between ecology and hydrology offers new chances: floodplains are both interesting parts of an ecological network and spaces in which part of the peak discharge can be stored.

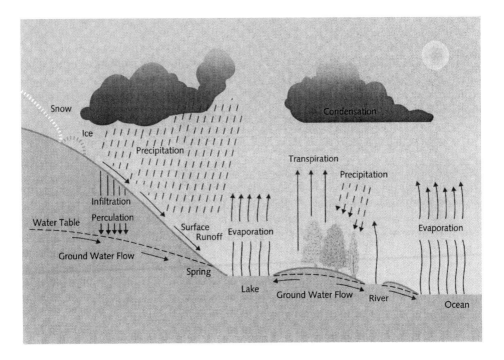

Fig. 3. The hydrological cycle.

In less than six months, the high-water working group came up with a policy statement which is supported internationally to reduce (damage through) high waters. This statement forms the basis of the Flood Protection Action Programme which consists of 10 principles, originally drawn up in Germany and taken over by the IRC (LAWA 1995, IRC 1995).

In short, the policy statement entails a cohesive programme of measures concerning both the basin and the river itself, i.e. (1) to influence the discharge regime and water levels, (2) to give warnings well in advance, (3) to limit the damage in the event of floods and (4) to improve public awareness of the risks of high waters. The latter issue is a good illustration of water management also being able to influence society. In spite of the measures to be taken, there will still be risks of which the community must be aware and against which it must protect itself.

The 10 principles for the IRCs Flood Protection Action Programme:
1) To retain water; every cubic metre counts;
2) To ensure the discharge of water, space for the river;
3) Protection against high water, geared to the potential damage;
4) To acknowledge limits, absolute safety does not exist, people must be aware of remaining risks;
5) To maintain protective facilities; present facilities must be kept in good repair;
6) To restrict potential damage, plans must take account of areas in which there is potential danger of flooding;
7) To make the public aware of the risks of high water; high waters are part of rivers, high waters occurring every 100 years may come back next week and the year after that as well;
8) To issue warnings of high water; warnings given well in advance will restrict the damage;
9) To improve private precautions; everybody will remain personally responsible;
10) Integrated approach.

Following the policy statement, an inventory was made of measures planned for the entire basin: the Bestandsaufnahme (IRC 1996a). On the basis of this inventory it will be decided which extra measures must be included in the Programme.

The options of further improving the high-water forecasting systems in the Rhine basin and of optimizing cooperation have been examined for the benefit of adequate operational high-water management. Because of the excellent cooperation between the hydrologists involved, it was possible to draw up a set of measures very quickly. These cover e.g. improvement of the data infrastructure, the uniformization of reporting and improvement of forecasting models (IRC 1996b). Making use of the public support that had come about, the measures were put into practice without delay. A new forecasting model for the water levels at Lobith, the site where the river Rhine enters the Netherlands, for example is being developed, which will allow for three- instead of two-day forecasts.

5. Conclusions

Water management that takes account of directive developments in terms of economy, ecology and sociology is indicated by the phrase "total water management". However, the development from integrated into total water management would appear to be a conceptual one rather than a chronological one: total water management has always existed.

In the last few decades, however, the claims of sectoral interests have grown to the extent that they can no longer all be honoured. A choice must be made and this will require the integrated weighing of such interests. The factors for the success of this integrated weighing of interests are scientific knowledge and public support. Progress has recently been made in both areas.

The use of ecotopes has facilitated the communication between engineers en ecologists. Ecotopes allow for finding a technological-scientific connection between nature, shipping and protection against floods in the river basin. Ecotopes are units with limited space, which makes them even more useful, because space is an important limiting factor in water management. The introduction of integrated surveys has been the first step of a joint planning process: integrated surveys provide a wide public with an insight into problems and solutions. Joint problem analysis is regarded as a condition for developing sufficient public support of water management decisions (Van Rooy 1995b).

Practical examples, such as the realization of a nature development project on the floodplains and international consultation on high-water protection, emphazise the importance of available knowledge and public support. Scientific knowledge has traditionally been well established at the water managing institutes. However, there is also a need for sociological knowledge to improve the communication between the various parties involved and to obtain a better insight into social processes determining the public support for decisions. In this context, one can learn a great deal from other large-scale landscaping projects carried out in the Netherlands, such as land consolidation. With projects such as Gelderse Poort, Grensmaas EIA and the Delta Act on Large Rivers, steps are being taken into the right direction.

References

Amoros, C., Roux, A.L., Reygrobellet, J.L., Bravard, J.P. & Pautou, G. 1987. A method for applied ecological studies of fluvial hydrosystems. Regulated Rivers 1: 17-36.

Anonymous. 1995. Declaration of Arles. By the Environment Ministers of France, Germany, Luxembourg and The Netherlands on tackling the problems caused by the high water level of Rhine and Meuse. Arles, 1995.

Buijse, A.D., Cals, M.J.R., Postma, R. & Den Held, J.J. 1996. Ecological restoration in the Netherlands: a cost-effective monitoring strategy for nature rehabilitation projects. (Submitted).

Buijsrogge, R.H. & Nieuwkamer, R.L.J. 1995. Integrated Surveys of Rhine Branches. Decision Supporting System. Ministry of Transport, Public Works and Water Management, LPR-report no.7, WL. ISBN no. 9036945453.

Cals, M.J.R. (ed.) 1994. Evaluation of the Duursche Waarden 1989 to 1993. Publications and reports of the "Ecological rehabilitation of Rhine and Meuse" project. Report EHR 60-1994, RIZA Lelystad.

De Bruijn, D., Hamhuis, D., Van Nieuwenhuize, L., Overmars, W., Sijmons, D. & Vera, F. 1987. Ooievaar. De toekomst van het rivierengebied. Stichting Gelderse Milieufederatie, Arnhem (in Dutch).

Duel, H., Pedroli, G.B.M. & Arts, G. 1995. Een stroom natuur. Natuurstreefbeelden voor Rijn en Maas. Watersysteemverkenningen 1996. Achtergronddocument B: 1-192. Ministry of Transport, Public Works and Water Management, Aquatic Outlooks project, RIZA working paper 95.173X (in Dutch).

Harms, W.B. & Roos-Klein Lankhorst, J. 1994. The future for nature in the Gelderse Poort, Planmaking and Evaluation. DLO-Staringcentrum, report 298.1.

IRC. 1987. Rhine Action Programm. Technisch-wissenschaftliches Sekretariat, Koblenz.

IRC. 1992. Ecological Master Plan for the Rhine "Salmon 2000". Technical-Scientific Secretariat, Koblenz.

IRC. 1994. 11. Rhein-Ministerkonferenz. Kommuniqué, International Commission for Protection of the Rhine (ICPR), Koblenz (in German).

IRC. 1995. Grundlagen und Strategie zum Aktionsplan Hochwasser. International Commission for Protection of the Rhine (ICPR), Koblenz (in German).

IRC. 1996a. Hochwasserschutz am Rhein – Bestandsaufnahme. International Commission for Protection of the Rhine (ICPR), Koblenz (in German).

IRC. 1996b. Bestandsaufnahme der Meldesysteme und Vorschläge zur Verbesserung der Hochwasservorhersage im Rheineinzugsgebiet. International Commission for Protection of the Rhine (ICPR), Koblenz (in German).

LAWA. 1995. Leitlinien für ein zukunftweisenden Hochwasserschutz. Länderarbeitsgemeinschaft Wasser (LAWA), Arbeitskreis Hochwasser (in German).

Ministry of Agriculture, Nature Management and Fisheries. 1989. Nature Policy Plan; Government decision. Lower Chamber 1989-1990, 21 149 nos. 2-3. SDU, The Hague.

Ministry of Agriculture, Nature Management and Fisheries. 1992. Structure Plan for the Rural Areas in the Netherlands. Natural areas worth the effort. Part 3. Cabinet opinion. Lower Chamber, meeting year 1992-1993, 22880, The Hague.

Ministry of Transport, Public Works and Water Management. 1985. Dealing with water, The Hague, The Netherlands

Ministry of Transport, Public Works and Water Management. 1989. Third National Policy Document on Water Management: water for now and later. Lower Chamber, meeting year 1988/1989, 21.250, nos. 1-2. SDU, The Hague, the Netherlands.

Ministry of Transport, Public Works and Water Management. 1990. Second Structure Plan for Traffic and Transport.

Ministry of Transport, Public Works and Water Management & Ministry of Housing, Physical Planning and the Environment. 1996. Space for Rivers, Policy Plan.

Pedroli, B. & Rademakers, J. 1995. Integrated Surveys of Rhine Branches. Landscape ecology. Ministry of Transport, Public Works and Water Management, LPR-report no. 5, WL and Grontmij. ISBN no. 9036945259.

Ploeger, B. 1992. Building on the Rhine; human intervention in the Rhine and its branches. Department of Public Works and Water Management-series no. 53.

Postma, R., Kerkhofs, M.J.J., Pedroli, G.B.M. & Rademakers, J.G.M. 1995. Een stroom natuur. Natuurstreefbeelden voor Rijn en Maas. Watersysteemverkenningen 1996: 1-102. Ministry of Transport, Public Works and Water Management, Aquatic Outlooks project, RIZA report 95.060, ISBN 9036945267 (in Dutch).

Postma, R., Pedroli, G.B.M. & Rademakers, J.G.M. 1996. Evaluation method for the Zandmaas EIA, assessment criteria for potential natural values based on ecotopes and species. RIZA-report 96.037, ISBN 9036945607.

Potman, H.P. 1995. Taking decisions on river dikes. Public Administration 95/8.

Project team NW4. 1995. Space for Water: a working paper. The Hague, the Netherlands. ISBN 90 369 0034 4

Quade, E.S. & Miser, H.J. 1981. Handbook of Systems Analysis. IIASA, Laxenburg, Austria.

Rademakers, J., Pedroli, G.B.M., Van Herk, J. 1995. Een stroom natuur. Natuurstreefbeelden voor Rijn en Maas. Watersysteemverkenningen 1996. Achtergronddocument A: 1-173. Ministry of Transport, Public Works and Water Management, Aquatic Outlooks project, RIZA working paper 95.172X (in Dutch).

Rademakers, J.G.M. & Wolfert, H.P. 1994. The River-Ecotope-System; a classification of ecologically relevant units of volume for the benefit of design and policy studies in the river area outside the dikes. Publications and Reports of the "Ecological Rehabilitation of Rhine and Meuse" project, no. 61-1994; edition: Department of Public Works and Water Management RIZA, Lelystad.

Reijnen, R., Harms, W.B., Foppen, R.P.B., De Visser, R. & Wolfert, H.P. 1995. Rhine Econet. Ecological networks in river rehabilitation scenarios: a case study for the Lower Rhine. Publications and reports of the "Ecological rehabilitation of Rhine and Meuse" project, report no. 58-1995. RIZA, Lelystad, 1995.

Schutte, L. & Van der Veen, R. 1996. Assessing roughness of winter bed on the basis of local vegetation. RIZA working paper 96.177x.

Silva, W. & Kok, M. 1996. Landscape Planning of the River Rhine in the Netherlands: Towards a balance in river management. Ministry of Transport, Public Works and Water Management, LPR-report no.1. RIZA and WL. ISBN 9036945348.

Schropp, M.H.I. 1995. Principles of designing secondary channels along the river Rhine for the benefit of ecological restoration. Water Science Technology 31 (8): 379-382.

Schropp, M.H.I. & Bakker, C. 1996. Secondary channels as a basis for the ecological rehabilitation of Dutch rivers. Aquatic Conservation: Marine and Freshwater Ecosystems (submitted).

Van Rooy, P.T.J.C. 1995a. Op weg naar totaal waterbeheer (2): knelpunten. H_2O 28 (10): 290-294 (in Dutch).

Van Rooy, P.T.J.C. 1995b. Op weg naar totaal waterbeheer (3): planvorming. H_2O 28 (22): 666-672 (in Dutch).

Van Rooy, P.T.J.C. & De Jong, J. 1995. Op weg naar totaal waterbeheer (1): ontwikkelingen. H_2O 28 (3): 62-66 (in Dutch).

Wolfert, H.P. 1996. Rijkswateren-Ecotopen-Stelsels: uitgangspunten en plan van aanpak. RIZA report 96.050, ISBN 9036950163 (in Dutch).

WWF. 1992. Living Rivers. Study commissioned by the World Wildlife Fund. ISBN 90-74595-01-4.

CONFLICTING FUNCTIONS IN THE MIDDLE-WAAL AREA: A PRELIMINARY STUDY

P.J.M. Van den Heuvel[1], N.G.M Ten Brink[1] & P.H. Nienhuis[1,2]
*[1] University Centre for Environmental Studies (UCM), Toernooiveld 1,
6525 ED Nijmegen, The Netherlands; [2] Department of Environmental Studies,
University of Nijmegen, P.O. Box 9010, 6500 GL Nijmegen, The Netherlands*

Abstract

Focal point of this article is the development in the Middle-Waal area between Gorinchem and Nijmegen in the Netherlands. The planned activities in this area range from the development of a network of nature reserves along the rivers, the so called Ecological Main Structure (EMS), the construction of an international rail connection for goods transport between Rotterdam and the German industrialized areas, to the development of an increasingly urbanized regional junction between the cities of Arnhem and Nijmegen (KAN). Integration of these plans might lead to major problems concerning the implementation of sustainable development in this region. Especially the construction of infrastructure to facilitate transport of goods and passengers will threaten the regional environment and the opportunities for nature protection and development.

1. Introduction.

The large European rivers Rhine and Meuse flow together in the Netherlands, where they form a complicated estuarine system, and finally discharge into the North Sea (East Atlantic). The catchment is bordered by the river Meuse in the South and by the Rhine in the North. The main branch of the river Rhine is the river Waal which flows between the Rhine proper and the Meuse, connecting the mainport of Rotterdam with the German industrial areas. The Waal area between the towns of Gorinchem and Nijmegen is called the Middle-Waal area (Fig. 1). Within this area many policy plans have been developed and many human activities dealing with town and country planning have to be realized in the near future. The planned activities range from the development of a network of nature reserves along the rivers known as the so called Ecological Main Structure (EMS), the construction of an international transport rail connection between Rotterdam and the German industrialized areas, to the development of an increasingly urbanized regional junction between the cities of Arnhem and Nijmegen (KAN). The main issue is that all these intended acts of environmental planning run separately, in order to meet their own specific conditions. Until now it is unknown how these major plans will be integrated and which priorities will prevail when unavoidable choices have to be made. An integrated vision of all developments and plans in the region is necessary in order to estimate the consequences for a sustainable socio-economic and ecological development in the Middle-Waal area. Therefore the University Centre for

New concepts for sustainable management of river basins, pp. 309–320
edited by P.H. Nienhuis, R.S.E.W. Leuven and A.M.J. Ragas
© 1998 Backhuys Publishers, Leiden, The Netherlands

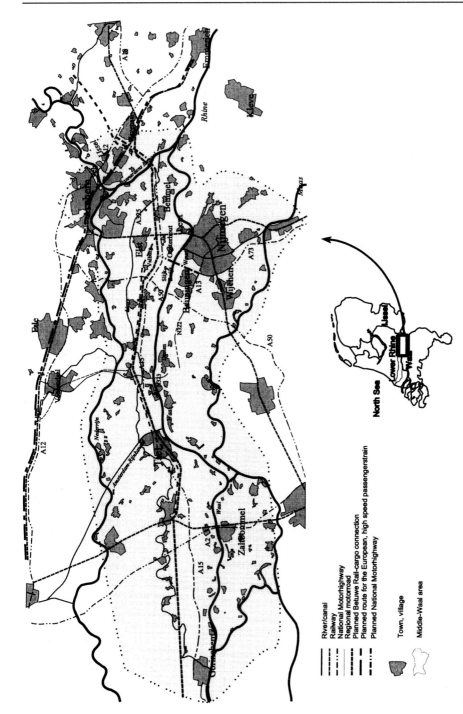

Fig. 1. The Middle-Waal Area, the section of the Rhine catchment between Nijmegen and Gorinchem.

Environmental Sciences (UCM) started a project in 1996 to integrate major aspects of physical planning in the area. The main aim of this project is to identify and analyze possible solutions for conflicts between nature-oriented functions and target views and between current and desired economic developments in the Middle-Waal area. It is impossible to achieve this goal by approaching the problems from a disciplinary perspective. Therefore, several disciplines starting from an ecological, economic or social focus are united in the UCM, and are working in co-operation on the problem. The research started with a general inventory of the existing plans for rural planning of the area. This was done mainly by studying the existing literature and interviews with experts and citizens on specific subjects. In the near future the results of the different studentgroups will be integrated in a report which will give an overall view. In this paper the preliminary results of the study of the UCM are presented.

Paragraph 2 gives an inventory of the current situation in the Middle-Waal area. In the third paragraph the future policy plans situated in this area will be described. Paragraph 4 discusses the conflicts between environmental, economic and social functions, followed by a number of preliminary conclusions.

2. Current situation in the Middle-Waal area

The Middle-Waal area comprises many social, economical, ecological and physical functions. The river Rhine discharges on average 2,000 m^3 water per second consisting of melting water from the mountains in Switzerland and rainwater from its tributaries in Germany, France, Belgium and the Netherlands. The river Waal transports the majority of the Rhine water discharge to the North Sea. During winter this discharge may increase to 15,000 m^3 water per second, which means that the man-made dikes alongside the river should be high and strong enough to protect the land outside the dikes from flooding (VROM-RWS 1996). During the dry summer period the river must contain enough water to facilitate transport of cargo by large ships (e.g. 'short-sea shipment'). This demands continuous dredging of superfluous sand and silt from the shipping channel in the centre of the river. The dredge of sand and silt from the shipping channel is combined with local nature rehabilitation plans in the floodplain of the river to avoid unnecessary transport of slush over long distances. A vast area of the land in the Middle-Waal area, both in the river delta and on the landside of the dikes, has an agricultural function (dairy farming, orchards and other agricultural products).

2.1. Ecological Main Structure

The Middle-Waal area is part of the Ecological Main Structure. This concept, which is published as a policy plan of the Dutch government (LNV 1990) comprises a network of main nature reserves in the Netherlands (to be extended all over Europe) which are connected with each other by ecological corridors. These corridors should enable animal and plant species to migrate from one reserve to the other and should therefore be suitable for passage. It is obvious that crossing these corridors by transport routes, towns and industrialized areas may cause serious problems for the functioning of the corridors. The more the corridors are fragmented, the more unlikely it will be that they will function as migratory routes. The floodplains within the winter-bed of the river are the main landscapes structuring the corridors. In the Middle-Waal area, these floodplains are situated between the larger nature reserves Fort Sint Andries near Zaltbommel in the west and the Gelderse Poort near Nijmegen in the east (Fig. 1). When analyzing the degree of fragmentation of the floodplain corridors and considering the large amount of ecological knowledge about the target species (being the species under study) it is theoretically possible to determine whether spe-cific target species can pass the area between the two main nature reserves (Lenders *et al.* 1998) The nature reserves under study show a great variety in types of land-scapes and consequently the area also has an important recreative function.

2.2. Other functions

The cities of Arnhem, Nijmegen and Tiel and several small towns and villages are located in the Middle-Waal area (Fig. 1). Many of these cities and villages are grow-ing rapidly because of the decreasing number of inhabitants per house and because of migration into the area. Historically the area between Arnhem, Nijmegen and Tiel has an agricultural function. The landscape is characterised by open farmland with many fruit orchards and meandering rivers lined with floodplains and enclosed by dikes thus protecting the low-lying farmland against flooding. The region is rich in clay, sand and gravel, resources which are extracted from the riverbed in large amounts for several economic purposes, thus creating small artificial lakes. These lakes are used as recreational areas and focal points for nature development but they are also used for storing ash, slags and contaminated sludge that is dredged from the riverbed.

2.3. Economic and social situation

The eastern part of the Middle-Waal area which is comprising more than half a mil-lion inhabitants has a high unemployment rate compared to the national level, vary-ing between 9% in the smaller villages and 16% in Nijmegen in relation to the national level of 7%. The gross regional product is 11% below the national standard and the region is therefore eligible for the European Regional Development Fund (ERDF) as an industrial region in decline (objective 2) and the European Social Fund (ESF-4) (Provincie Gelderland 1996). The prognosis is that the human population in the region (KAN area) will grow with approximately 7% in 2005 until 11% in 2015 compared to 1995 (KAN 1997). Moreover, the "depletion" of the number of persons per household coupled with the ageing of the society continues. The consequence of all physical claims on the environment is that the tension between urbanization, industrial development and nature development is getting more and more severe.

3. Future plans

Decision-making concerning the multiple use of our environment is usually a top-down process: European and national governments design overall plans for land use of the rural environment while regional and local governments are implementing these resolutions on the level of their own region. This paper follows the sequence of European, national and regional planning.

3.1. European plans

The European concept for nature conservation and -development is the Ecological Main Structure (EMS), a network of major nature reserves (core areas), connected with corridors (Jongman 1998). The consequences of the European EMS ask for national policy decisions and actions of nature management. In some cases, a core area of the EMS is a border-crossing nature reserve (e.g. Gelderse Poort), demanding international management planning (Reijnen *et al.* 1995).

A second European concept is the so called modal split, meaning that transport over long distances should go by rail or by ship, while short distance transport can be done by roadcarriers. The rationale is that along this way the pollution and nuisance of transport by road can be diminished as much as possible, and moreover, the European market is made accessible for many nations. To reach this goal harbours and ship-terminals, and connecting transport routes for road cargo and rail cargo are needed to transfer the goods from one transport modality to the other. These policy considerations led to the design of the Betuwe rail-cargo connection which crosses the Middle-Waal area from west to east (see section 3.2). This has a great potential impact on this rural agricultural area. Parallel to the rail-cargo connection a high-speed passenger train connection is planned between the Dutch main cities in the west and German cities in the east. The high-speed passenger train network is planned to replace short distance air transport of passengers between West European capitals.

3.2. National Plans

In addition to European plans the Dutch national government has made precise plans on nature development and rehabilitation according to the EMS. In the Dutch Nature Policy Plan (LNV 1990), the floodplains in the Middle-Waal area are meant to function as a major corridor between Dutch and German nature reserves. The Dutch government presented also plans on the development of the economic transport-oriented infrastructure. The two policy plans conflict in essence and both plans severely affect the Middle-Waal area. The transport-navigation route in the winding river Waal is continuously improved by widening and deepening the channel to create more transportation capacity and to decrease risks of accidents. The Betuwe rail-cargo connection is already in the "Second Structure Schedule Traffic and Transport" envisaged (V&W 1988).The project is meant to strengthen the position of Rotterdam as mainport by improving the connections with the Dutch hinterland and Germany, and to stress the role of the Netherlands as a distribution-oriented country. Compared to road-cargo transport, a railway is considered a better option to meet the predicted increase in goods transport in an efficient way to avoid future traffic congestion and to respect the environment by using less fossil energy which will decrease emissions.

The Betuwe rail-cargo connection (BRC) should consist of three branches (V&W 1992; Provincie Gelderland 1993b; Fig. 2):
– West-East connection between Rotterdam-Zevenaar-Emmerich (Germany) of about 130 km in between the river Waal and the river Lower-Rhine (BRC-main);
– North connection between Zevenaar-Oldenzaal-Rheine (Germany) (BRC-North).
– South connection Valburg-Venlo-Köln (Germany) (BRC-South).

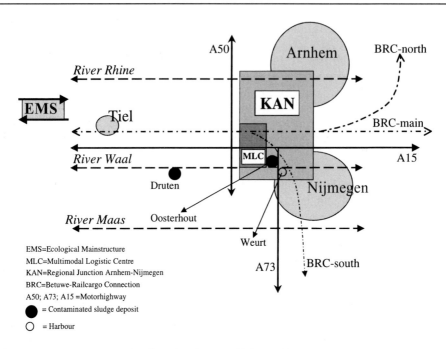

Fig. 2. Schematic overview of policy plans in the Middle-Waal area.

The national and regional governments have already approved policy plans for the construction of the main West-East connection. Some local authorities still fight the Betuwe rail-cargo connection but this battle seems to be lost. The costs of the main connection are estimated at 8.4 billion Dutch guilders (9.4 billion in case of 'Double-Stacking'). These estimates are this high because of the mitigating measures that have to be taken to avoid unnecessary damage to the natural environment. The economic costs of the southern connection are still unknown. The costs of the northern connection are estimated at 4 billion Dutch guilders.

3.3. Regional Plans

Although derived from national schemes, many policy plans have a regional status originating from the administration of the province of Gelderland and the administration of the regional junction Arnhem-Nijmegen where urban expansion is the main item (KAN). A number of policy plans on the physical and economic development of the KAN region were published in the course of the years; "Seizing opportunities " (IBBC-KAN 1992); Regional Junction Arnhem - Nijmegen (KAN 1993); Regional Structure Plan –RSP- (KAN 1997). These policy plans have led to a series of documents covering the following items to be realized in the (near) future (see also Fig. 1 and Fig. 2):
a) The construction of at least 56,000 and maximum 63,000 houses until the year 2015. Most houses will be located North of Nijmegen (Waalsprong) and South of Arnhem (Schuytgraaf). These areas have been designated VINEX-locations

(VROM 1988) which means that the national government has decided that these regions should be used as expansion areas for concentrated urban developments in contrast to neighbouring areas where the open agricultural landscape will be maintained.

b) The construction and clustering of offices and industrial zones for eventually 20,000 employees. The "quality KAN locations" should discourage the use of automobiles. This means that locations with a high employment density per square meter (A-locations) are planned nearby central railway stations. B-locations are located within a 15 minute walk from a railway station and C-locations are accessible by car and within 500 meters from a bus-stop.

c) The present area accommodates a considerable number of greenhouse complexes. In future plans these greenhouses have to be moved to and concentrated near Huissen (800 ha) and Oosterhout (50 ha), where new horticulture enterprises have to be started.

d) The construction of a Multimodal Logistic Centre (MLC) is envisaged Southwest of Valburg, and near Oosterhout and Slijk-Ewijk at the junction of road-, rail- and water-transport. This centre includes a shipping harbour a Rail Service Centre (RSC) and a location for Value Added Logistics (VAL), altogether employing 8,000 workers. The total area will be approximately 350 ha.

e) In connection with the economic activities in the KAN area existing infrastructure will be improved and extended, such as (1) the extension of the motorway A73 to the A50, including a new motorhighway bridge over the river Waal, (2) extension of motorway A15 to the A12, (3) construction of the N837 between Arnhem-South and Heteren, (4) modification of the railway track Zevenaar-Arnhem-Nijmegen-Wijchen into a Light Rail System.

f) The Betuwe Canal should be constructed for sailing and pleasure yachting. This canal between the Waal near the entrance of the Maas-Waal canal and the Pannerdensch canal is supposed to prevent obstruction of the heavy cargo traffic on the river Waal by pleasure boats.

g) A green zone is planned between Arnhem-South and the Waalsprong along the river the Linge to avoid the new city quarters to coalesce and at the same time to function as a recreational area and as a corridor for the EMS.

h) Two sludge deposit sites will be developed (near Druten and Oosterhout). These sites were originally used as sand and gravel exploitation centres and will be used to store contaminated sludge from the river and its floodplains.

i) A harbour is planned near Weurt to facilitate a resting side for passing skippers and their families.

All described plans are in different phases of policy and administrative procedures, including public participation. At this stage it is not clear which plans will actually be carried out.

4. Discussion

Larger cities show some specific problems (VROM 1988, RAVO 1993): unemployment is often high. Traffic jams and road congestion around the centre cause much annoyance. The centres of the cities no longer have a residential function and slowly deteriorate while other quarters of the city are only accessible for the wealthier people. This means a higher risk of segregation. The construction of "regional junctions" is thought to catch up on economic arrears (Borman 1995). These regional junctions are cooperations of several smaller and larger communities which cooperate in order to establish their main goal of economic development for the whole region. This policy not only considers cities as problem areas but also as the motors for economic development and has some important consequences. Vital in this model is that authorization rights on physical planning and economics are handed over from the municipality to a "junction board" that decides how the region will be developed. The regional junction Arnhem-Nijmegen is facing the challenge of new developments. At the same time however it is clear that the policy plans may evoke frictions between all existing independent municipalities.

4.1. Nature development within the Ecological Main Structure

Lenders *et al.* (1998) gave an extensive description of the degree to which the floodplains in the Middle-Waal area are suitable as a corridor for a number of endangered bird species and mammals. Infrastructural projects introduce the risk of an ever increasing fragmentation of habitats for plants and animals in the Middle-Waal area.

The existing valuable nature reserves in the planning area should be protected, but it is, however, questionable whether these isolated and not connected areas, are large enough to maintain viable populations of animals and plants. Nature development and recreational areas have been planned between Arnhem-South and the Waalsprong to function as a corridor for the EMS.

Fragmentation of (potential) nature reserves and mainly floodplains, is significantly altering the habitat demands of specific target species such as Bluethroat, Cormorant, and Little ringed plover. These species cannot form viable populations in the area because the size of the remaining swamps and wetlands is insufficient. Small mammals like the Water-shrew are unable to perform their natural migratory behaviour because of the physical barriers in their fragmented habitat. The dimension of this problem will increase with the construction of the shipping harbour of the MLC.

Although many initiatives are carried out to protect and develop nature in the river floodplains the coordination and cooperation between parties involved is still limited which jeopardises the economic and political feasibility of the projects.

4.2. Economic development in the regional junction Arnhem-Nijmegen

Economic development of the region is said to be based on two pillars: distribution and logistics, and general services. The first pillar is initiated and promoted by the mainport of Rotterdam. This harbour which is the largest in the world is in need of space to expand its activities (Projectorganisatie Maasvlakte 1997), therefore the harbour authorities are looking for solutions to solve this problem. They try to build a network of cooperating harbours along the river Rhine, e.g. Rotterdam, Valburg (Middle-Waal), Emmerich and Duisburg (Germany) to create an efficient logistic structure to compete with other European harbours.

The Rotterdam harbour authorities are in favour of a first priority construction of the Betuwe rail-cargo connection to avoid too much dependency on one transport system (cargo over water) and maintain their leading position on the world trade and distribution market.

The estimated volume of annually transported goods through the Netherlands is given in Table 1. The estimates used by Knight Wendling (1992) are based on the "European Renaissance" scenario outlined by the Netherlands Bureau for Economic Policy Analysis (CPB) which estimates the economic growth on an average level. New estimates (CPB 1995) point out that considerably less goods will be transported than indicated by the prognosis which led to the decision to build the Betuwe rail-cargo connection.

The Betuwe connection will only gain profit after 25 years (CPB 1995) due to many investments concerning the compensation and mitigation of environmental annoyance. This is counteracted by the considerable increase of the road transport volume. Rail transport in the Netherlands is captive between road transport on the one hand at much lower handling costs, flexibility and superior accessibility and transport over water at low variable costs. The economic arguments in favour of the Modal-Split might be invalid since only a small part (1%) of all freight transports will use the Betuwe-connection (CPB 1995).

Until 2015 the transport capacity on existing railway tracks in the Central and Western part of the Netherlands is sufficient, but in the meantime more modern transport systems and logistic concepts will be developed. Especially the underground dimension of public and private transport will be explored and new techniques that have less impact on the landscape will be applied, leading to the construction of underground transport systems such as the transport of units through pipelines (V&W 1996). These systems might not be competitive at this moment but they may take the lead in the near future.

Although economically uncertain, the construction of the Betuwe railway connection has already started in 1997. In order to gain profit from the large investments in Dutch railway connections the MLC must be built and coupled to the Betuwe connection. The main risks in constructing all the necessary infrastructure to develop the regional junction Arnhem-Nijmegen to a Multi Modal distribution area are (1) narrowing the economic focus of the region for decades because infrastructural works are usually built to last for one or two generations, and (2) the focusing of this region on distribution services concomitant with other national and international (German) -competing- developments (Buck consultants 1996). This could lead to an overcapacity in transshipment facilities. The regional junction Arnhem-Nijmegen wants to be put on the European map hereby ignoring the social-economic relations with its neighbouring regions in the Netherlands and Germany: instead of the cooperation-

Table 1. Estimated volumes of transported goods in 2015 (in mln tons)

Direction	Knight Wendling (1992)	CPB (1995)
East-West	47	28
North-South	18	11
Rest	5	3
Total	70	42

model as suggested in the first paragraph of section 3.2, the opposite competition-model might become reality which puts the huge investments at risk.

The area around Valburg and the neighbouring villages are confronted with several infrastructural plans which not only put pressure on the landscape but also on the inhabitants. Public participation in this policy process is only marginal: the clash between the traditional agricultural, rural society and the transport and distribution-oriented future society with industries, noisy railway connections and motor-highways is obvious.

4.3. The East-West, North-South conflict

VINEX-locations are basically appropriate for the sustainable (ecological) construction of residential areas and houses but the criteria to be used for these new building concepts in the KAN-area are not clear. Neither are the effects of this massive North-South oriented urban zone on the functioning of the east-west oriented Ecological Main Structure. The KAN urban planning models are in conflict with the principles of the VINEX-philosophy. There is a contrast between the concepts of the compact cities surrounded by an open landscape (VINEX) and the ample opportunities to build houses and develop business activities in the KAN concepts (RPD 1996). Especially the eastern part of the Middle-Waal area will be fragmented by infrastructure and industrial areas (Dijkstra 1996) thus considerably damaging the open country and decreasing the livability of the eastern region. The earliest policy plans on the environment and economic development of the KAN region already claim that the Waalsprong is not consistent with the construction of the MLC harbour in the west. (Provincie Gelderland 1993a).

Moreover, in the KAN concept greenhouses must make room for newly built houses, introducing the problem of the heavily contaminated soil underneath the greenhouses which is incompatible with the residential housing function. The other side of this problem is positive, viz. the possibility to develop new locations where sustainable agriculture in greenhouses could be possible. The original investments are high, but in the long run it might be an economically sound enterprise because of the tendency in society to move towards ecological or biodynamic forms of agriculture (LNV 1996).

Fig. 2 summarises all the land-use plans for the Middle-Waal area, showing the conflict between the North-South urban and industrial developments including the continuous MLC-activities which require 24 hours (day)light and the east-west corridor function in the EMS. The total area planned for urban, industrial, logistic and recreational purposes is relatively large which means a complete change of the regional junction area. Future developments are focusing more and more on the use of the "third dimension" the underground infrastructure, to decrease the pressure on the open landscape. Underground transport and distribution systems are designed at this very moment (V&W 1996) and it is just a matter of time before these systems may compete with the traditional transport systems. Therefore infrastructural projects such as the Betuwe railway connection will probably be outdated before they will function in the year 2005.

5. Final Remarks

So far results lead to the following indications:
- The characteristic free open landscape of the Middle-Waal area will change into an industrialized and urban region. This will have many social consequences for the rural communities.
- Migration or establishing reproductive units for specific species as the Great reed warbler (*Acrocephalus arundinaceus*) and Otter (*Lutra lutra*) in the flood-plains will be impossible (Lenders *et al.* 1998)
  The main risk of the huge investments in infrastructure is the enlarged dependency on the global economic development and on conjuncture. Spreading these risks is only possible through investments in the traditionally strong sectors of the Arnhem- Nijmegen region. (i.e. education and healthcare).
- The risk of economic failure is high because of the lower expectations on transport quantity and higher quality and competition with neighbouring national and German regions. Developments such as postponed manufacturing, "just-in-time"-production and product-differentiation will lead to a demand for fast and flexible transportation in smaller units.
- More attention should be paid to develop more compact cities by strengthening the functions of the inner-cities with good connections and public transport instead of the extensive use of free open space which will inevitably lead to more (car)mobility.
- More and earlier participation of all end users in the decision process is necessary.
Economic development is the main goal for improving this region. It must be clear that consequences for nature and environment should be calculated thoroughly. There is still a long way to go before a sustainable development of this region is achieved. Success will depend on effective communication between the interest groups and the wish to find new compromises between economic and ecological targets.

References

Borman, C. 1995. Kaderwet bestuur in verandering, Tekstuitgave, Tjeenk Willink, Zwolle (in Dutch).
Buck-consultants. 1996. Inlandterminals voor intermodaal transport. Nijmegen (in Dutch).
CPB. 1995. Economische effecten van de Betuweroute op basis van recente informatie. Centraal Planbureau (CPB), Werkdocument 75, Den Haag (in Dutch).
Dijkstra, G. 1996. Ruimte versnipperd; kwaliteit en versnippering in het Midden-Waalgebied, studentrapport vakgroep Planologie Katholiek Universiteit Nijmegen, Nijmegen (in Dutch).
IBBC-KAN. 1992. Kiezen voor kansen. Interbestuurlijke Begeleidingscommissie van het Knooppunt Arnhem-Nijmegen (IBBC-KAN), Nijmegen (in Dutch).
Jongman, R.H.G. 1998. Rivers: key elements in European Ecological Networks. In: Nienhuis, P.H. Leuven, R.S.E.W. and Ragas, A.M.J. (eds). New Concepts for Sustainable Management of River Basins, pp. 53-66. Backhuys Publishers, Leiden, The Netherlands.
KAN. 1993. Ontwikkelingsvisie; een ruimtelijk economisch perspectief. Knooppunt Arnhem-Nijmegen (KAN), Nijmegen (in Dutch).
KAN. 1997. Ontwerp Regionaal Structuurplan 2015. Knooppunt Arnhem-Nijmegen (KAN), Nijmegen (in Dutch).
Knight Wendling. 1992. Onderbouwing Masterplan EuroTransPort Knooppunt Arnhem - Nijmegen. Arnhem Provincie Gelderland (in Dutch).

Lenders, H.J.R., Leuven, R.S.E.W., Nienhuis, P.H., Oostinga, K.D. & Van den Heuvel, P.J.M. 1998. Ecological rehabilitation of floodplains along the middle reach of the river Waal: a prosperous future for fauna target species? In: Nienhuis, P.H. Leuven, R.S.E.W. and Ragas, A.M.J. (eds). New Concepts for Sustainable Management of River Basins, pp. 115-130. Backhuys Publishers, Leiden, The Netherlands.

LNV. 1990. Natuurbeleidsplan Regeringsbeslissingen. Ministerie van Landbouw, Natuurbeheer en Visserij (LNV), SDU-uitgeverij, Den Haag (in Dutch).

LNV. 1996. Plan van aanpak Biologische Landbouw. Ministerie van Landbouw, Natuurbeheer en Visserij (LNV), Den Haag (in Dutch).

Projectorganisatie Maasvlakte. 1997. Maasvlakte 2; Tussenrapportage fase 1B. Projectorganisatie Maasvlakte 2, Rotterdam (in Dutch).

Provincie Gelderland 1993a. Ontwikkelingsvisie stedelijk Knooppunt Arnhem-Nijmegen. Provincie Gelderland, Arnhem (in Dutch).

Provincie Gelderland. 1993b. Provincie Gelderland, Limburg en Overijssel en het ministerie van Stadsontwikkeling en Verkeer van Nordrhein-Westfalen. Gemeenschappelijke verklaring met betrekking tot de geplande railverbinding Randstad The Netherlands-Rhein-Ruhr met de noord-tak Zevenaar-Oldenzaal-Rheine en de zuidtak Valburg-Venlo-Köln. Provincie Gelderland, Arnhem (in Dutch).

Provincie Gelderland. 1996. Proviciale Economische Verkenning. Provincie Gelderland, Arnhem (in Dutch).

RAVO. 1993. Advies inzake de nota Bestuur op niveau II en het voorontwerp interimwet bestuur stedelijke gebieden. Raad voor de Volkshuisvesting (RAVO), Zoetermeer (in Dutch).

Reijnen, R., Harms, W.B, Foppen, R.P.B., De Visser, R., & Wolfert, H.P. 1995. Rhine-Econet; ecological networks in river rehabilitation scenario's: a case study for the lower Rhine. Lelystad, RIZA.

RPD. 1996. Ruimtelijke Verkenningen 1996. Jaarboek van de Rijksplanologische Dienst (RPD), Ministerie van Volkshuisvesting, Ruimtelijke Ordening en Milieubeheer, 's-Gravenhage (in Dutch).

V&W. 1988. Tweede Structuurschema Verkeer en Vervoer. Ministerie van Verkeer en Waterstaat (V&W), SDU-Uitgeverij, Den Haag (in Dutch).

V&W. 1992. Overeenkomst tussen het Ministerie van Verkeer en Waterstaat en de Bondsminister van Vervoer van de Bondsrepubliek Duitsland inzake de verbetering van het Nederlands- Duits railgoederen en railpersonenvervoer. Ministerie van Verkeer en Waterstaat (V&W), Warnemünde (in Dutch).

V&W. 1996. Unit Transport per Pijpleiding. Ministerie van Verkeer en Waterstaat (V&W), Den Haag (in Dutch).

VROM. 1988. Vierde nota over de ruimtelijke ordening: op weg naar 2015. Ministerie van Volkshuisvesting, Ruimtelijke Ordening en Milieubeheer (VROM), SDU-uitgeverij, 's-Gravenhage (in Dutch).

VROM-RWS. 1996. Beleidslijn Ruimte voor de Rivier. Ministerie van Vokshuisvesting, Ruimtelijke Ordening en Milieubeheer (VROM) & Rijkswaterstaat (RWS), VROM, Den Haag (in Dutch).

WATER QUALITY MANAGEMENT OF THE LOWER REACH OF THE VISTULA RIVER IN POLAND

P.H. Nienhuis[1], N.J.W. Hofman[2], M.G. Rietbergen[1], S.S.H. Ligthart[2] & T. Prus[3]

[1]Department of Environmental Studies, Faculty of Science, University of Nijmegen, P.O. Box 9010, 6500 GL Nijmegen, The Netherlands; [2]Department of Environmental Policy Studies, Faculty of Policy Sciences, University of Nijmegen, P.O. Box 9108, 6500 HK Nijmegen, The Netherlands; [3]International Centre of Ecology, Polish Academy of Sciences, Ul. Marii Konopnickiej 1, Dziekanow Lesny n. Warsaw, 05-092 Lomianki, Poland

Abstract

A tentative overview of the water management of the lower reach of the Vistula, Poland's main river, is given. The Vistula plays an important role in the economic infrastructure of Poland. The river is heavily polluted, both from point discharges as well as from diffuse sources; it has maintained its natural, wild character, especially in the middle section of the catchment, and the diversity and integrity of habitats is large. Poland has a water quality monitoring programme for lakes and rivers based on physical, chemical and biological criteria: class I (good quality) to class III (bad quality). The largest part of the Vistula belongs to class III. Water quantity management is still in its infant stage. The ecological values of the river are fully recognized in theory, but in practice economic counteracting motives are still dominating. The area of tension between economic growth and ecological restoration is overshadowed by the drastic changes in environmental policy and management occurring in Poland since 1989. The institutional structure of the Polish environmental management is still characterized by central and hierarchical structures, but there is a strong tendency towards decentralization and privatization, thereby increasing the role of local governments. All over Western-Europe river environments have often been irreversibly abused in favour of economic growth. It is anticipated that the Polish authorities promote wise use of water resources, and concomitant preservation of Vistula river ecosystems.

1. Introduction

The Vistula is the largest river in Poland and has a length of 1047 km; it is a unique feature in Poland, and to a great extent also in Europe, as it is one of the largest continental rivers which has maintained an almost natural character, as far as physical properties are concerned, over a large part of its reach. Next to the Neva, the Vistula is the second largest river discharging into the Baltic Sea basin, and it plays an important role regarding the volume of the water conveyed, and the quantity of sediments transported to the sea. The Vistula drainage basin covers an area of 194,410 km^2, and of that area approximately 90% is situated in Poland (Kajak 1992; Jedraszko-Dabrowska *et al.* 1995; Fig. 1).

The Vistula river bed has only been channelized partially, chiefly in the upper and the lower river sections. Large dams and reservoirs are mainly concentrated in

New concepts for sustainable management of river basins, pp. 321–332
edited by P.H. Nienhuis, R.S.E.W. Leuven and A.M.J. Ragas
© *1998 Backhuys Publishers, Leiden, The Netherlands*

Fig. 1. Map of Poland (geographic situation before 1989) showing the Vistula drainage basin (dashed). Dotted lines: boundaries between drainage basins; triangles = reservoirs (Kajak 1992).

the upper, montaneous part of the river. In the lowlands there are embankments along wide stretches of the river valley to prevent floods. Consequently the middle Vistula has retained its natural character, harbouring a diverse flora and fauna, and it also forms an extremely important pathway for bird migration (Tomialojc 1993). The middle part of the Vistula is dynamic, with braided channels, permanent and temporary islands and rich vegetation in the valley. This part is a very important habitat for breeding birds. Downstream from Wloclawek, south of Torun (Fig. 1) the regulation works of the nineteenth century changed the braided type into the meandering type. In some places the banks are regulated, and partial dams are built across the river bed to straighten the channel.

A total population of 24 million people lives in the Vistula drainage basin, which discharge its mostly untreated sewage water into the river. The basin comprises 48% arable land, 14% meadows and pastures, 27% forests, and 11% other categories, among which water (CML 1995).

In the course of the years the riverbed has silted up. At present scientists and engineers have contradictory opinions about the idea to restore the Vistula as a way of transport. Besides the management of the lower Vistula (the Lower Vistula Cascade project), there exists a plan to regulate the middle part of the river. This part of the river is to be included into a planned East-West water route which should connect the Odra river via the Vistula basin to the Dniestr river in the Ukraine. The opponents of this idea are afraid that it might destroy the natural conditions of the river as well as its self-purification abilities (Niemirycz 1994). Recently this plan has been fully abandoned (personal communication prof. Kajak). There is a great area of tension between the present economic growth in Poland and the ecological restoration of disturbed and polluted habitats, such as the river Vistula. Superimposed on that conflict are the drastic changes in environmental policy and management in Poland, affecting the management strategies to be preferred for river rehabilitation.

The aim of this paper is to give a short, tentative overview of the water management of the lower reach of the river Vistula. The paper starts with an introduction of the Vistula environmental problems, followed by a brief survey of the present status of the water quality of the Vistula. Next, current water management strategies are presented, and the paper ends with some considerations for future management.

2. Water quality of the Vistula river

From the beginning of the Polish state the Vistula river has played an essential role in the welfare, health, safety and prosperity of the human population. The Vistula serves as a source of drinking water for most of the towns located along it. At the same time the river receives the sewage of industry and households. Because of the fact that on average 70% of the sewage is untreated or treated unsatisfactory, the concentrations of pollutants are very high and may affect human health (Dojlido & Woyciechowska 1989). The Vistula has become one of the most polluted rivers in Europe, both the water and the sediments. The pollution level is so alarmingly high that none of the cities downstream from Warsaw use the river water for drinking purposes. Due to chlorides, sulphates, heavy metals and toxic organic substances, the water is not only inappropriate for drinking, but also for irrigation purposes (Kaniewska-Prus 1983, Kownacki *et al.* 1994, CML 1995).

The water quality problem is strictly related to the problem of water resources. Because of the high demand for water from the Vistula and due to its irregular flow, there is a great need for water retention in several reservoirs along the Vistula. On the one hand these reservoirs may be regarded as positive, because they act like natural sedimentary ponds, where pollutants can be stored and not need to be removed. Furthermore, in this way the contribution of the Vistula to the Baltic pollution is reduced. On the other hand, the sediments accumulating in the Wloclawek reservoir have already proved to be very dangerous. Due to dredging and consequent resuspension of particles with adhered pollutants, an ecological catastrophe took place in 1986, resulting in mass mortality of fish in this reservoir (Kajak 1993, CML 1995).

A problem specific to Poland is excessive salinity, which impairs water use in several ways, including reduction of self-purification processes in rivers, corrosion of water factories, ships and barges as well as water supply and cooling systems. The salinity of river water in Poland originates from the region of Upper Silesia (Southern Poland), mainly from coal mine water discharged to surface waters. The salt load discharged to surface waters is approximately 9,000 tons year[-1] and is still growing (MEPNR&F 1991a,b).The largest loads (almost 50% of the Vistula catchment) come from five mines, and for the year 2000 a further increase with 60% to

15,000 tons year^{-1} is anticipated (Baginski 1993). The concentration of sodium chloride in the river reach that passes Cracow, approximately 80 km away from Silesia, is sometimes higher than in the receiving water of the Baltic Sea. Construction of desalination plants for the five main contributing mines would reduce the load discharged to the Vistula river with roughly 40% (Makinia *et al.* 1996).

Poland's potential impact on the Baltic sea is reflected in the facts that: (1) about 99.7% of Poland's area belongs to the Baltic Sea drainage basin; (2) over 50% of the entire basin population live in Poland; and (3) approximately 40% of the entire basin's farmland is situated in Poland. The average combined discharge of the Vistula and Odra rivers to the Baltic Sea is 1,640 m^{3}sec^{-1}, of which 65% flows through the Vistula river (Central Statistical Office 1993, MEPNR&F 1991a,b). Poland's organic load, expressed as biological oxygen demand (BOD5), is 22% of the total load discharged by all countries surrounding the Baltic. Nutrient leaching from the Polish land is also high, representing 30% and 40% respectively, of the total nitrogen and phosphorus discharged to the Baltic Sea. The loads per capita in Poland, however, are two to four times lower than those from all Scandinavian countries (Makinia *et al.* 1996).

The Baltic coast is an important tourist attraction, and the elimination of bacteriological contamination of the beaches of the Baltic has a high priority. Of the five Polish seaside voivodships (provinces) in 1993 only one (Koszalin) allowed bathing on all beaches. The largest sources of bacteriological contamination are the direct sewage outlets and small rivers and streams entering the sea. In recent years bacteriological contamination was the main reason for closing the beaches in the region of Gdansk (Olanczuk-Neyman *et al.* 1992), although some beaches in this area have been reopened since (Makinia *et al.* 1996).

3. Strategies of current water management

3.1. Water quality classification

Poland has a water quality monitoring programme, designed to assess current water quality and trends of 30,000 km of rivers and over 300 lakes (Koblak-Kalinska 1992). The quality classification of water in Poland is based on regulations of the Ministry of Environmental Protection which define water purity according to specific physical-chemical and biological criteria. Class I waters (good quality) apply to human consumption and food processing uses, class II waters (moderate quality) are applicable for animal consumption and human recreation, and class III waters (bad quality) are used only for irrigation and general industrial purposes (Makinia *et al.* 1996).

Among all rivers in Poland, the two largest, Vistula and Odra, are of special interest as they discharge almost 90% of Poland's pollutant load to the Baltic Sea. In the Vistula river, changes in water quality have been investigated carefully for over 50 years (Szymanska 1975, 1987; personal communication prof. Kajak). An analysis of physical-chemical data shows increasing degradation of the river until the 1990s, when a slight improvement was observed. The degradation was especially evident in the late 1970s and the early 1980s when all monitored waters were classified level III or worse, "out of class" (very bad quality). Since the mid-1980s the length of both class II and "out of class" waters has increased. In 1991, 77% of the total length of the river was "out of any class" and none in the first class (Central Statistical Office 1993), but dissolved substances characterizing salinity, such as chlorides and sulphates, have a crucial impact on this classification. Elimination of these pollutants would shift over 50% of "out of class" river stretches to higher classes (Makinia *et al.* 1996).

Based on physical-chemical criteria only, data from the early nineties show that approximately 2% of Poland's monitored river stretches meet class I standards, while 60% do not even meet class III. When biological criteria are applied, these values drop to 0% and increase to 88%, respectively (Central Statistical Office 1993). Changes of riverwater quality over the period 1964-1992, based on physical-chemical criteria indicate a dramatic drop (up to 10 times) in the length of the river stretches in class I, while the proportion in the other classes has varied without noticeable tendency (Makinia *et al.* 1996).

Kudelska *et al.* (1997) elaborated this classification for Polish lakes, which are often part of the catchment of larger rivers. Lake quality assessment and monitoring is performed according to the Lake Quality Evalution System (LQES) developed by the Institute of Environmental Protection in Warsaw. The system represents an ecosystem approach to lake quality evaluation, considering not only the characteristics of the water contained in the lake basin, but also the morphometric, hydrographic and catchment parameters on which the state of the lake is dependant. The system which has three principal classes of water quality and three categories regarding the sensitivity of lakes to ecosystem degradation, gives general guidelines on how lakes and connected river basins should be managed, protected and restored. The LQES is widely used in lake monitoring in Poland, and, according to Kudelska *et al.* (1997), has proved to be a useful decision making tool for effective lake quality control and management.

The water quality classes are based on different ranges of 18 (physical, chemical and biological) parameters indicative of general water conditions in the lake. Among them are commonly used indices of trophic status, such as phosphate and nitrogen concentration, oxygen saturation, chlorophyll-a concentration, BOD_5, as well as the concentration of toxic chemicals, and the density of coliform bacteria.

When massive mortalities of aquatic organisms (e.g. fish kills or death of other aquatic organisms) are visibly detected in the catchment, they may place the basin "beyond" the principal three classes, regardless of the range of other parameters. The second element of the LQES concerns the lake's sensitivity to ecosystem degradation, showing the reaction of the water body to various human impacts, such as pollution, according to its morphometric and hydrographic properties and catchment land use. The three successive categories (I to III) give information on the habitat quality and correspond to decreasing values of mean depth, the ratio of lake volume to shoreline length, and the relative volume of the unmixed layer, and to increasing values of the water renewal coefficient, and the percentage area of cultivated fields versus forests in the catchment. The values of these lake sensitivity parameters are transferred into a point scale and, as in the water quality classification method, a cumulative index determines the category of the lake (I to III).

Lakes and river basins classified as having class I and category I have clean water, and optimal morphometric and catchment conditions. Control of the present state is needed and use of water is allowed according to "special protection" principles. Lakes and river basins having class III and category III are highly polluted, and mostly hypertrophic, having the worst catchment situation and morphometric properties. Fundamental changes in the use of these lakes and river basins are absolutely necessary, with restoration activities such as the removal of the upper layer of bottom sediments probably the most effective (Kudelska *et al.* 1997).

Until now a Vistula rehabilitation project at the level of the entire river is not feasible: the unidirectional flow of water necessitates a catchment approach. Water quality of the river Vistula will improve after the process of sewage purification by treatment plants is completed. Part of the town of Warsaw has treatment plants already, and others are under construction (Prus 1996).

3.2. Pollution control and water management

The Vistula is important not only to Poland but to all Baltic countries, that have interests in the abatement of Baltic sea pollution. Most of the Vistula pollution undoubtedly comes from industry and towns. More and more villages are now getting a centralized water supply; unfortunately many of these settlements are not provided with sewage-treatment plants. There is an urgent need for sewage purification and modern technology, and the situation is improving year after year. Diffuse pollution input into the Vistula is also important, and according to Kajak (1993) this can be significantly diminished by vegetation belts along rivers. The Vistula has embankments up to hundreds of meters in width along most of its length, where extensive floodplains are covered with abundant vegetation. This vegetation together with the fertile soil, probably absorbs most of the dispersed pollution flowing into the Vistula. It might be that Kajak (1993) is too optimistic about the nutrient- and pollutant-absorbing capacity of river floodplains. The geomorphology of the main river course is continuously changing: the river is braiding and meandering, and extreme river floods, such as the event of July 1997, could wash out all kinds of dissolved elements from the sediments, and among them nutrients.

The most important action now is pollution control at the source. This should be incorporated in the ongoing privatization, restructuring and modernization of the individual water-use activities of farms, factories and municipalities. The pollution of diffuse sources is an important problem, especially with respect to the agricultural sector. According to Kindler (1994) protective measures should be taken against the uncontrolled rise in the use of chemical fertilizers.

It has become clear that water quality problems can have an important impact on human health, economic growth and nature conservation. In an integrated management study the water of the river should be studied in relation to the underwater bottom, the adjacent land and the biota in the habitats. The major subject of research will, however, be the water quality management of the Vistula. But where the water quality problem is directly linked with water quantity problems (i.e. the accumulation of pollutants in reservoirs or the effect on auto-purification), the latter should be taken into consideration as well.

In the framework of a better control of point sources, in 1990 the "list of 80" most polluting industrial plants in Poland was published, and among them many discharging on the Vistula basin. By decision of the respective voivodships these factories are subjected to strict control measures of their activities. The plants were obliged to implement environmental-friendly technologies and to install environmental protection equipment. The results of these measures were considerable: a 70% lower chemical oxygen demand (COD) charge in waste water (RECCEE 1995). The introduction of a computer system to control water consumption by industries and communities, water quality and amount of wastes, connected to charges for the water consumption and penalty fees for degradation, is also a step forwards (Pawlowski & Dudzinska 1994).

Since 1989 Poland is going through several political, social and economic changes. These developments initiated a process of evolution in water management: a new water law that applies to the new organizational water management structure, is anticipated. Because of the changes in the organization and contents of the water management, sometimes the division of responsibilities and tasks between different authorities and institutions is unclear.

Three governmental levels can be distinguished in water management, national, regional and local level (RECCEE 1994, 1995; CML 1995). The responsibilities of the separate authorities, especially with respect to local level activities, are rather diffuse. On national level the Ministry of Environmental Protection is the main executor responsible for water management. The tasks of this Ministry are the setting of water quality objectives, the implementation of plans on national level and the formulation of water quality standards. The Ministry of Agriculture and Food Management is responsible for the management of the rural river stretches, for river regulation, land reclamation and flood protection (CML 1995).

On regional level a distinction can be made between general water management and river basin management. Regarding general water management, 49 voivodships are responsible for the regional water management, i.e. they have jurisdiction to provide licences, to implement the water law, in order to manage the water quality. River basins of Poland's main rivers are managed by the Regional Water Management Authority. This new administrative body was created in 1992 because of tuning problems between different voivodships and different governmental levels. Because river catchment boundaries did not correspond with administrative provincial units, the division of tasks between different voivodships was not clear. The lower Vistula is now managed by a number of Regional Water Management Boards (of Gdansk and Warsaw, and other cities; CML 1995).

3.3. Flood protection and water quality

The Vistula river is partly regulated for the purpose of navigation and flood risk control. The anti-flood dikes protect the population in the lowlands of the river basin. Most of the dikes were built in the nineteenth century. Their present technical construction is not good, and the height of the dikes is decreasing by the process of subsiding. So a large area is constantly endangered by floodings and consequent negative effects of the bad water quality of the river. Due to bad management and river regulation, ice jams can cause destruction of dikes with an increasing risk of flooding. In January 1982 the largest and most detrimental flooding occurred in the Wloclawek reservoir. More than 100 km² of the valley was under water and 14,000 people had to be evacuated (CML 1995).

In July 1997 large parts of the Czech Republic, Germany and Poland suffered from very serious river floods, caused mainly by extreme rain fall: two severe depressions brought in a few weeks time an amount of rain, falling under normal circumstances in half a year. A secondary cause, presumably amplifying the rainfall, was the quick run off of river water, connected to the recent changes in upstream land use. The flood wave which originated in the mountains, ran in a few weeks time through the basin of the rivers Vistula and Odra, and reached the Baltic Sea in the last week of July. The river floods caused a disaster in Poland. There were more than 50 casualties, large parts of cities and villages were flooded, and hundreds of thousands of hectares of land were flooded with polluted and toxic waste water. Lack of administrative coordination and lack of adequate funds decided the size of the catastrophe. Besides that the recent floods in Poland demonstrated the continued vulnerability of the country to natural hazards. In the lower reaches of the Odra river the dikes bordering the river appeared to be too low and were improperly maintained, while the river itself suffered from postponed and insufficient dredging (Anonymous 1997).

4. Considerations for future Vistula management

4.1. Policy considerations for river management

According to Spaargaren *et al.* (1993) the political changes in Central- and Eastern Europe have had serious consequences for the international political agenda. Environmental care, especially care for public health has priority now. The Polish National Environmental Policy Plan of 1990 puts the implementation of "sustainable development" in a central place: (1) maximum use of market mechanisms in environmental management, and maintenance by the goverment, and gradual introduction of a system of anti-pollution levies (the polluter pays); (2) decentralization of environmental policy, giving regional governments ample responsibilities to erect their own environmental standards; (3) the necessity of international cooperation in environmental issues, including ecological modernisation of the Polish industry. The institutional structure of the Polish environmental management is still characterized by central and hierarchical structures, whereas the resistance of local authorities against that system is increasing. On paper the authorities are working on drastic policy changes, but in practice the turn occurs very slowly, and continuity and desintegration seem more prominent than policy changes and build-up programmes (Spaargaren *et al.* 1993).

Poland is facing serious problems with water resources, and the Vistula is playing a central role in that process. The water demands doubled between 1960 and 1970 because of large industrial investments and the increase in the human population (Mikulski 1990). The relative water use in the industry is 2-3 times higher than in most industrialized countries. Inefficient use of water resources and the lack of a realistic pricing policy have led to high water demands. The opinion in the eighties was that if nothing is done about this problem there will be a considerable water deficit in the next century which may even inhibit further economic development (CML 1995). Recent information, however, points to a stabilization of the water resources and distribution problem in Poland (personal communication prof. Kajak).

It is suggested that one of the ways to manage the Vistula water quantities, is the Lower Vistula Cascade project (LVC), meant to promote the socio-economic development of the Lower Vistula region (CML 1995). In the lower section of the Vistula, between the cities Plock and Wloclawek, a dam reservoir has been built. The concept furthermore anticipates the building of seven large dams in the lower Vistula between Warsaw and Gdansk within 20 years. The project is controversial, because of the conflict between the supposed economic gains, generation of clean energy and better conditions for irrigation, and the irreversible changes provoked in the Vistula environment. In general people agree that something should be done regarding flood risk control and water supply of the Vistula basin. An integrated river basin management plan, and not a lower Vistula plan only, may enhance solutions.

To sum up, the recognition of water problems, the formulation of a comprehensive water policy, and the building of an institutional basis for water management are three elements for improving the water policy implementation (CML 1995, Hofman & Rietbergen 1996). To develop water management strategies, some key elements of the ongoing transition must be taken into account:

1. There is a movement towards decentralization and privatization. Centralized strategic and financial planning by the state has therefore largely been abandoned.
2. With the increasing role of local governments, the institutional system is slowly, but significantly changing. In Poland new river basin authorities are created, just like environmental agencies. New environmental legislation has been introduced, and state-owned regional water and waste water companies are in the process of disappearing.
3. The decision making has been largely decentralized. Due to lack of experience and institutional structure, some problems will emerge. One example: it will take quite some time to decide about building the LVC, as many different interest groups are involved in the process of decision making, without a clear structure of competences and responsibilities.

Water quality management was discussed in the first place in this paper. Many aspects of water quantity management are unknown, and need further research. The improvement of river basin management of the Vistula needs a clear study of the administrative structure of the water management. The Ministry of Environmental Protection published recently a report about the present state of the water management in Poland and tendencies of change (Hydroprojekt 1996). The consequences of this report have not been evaluated by us.

4.2. Future ecological restoration

In 1995 an international seminar was held in Warsaw devoted to the protection of the Vistula river valley in the light of economic investments. The meeting concluded (Prus 1996):

1. The river Vistula valley is of great international importance in the system of national protected areas both in Poland and in Europe. The valley contains a harmonious set of ecosystems with high ecological diversity, resulting from diversified habitats stretching along the river. This area is of great ecological value, and functions also as a corridor connecting other wetlands with a high natural value.

Several international conventions indicate the need to create protected areas in order to maintain ecological values, both at national and continental level.

2. In order to ensure effective nature protection in the region of the Vistula river valley, certain strategic decisions are claimed, such as: (a) consideration of the Vistula valley region as part of the national and European system of areas of protection; (b) ensuring the longitudinal river continuum, thus abandoning the ideas about the construction of thresholds in the river between Warsaw and Plock; (c) resigning from continuation of regulatory constructions according to plans of 1969-1970 for the mid-course of the Vistula; (d) compulsory preparation of ecological expertise for economic investments regarding river regulation (*cf.* Environmental Impact Assessment; Prus 1996).

It may be concluded that the ecological values of the Vistula are fully recognized in theory, but in practice economic counteracting motives are still dominating. The river Vistula plays an important role in the economic infrastructure of Poland. In this respect it can be compared to the river Rhine, that has an important infrastructural function in Europe. Both river systems are roughly under the same cold temperate climatic regime, but have a completely different historical background. During the nineteenth century most of the large European rivers, including the Rhine, were being regulated by numerous dams and weirs, mainly for navigation and transport purposes (Nienhuis & Leuven 1998). As the Polish economic development during the past 70 years diverged negatively from the expansion in Western European states, only a few dams were built in the middle and lowland sections of the river, and consequently in these areas the Vistula has maintained its natural, wild character.

A comparison between the river basin management of the Rhine (where water quality has improved, but habitats have been annihilated), and the river Vistula (where water quality is still bad, but the diversity and integrity of habitats is large) leads to the conclusion not to destruct the Vistula floodplains irreversibly for short-term economic profits, but to save the river basin for future long-term profits. These long-term profits comprise healthy ecosystems, "spongy" wetlands for quantitative water management, self purification properties, and nature conservation perspectives. The area of tension between economic growth and ecological restoration is overshadowed by the drastic changes in environmental policy and management occurring in Poland since 1989. History learns us that river environments are often irreversibly abused in favour of economic growth. We may only hope that the Polish authorities promote the wise use of water resources, and concomitant preservation of river ecosystems.

Acknowledgement

We thank Prof. Dr. Z. Kajak, Polish Academy of Sciences, Warsaw, for critically reading the paper.

References

Anonymous. 1997. Powodz. pp.1-128. Amber, Warszawa, Poland (in Polish).

Baginski, L. 1993. The main problems of water resources protection in Poland. In: L. Pawlowski (ed.) – The main environmental problems of nowadays Poland. Srodkowo – Europejski Instytut Badan nad Srodowiskiem, Lublin, pp. 31-42.

Central Statistical Office. 1993. Environmental Protection, Warsaw (in Polish).

CML. 1995. Lower Vistula management: towards sustainable development. Centre of Environmental Science (CML), European Postgrad. Course Environment. Management, pp. 1-108, Leiden University, The Netherlands.

Dojlido, J. & Woyciechowska, J. 1989. Water quality classification of the Vistula river basin in 1987. Ekologia Polska 37: 405-417.

Hofman, N.J.W & Rietbergen, M.G. 1996. Water management in the lower reach of the Vistula River in Poland. Reports Environmental Studies no. 127: 1-88, Department of Environmental Studies, Faculty of Science, University of Nijmegen, The Netherlands.

Hydroprojekt. 1996. Strategia Gospodarki Wodnej w Polsce (Strategic Water Management in Poland), Warszawa (in Polish).

Jedraszko-Dabrowska, D., Bukacinski, M., Bukacinski, D. & Cygan, J.P. 1995. Vistula river (Poland) – Concepts of Management. Arch. Hydrobiol. Suppl. 101, Large Rivers 9: 675-678.

Kajak, Z. 1992. The river Vistula and its floodplain valley (Poland): its ecology and importance for conservation. In: P.J. Boon, P.Calow & G.E. Petts (eds.) – River conservation and management, pp. 35-49. Wiley, Chichester.

Kajak, Z. 1993. The Vistula river and its riparian zones. Hydrobiologia 251: 149-157.

Kaniewska-Prus, M. 1983. Ecological characteristics of the polysaprobic section of the Vistula river below Warsaw. Pol. Arch. Hydrobiol. 30: 149-163.

Kindler, J., 1994. Some thoughts on the implementation of water quality management strategies for Central- and Eastern-Europe. Water Science Technol. 30: 15-24.

Koblak-Kalinska, E. 1992. Problems of water protection against pollution. Gospodarka Wodna 10: 222-229 (in Polish).

Kownacki, A., Kajak, Z., Lajczak, A. & Wlodek, J.M. 1994. Natural science bibliography of the river Vistula (Poland). Acta Hydrobiol. (Krakow) 36: 409-465.

Kudelska, D., Soszka, H. & Cydzik, D. 1997. Polish practice in lake quality assessment. In: P.J. Boon & D.L. Howell (eds.) – Freshwater Quality: defining the indefinable, pp. 149-154. The Stationery Office, Edinburgh.

Makinia, J., Dunnette, D. & Kowalik, P. 1996. Water pollution in Poland. Europ. Water Pollut. Control 6: 26-33.

MEPNR&F. 1991a. The state of the environment in Poland – damage and remedy. Ministry of Environmental Protection, Natural Resources, and Forestry (MEPNR&F), Warsaw (in Polish).

MEPNR&F. 1991b. Regulation of the Minstry of Environmental Protection, Natural Resources and Forestry (MEPNR&F), 1991, concerning water classification and conditions required for wate-water discharged to water and ground, Dziennik Ustaw 116/1001, pos. 503 (in Polish).

Mikulski, Z. 1990. Water resources and management in Poland. In: B. Mitchell (ed.) – Integrated water management, international experiences and perspectives, pp. 172-187, Belhaven Press, London.

Niemirycz, E. 1994. The Vistula river of Poland, environmental characteristics and historical perspective. Plenary Present. Intern. River Quality Symp., Portland, Oregon, USA, March 21-25, 1994.

Nienhuis, P.H. & Leuven, R.S.E.W. 1998. Ecological concepts for the sustainable management of river basins: a review. In: P.H. Nienhuis, R.S.E.W Leuven & A.M.J. Ragas (eds.) – New concepts for sustainable management of river basins, pp. 7-33. Backhuys Publishers, Leiden, Netherlands.

Olanczuk-Neyman, K., Czerwionka, K. & Gorska, A. 1992. Bacteriological pollution of coastal water and sand in the region of the Gdansk Bay. Proceed. Symposium Research on Hydraulic Engineering, University of Zagreb, Zagreb, pp.165-169.

Pawlowski, L. & Dudzinska, M.R., 1994. Environmental problems of Poland during economic and political transformation. Ecol. Engineering 3: 207-215.

Prus, T. 1996. Present and former state of the river Vistula (Poland). In: Sprengers, S.A., Nienhuis, P.H. & Elias, P. (eds.) – Report of the workshop "Sustainability of Ecosystems: Ecological and Economic Factors", Bratislava, 1995, pp. 156-157. Royal Netherlands Academy of Arts and Sciences, Amsterdam.

RECCEE. 1994. Government and Environment, a directory for Central and Eastern Europe, Regional Environmental Centre for Central- and Eastern-Europe (RECCEE). Contacts for Government Ministries with Environmental Responsibilities, Budapest.

RECCEE. 1995. The Emerging Environmental Market. A survey in the Czech Republic, Hungary, Poland and the Slovak Republic, Regional Environmental Centre for Central- and Eastern-Europe (RECCEE), Budapest.

Spaargaren, G., Liefferink, J.D., Mol, A.P.J., Brussaard, W & Kakebeeke, W.J. 1993. Internationaal Milieubeleid, Sdu Uitgeverij, Den Haag, pp. 1-253 (in Dutch).

Szymanska, H. 1975. Comparison of the Vistula water purity in years 1964-1972. Gospodarka Wodna 5: 166-168 (in Polish).

Szymanska, H. 1987. Comparison of the Vistula water purity in years 1972-1983. Gospodarka Wodna 12: 282-285 (in Polish).

Tomialojc, L. (ed.). 1993. Nature and environment conservation in the lowland river valleys of Poland. Polska Akademia Nauk Komitet Ochrony Przyrody (in Polish).

POSSIBILITIES AND DIFFICULTIES IN QUANTIFYING THE GENERAL NOTION OF ENVIRONMENTAL UTILISATION SPACE (EUS) FOR WATER SYSTEMS

M.W.H. Thörig[1] & R.A.P.M. Weterings[2]

[1]Department of Environmental Studies, University of Nijmegen, P.O. Box 9010, 6500 GL Nijmegen, The Netherlands; [2]TNO Centre for Strategy, Technology and Policy (TNO-STB), P.O. Box 541, 7300 AM Apeldoorn, The Netherlands

Abstract

This paper explores the possibilities and difficulties in quantifying the general notion of Environmental Utilisation Space (EUS) for water systems. EUS is a concept that expresses the idea that at any point in time, there are limits to the degree of environmental pressure the earth's ecosystems can handle without unacceptable of irreversible damage to these systems, or to the life support functions that they enable. In this paper, EUS is used as a conceptual framework for identifying and describing the conflicting claims between recreation and nature conservation in a former estuary called Lake Grevelingen (the Netherlands).

In order to determine the level of recreation possible within the boundaries of the EUS, the population sizes of individual species (birds) have been chosen as indicators. For each indicator species, a weak and a strong sustainability level in population size were determined. The 'distances' between current population size and both sustainability levels are measures for sustainability. Our case study of Lake Grevelingen shows that sustainability levels are dynamic in time and space, with levels of ecosystem vulnerability varying during the season. It is concluded that EUS can be of help in visualising the dynamic (im)balance between recreation and nature conservation.

1. Introduction

Environmental Utilisation Space (EUS) is a concept that expresses the idea that at any point in time, there are limits to the degree of environmental pressure the earth's ecosystems can handle without unacceptable or irreversible damage to these systems, or to the life support functions that they enable. The boundaries of the EUS reflect critical levels for environmental use beyond which ecosystems cannot cope or repair the damage. Within this limited space, the biosphere provides society with a variety of societal functions. Beyond these boundaries, natural species become extinct, resources are exhausted and biological processes are disrupted.

This paper explores the possibilities and difficulties in quantifying the general notion of EUS for water systems. It focuses on the search for critical levels beyond which water system use can no longer be called sustainable. The paper is based on the observations in a case study of sustainable water management in a former estuary called Lake Grevelingen (Thörig 1996, Thörig *et al*. 1996). The challenge for water management in Lake Grevelingen is to create a sustainable balance between

New concepts for sustainable management of river basins, pp. 333–341
edited by P.H. Nienhuis, R.S.E.W. Leuven and A.M.J. Ragas
© 1998 Backhuys Publishers, Leiden, The Netherlands

recreation and nature conservation. This calls for an assessment of critical levels for recreation, beyond which it results in unacceptable and irreversible effects on the development of ecosystems and natural species in Lake Grevelingen.

Box 1. Introduction to Lake Grevelingen.

Lake Grevelingen is a former estuary in the delta of the river Rhine in the province of Zeeland (The Netherlands). The lake's water surface is 10,800 hectare, with an average depth of 5.4 meters. In order to prevent inundation during storm floods, the influence of tidal movements has been removed by the construction of two dams (Grevelingendam at the inland side and Brouwersdam at the North Sea side of the Lake). At present, the lake is stagnant, it is oligotrophic and has a low turbidity. During the winter period, the sluices are opened and exchange with coastal water takes place. Because of its isolated position, the lake has not been seriously polluted during the seventies. The following functions have been assigned to it (Ministerie van Verkeer en Waterstaat 1989):
– swimming water, waterside recreation and recreational sailing;
– professional and sports fisheries;
– nature conservation;
– transport of water, ice and sediment.
The number of tourists visiting the lake is increasing, and they tend to visit the area all year round. The diversity of recreational activity is also increasing. At peak times during the summer, approximate 3,000 recreation yachts, 500 surfers, 18 jet skiers and 400 sports divers use the lake, while approximate 10,000 persons are swimming and sunbathing, mostly at the Brouwersdam and Grevelingendam (Morren 1996, Wattel 1996). Hiking and biking are practised by approximate 20% and 10% of the visitors, respectively, mostly in addition to other kinds of recreation.
In order to regulate the water system use, areas with recreational functions have been separated from those that function as a nature reserve by means of zoning. The nature zone consists of an open landscape, with shallow water, shell banks and fowl which depend on this type of landscape. Because of the landscape's open character, the birds living in this area are easily disturbed.
The growth of recreation is resulting in an increasing environmental pressure, which in time might lead to malfunctioning zoning (Morren 1996).

2. Dimensions and indicators of the EUS

Weterings & Opschoor (1994a) suggested that the general approach to defining boundary conditions for the EUS consists of two steps: (i) distinguishing broad dimensions of the EUS and (ii) selecting specific environmental issues for which sustainability levels can be determined. It was established that at least three dimensions of the EUS should be represented (Weterings & Opschoor 1994a,b):
a. pollution of natural systems with xenobiotic substances or with natural substances in unnatural concentrations;
b. depletion of natural resources: renewable, non-renewable and semi-renewable;
c. loss of naturalness: integrity, biodiversity and absence of disturbance.
These three dimensions of the EUS allow more focused research into boundary conditions, based on assumptions as to what constitutes a sustainable level of environmental impact. Our search for boundary conditions for EUS for recreation focused on only one of the above three dimensions, viz., the loss of naturalness, in

terms of disturbance of natural systems. In Lake Grevelingen, recreation poses one of the major threats to the integrity of the natural systems and species. Therefore, the case study focused on the main impact of recreation, i.e. the disturbance resulting from recreational activities such as swimming, fishing and sailing. Of course, recreation results in other types of impact on the natural systems of Lake Grevelingen as well, but disturbance seems to be the major one (Morren 1996, Wattel 1996).

In order to define the boundaries of the EUS, sustainability levels have to be determined for a set of environmental indicators reflecting the key impacts of recreation. An environmental indicator can in general be defined as a measurement, statistic or value that provides a proximate gauge or evidence of the effects of environmental management programmes or of the state or condition of the environment (US Environmental Protection Agency 1997). Environmental indicators can be either descriptive or normative. Descriptive indicators reflect actual or factual conditions, such as the state of the environment or environmental pressure. Normative indicators compare actual or factual conditions with reference conditions. The indicators defined in this paper are normative in the sense that they compare current environmental conditions to a specific set of sustainability levels. The ideal is to develop a set of indicators which captures all relevant aspects of environmental pressure of recreation in the former estuary. In practice, this is very difficult, as we will show below.

3. Sustainability levels

For each of the environmental indicators, sustainability levels can be defined. These sustainability levels are reference values for the environmental quality required for sustainability. Sustainability can be defined as a situation where no unacceptable harmful impacts of human activities for humans, plants, animals and goods occur either now or in the future (Ragas *et al.* 1995). In defining sustainability levels, we can start from different interpretations of sustainability, ranging from so-called strong to so-called weak sustainability (Serageldin *et al.* 1994). Within strong sustainability, the ecological dimension is considered to be conditional for sustainable development. According to this interpretation, sustainability levels equal the environmental quality at which the naturalness of ecosystems is not being affected. Within weak sustainability, a certain loss of naturalness is considered acceptable if this results in an equivalent growth of socio-economic types of capital. More environmental pressure will lead to unacceptable and irreversible damage to ecosystems. In general, the weak sustainability level will allow a higher degree of activity, because the ecological damage accepted will be higher. In the present case study, it was left open what level of sustainability should be applied in water management.

Fig. 1 illustrates two theoretical relationships between environmental stress and environmental quality. Our search for sustainability levels is based upon these relationships. Within the strong interpretation of sustainability, the extent of environmental stress at which the environmental quality is not yet affected is considered the boundary of the EUS. Environmental stress values corresponding with the strong sustainable environmental quality are considered indicators for strong sustainabili-

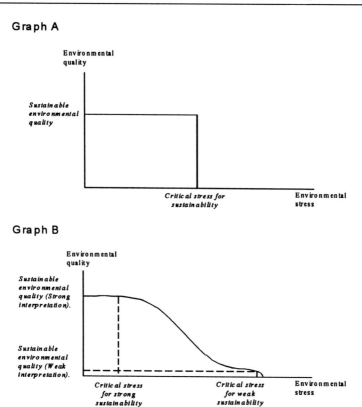

Fig. 1. Two possible relationships between environmental quality and environmental stress. Graph A: Block response to environmental stress: the level of environmental stress referring to a sustainable environmental quality (no observed effect) can be pointed out univocally. Graph B: Sigmoid response to environmental stress: the locus of the critical stress for sustainability depends on the interpretation of sustainability. Within a strong interpretation of sustainability no observed environmental effect is considered sustainable. Within a weak interpretation of sustainability no extinction of species or no irreversible damage to environmental quality is considered sustainable.

ty. The extent of environmental stress matching the locus of the ecological minimum (for example the biological minimum population size of a species) is considered a boundary of the EUS according to the weak interpretation. Indicator values reflecting this kind of situation are considered weak sustainability levels. As regards recreation at Lake Grevelingen, environmental stress can be expressed as the numbers of leisure visitors present in an area or as the total surface being disturbed by such visitors. Environmental quality can be expressed as the available habitat or ecotope units or as the abundance of one species.

It is theoretically possible that both the weak and the strong sustainability level refer to the same level of environmental pressure. This is the case if increasing pressure results into a block response (graph A in Fig. 1). However, a block response rarely occurs, and sigmoid responses are in general more adequate for describing environmental response patterns (graph B in Fig. 1). In this case, the strong and the weak sustainability levels each reflect a different extent of environmental stress. Actually measured indicator values have to be interpreted towards both sustainability levels. If indicator values do not cross the strong sustainability level, the environmental system is considered the be in a state of absolute sustainability. Activities take place within the boundaries of EUS. If indicator values measured cross the weak sustainability level, the environmental system is in an absolute unsustainable state. Activities have led to boundaries of EUS being crossed. The levels in-between strong and weak sustainability levels provide a margin for setting management targets aiming at (politically) chosen sustainability. Fig. 2 is a graphic representation of the indicator and the sustainability levels.

4. Defining environmental indicators for Lake Grevelingen

As discussed above, this paper focuses on the disturbance resulting from recreational activities in Lake Grevelingen. Hence, we will have to develop a set of indicators that captures all relevant aspects of disturbance of natural species and ecosystems resulting from recreational activities.

In the case study, the disturbance of individual species (birds) was chosen as indicator for environmental pressure caused by recreation. Disturbance of birds has been regarded as a major disturbance issue (Wattel 1996). Of course, disturbance of birds does not capture all relevant aspects of environmental pressure, but we assume

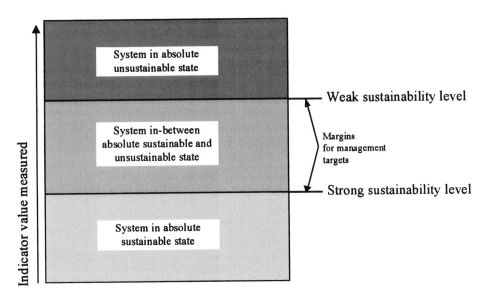

Fig. 2. Graphic representation of the environmental indicator values possible in relation to weak and strong sustainability levels. Indicator values measured smaller than the strong sustainability level, refer to an absolute sustainable situation. If indicator values measured exceed the weak sustainability level, the system is considered to be in an absolute unsustainable state. The levels in-between the strong and weak sustainability level provide margins for management targets, aiming at a politically chosen sustainability level.

that disturbance adequately reflects the level of recreation in Lake Grevelingen. A practical reason for selecting birds as indicator species is that these animals have been relatively well described for Lake Grevelingen.

The case study has taken a closer look at recreational activities on Hompelvoet Island and the surrounding shallow waters. At present, the pressure that recreation puts on the Island is insignificant: the surrounding water is too shallow to be sailed by yachts and the islands are closed to the public. Disturbance only occasionally occurs. The area is located within the nature conservation zone. Because of its sensitivity to recreation, the Sandwich tern (*Sterna sandvicensis*) was chosen as the environmental indicator for land recreation on the Island and the surrounding water. The sustainability levels assessed concern the period April-July. During this period, one person visiting the island can do as much damage as a group of persons. The worst response would be that the birds fail to found a colony. This response fits the block response of Fig. 1. This allows the conclusion that the critical level for land recreation at Hompelvoet Island during the breeding period approaches zero. As was shown above, disturbance can also occur as a result of recreation on the shallow waters around the island (for example surfing and canoeing). However, the impact of this activity on the colony is expected to be less manifest and abrupt: a sigmoid response would be expected (Thörig 1996). Therefore, the weak and strong sustainability levels refer to a different extent of recreation. Because of the limited scope of the case study, the critical levels for water recreation on the shallow water area, were not quantified.

Similar results were found for critical levels of recreation near the Brouwersdam during the winter (Thörig 1996). In this case, the wintering Great crested grebe (*Podiceps auritus*) was chosen as environmental indicator. Large numbers of this bird are found in the area, because of the favourable food situation nearby the sluices of the dam. The 1% norm of the Ramsar convention for waterfowl populations of international importance is being exceeded by a factor of 12 (the 1% norm means that more than 1% of the world population of a waterfowl regularly uses a particular wetland). Occasional disturbance, for example by motorboats, can have a severe impact on the amount of birds present. The response approaches a block response, which implies that during the winter period the weak and strong sustainability levels correspond to a critical level for aquatic sports which approaches zero.

We also evaluated an indicator species relevant to recreation on a larger geographic scale, viz. the Black-necked grebe (*Podiceps nigricollis*). These birds moult in the period June – July and during this period they are easily disturbed. Hence they concentrate on the quiet shallow water areas near the islands of Hompelvoet and Markenje (see Fig. 3, map A). After the moulting period, the birds spread out over the lake (see Fig. 3, map B). The movement of the birds from the shallow waters towards the moulting areas is considered a response to recreational activity (Wattel 1996). Increased recreation on the shallow waters near Hompelvoet will result in substantial degradation of the lake's moulting function (Wattel 1996). From this it can be concluded that such a development would lead to the strong sustainability level being exceeded. As to the current situation for Lake Grevelingen, it can be concluded that the indicator value is now located in-between the strong and weak sustainability levels (Thörig 1996).

A   B

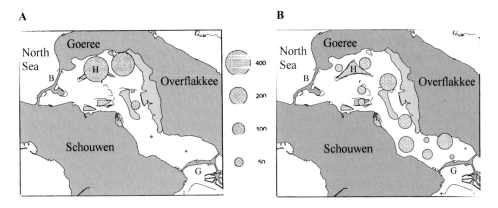

Fig. 3. Dispersal of the Black-necked grebe (*Podiceps nigricollis*) in the Grevelingen area during July 1994 (map A) and August 1995 (map B). Legend: H = Hompelvoet Island; B = Brouwersdam; G = Grevelingendam.

5. Discussion

An important observation from the case study (Thörig 1996) is that it is very difficult to define a comprehensive set of indicators that captures the complex web of interactions between recreation, ecosystems and natural species. As has been observed by several other authors (Opschoor & Weterings 1994, Musters *et al.* 1994, Buise *et al.* 1995) there are fundamental gaps in the available information with regard to key processes and mechanisms in this complex web of interactions. Although the concept of EUS was introduced to explicitly take into account multiple stress-related response mechanisms, there is a general lack of information in this respect. Therefore, it will be very difficult to define and quantify a comprehensive set of indicators, covering all relevant aspects of ecosystem response.

A second important observation from the Grevelingen case study is that boundary conditions for EUS are dynamic in time and space, with levels of ecosystem vulnerability varying during the season. This can be illustrated using the Sandwich tern (*Sterna sandvicensis*). This bird uses Hompelvoet Island, at the North side of Lake Grevelingen, as a breeding area. At the beginning of the breeding period (April) the birds are extremely sensitive to disturbance caused by land recreation, so that the critical level for recreation on Hompelvoet approaches the zero stress-level. After the breeding period (July) the degree of sensitivity decreases and the critical level for recreation at Hompelvoet rises. During the breeding period, aquatic sports on the shallow waters around Hompelvoet Island can also disturb the birds, although the sensitivity to aquatic sports is less than that to recreation on the island itself. Therefore, in addition to the differentiation in time, spatial differentiation should also be included in our search for critical levels of recreation. The critical level of recreation at Hompelvoet Island is substantially lower than that of recreation on the shallow waters around Hompelvoet, which in turn is substantially lower than the critical level of recreation in the more distant deep waters.

The case study described here is a first impetus towards quantifying EUS for Lake Grevelingen. Boundary conditions for recreational use of lake Grevelingen are strongly determined by the level of disturbance possible within a sustainable environmental quality. From the case study, it can be concluded that the numbers of fowl present in particular areas of Lake Grevelingen indicate the level of disturbance within these areas. However, indicator values measured can only be correctly interpreted if the disturbance by other activities, such as fishery, is of minor importance compared to disturbance by recreation. As regards the case study, environmental stress of activities other than recreation is insignificant. An other criterion for selecting an indicator species is the existence of an unambiguous relationship between fluctuations in the numbers of an indicator species and the extent of environmental stress (in our example recreation). In practice, quantification of these relationships showed to be difficult, because of the lack of information referred to above.

6. Conclusions

In Lake Grevelingen, a vulnerable balance exists between the recreational functions and nature conservation. The combination of these functions within the lake inevitably gives rise to conflicting claims. The EUS presents a conceptual framework for identifying and describing these conflicting claims, and helps to visualise and comprehend the dynamic nature of the balance between recreation and nature conservation. In operationalizing this conceptual framework, it is necessary to develop a set of environmental indicators that captures all relevant aspects of environmental pressure and to define sustainability levels for each of these indicators. However, the information needed on the key ecological processes and mechanisms is largely lacking, making choices and assumptions inevitable in defining indicators and sustainability levels.

Because of the above limitations, only a fragmented image of the boundary conditions for the EUS of Lake Grevelingen could be assessed. Nevertheless, it can cautiously be concluded that the area of Hompelvoet deserves special attention with regard to recreation during the period April-July. In this period, the critical ecological functions of this area include the breeding of the Sandwich tern (*Sterna sandvicensis*) and the moulting of the Black-necked grebe (*Podiceps nigricollis*). Increasing recreational activities in the area can result in weak sustainability limits being exceeded for both species. The dispersal pattern of the Black-necked grebe during the moult indicates that the strong sustainability level of recreation is already being exceeded locally during this period. During the winter period special attention concerning the water sports is recommended for the area near the Brouwersdam: even occasional motor boat traffic can have a large influence on the wintering Great crested grebe (*Podiceps auritus*). Because of the dynamic nature of the EUS, management targets have to be differentiated for different geographical and temporal scale levels. In the example of the moulting of the Black-necked grebe, this means that in judging the acceptability of environmental pressure from the shallow waters nearby Hompelvoet Island, the dispersal pattern over the entire lake has to be accounted for.

Acknowledgements

A part of the case study has been financed by the National Institute for Coastal and Marine Management (RIKZ; project number 22961088).

References

Buise, C.L., Eijkenboom, R.G.F.T.M., Van de Heuvel, P.J.M., Knapen, M.J & Ragas, A.M.J. 1995. Knelpunten bij toepassing van het concept milieugebruiksruimte voor het bepalen van de duurzaamheid van produktsystemen. Milieu 10: 33-40 (in Dutch).

Ministerie van Verkeer en Waterstaat. 1989. Derde Nota Waterhuishouding. Sdu-uitgeverij, Den Haag, The Netherlands (in Dutch).

Morren, W. 1996. De Grevelingen: gebruik en grenzen. Gebruikersevaluatie van de Grevelingen. Achtergronddocument milieugebruiksruimte-onderzoek. Vakgroep Milieukunde, Katholieke Universiteit Nijmegen, Verslagen Milieukunde nr. 115, Nijmegen, The Netherlands (in Dutch).

Musters, C.J.M., De Graaf, H.J., Noordervliet, M.A.W. & Ter Keurs, W.J. 1994. Measuring environmental utilisation space: can it be done? Netherlands Journal of Environmental Sciences 9: 213-220.

Opschoor, J.B. & Weterings, R. 1994. Environmental utilisation space: an introduction. Netherlands Journal of Environmental Sciences 9: 198-205.

Ragas, A.M.J., Knapen, M.J., Van den Heuvel, P.J.M., Eijkenboom, R.G.F.T.M., Buise, C.L. & Van de Laar, B.J. 1995. Towards a sustainability indicator for production systems. Journal of Cleaner Production 3: 123-129.

Serageldin, I., Daley, H. & Goodland, R. 1994. The concept of environmental sustainability. The World Bank, Washington DC, United States of America.

Thörig, M.W.H. 1996. Verkenning van het begrip Milieugebruiksruimte. Case studie Grevelingenmeer. Vakgroep Milieukunde, Katholieke Universiteit Nijmegen, Verslagen Milieukunde nr. 135, Nijmegen, The Netherlands (in Dutch).

Thörig, M.W.H., Knapen, M.J., Van der Laar, B.J. & Ragas, A.M.J. 1996. A design for a sustainability indicator based on environmental utility space: two cases. In: ERP Environment, The 1996 International Sustainable Development Research Conference, Conference Proceedings. pp. 249-254, ERP Environment, Shipley, UK.

U.S. Environmental Protection Agency. 1997. Terms of environment. Revised October 30, 1997 (http://www.epa.gov/OCEPAterms/).

Wattel, G. 1996. Grevelingenmeer: Uniek maar kwetsbaar. De ontwikkelingen in de periode 1990-1995. Rijksinstituut voor Kust en Zee (RIKZ), Rapport nr. RIKZ-96.014, The Netherlands (in Dutch).

Weterings, R. & Opschoor, J.B. 1994a. Environmental utilisation space and reference values for performance evaluation. Netherlands Journal of Environmental Sciences 9: 221-228.

Weterings, R. & Opschoor, J.B. 1994b. Towards environmental performance indicators based on the notion of environmental space. Advisory Council for Research on Nature and Environment (RMNO), Publication nr. 96, Rijswijk, The Netherlands.

RIVER MANAGEMENT AND PRINCIPLES OF ENVIRONMENTAL LAW

H.J.A.M. Van Geest & P.J. Hödl
Department of Public Law, Administrative Law Section, University of Nijmegen, P.O. Box 9049, 6500 KK Nijmegen, The Netherlands

Abstract

On 6 October 1996 the Treaty of Helsinki became effective. This treaty sees on prevention of water pollution. Therefore, in dealing with pollution problems the parties to the treaty shall be guided by three principles: the precautionary principle, the polluter-pays principle and sustainable development.

The precise meaning of the precautionary principle for the river management is not clear yet. Different international documents bring along different definitions. At least, it means that the absence of causal proof of pollution resulting from an activity is not an argument to abandon action. The polluter-pays principle which was originated by the OECD has more or less three aspects. We discuss prevention, the economic aspect and liability. Sustainable development gets more and more an important meaning, not only in river management, but in international environmental policy and law as well. Connected to this last principle is a duty to care for both states and individuals. Rivers play in this contribution a leading role.

1. Introduction

On 6 October 1996 the Convention on the protection and use of transboundary water courses and international lakes (Treaty of Helsinki) became effective (the parties agreed upon this treaty on 17 March 1992, Tractatenblad 1992, 199). This treaty is not restricted to prevention of water pollution, but it also aims at ecologically responsible and rational management, protection of the environment and restoration of ecosystems. This convention obliges parties to take all appropriate measures to prevent, control and reduce transboundary impact. In the treaty, a framework for riparian co-operation is developed.

We are interested in principles of environmental law, because they should be the cornerstones of (inter)national environmental policy and law in general and of international river management in particular. Article 2, subsection 5 of the Treaty of Helsinki lays down that the Parties shall be guided by the following principles: a) the precautionary principle, b) the polluter-pays principle and c) sustainable development. Besides these principles the Parties agreed to act upon 'best available technology', which is defined in annex 1 to the convention.

In this contribution we discuss the Helsinki-principles. We focus on the meaning of these principles and present possibilities to implement them. First of all however we discuss the meaning of principles of environmental law in general.

New concepts for sustainable management of river basins, pp. 343–352
edited by P.H. Nienhuis, R.S.E.W. Leuven and A.M.J. Ragas
© 1998 Backhuys Publishers, Leiden, The Netherlands

2. Principles

Environmental law forms a part of the law in general and it must follow general legal principles. Focusing on environmental law in particular it can be stated that environmental law contains the instruments to reach the goals decided on in environmental policy. Of course the basic legal values must be met, but in general it can be said that environmental law is instrumental in environmental policy. In laying down policies, the regulator is free to choose a legal instrument to reach a given goal.

25 Years after the Stockholm Declaration on the Human Environment (adopted 16 June 1972, UN Doc. A/CONF. 48/14/Rev. 1) it is common knowledge that principles are developed in environmental policy. In the development of (international, supranational or national) environmental policy one can distinguish more or less regular patterns which have grown to so-called principles. These principles, once recognised, are steering the further development of environmental policy and management. These principles are not legal principles, but basically policy principles. Such a principle might meet the demands of legal principles (the principle 'the polluter pays' may be understood as justification) but the law itself is not the basis of those principles. Those principles are originated in policy.

Once a principle is acknowledged on the national, supranational or international level, it will be the basis for environmental policy and law. Based on environmental policy, environmental law will be formulated and/or changed. Policy principles will penetrate environmental law. In article 130R of the EC-treaty, for instance, some principles are laid down. These principles get a legal status by being laid down in the treaty. But a lot of those principles are not binding, have no direct legal effect. In national environmental law these principles must be implemented. The realisation of the polluter-pays principle, for instance, might be by way of strict-liability or taxation or both. The instrument to realise a principle might be different in France or the Netherlands, amongst others because of juridical traditions. Even within a national legal system realisation of a principle does not need to be uniform.

3. Precautionary principle

Regarding the precautionary principle the Treaty of Helsinki reads:

> "The Parties shall be guided by the following principles: a) The precautionary principle, by virtue of which action to avoid the potential transboundary impact of the release of hazardous substances shall not be postponed on the ground that scientific research has not fully proved a causal link between those substances, on the one hand, and the potential transboundary impact, on the other hand ...".

Principle 15 of the Rio Declaration on Environment and Development (adopted 14 June 1992, A/CONF. 151 /5/Rev. 1) contains a similar principle:

> "In order to protect the environment, the precautionary approach shall be widely applied by States according to their capacities. Where there are threats of serious irreversible damage, lack of full scientific certainty shall not be used for postponing cost-effective measures to prevent environmental degradation".

Article 130R of the EC-Treaty states that community policy shall be based amongst others on the precautionary principle. These examples show that the precautionary principle is widely recognised.

Apparently the contents of the precautionary principle are clear: lack of scientific proof with regard to the causal link between pollution and effects on the environment does not justify delaying action. However, according to Krämer (1995) this principle has not much added value because of the overlap with the principle of preventive action.

We do not agree with Krämer because the underlying reason of the precautionary principle is that it should be prevented that measures are postponed until full scientific certainty exists with regard to the consequences for the environment of the activity concerned. Waiting for that moment might mean that the damage has become so serious that restoration is no longer possible. According to Gilhuis & Verschuuren (1996) every form of pollution that may be caused by a particular activity should be prevented, even if no clear indications exist that pollution will actually occur. A reasonable suspicion of negative effects on the environment is, in their view, sufficient to take preventive measures. In their opinion, a policy based on the precautionary principle is possible only if legislation offers the possibility of anticipating uncertainties as much as possible. Planning with vision is indispensable in this matter.

Without stating it explicitly, they go in the direction of the German 'Vorsorgeprinzip'. This German principle indicates that environmental policy should not only aim at restoration and prevention but also at preventing that pollution can arise. According to this 'Vorsorgeprinzip' a comprehensive approach is presupposed, because a fair insight into the potential risks for the environment as a whole, can only be gained if one takes such an approach. In the German doctrine, planning indeed seems necessary (Hoppe & Beckman 1989):

> "Das Vorsorgeprinzip besagt, dass Umweltpolitiek sich nicht in der Beseitigung eingetretener Schäden und der Abwehr Gefahren erschöpft; vielmehr soll bereits des Entstehen von Umweltbelastungen unterhalb der Gefahrenschwelle verhindert werden. ... in der rechtswissenschaftliche Literatur zum Teil nur zwei Systemvarianten des Vorsorgeprinzips, nämlich eine planerische und eine risikovorsorgende Unterschied".

There is no uniform understanding of the meaning of the precautionary principle. At the most general level, it means that states agree to act carefully and with foresight when taking decisions which concern activities that may have an adverse impact on the environment (for instance granting a permit for discharging polluted water into a lake). A more to the point interpretation provides that the principle requires activities and substances which might pollute the environment to be regulated, and possibly prohibited, even if no conclusive or overwhelming evidence is available as to the harm or possible harm they may cause to the environment (Sands 1995). Sands points out that a fundamental change would be adopted by an interpretation of the precautionary principle which would shift the burden of proof. According to current practice the burden of proof lies with the person opposing an activity to prove that it does or is likely to cause environmental damage. A new approach would shift the burden of proof and require the person who wishes to carry out an activity to prove that it will cause no harm to the environment (Sands 1995):

"This interpretation would require polluters, and polluting states, to establish that their activities and the discharge of certain substances would not adversely or significantly affect the environment before they were granted the right to release the potentially polluting substances or carry out the proposed activity".

In international environmental law, there is some evidence for this interpretation of the precautionary principle. According to the EC Urban Waste Water Directive (Directive 91/271) certain urban waste water discharges may be subjected to less stringent treatment than generally required, providing that 'comprehensive studies indicate that such discharges will not adversely affect the environment'.

In the Rio Declaration, the measures to be taken in the framework of the precautionary principle should be cost-effective. In the Treaty of Helsinki, an aspect of economic balancing is not introduced in the principle itself. However, according to article 3 of the treaty, limits for waste water discharges stated in permits are based on the best available technology for discharges of hazardous substances. In annex 1 the term 'best available technology' is defined. This term:

"1. is taken to mean the latest stage of development of processes, facilities or methods of operation which indicate the practical suitability of a particular measure for limiting discharges, emissions and waste. In determining whether a set of processes, facilities and methods of operation constitute the best available technology in general or individual cases, special consideration is given to: ... c) the economic feasibility of such technology; ...

2. It therefore follows that what is 'best available technology' for a particular process will change with time in the light of technological advances, economic and social factors, as well as in the light of changes in scientific knowledge and understanding."

In the definition of 'best available technology' the economic aspect is introduced in granting a permit. In our opinion this is correct: environmental policy does not exclude economic factors.

In the Dutch Environmental Management Act, the precautionary principle is not laid down. In that Act of Parliament, the so-called ALARA (as low as reasonable achievable) principle has a prominent place. In the Environmental Management Act, this principle is laid down in section 8.11, subsection 3:

"A licence shall be subject to any regulations which are necessary to protect the environment. If any adverse effects on the environment caused by making the licence subject to such regulations cannot be avoided, the licence shall be made subject to such additional regulations as may be necessary to provide the greatest possible protection to the environment from the said effects, unless this cannot reasonably be required".

In the parliamentary papers, the minister emphasised that 'best technical means' was meant in a most literal sense. In certain cases using 'best practicable means' could be appropriate. However, according to the act interests should always be weighed. In our view, using 'best technical means' is only acceptable in specific situations such as a highly contaminated soil or a damaging degree of water pollution. We think that if some ecosystem is in real danger an approach using best technical means might be the right approach. The ALARA principle cannot be understood as an implementation of the precautionary principle.

An implementation of the precautionary principle indicates an integral approach. One of the contracting parties to the Treaty of Helsinki is the European

Union. Almost all Member-States are party to the convention, too. It is interesting to remark that at the end of 1996 the Council Directive concerning Integrated Pollution Prevention and Control became effective (Directive 96/61/EC of 24 September 1996). The purpose of this directive is to achieve integrated prevention and control of pollution arising from activities listed in annex 1. To perform such an activity the operator needs an integrated permit. According to the Dutch Environmental Management Act, the operator of an establishment needs an almost integral permit (the water compartment is not included in this Act).

4. Polluter-pays principle

The polluter-pays principle was originated by the Organisation for Economic Co-operation and Development (OECD). The principle is based on the idea that charging polluters for the costs of action to fight the damage they cause, will encourage them to reduce pollution and stimulate them to find clean production processes or technologies. In article 2, paragraph 5, under b, of the Helsinki-treaty the principle is defined:

> "The polluter-pays principle, by virtue of which costs of pollution prevention, control and reduction measures shall be borne by the polluter".

In the following, three aspects of the polluter-pays principle shall be dealt with. The prevention aspect is the first we will discuss. Second, the economic aspect of the principle will be mentioned. The third aspect to be dealt with is liability. The question who is liable for the damage caused, will play a central role.

One may notice the similarity between the OECD and Helsinki explanations. However, the Treaty of Helsinki mentions the aspect of prevention, and for that reason may have a broader scope than the meaning of the OECD in the seventies. It appears that prevention has become a part of the polluter-pays principle. Another example of this broader interpretation is the Treaty of Strasbourg concerning the collection, disposal and reception of waste in the Rhine and inland navigation (Übereinkommen über die Sammlung, Abgabe und Annahme von Abfällen in der Rhein- und Binnenschiffahrt, 9 September 1996, see Tractatenblad 1996, 293 for the Dutch, French and German text). All contracting Parties (Germany, Belgium, France, Luxembourg, The Netherlands and Switzerland) commit themselves to set a uniform fee for the reception and disposal of shipping waste ('Schiffsabfall'). According to article 6, subsection 3, of the treaty, the payment of the fee gives a right to dispose oil and grease containing shipping waste in a reception unit. The shipmaster who pollutes has the duty to pay before the shipment takes place. By developing this system, the aspect of prevention is obvious. When there is less waste to get rid off, the payment will also be less. Preventive behaviour has got a financial benefit. A shipmaster has a choice whether to pollute (or better: to pay) or not. Thus, the polluter-pays principle set in other words means the payer pollutes. The payer obtains a right to pollute. One might doubt this explanation of the polluter-pays principle, but in fact it is what article 6, paragraph 3, of the Strasbourg-treaty states. This may be a rather inconvenient effect of defining the principle. Inconvenient if not alarming because it becomes a problem in case the sum of money to pay is lower than the benefits connected with polluting.

A few remarks with regard to economic (and fiscal) aspects of the polluter-pays principle will be made. The fifth EC Action Programme indicates the strategy for environmental policy in the European Union (EC 1993). More and more the fundamental aim of both economic and fiscal instruments will be to internalise all external environmental costs incurred during the whole life-cycle of products. An important category of economic instruments consists of charges. They are, in line with the polluter-pays principle, appropriate to discourage pollution at source as well as encourage clean production processes. Such charges are well understood and used, for instance in the field of water pollution (see chapter 7.4 of the Action Programme). The Treaty of Helsinki elaborates on these ideas, it sets out a charge for pollution system. The payment of the fee should be seen as a charge.

In chapter 7.7 of the Action Programme (Financial support mechanisms) one of the objectives is mentioned: getting the prices right. With regard to state aids, the target "application of polluter pays principle" is set. In this respect the polluter-pays principle forms a guidance to develop financial support mechanisms (taxation systems). The Helsinki-treaty does not refer to the EC Action Programme, so the mutual influences are not quite clear. But apparently, the polluter-pays principle nowadays gets a place in official policy documents, which set out the meaning of the principle in general. In that sense, official recognition is most important.

Another remark on the economic aspect should be made. As a matter of principle no state aid should be paid to clean up environmental pollution. The polluter-pays principle would be put under pressure, since in that case, in the end the tax payer will pay the bill.

Last subject that will be discussed in this paragraph is liability. Article 7 of the Helsinki-treaty reads:

"The Parties shall support appropriate international efforts to elaborate rules, criteria and procedures in the field of responsibility and liability".

This rather vague assignment cannot be named legal obligatory. We do not read any obligation in the term "shall support efforts". An environmental accident can cause different kinds of damage. Some of the consequences are directly quantifiable in monetary terms, for instance cleaning costs. An oil spill accident might also have indirect effects that cannot be calculated very easily. The harmed image or reputation of a coastal area may lead to a down-grade of hotel bookings. However, this damage might be compensated. Damage to the environment as such will be more difficult (or perhaps impossible) to calculate as well as compensate.

Questions of liability have been dealt with both on national and international levels. The background ideas on liability for environmental damage have not taken their definite shape yet. Whether or not to choose a system of strict or fault-based liability is up to the contacting parties.

An (international) example is the Council of Europe's Convention of civil liability for damage resulting from activities dangerous to the environment (Convention of Lugano, 22 June 1993; for Dutch information see Staatscourant 1993, 29 and 115). This is the first general convention on civil liability. The convention aims at ensuring adequate compensation for environmental damage and also provides for means of prevention and reinstatement.

In the preamble of the Convention of Lugano, the polluter-pays principle is mentioned explicitly. By taking the environmental costs into account in the prices of a product or an economic activity pollution will bring along a higher price in the end. Essential in this respect is that the damage is quantifiable in monetary terms.

A last remark on liability sees to the solutions one might seek to repair the damage. A penal conviction of the polluter does not mean the damage will factually be repaired. If a company appears to be insolvent, problems will certainly rise. Two solutions should be named: insurance and fund. With regard to a fund we shall mention one example. In the Netherlands, there is a Fund Air Pollution, based on title 15.5 of the Environmental Management Act. Everyone who suffers damage because of suddenly occurring air pollution can be compensated. Besides polluting industries, all Dutch car drivers contribute to the Fund.

5. Sustainable development

The third principle mentioned in the Treaty of Helsinki is generally known as sustainable development: "Water resources shall be managed so that the needs of the present generation are met without compromising the ability of future generations to meet their own needs". Already in the Stockholm Declaration something like sustainability was formulated in principle 1: "Man has the fundamental right to freedom, equality and adequate conditions of life, in an environment of a quality that permits a life of dignity and well-being, and he bears a solemn responsibility to protect and improve the environment for present and future generations" (UN Conference on the human environment, Stockholm 16 June 1992, UN Doc. A/CONF.48/14/Rev. 1). States decided on a solemn responsibility to protect and improve the environment for present and future generations.

Four elements appear to comprise the legal elements of the concept of sustainable development in international agreements. First the need to preserve natural resources for the benefit of future generations (intergenerational equity). Second the goal of exploiting natural resources in a manner which is 'sustainable', or 'prudent', or 'rational', or 'wise' or 'appropriate'. Third the 'equitable' use of natural resources, which implies that use by one state must take into account the needs of other states. And fourth the need to ensure that environmental considerations are integrated into economic and other development plans, programmes and projects and that development needs are taken into account in applying environmental objectives (the principle of integration; Sands 1995).

We shall not discuss at length the legal consequences of sustainable development. We shall focus in this paragraph on the intergenerational equity which implies that mankind is responsible for sustainability. In legal terms, this means a duty to care for the environment. Article 21 of the Dutch Constitution reads:

> "It shall be the concern of the authorities to keep the country habitable and to protect and improve the environment".

In the doctrine it is generally stated that this provision obliges the government to formulate an environmental policy, but does not give any indication about the contents of this obligation. Besides, it is emphasised that this provision cannot successfully be called upon in court. However, in the Benckiser-case (Hoge Raad, 1987) the Dutch Supreme Court made reference to this article 21. In this case, the Dutch authorities sued the German company Benckiser for an unlawful act, namely dumping polluted plasters in the Netherlands. It was questionable whether the claim of the government was admissible. The Court ruled: the government is guardian of the general interest. Article 21 of the constitution obliges the public authorities to take care of the environment. Taking into account the circumstances of the case and the constitution, the claim was admissible.

In Germany, the duty of care was recently laid down in the constitution. Before this occurred the courts constructed something of the kind. The Constitutional Court deduced such a duty from the right to life and personal integrity. In the Kalkar-case (Bundesverwaltungsgericht 1978) an individual called upon the changed opinions with regard to the danger of nuclear energy. He pointed out that these opinions could not longer hold the decision by which the location for the building of that installation was decided. The court accepted that the duty to protect constitutional rights implicates that the competent authority tests the foundation of the decision. Question was whether changed opinions should have consequences for the location-decision. The duty to do so, has to be read in article 2, subsection 2 of the applicable German Constitution ("Jeder hat das Recht auf Leben und körperliche Unversehrtheit").

A duty to care for individuals can also be laid down in the constitution. The Portuguese Constitution reads: "all have ... the duty to protect the environment". In the Netherlands, this general duty to care is laid down in the Environmental Management Act: "Every person shall treat the environment with due care". It is hard to deduce a specific action or refraining from action, from this general duty. It may be too general to impose specific rights and/or obligations. Perhaps one should go one step further: a general duty to care for citizens is more like a moral obligation.

If a duty to care should be effective, it must be more specific. Article 13 of the Dutch Soil Protection Act reads:

> "Any person performing acts on or in the soil ... and who is aware or can reasonably suspect that such acts are likely to contaminate or impair the soil shall be obliged to take any measures that can reasonably be required of him in order to prevent the soil being so contaminated or impaired or, in the event of such contamination or impairment occurring, to take remedial action to limit and to eliminate as much as possible the impairment or the direct consequences thereof. If the contamination or impairment is the result of an unusual event, the measures shall be taken forthwith."

In a recent case the Dutch administrative court ruled that this duty to care has an autonomous meaning, giving the public authorities the possibility to enforce (administrative) environmental law by administrative actions (Raad van State 1994). Article 13 of the said act makes criminal prosecution in case of activities, which do contaminate the soil, possible, too.

A duty to care is a legal instrument to impose or strengthen self-responsibility. In the Netherlands, the public authorities try to enlarge the self-responsibility of the entrepreneur. According to the Environmental Management Act groups of establishments can be regulated by general rules, laid down in a Royal Decree. In a recent (draft) Royal Decree, regulation with regard to certain establishments is formulated in terms of duties to care (Ontwerp-besluit detailhandel en ambachtsbedrijven milieubeheer, Staatscourant 1996, 116). The operator of an establishment 'takes due care for the environment' (article 3). This general duty to care is made more specific in other provisions, for instance: 'production of waste will be prevented as far as possible'. This more specific duty to care is followed by a set of duties how to prevent production of waste. The draft is rather global and flexible leaving the responsibility with the operator of an establishment. Research on behalf of the Evaluation committee Environmental Management Act (EC EMA) shows that operators of more specialised establishments want to be self-responsible. In case of more standardised establishments, it seems more appropriate to decide on precise regulations (Evaluatiecommissie Wet milieubeheer 1996a,b).

Duties to care are not only developed in the Netherlands. In section 34 of the UK Environmental Protection Act (1990) a duty of care on anyone (other than an occupier of domestic property as respects the household waste produced on that property) 'who imports, produces, carries, keeps, treats or disposes of controlled waste or who, as a broker, has control of such waste' is imposed. This duty to care is specified in more precise regulations, such as 'to prevent the unlawful disposal or treatment of the waste by any other person'.

6. Conclusion

In this contribution we discussed the three principles which are laid down in the Treaty of Helsinki: the precautionary principle, the polluter-pays principle and sustainable development. In (inter)national environmental law more principles can be distinguished, such as the stand still-principle and rectified at source-principle. Principles are important to steer environmental policy and law. However, one should not overestimate the importance of these principles: they must be translated in (inter)national law. This might be done in diverse ways. In the end, implementation of the law brings principles alive.

The real and precise meaning of the precautionary principle is not quite clear yet. It may become one of the most important principles, not only in international river management but also in (international) environmental law in general. One interpretation of this principle may lead to shift the burden of proof. In paragraph 3 we gave an example in the international sphere. Here we must remark that on the national level someone who wants to undertake an activity which might harm the environment (rivers) has to clarify the effects of that activity. Not only by way of environmental impact assessment but also in his request for the permit (or decision). In the Netherlands, such a permit can be refused 'in the interest of protecting the environment' (section 8.10 Environmental Management Act). This system might, afterwards, also be interpreted as resulting from the precautionary principle.

Dealing with the polluter-pays principle we mentioned three aspects. First: prevention as part of this principle. It seems a new development within the scope of the polluter-pays principle. One should recognise it as a logical step certainly in combination with the principle of preventive action. A second aspect we discussed were economic instruments. As was shown the polluter pays may become the payer pollutes. Not all pollution can be prevented: if pollution cannot be prevented (for instance driving cars) paying a fee may be a solution. The third aspect we mentioned was liability. It looks as if strict-liability with regard to environmental affairs (for instance river management) will be the tune of the future.

From sustainable development a duty to care was deduced. We showed a number of ways to implement such a duty to care which might be helpful in river management. A very agreeable side-effect of this duty is enlarging self-responsibility. Not only the state is responsible with regard the environment but all individuals are.

References

Bundesverwaltungsgericht, 1978. Verwaltungsrecht, BVerwGE 54, 211 (224) (in German).
Commission of the European Communities 1993. Towards sustainability: a European Community programme of policy and action in relation to the environment and sustainable development. Directorate-General XI: Environment, Nuclear Safety and Civil Protection. Office for Official Publications of the European Communities, Luxembourg.
Evaluatiecommissie Wet milieubeheer 1996a. De milieuvergunning in bedrijf, fase 3: milieugedrag en bevoegd gezag. Achtergrondstudie nr. 25, Ministerie van Volkshuisvesting, Ruimtelijke Ordening en Milieubeheer, Den Haag (in Dutch).
Evaluatiecommissie Wet milieubeheer 1996b. Vergunnen met beleid: advies over de milieuvergunning in bedrijf. Advies nr. 11. Ministerie van Volkshuisvesting, Ruimtelijke Ordening en Milieubeheer, Den Haag (in Dutch).
Gilhuis, P.C. & Verschuuren, J. 1996. The codification of the Rio principles in national environmental law. Publikatiereeks milieubeheer nr. 1996/1, Ministry of Housing, Spatial Planning and the Environment (VROM), Den Haag.
Hoge Raad, 1987. Uitspraak inzake Benckiser-zaak, 25 juni 1987, Jurisprudentie-katern, Tijdschrift voor Milieu en Recht 1988: 31 (in Dutch).
Hoppe, W. & Beckman, M. 1989. Umweltrecht. Beck, München (in German).
Krämer, L. 1995. E.C.-Treaty and environmental law. Sweet and Maxwell, London.
Raad van State, 1994. Administratief Rechterlijke Beslissingen. Afdeling Bestuursrechtspraak, 5 July 1994, AB 1994, 636 (in Dutch).
Sands, Ph. 1995. Principles of international environmental law. Volume 1. Manchester University Press, Manchester.

DISCUSSION AND STATE OF THE ART: NEW CONCEPTS EMERGING

P.H. Nienhuis, R.S.E.W. Leuven & A.M.J. Ragas
Department of Environmental Studies, Faculty of Science, University of Nijmegen, P.O. Box 9010, 6500 GL Nijmegen, The Netherlands

1. Introduction

In this final chapter we will discuss the major results obtained in this book. The sequence of topics follows the outline given in the introduction (Nienhuis *et al.* 1998a) and covers also roughly the three parts of the book, viz. (a) Ecological concepts and habitat quality, (b) Emission- and water quality-based approaches, and (c) Integrated river basin management.

(1) Habitat quality is exemplified as the environmental quality of a spatial unit, either defined at the level of the landscape, ecosystem, ecotope or habitat.

(2) Water quality covers the classical restoration issues, viz. environmental pollution and water- and sediment quality, and focuses in this book on effects of emissions of chemical elements, such as heavy metals and nutrients, but also on diffuse loadings and their (cumulative) impact on the receiving water bodies and on populations of plants and animals.

(3) Integrated river basin management as presented in this book is characterized by a preliminary approach, either dealing with Dutch case studies (Van de Kamer *et al.* 1998, Van den Heuvel *et al.* 1998) or policy (Thörig & Weterings 1998) and legal aspects (Van Geest & Hödl 1998). Ideally integrated river basin approaches include the conservation, enhancement and restoration of the total river environment through effective land and resource planning, across the whole catchment area.

2. Ecological concepts and habitat quality

2.1. Ecological concepts as a basis for river management

It is evident that rivers constitute ecological continua from the source, via their upper and lower basins, down to the estuaries and the sea: in a natural river a continuous shift of habitats can be found (River Continuum Concept; Vannote *et al.* 1980). However, the ecological connectivity in the basins of the large European rivers is severely weakened by human impact. The construction of weirs and dams, and the continued regulation of the streambed and the intensive agricultural use of the endiked floodplains caused dramatic geomorphological and hydrological changes in the river basin, and consequently many riverine habitats were lost or deteriorat-

New concepts for sustainable management of river basins, pp. 353–367
edited by P.H. Nienhuis, R.S.E.W. Leuven and A.M.J. Ragas
© *1998 Backhuys Publishers, Leiden, The Netherlands*

ed. Together with their original habitats the characteristic river communities disappeared. Already in the beginning of this century most of the characteristic riverine flora and fauna of the Dutch rivers was lost. Biota in rivers are not only affected by the loss of habitats but also by the degradation of water and habitat quality. Around the seventies the aquatic nature of Dutch rivers was very poor. Later on, water quality slowly improved and density and species numbers of macro-invertebrates again increased. Recently, however, this recovery does not progress anymore, probably because of lack of sufficient suitable habitats (Hendriks *et al.* 1997, Nijboer *et al.* 1998), and impact of multiple stressors (Nolan *et al.* 1998, Leuven *et al.* 1998a).

Natural and anthropogenic processes in river systems show a large variation in physical, chemical and biological parameters. Consequently, river science is in most countries still in its descriptive phase. Ecological knowledge at the level of plant- and animal-individuals and populations living in and around rivers is quite extensive; ecological knowledge of the structure and functioning of entire river ecosystems is restricted, and the empirical underpinning of large-scale nature development at landscape level is almost lacking (Harper & Ferguson 1995).

The challenge lies in defining prescriptive restoration measures for river processes and structures, and predictive, properly calibrated and validated ecological models of physical, chemical and biological system parameters. Theoretical considerations for ecological river management are amply available. A considerable number of (holistic) ecological concepts for river management have been published recently (Townsend 1996), and in our opinion there is only restricted need for the development of new concepts. What presently counts is the recognition and practical application of ecological principles and the ambition of scientists to cooperate internationally at the catchment level.

Integrated river catchment management implies standard setting at ecosystem level, the use of ecological indicators and risk analysis of multi-stress effects on river systems (Leuven *et al.* 1998a). Most of these parameters are still beyond common knowledge in river science, and progress obtained in open, unidirectionally flowing river systems is lagging behind, compared to knowledge obtained in homogeneous, isolated water systems like shallow lakes and reservoirs (Scheffer 1998).

The Dutch policy regarding ecological restoration of rivers is characterized by a rather advanced combination of methodologies such as AMOEBA, Ecological Dow Jones Index and ecotope classification (Luiten 1995, Ten Brink *et al.* 1991, Ten Brink & Woudstra 1991, Wolfert 1996). But owing to the use of the Dutch language in most of the publications, the progress in river restoration in the Netherlands finds itself internationally in a rather isolated position (Nienhuis & Leuven 1998). Several useful contributions in this book are widening our knowledge in favour of ecological restoration of Dutch large rivers. In the framework of a number of nature rehabilitation projects along the river Rhine, Harms & Wolfert (1998) developed a GIS-based landscape ecological decision support system, LEDESS, to assess the ecological impact of geomorphological changes in the floodplain on vegetation and fauna.

Riparian ecosystems along the lower Rhine have become fragmented, owing to human interference, and small relics have remained in between larger nature reserves. These fragments are in many cases to small to maintain vital populations of characteristic river-bound species. In order to restore the corridor function of the lower Rhine theoretical models have been constructed based on existing knowledge

(Foppen & Reijnen, 1998; Lenders *et al.* 1998a) predicting the viability of fragmented populations. In a later phase these results will be used to implement practical nature rehabilitation measures along the river.

Ecological restoration of river ecosystems is driven by different principles. Ecologist generally take the rigorous target image: the wild, historical river should return, which means a minimalisation of human interference (Lenders *et al.* 1998b). Undoubtedly the metaphor "naturalness is good" or "let nature have its way" has its intrinsic value; the advantage of such an approach is that we will gain new insight into the natural recovery of river ecosystems. However, the approach also has its limits: the river ecosystem might not recover as planned. This might result in disappointment of stakeholders involved, e.g. if target species such as the Beaver or the Salmon do not recover as planned. Disappointments like these can be prevented by good communication and avoiding unrealistic expectations. Another limit of "-nature having its way", is that it may have unexpected consequences. Especially where public safety is concerned, e.g. in flood defence, we should be alert for these unexpected consequences.

In some cases river managers take a rather realistic point of view. Pedroli & Postma (1998) argue that river rehabilitation should be guided by the present-day ecological potential of the river and its floodplains. This means that not the past historical reference image of the river should dictate the future image, but a more realistic image. European lowland rivers have changed irreversibly, and hydrodynamic and hydromorphological characteristics of the rivers under current conditions should be used as a starting point to determine which ecological target image can be realized.

Verhoeven *et al.* (1998) sketch the consequences of future river management for the development of floodplain ecosystems in the lower reaches of the Rhine and Meuse. These areas are only rarely being flooded due to the protection provided by so called summer dikes, man-made levees bordering the river channel. Restoration projects will restore the connection between the floodplains and the river, by removing the summer dikes and lowering the floodplains. A consequent increase in the frequency of flooding of the floodplains will result in enrichment of the soil with both N- and P-nutrients. This eutrophication will decrease the potential for an increased plant diversity in grasslands bordering the river.

According to Van de Steeg & Blom (1998) an analysis of the ecology of the floodplain vegetation along the river Rhine shows that floodplain rehabilitation may restore the dynamic softwood floodplain forests, but not the more complex and less dynamic, but constant former hardwood floodplain forests. This is due to the artificial managed hydrological and geomorphological characteristics of the embanked floodplains along the river Rhine in the Netherlands.

Nijboer *et al.* (1998) are developing an integrated indicator for the quality of river ecosystems, a classification of aquatic habitats and habitat systems based on aquatic macrofauna assemblages to be found in rivers. This indicator-system is still in its initial stage, and can ultimately be used as a practical instrument for river managers. The unpredictable ecological impact of exotic species in the Rhine basin is substantial, as is shown by Van der Velde *et al.* (1998). The recent mass colonization of *Corophium curvispinum* in the river Rhine has resulted in a drastic decline of an earlier exotic species, the Zebra mussel, *Dreissena polymorpha*. Both species are filter feeders, but *Corophium* deposits a thick layer of silt on the stones, chang-ing the benthic habitat and the benthic foodchain, thus outcompeting *Dreissena*.

Ecology scores better nowadays than it did decades ago. One of the causes for that change is simply the costly mistakes that have been made in the past by ignor-ing natural processes when designing dams, levees, channel stabilization and flood protection schemes. Another factor behind the higher valuation of ecology is the rise of the environmental impact assessment (EIA). Environmental impact legisla-tion in the European Union and many other countries now makes it mandatory to carry out formal EIAs of any major scheme likely to alter river systems. This includes dams and channel realignments, the physical planning of floodplains and dike reinforcement projects. The outcome of this process is a generation of engi-neer-designers who simply have to know about ecology, hydrology, soil science, environmental economics, sociological processes, and planning and land use chang-es (Hey 1995).

Notwithstanding the improved position of ecological knowledge the integration of concepts is necessary to accelerate progress. For instance, the "ecotope system", developed by scientists commissioned by the Ministry of Transport and Water Management for terrestrial biological communities and river basin landscape units (Rademakers & Wolfert 1994, Wolfert 1996), should be integrated with the "habitat system" developed by scientists commissioned by the Ministry of Agriculture, Nature Conservation and Fisheries, for aquatic communities (Nijboer *et al.* 1998). Up to now both classification systems have been developed completely separated. It is remarkable that concepts and theories regarding the spatial segregation of terrestrial and aquatic ecosystems along Dutch rivers for nature management purposes, are not originating from the purely scientific context of the Dutch universities, but stemming from the applied scientific atmosphere of not-university connected State Research Centres. The tradition in the United Kingdom is a different one: universities are lead-ing the conceptual discussion resulting in applications in nature management and conservation (e.g. Harper *et al.* 1995). Dutch universities should play a larger role in the underpinning of nature management in the Netherlands. A recent Dutch initiative is to be mentioned here: the foundation of the Dutch Centre of River Science in 1998, where governmental organisations and universities together bundle their knowledge in order to be prepared to face future challenges in river management.

2.2. Flood protection and ecological concepts

Alarmed by the extreme Rhine and Meuse discharges of 1993 and 1995, triggering a nearly-flooding disaster, the national policy suddenly changed from ecological res-toration of silted up river beds and floodplains, to safety for the population and con-sequent deepening of the floodplains and allowing more space for the river. Flood protection became a high-priority issue (e.g. recent Dutch legislation: Delta Act Large Rivers, 1995; policy guideline "Space for the River", 1996; Flood Protection Act, 1996). During a process that started centuries ago, the Dutch lowland rivers have been pressed in a too narrow channel between the winter-dikes. The river man-ager has to face several problems simultaneously: the navigation channel proper is eroding and deepening, the floodplains are silting up, and the inland polders consist-ing of river clay, are subsiding owing to a lowering of the groundwater table.

Deepening the winterbed does not solve the problem of the increasing flooding risks, unless it occurs over the entire length of the river section in a relatively short time span, which seems not to be feasible in practice (Middelkoop 1997). In dealing with the most recent trends in Dutch policy plans for river management, it should be realized that the deteriorated large rivers as we know them nowadays leave only little space for restoration measures without violating the basic rule of safety.

Nowadays Dutch river stretches are harnassed by high dikes, avoiding flooding of the hinterland in case of extremely discharges of river water. In the future the maximum discharge of the rivers Rhine and Meuse will increase (Kwadijk & Middelkoop 1994), placing the Dutch river managers in the situation to make the policy choice whether the dikes along the rivers should be heightened or the level of the floodplain should be lowered. One of the policy-driven boundary conditions of the target image of the river is that ecological rehabilitation may not lead to higher Standard Highwater Levels in the river (Silva & Kok 1996). This means that river lowland forests, following their natural succession, i.e. dominating after roughly 30 years, are only allowed to develop over very limited areas, bound by safety precautions. Forest growth increases the roughness of the riverbed, hence decreasing the velocity of the discharged river water, and presumably increasing the Standard Highwater Level. Nature development introduces in this context a number of ecological dilemmas: large-scale floodplain excavation will lead to a sediment balance beyond control of the river managers, and the spontaneous developments of nature leading to softwood and hardwood forests in the flood plains should continuously be managed and removed by grazing and cutting. Ecologically "Space for the river" can only be interpreted as widening and vacating floodplains, and having spillways and overflows available in case of extreme river floods.

Pleas for widening of the riverbed, and consequent vacation of the floodplains, are frequently advocated, mainly in the American literature (Gore & Shields 1995). The challenge for European river managers is to protect uncolonized floodplains by re-establishing periodic overbank flooding, allowing the river to rebuild the original habitats. Elsewhere, incentives will be needed to get people to vacate floodplains so that the revetments can be removed allowing reconnection of channels and floodplains. If that is not practical or desired by stakeholders, development of strategies for reconnection of several lowland floodplain wetlands and backwaters by using lateral flow control structures (sluices; culverts) may be useful (Gore & Shields 1995).

An analysis of Dutch river management up to 1997 shows exactly the opposite strategy: the rivers Rhine and Meuse are irreversibly canalized, and the formerly uncolonized floodplains are in recent times intensively used for the building of houses and other urban infrastructure (Hensens *et al.* 1997). The public debate about floodplain lowering and spillway and overbank flooding has been started recently, and massive counter actions from society are anticipated, because it is mainly agricultural land that should be "sacrificed" to the river.

3. Emission- and water quality-based approaches

The European policy concerning the improvement of water quality of the catchments of large rivers is rather successful in several countries. In the past decades the protection of water quality mainly focused on the abatement of organic pollution, and the significant toxic elements, such as heavy metals and non-degradable organic constituants, to protect drinking water supplies, fish production and recreation facilities. The result is that the water quality of most large rivers in Western Europe has improved significantly over the last two decades, mainly due to the drastic clean-up of point-source discharges. Policy makers are eager to illustrate this quality improvement with colourful graphs of decreasing pollutant concentrations, e.g. for cadmium, PCBs, PAHs and phosphate. As a consequence, the priority in river restoration is slowly shifting from classical pollution issues to issues of nature restoration and development. Although this shift in priorities is sensible, we should be aware of the fact that only part of all pollution problems have been solved (Leuven *et al.* 1998a).

The pollution problems that remain to be solved can be typified as persistent, relatively inconspicuous and difficult to master. Prolonged ignorance of these pollution problems may severely endanger the successful implementation of nature restoration and development projects, and other river functions. Some of the problems and promising new concepts to deal with them, will be discussed below: (a) mixing zones around point-source discharges, (b) discharges of unknown substances, (c) diffuse pollution, (d) effects of multiple-stressors and (e) accumulation of pollutants in sediments and deposits.

(a)   In European discharge permits, emission limits are based on the technological possibilities for emission reduction and/or on general environmental quality objectives (EQOs) in combination with the assumption of complete mixing (Haans *et al.* 1998, Ragas *et al.* 1998). In most situations, these emission limits are less stringent than the ambient EQO. The result is a mixing zone in which the ambient EQO is exceeded. The European countries lack national regulations concerning the maximum size of these mixing zones. Nonetheless, it is evident that prolonged exceeding of EQOs in a considerable part of the river may result in disturbance of the river ecosystem. Migrating fish species like the Atlantic salmon (*Salmon salar*) may be deterred by toxic concentration levels in mixing zones impeding the passage of the point discharge and colonization of upstream habitats. Furthermore, sessile organisms, like mussels and water plants, may be impeded to colonize habitats in the neighbourhood of the discharge or they may accumulate toxic substances up to dangerous levels. It is remarkable that relatively little scientific research has focused on the effects of mixing zones on river ecosystems. Stimulation of this type of research and the consequent derivation of scientifically sound mixing zone criteria is strongly advised. The criteria should not only aim at chronic toxicity, but also at acute toxicity. The mixing zone policy advocated by the Environmental Protection Agency of the United States of America can serve as an example (US-EPA 1991).

(b)   Another environmental problem that remains to be solved is the pollution with unknown substances. Toxicity tests with concentrated river water clearly indicate that a considerable part of the toxicity is caused by yet unknown substances (Hendriks *et al.* 1994, Leuven *et al.* 1998a). Apparently, our current knowledge about the presence and the detection of toxic substances is limited and, consequently, toxicity predictions based on measurements of separate parameters are likely to result in underestimation of real risks. This militates in favour of stringent source-oriented regulation of discharges and the introduction of sophisticated effluent toxicity tests. These tests should not only concentrate on acute toxicity, but also on long term effects like mutagenicity and bioaccumulation. The test for whole effluent environmental risk (WEER) as proposed by Tonkes & Botterweg (1994) seems promising in this respect.

(c)   As stated above, the current improvement of river water quality can mainly be attributed to emission reductions realized by point sources. The quality improvement is significantly less for substances predominantly emitted by non-point sources, such as pesticides and fertilisers (Verhoeven *et al.* 1998). Consequently, the relative contribution of non-point sources to river pollution is increasing (Leuven *et al.* 1998a). This confirms that non-point pollution is much more difficult to regulate than point source pollution. This is not only due to the multitude of small, widespread and often intermittent sources which are difficult to control, but it is also due to lack of adequate instruments to trace, identify and quantify non-point pollution sources. The river basin approach as outlined by Dogterom *et al.* (1998) seems a promising instrument to tackle the latter problem. The overall amount of toxic substances leaving the river basin at the point of discharge and through degradation and volatilisation is quantified and balanced with the amount entering the river basin through waste water discharges, leaching, deposition and agricultural activities. In this way, the contribution of the various sources to the overall river water quality can be assessed. If the major sources are identified, the next step is to draw up a plan for emission reduction. Since adequate legislative instruments for controlling diffuse sources are still lacking, emission reduction tends to be more successful when the stakeholders are involved. The plan should therefore be based on mutual respect, scientifically sound information, education, flexibility and a common sense of responsibility (McGuire 1994).

(d)   Traditionally, toxicity tests focus on the exposure of individual organisms to individual substances. In reality, however, the river ecosystem is not affected by a single toxic substance, but by a cocktail of various substances and other agents which may have a detrimental effect, e.g. heat discharges, radiation, noise pollution and human disturbances. Extrapolation of the results of the simple laboratory toxicity tests to field conditions is therefore uncertainty-ridden and may result in underestimation of the real risk. For example, experimental data indicate that in fish species which naturally occur in the Rhine (historical records), exposure to water of the lower Rhine leads to physiologically and toxin induced cell death of fish skins (Nolan *et al.* 1998). We may hypothesize that the present water quality does not allow the return of organisms high in the food chain.

Scientific studies concerning the overall effect of a combination of stress factors (multiple-stressors) are rare, probably because of the complexity involved. As illustrated by Leuven *et al.* (1998b) most of these studies focus on the mixture toxicity of a few well known substances and they seldom include physical and biological stressors. However, if we are to produce reliable predictions of the human impact on river ecosystems, we need detailed insight into the possible interactions between stressors and their cumulative effects. Increase of scientific research in this area and the development of methods to predict effects of multiple-stressors should therefore be stimulated. As long as reliable methods are lacking we should treat the results of ecological risk assessments with caution.

The lack of knowledge on pollution impacts does not only apply to the stressors involved, but also to the structure and functioning of ecosystems. Almost all our current ecotoxicological knowledge stems from single species tests. Empirical data on indirect ecological effects, involving interactions such as competition and predation, are scarce. On the one hand, the effects observed in single species tests may never occur in the field due to compensating mechanisms, e.g. avoidance of exposure by selection of uncontaminated food or habitats. On the other hand, effects which remain unnoticed in single species tests or which do not occur in these tests, may manifest itself in the ecosystem e.g. due to changes in sensitive competitive relationships between species (e.g. Van der Velde *et al.* 1998). Consequently, ecological risk assessment based on extrapolation of single species tests is incomplete and uncertain. Most EQOs for toxic substances are cursed with this shortcoming. The problem can be solved if our understanding of ecosystem functioning is improved and combined with ecotoxicological knowledge e.g. in integrated models for ecological risk assessment which include ecological processes such as population dynamics, competition and predation. A huge amount of scientific questions remains to be answered before such models will produce reliable predictions, representative for ecosystems under field conditions.

(e)   Another major river basin pollution problem that remains to be solved is the pollution that has accumulated over the last few decades in river sediments and deposits. If this pollution is not removed, it is likely to remain a source of non-point pollution affecting river water quality for many years. Furthermore, the recovery of sediment-based ecosystems is likely to be impeded and the pollution accumulated in the deposits may enter the human food chain through agricultural activities in the river flood plains. However, removing the polluted sediments and deposits is a risky undertaking. The accumulated pollution that is relatively immobile under the current environmental conditions may become mobile when it is dug up, transported and stored under different conditions. Furthermore, cleaned-up areas may become polluted again due to redistribution of polluted sediments from other areas during large floods. The re-mobilisation of pollution is also a serious threat to the successful implementation of river restoration and flood defence projects that involve the transfer of large amounts of river sediments and deposits, e.g. river bed deepening, flood plain excavation and the creation of side channels. The adverse side effects of such large projects should be studied carefully before they are implemented (cf. Hendriks *et al.* 1997).

The problems outlined above underline that river pollution deserves our full and continued attention. The fact that river water quality is improving does not imply that all pollution problems have been solved, nor that we fully understand how pollution affects the river ecosystem. The enthusiasm about the river water quality improvement due to point source regulation should not result in ignorance of the remaining problems, but it should be a stimulus for further quality improvements and scientific research aiming at a better understanding of river ecosystem functioning. The current priority for nature restoration and development along large

West European rivers should go hand in hand with pollution prevention and control. The scientific integration of these fields can be realized by developing integrated models for ecological risk assessment. Such models should combine chemical, hydrological, toxicological and ecological knowledge about river ecosystem functioning. The ultimate goal of these models should be to produce a reliable prediction of the structure and functioning of a river ecosystem which is liable to a manifold of stressing agents, e.g. toxic substances, human disturbances and migration barriers.

4. Integrated river basin management

A number of European policy documents on multifunctional water management appeared in the eighties (Higler & Van Liere 1997, Nienhuis & Leuven 1998). These documents functioned as inspiring sources for the development of concepts and instruments for integrated water management of lowland river basins. The excitement about the first spectacular results, however, is fading away. Considering the complexity of the remaining environmental problems in river catchments, it is becoming more and more difficult to gain positive and predictable results. To give an example: in the lowland section of the Rhine-Meuse catchment the emissions of harmful elements are decreasing slowly, and continuously, but the emissions of some heavy metals and nutrients on the Dutch surface waters are slightly increasing again (comparison of 1994 and 1995; Anonymous, 1998). The curve of the societal costs of integrated water management against the results gained, shows signs of diminishing returns. Several Western European riparian states have recently started to lift the strict environmental quality objectives (EQO) for surface water, that are defined in policy plans and legislation. They are being replaced by targets that merely function as guidelines, but which are not legally binding (personal communication J. Haans, University of Nijmegen).

One of the major reasons for the continued widespread degradation of environmental conditions in streams and rivers throughout the developed world is the inadequate input, transfer and application of ecological knowledge to decisions concerning the management of rivers and their biota. Only a small percentage of the results of projects dealing with environmental management and nature development along European rivers is accessible through international journals (De Waal *et al.* 1995, Maitland & Morgan 1997). The proper communication of their research findings should be a challenge to river scientists. Much of the research of river scientists is still curiousity-driven, and few scientists attempt to interpret their results in a management framework. Most of the applied, management oriented publications on (scientific) findings in rivers end up in "grey" reports or in papers written in the national language. This should not be the final step in the scientific process, but the beginning of the flow of internationally available information to managers and the general public.

But there is also a deficit in whole-river ecological knowledge. Notwithstanding the fact that we possess many ecological concepts now for river management (cf. Townsend, 1996), the large-scale empirical underpinning of nature development along rivers is considerably lacking, and consequently the knowledge about the ecological functioning of entire river ecosystems is restricted. The unpredictability in biological changes (invasions) connected to the almost unchangeable boundary conditions of river systems, such as increased water temperature and salinity, disrupted and fragmented habitats, and the geological uni-directional development of the "old" river (cf. Ripl *et al.* 1994), and moreover various societal demands, leave little space for rejuvenation and "nature development". The goals for ecological restoration that could be anticipated considering the reference images, are strongly jeopardized by the multi-functional characteristics of large rivers.

A fact is that most river-monitoring systems are descriptive and at a maximum prescriptive but not predictive. In reality calamities are still determining the agenda of the water manager. The Rhine and Meuse floods of 1993 and 1995 provide a near-perfect laboratory experiment for crisis management. The main objective was to enhance systematic understanding of national differences and similarities in flood management (Rosenthal & Hart 1998). The most recent floods in 1997 in the Czech Republic, Poland and Germany demonstrated once again the continued vulnerability of modern societies to natural hazards.

A major shortcoming of the current modelling exercises concerning river restoration is lack of validation data. As a result, the reliability of the model predictions, e.g. of metapopulation models and scenario studies, is often unknown. Most modellers are well aware of this shortcoming but, nevertheless, they all defend the application of their results for policy making. But is it wise to base a policy decision on a prediction whose likelihood is unknown? We could, for example, imagine a sequence of events which will eventually result in the destruction of the earth within 10 years. However, if we evaluate the probability of this sequence of events as one in a billion, we are unlikely to consider this event in policy making. Leaving the probability of model predictions out of consideration when taking policy decisions is obviously to result in misconception and unexpected results. To overcome these problems ecological modellers should consider to make better use of probabilistic modelling techniques. Furthermore, if predictions of ecological models are to be used for policy making they should be accompanied by a detailed uncertainty analysis.

International cooperation and combination of knowledge is a prerequisite for truly bordercrossing management of large rivers. Although the Netherlands, Germany, and France share important international rivers, all countries use diverging systems for integrated river management (Harper & Ferguson 1995, Nienhuis & Leuven 1998). River management usually stops at the borders of a country. A positive exception is the transboundary management for the river Rhine, resulting in the Rhine Action Programme in 1986, having as an aim to restore the Rhine habitat into a healthy system, where once extinguished species, such as the Salmon may fulfill part of their life cycle.

There is an increasing trend during the last decade in some European countries to extensify agricultural production and to set-aside agricultural land in river floodplains. This tendency has increased the awareness of the importance of river and watershed restoration. A naturally functioning river is a plea in favour of catchment management, because nutrient retention will be enhanced, and the water discharge will be more evenly spread over the year. The latter aspect overcomes the problem of reduced summer discharge, and increases the floodwater storage capacity of the river, hence reducing the river maintenance costs (Nielsen 1996, Nienhuis *et al.* 1998a).

Experience with the rehabilitation of large rivers is rare relative to smaller streams, due to the large number of interwoven societal demands on the river, the connected economic costs and the complexity of the physical and biological systems involved. Proposals and concepts for large river restoration are much more abundant than are demonstrations in the field. However, it had been demonstrated that localized rehabilitation projects can be successful (Maitland & Morgan 1997, Cals *et al.* 1998).

Concepts from landscape ecology and population dynamics provided nature conservation strategies with a scientific basis. A Europe-wide descriptive system is evolving in which ecological networks play a significant role (Jongman 1998). The description of these ecological networks stands for a recent pan-European development in nature conservation and spatial planning. The advantage of ecological networks is the international use of unequivocal landscape units and descriptions. The principles on which they are based stem from the theory of island biogeography and the metapopulation concept, and a keyrole is played by rivers as ecological corridors. Area reduction of "wild" river habitats, or stringent habitat fragmentation, as was the case in the agriculture-dominated floodplains of most European lowland rivers, increase the risk of extinction of highly valued plant- and animal species. An ecological network is composed of core areas, surrounded by buffer zones and connected by ecological corridors. Areas with proper living conditions to be inhabited by a sustainable population of a plant- or animal species can be defined as core areas for that particular species. The size of the core area differs per species (Lenders *et al.* 1998b) and in general larger species need larger areas, and predators need larger areas than herbivores.

Far out most of the work presented in this book is dedicated to Dutch stretches of international rivers. Case studies of the rivers Vistula (Nienhuis *et al.* 1998a) and Danube (Pedroli & Postma 1998) are included for reasons of comparison. Future Dutch river management should more optimally include the knowledge gained in relatively "natural" rivers such as the Odra, Vistula and Danube. A comparison between the river basin management of the Rhine (where water quality has improved, but habitats have been annihilated), and the river Vistula (where water quality is still bad, but the diversity and integrity of habitats is large), leads to the conclusion not to destruct the Vistula floodplains irreversibly for short-term profits (as has been done by the Rhine), but to save the river basin for future long-term profits. These long-term profits comprise healthy ecosystems, "spongy' wetlands for quantitative water management, self-purification properties, and nature conservation perspectives. The area of tension between economic growth and ecological restoration is overshadowed by the drastic changes in environmental policy and management occurring in Poland since 1989. History learns us that river environments have often been irreversibly abused in favour of economic growth. We may only hope that the Polish authorities promote the wise use of water resources, and concomitant preservation of river ecosystems (Nienhuis *et al.* 1998b).

5. General conclusions

(a) The inadequate input, transfer and application of ecological knowledge to decisions concerning the management of river basins is one of the major reasons for the continued degradation of these ecosystems.

(b) On the basis of the evidence collected in this book the present management practice of most European rivers does not deserve the label 'sustainable', although signs of a changing policy, from technological to ecological management, are visible.

(c) A considerable number of ecological concepts for river management have been summarized in this book. What counts is the recognition and practical application of ecological principles and the ambition of scientists and managers together, to cooperate internationally at the scale of the river basin.

(d) The enthusiasm about the river water quality improvement due to point source regulation should be a stimulus for further quality improvements and scientific research aiming at a better understanding of river ecosystem functioning. Scientific integration can be realized by developing integrated models for ecological risk assessment.

(e) Ecological modellers should make better use of probabilistic modelling techniques, including an uncertainty analysis.

(f) It has been demonstrated that local river rehabilitation projects can be successful but concepts and designs for sustainable restoration of large rivers are much more abundant than demonstrations in the field.

(g) Sustainable river management, in the meaning of WCED (1987), is far beyond the practical goals to be set in an international context (cf. Nienhuis *et al.* 1998a). Metaphorically we might state that sustainability is held prison in the triangle "ecology-economy-sociology" (see Fig. 1 in Van de Kamer *et al.* 1998), in which strong, ecological sustainability is the victim of weak, economic sustainability.

References

Anonymous. 1998. Emissie naar water en lucht 1995. H$_2$O 31 (2): 9 (in Dutch).

Cals, M.J.R., Postma, R., Buijse, A.D. & Marteijn, E.C.C. 1998. Habitat restoration along the river Rhine in The Netherlands: putting ideas into practice. Aquatic Conserv.: Mar. Freshw. Ecosystems 8: 61-70.

De Waal. L.C., Large, A.R.G, Gippel, C.J. & Wade, P.M. 1995. River and floodplain rehabilitation in Western Europe: opportunities and constraints. Arch. Hydrobiol. Suppl. 101 – Large Rivers 9 (3/4): 679-693.

Dogterom, J., Van der Wiele, P.J. & Buijs, P.H.L. 1998. Diffuse loadings as a yet unsolved problem for receiving water bodies (rivers). In: Nienhuis, P.H., Leuven, R.S.E.W. & Ragas, A.M.J. (eds), New concepts for sustainable management of river basins. pp. 211-228. Backhuys Publishers, Leiden, The Netherlands.

Foppen, R.P.D. & Reijnen, R. 1998. Ecological networks in riparian systems: examples for Dutch floodplain rivers. In: Nienhuis, P.H., Leuven, R.S.E.W. & Ragas, A.M.J. (eds), New concepts for sustainable management of river basins. pp. 85-93. Backhuys Publishers, Leiden, The Netherlands.

Gore, J.A. & Shields J.F.D. 1995. Can large rivers be restored ? BioScience 45:142-152.

Haans, J.L.M., Leuven, R.S.E.W. & Ragas, A.M.J. 1998. Immission assessment procedures for discharge permitting. In: Nienhuis, P.H., Leuven, R.S.E.W. & Ragas, A.M.J. (eds), New concepts for sustainable management of river basins. pp. 179-189. Backhuys Publishers, Leiden, The Netherlands.

Harms, W.B. & Wolfert, H.P. 1998. Nature rehabilitation for the river Rhine: a scenario approach at different scales. In: Nienhuis, P.H., Leuven, R.S.E.W. & Ragas, A.M.J. (eds), New concepts for sustainable management of river basins. pp 95-113. Backhuys Publishers, Leiden, The Netherlands.

Harper, D.M. & Ferguson, A.J.D. (eds.) 1995. The ecological basis for river management. Wiley, Chichester. pp. 1-614.

Harper, D., Smith, C., Barham, P. & Howell, R. 1995. The ecological basis for the management of the natural river environment. In: Harper, D.M. & Ferguson, A.J. (eds), The ecological basis for river management, pp. 219-238. Wiley, Chichester.

Hendriks, A.J., Cals, M.J.R., Cazemier, W.G., Van Dijk, G.M., Higler, L.W.G., Marteijn, E.C.L., Pieters, H., Postma, R. & Wolfert, H.P. 1997. Ecological rehabilitation of the rivers Rhine and Meuse: Summary Report 1994-1995. Ecological Rehabilitation of the Rivers Rhine and Meuse, no 67-1997: 1-34. DLO / RIVM / RIZA, Lelystad.

Hendriks, A.J., De Jonge, J. Den Besten, P. & Faber, J. 1997. Gifstoffen in het rivierengebied. Een belemmering voor natuurontwikkeling? Landschap 14 (3): 219-233 (in Dutch).

Hendriks, A.M., Maas-Diepeveen, J.L., Noordsij, A. & Van der Gaag, M.A. 1994. Monitoring response to XAD-concentrated water in the Rhine delta: a major part of the toxic compounds remains unidentified. Water Research 28: 581-598.

Hensens. G., Nienhuis, P.H. & Thörig, M.H.W. 1997. Ruimte voor de Maas: veranderingen in de afvoerfunctie in relatie tot de hoogwaterproblematiek. H$_2$O 30: 496-499+515 (in Dutch).

Hey, R. 1995. River processes and management. In: T. O'Riordan (ed) – Environmental Science for Environmental Management. Longman, Singapore. pp. 131-150.

Higler, L.W.G. & Van Liere, L. 1997. Freshwater quality in Europe: tales from the continent. In: P.J. Boon & D.L. Howell (eds) – Freshwater quality: defining the indefinable? The Stationery Ofice, Edinburgh, pp. 59-68.

Jongman, R.H.G. 1998. Rivers: key elements in European ecological networks. In: Nienhuis, P.H., Leuven, R.S.E.W. & Ragas, A.M.J. (eds), New concepts for sustainable management of river basins. pp. 53-66. Backhuys Publishers, Leiden, The Netherlands.

Kwadijk, J. & Middelkoop, H. 1994. Estimation of impact of climate change on the peak discharge probability of the river Rhine. Climatic Change 27: 199-224.

Lenders, H.J.R., Leuven, R.S.E.W., Oostinga, K.D., Nienhuis, P.H. & Van den Heuvel, P.J.M. 1998a. Ecological rehabilitation of floodplains along the middle reach of the river Waal: corridors or unbridgeable barriers for target species? In: Nienhuis, P.H., Leuven, R.S.E.W. & Ragas, A.M.J. (eds), New concepts for sustainable management of river basins. pp. 115-130. Backhuys Publishers, Leiden, The Netherlands.

Lenders, H.J.R., Aarts, B.G.W., Strijbosch, H. & Van der Velde, G. 1998b. The role of reference and target images in ecological recovery of river systems: lines of thought in the Netherlands. In: Nienhuis, P.H., Leuven, R.S.E.W. & Ragas, A.M.J. (eds), New concepts for sustainable management of river basins. pp. 35-52. Backhuys Publishers, Leiden, The Netherlands.

Leuven, R.S.E.W., Haans, J.L.M., Hendriks, A.J., Lock, R.A.C. & Wendelaar Bonga, S.E. 1998a. Assessing cumulative impacts of multiple stressors on river systems. In: Nienhuis, P.H., Leuven, R.S.E.W. & Ragas, A.M.J. (eds), New concepts for sustainable management of river basins. pp. 241-259. Backhuys Publishers, Leiden, The Netherlands.

Leuven, R.S.E.W., Zwart, W.A., Kesseleer, J.M.A. & Nienhuis, P.H. 1998b. Emission of metals from mine stone in hydraulic engineering structures in Dutch river basins. In: Nienhuis, P.H., Leuven, R.S.E.W. & Ragas, A.M.J. (eds), New concepts for sustainable management of river basins. pp. 179-189. Backhuys Publishers, Leiden, The Netherlands.

Luiten, J.P.A. 1995. The ecological basis for catchment management. A new Dutch project: the Water System Explorations. In: D.M. Harper & A.J.D. Ferguson (eds.) – The ecological basis for river management. John Wiley & Sons, Chichester, pp. 453-473.

Maitland, P.S. & Morgan, N.C. 1997. Conservation Management of Freshwater Habitats. Conservation Biology Series 9: 1-233. Chapman & Hall, London.

McGuire, R.T. 1994. A new model to reach water quality goals. Choices 9 (2): 20-25.

Middelkoop, H. 1997. Embanked floodplains in The Netherlands. Geomorphological evalution over various timescales. Ph. D. Thesis University Utrecht, Netherlands Geographical Studies no. 224: 1-341. University Utrecht.

Nielsen, M.B. 1996. River restoration: report of a major EU Life demonstration project. Aquat. Conserv.: Marine Freshwat. Ecosyst. 6: 187-190.

Nienhuis, P.H. & Leuven, R.S.E.W. 1998. Ecological concepts for the sustainable management of owland river basins: a review. In: Nienhuis, P.H., Leuven, R.S.E.W. & Ragas, A.M.J. (eds), New concepts for sustainable management of river basins. pp. 7-33. Backhuys Publishers, Leiden, The Netherlands.

Nienhuis, P.H., Leuven, R.S.E.W. & Ragas, A.M.J. 1998a. General introduction. In: Nienhuis, P.H., Leuven, R.S.E.W. & Ragas, A.M.J. (eds), New concepts for sustainable management of river basins. pp. 1-6. Backhuys Publishers, Leiden, The Netherlands.

Nienhuis, P.H., Hofman, N.J.W., Rietbergen, M.G., Ligthart, S.S.H. & Prus, T. 1998b. Water management of the lower reach of the Vistula river in Poland. In: Nienhuis, P.H., Leuven, R.S.E.W. & Ragas, A.M.J. (eds), New concepts for sustainable management of river basins. pp. 321-332. Backhuys Publishers, Leiden, The Netherlands.

Nijboer, R.C., Verdonschot, P.F.M. & Bisseling, C.M. 1998. Habitat systems as quality indicator in large rivers; a first step to construct an instrument for river nature management. In: Nienhuis, P.H., Leuven, R.S.E.W. & Ragas, A.M.J. (eds), New concepts for sustainable management of river basins. pp. 145-157. Backhuys Publishers, Leiden, The Netherlands.

Nolan, D.T., Hadderingh, R.H., Jenner, H.A. & Wendelaar Bonga, S.E. 1998. The effects of exposure to Rhine water on the Sea trout smolt (*Salmo trutta trutta L.*): an ultrastructural and physiological study. In: Nienhuis, P.H., Leuven, R.S.E.W. & Ragas, A.M.J. (eds), New concepts for sustainable management of river basins. pp. 261-271. Backhuys Publishers, Leiden, The Netherlands.

Pedroli, G.B.M. & Postma, R. 1998. Nature rehabilitation in European river ecosystems. In: Nienhuis, P.H., Leuven, R.S.E.W. & Ragas, A.M.J. (eds), New concepts for sustainable management of river basins. pp. 67-84. Backhuys Publishers, Leiden, The Netherlands.

Rademakers, J.G.M. & Wolfert, H.P. 1994. Het Rivier-Ecotopen-Stelsel. Ecological rehabilitation of the Rivers Rhine and Meuse, no. 61-1994: 1-77. DLO /RIVM / RIZA, Lelystad.

Ragas, A.M.J., Van de Laar, B.J., Van Schijndel, A.M.J., Klapwijk, S.P. & Stortelder, P.B.M. 1998. Application of the water quality-based approach in water pollution control: possibilities and restrictions. In: Nienhuis, P.H., Leuven, R.S.E.W. & Ragas, A.M.J. (eds), New concepts for sustainable management of river basins. pp. 191-209. Backhuys Publishers, Leiden, The Netherlands.

Ripl, W., Pokorny, J., Eiseltova, M. & Ridgill, S. 1994. A holistic approach to the structure and function of wetlands, and their degradation. IWRB Public. 32: 16-35.

Rosenthal, U. & Hart, P. (eds). 1998. Flood response and crisis management in Western Europe. A comparative analysis. Springer, Berlin, 236 pp.

Scheffer, M. 1998. Ecology of Shallow Lakes. Chapman & Hall, London, pp. 1-357.

Silva, W. & Kok, M. 1996. Integrale Verkenning inrichting Rijntakken. Hoofdrapport; IVR-rapport nr.1. Ministerie van Verkeer en Waterstaat – RIZA, Arnhem en Waterloopkundig Laboratorium, Marknesse (in Dutch).

Ten Brink, B.J.E., Hosper, S.H. & Colijn, F. 1991. A quantitative method for description and assessment of ecosystems: the AMOEBA-approach. Mar. Pollut. Bull. 23: 265-270.

Ten Brink, B.J.E. & Woudstra, J.H. 1991. Towards an effective and rational water management: the Aquatic Outlook Project – integrating water management, monitoring and research. Europ. Wat. Pollut. Control 1: 20-27.

Thörig, M.W.H. & Weterings, R.A.P.M. 1998. Possibilities and difficulties in quantifying the general notion of environmental utilisation space for water systems. In: Nienhuis, P.H., Leuven, R.S.E.W. & Ragas, A.M.J. (eds), New concepts for sustainable management of river basins. pp. 333-341. Backhuys Publishers, Leiden, The Netherlands.

Tonkes, M. & Botterweg, J. 1994. Totaal effluent milieubezwaarlijkheid. Beoordelingsmethodiek milieubezwaarlijkheid van afvalwater: literatuur- en gegevensevaluatie. Report 94.020, Institute of Inland Water Management and Waste Water Treatment (RIZA), Lelystad, Hageman Verpakkers, Zoetermeer, The Netherlands (in Dutch).

Townsend, C.R. 1996. Concepts in river ecology: pattern and process in the catchment hierarchy. Arch. Hydrobiol. Suppl. 113, Large Rivers 10: 3-21.

US-EPA. 1991. Technical support document for water quality-based toxics control. United States Environmental Protection Agency, Office of Water, Report EPA/505/2-90-001, Washington DC, USA.

Van de Kamer, S.P.G., Postma, R., Marteijn, E.C.L. & Bakker, C. 1998. On the way to total water management for large rivers in the Netherlands. In: Nienhuis, P.H., Leuven, R.S.E.W. & Ragas, A.M.J. (eds), New concepts for sustainable management of river basins. pp. 291-307. Backhuys Publishers, Leiden, The Netherlands.

Van de Steeg, H.M. & Blom, C.W.P.M. 1998. Impact of hydrology on floodplain vegetation in the Lower Rhine system: implications for nature conservation and nature development. In: Nienhuis, P.H., Leuven, R.S.E.W. & Ragas, A.M.J. (eds), New concepts for sustainable management of river basins. pp. 131-144. Backhuys Publishers, Leiden, The Netherlands.

Van den Heuvel, P.J.M., Ten Brink, N.G.M. & Nienhuis, P.H. 1998. Conflicting functions in the Middle-Waal area: a preliminary study. In: Nienhuis, P.H., Leuven, R.S.E.W. & Ragas, A.M.J. (eds), New concepts for sustainable management of river basins. pp. 309-320. Backhuys Publishers, Leiden, The Netherlands.

Van der Velde, G., Rajagopal, S., Van den Brink, F.W.B., Kelleher, B. Paffen, B.G.P., Kempers, A.J. & Bij de Vaate, A. 1998. Ecological impact of an exotic amphipod invasion in the River Rhine. In: Nienhuis, P.H., Leuven, R.S.E.W. & Ragas, A.M.J. (eds), New concepts for sustainable management of river basins. pp. 159-169. Backhuys Publishers, Leiden, The Netherlands.

Van Geest, H.J.A.M. & Hödl, P.J. 1998. River management and principles of environmental law. In: Nienhuis, P.H., Leuven, R.S.E.W. & Ragas, A.M.J. (eds), New concepts for sustainable management of river basins. pp. 343-352. Backhuys Publishers, Leiden, The Netherlands.

Vannote, R.L., Minshall, G.W., Cummins, K.W., Sedell, J.R. & Cushing, C.E. 1980. The river continuum concept. Can. J. Fish. Aquat. Sci. 37: 130-137.

Verhoeven, J.T.A., Bogaards, H., Van Logtestijn, R.S.P. & Spink, A. 1998. Initial estimates of nutrient-related process rates in floodplains along modified rivers in the Netherlands. In: Nienhuis, P.H., Leuven, R.S.E.W. & Ragas, A.M.J. (eds), New concepts for sustainable management of river basins. pp. 229-240. Backhuys Publishers, Leiden, The Netherlands.

WCED. 1987. Our Common Future, pp. 1-11. World Commission on Environment and Development, Oxford University Press, Oxford.

Wolfert, H.P. 1996. Rijkswateren-Ecotopen-Stelsels: uitgangspunten en plan van aanpak. RIZA Nota nr. 96.050 (in Dutch).

INDEX OF AUTHORS

SUBJECT INDEX